HALTON

The story of an East Leeds village

JOHN GILLEGHAN
MBE

THE KINGSWAY PRESS LEEDS

Dedication

To my dear Mum, the Halton Pharmacist who passed away aged 97 on Boxing Day 2001 whose many memories were the inspiration for this story.

Cover photograph: John Gilleghan. High Street (Selby Road) 1964

Printed in Victoria, BC, Canada

Note for Librarians: a cataloguing record for this book that includes Dewey Decimal Classification and US Library of Congress numbers is available from the Library and Archives of Canada. The complete cataloguing record can be obtained from their online database at: www.collectionscanada.ca/amicus/index-e.html
ISBN 1-4120-2945-7

TRAFFORD

This book was published *on-demand* in cooperation with Trafford Publishing. On-demand publishing is a unique process and service of making a book available for retail sale to the public taking advantage of on-demand manufacturing and Internet marketing. On-demand publishing includes promotions, retail sales, manufacturing, order fulfilment, accounting and collecting royalties on behalf of the author.

Offices in Canada, USA, UK, Ireland, and Spain
book sales for North America and international:
Trafford Publishing, 6E–2333 Government St.
Victoria, BC V8T 4P4 CANADA
phone 250 383 6864 toll-free 1 888 232 4444
fax 250 383 6804 email to orders@trafford.com
book sales in Europe:
Trafford Publishing (UK) Ltd., Enterprise House, Wistaston Road Business Centre
Crewe, Cheshire CW2 7RP UNITED KINGDOM
phone 01270 251 396 local rate 0845 230 9601
facsimile 01270 254 983 orders.uk@trafford.com
order online at:
www.trafford.com/robots/04-0773.html

10 9 8 7 6 5 4 3 2 1

Introduction

I was born at the Halton Pharmacy and have fond memories of life in Halton when it was a true village. There were friendly policemen, lamplighters, doctors who seemed to spend much of their time in our shop and home as well as at Gilsyke House with bus drivers and conductresses on the yellow bus who stopped for a cup of tea when weather was inclement. There was a strong community spirit and I always remember being spoken to on my frequent walks to catch the tram at the Irwin Arms, to Cross Gates School across valley bridge and along Bridlepath and helping Harry Taylor with his horse drawn cart milk round. Perhaps wartime knitted together the Halton community: there was an air raid shelter at the bottom of Wilfred Avenue although Mum and Dad had adapted part of the shop cellar as a shelter, used in March 1941 when an air raid hit the city.

These were the days prior to television and there was so much enjoyment to be had in appreciating the simpler things of life: street games, walks and visiting the Ritz or Regal in Cross Gates as a special treat. I used to save my tram fare for getting Dandy first published in 1937, Champion, Hotspur, Radio Fun and Film Fun comics and later Eagle first published on April 14th 1950 and had much pleasure in taking my Ian Allen spotter book to Cross Gates or cycling down to Neville Hill sheds to underline the engine numbers "copped".

I always wore my school uniform for both Cross Gates (red cap with a blue outline of the gates) and Leeds Grammar School from Easter 1945 both on school days and quite often on holidays. The trusty gabardine raincoat, banana skins cap and polished black shoes were a constant feature of my early life.

My childhood was very happy with Miss Norah Ann Lancaster at Cross Gates Boy's School: she had been appointed in 1925 from Seacroft CE School as a 24 year old teacher, music lessons with Eva Bennion at her house on Cold Well Road and helping Mrs Hemming and Mrs Levitt to stamp the books out at Cross Gates Children's Library. I was in the choir at Whitkirk Church and there were Friday practices in the old tithe barn with Sunday School held in a wooden hut on Station Road.

I remember Mr Button and waiting to have my hair done listening to the village gossip at his shop on Primrose Road and visiting

Ossie Bell's little shop on Woodman Street or Alec Cowell's shop opposite our own on Cross Green Lane. Jack Stuart White looked after my teeth, I never did like the gas prior to treatment. A walk to Cross Gates often included a visit to Booth & Horsfall's shop at the Ritz or on Austhorpe Road.

It was in Halton that I lived and grew up with so many shops: Tomlinson's hardware, Vamplew's cycles, Charlie Frame's butchers, Schofield's newsagents and Alec Cowell's shop. Our butchers were Lees near the Irwin where my parents obtained good deals in the war years and we visited the greengrocers shops run by the Ball family. Florrie Ball lived on Wilfred Avenue and for many years was our shop, house cleaner and friend who I always looked up to; we had a garage on that street where I kept Snowy my pet rabbit.

Memories of old Halton must include the effects of the great snows of 1947 when I helped to dig a track through the drifts to the shop; putting ship halfpennies on the tram lines and the wonder of Christmas when the Congregational Chapel choir came around the village.

These are some of the reasons why I have decided to write the story of a village from the early beginnings to the present day. Enjoy the memories which my dear Mum so often enjoyed with me.

John Gilleghan at Bridlington 1939

INTRODUCING HALTON VILLAGE

The name Halton comes from "farmstead in a secluded nook" and was Halletun in the Domesday Book of 1086, Haleton (1200), Halghton (1235), Haulton (1322) and Hawton in 1677. There is a suggestion that the name refers to a church in the area described by the Venerable Bede in the 7th century. There were four main field systems in Halton: Gill Syke, Garth End, Cross Field and New Field.

EARLY DAYS

In about 4000BC farmers were clearing the oak and birch woodlands of the area to grow their crops and to raise animals. Flint implements that have been unearthed at the Skelton Grange site offer evidence of occupation from this period. Grim's Dyke which forms the eastern edge of the Temple Newsam estate was partly revealed and archaeologically investigated during the construction of the AI/MI link road from 1996.
A dig was carried out by the Yorkshire Archaeological Society during summer 1957: it also investigated digs from 1977 to 1983. The best preserved section of the ditch parallel to Bullerthorpe Lane on the site of the old car park was surveyed in 1977. The ditch at Thorp Park was dated to the Bronze Age (2000BC-500BC) with construction taking place about 1000BC/900BC by farmers who worked the land from their isolated farmsteads: the original idea could have had pagan religious connections. Samples from the ditch on Bullerthorpe Lane were dated to the Roman

period. A Bronze Age cemetery was discovered north of Garforth with the cremated remains in an almost intact collared urn found within a small ring barrow. Stile Hill/Colton Common was archaeologically investigated from November 1994 to February 1994 and produced evidence of Bronze Age activity with two circular huts and their post holes; the site became the car parking area to the Colton Retail Park (Sainsbury's Store opened in November 1994) with the new road called Stile Hill Way: a local name has been Lately Hill. A late Iron Age/Romano-British site north of Swillington Church was archaeologically investigated in 1991-92: there was a double enclosure with two ditches and a roundhouse. An amount of pottery suggested an established community and a bronze ring was dated to the 1st century AD. An Iron Age site was uncovered in the shadow of Ferrybridge Power Station during the building of a motorway. An Iron Age chariot was found in a burial site in late 2003 which included a man's skeleton and a spearhead together with the bones of over 250 cattle.

A large scale dig was undertaken in 2002 at Temple Point on Stile Hill Way. The dig has given an insight into how land use has changed from the early Bronze Age to late Roman and perhaps post-Roman periods. It is likely that the land was first used as a burial ground in the Bronze Age and then became a settlement. Discovered were the remains of round barrows used as burial mounds together with artefacts including cremation urns. Part of the enclosure may have been used for livestock in the early post-Roman period. The archaeological investigation on a site north of Bullerthorpe House on Bullerthorpe Lane revealed late Iron Age pits and fragments of querns. The material also showed occupancy from the mid-2nd century to the early 4th century AD. Other sites in the area showed both 1st/2nd century and 3rd/4th century artefacts.

THE ROMANS TO THE NORMAN CONQUEST

The Roman road in the area was Ermine Street from Castleford (Legolium) to Aberford and the north. The Ridge Road runs east of Kippax and was investigated by the archaeologists at Hook Moor. This revealed an agger or bank of interleaved layers of sub-soil and limestone about 6 metres wide and a metre high. It was therefore no surprise to discover a Romano-British farm to the east of Temple Newsam: they grew corn and bred animals. Excavations at Aberford Road north-east of Garforth revealed a sequence of enclosures yielding a large amount of Roman pottery, building materials and animal bones. This site also had a small Roman cemetery with six burials; there were other sites revealing Roman pottery along Bullerthorpe Lane and at Swillington Common.

The end of the Elmetian period was 637AD when the Saxons finally took over the old kingdom created following the departure of the Romans in

410AD. The Elmetian folk tried to prevent invasion by re-using the man-made ditches/embankments found at Becca Banks and Grim's Ditch. The Aberford Road archaeological site revealed a find of national importance: two early Anglo-Saxon grubenhausen which were the first to be discovered in West Yorkshire. These huts had Germanic origins and were dated to the 5th century AD: they were pit houses with the earth at its base grubbed away to form a shallow depression over which the house was built in wood and thatch. The sunken-floored huts represent a change from round shape to rectangular huts with rare pottery also being discovered on the same site.
The West Yorkshire Archaeology Service investigated 34 sites along 8 km of the road which revealed evidence of ancient rural landscape from the Bronze Age, developed during both the Iron Age and the Roman period. The £200 million link road was opened on Thursday February 4th 1999.

THE KNIGHTS TEMPLARS

In the period prior to the Norman Conquest the Newhusum area was farmed by the Saxons of the area. Dunstan and Glunier mentioned in the Domesday Book had three acres of meadow with wood and pasture together with eight carucates of land and four ploughs. Halton was where Morfari had six carucates worth 20 shillings in 1066 and only worth 2 shillings in 1086 after the Harrying of the North. The Norman Ilbert de Lacy was given the lands after the Conquest and administration was from Pontefract Castle; they had many people who worked the land on their behalf. The centre of Newhusum was at Newsam Green, where earthworks have suggested the existence of a settlement: there were still eleven houses in the 18th century.
In the area around Temple Thorp Farm on the north side of the River Aire in 1155 the Knights Templars founded their preceptory (farm and chapel) on 16 carucates of land which had been presented to them by William de Villiers. They were to hold a "knight's fee in Newsom, Halghton, Colton and Skelton". Following the first Crusade the Christian kingdoms in the Middle East were insecure and pilgrims were being attacked on their way to Jerusalem. A group of knights got together in order to offer these pilgrims some protection. They were offered lodgings at the King's Palace at Jerusalem in 1128 which was believed to be the site of Solomon's Temple: they became known as Knights Templars or the Templars. In Europe the Templars gained the backing of the Cistercians and in support of their life in church and farm, they wore a white tunic with a red cross (granted 1146) over their armour. The Knights Templars also owned land at Wetherby and Ribston as well as Temple Newsam, where they were granted free warren in 1248. The Templars were given the Manor of Whitkirk and lived, trained and

farmed the area, gaining the money needed to live and to finance their journeys in the Holy Land. The Knights Templars were arrested by order of Edward II and their estate at Temple Newsam was confiscated in 1308 and by 1312 their preceptory was abandoned: the last preceptor was Geoffrey de Arches who with some of his fellow Templars went to Kirkstall Abbey. The lands were leased to Robert Holland and Edward II granted Temple Newsam to Mary de St Paul Countess of Pembroke in 1327. This followed her marriage and widowhood in exchange for the castles and towns of Haverford and Hertford.

Halton was part of the great estate of Temple Newsam and the story of the families is an important part of the village history.

THE DARCY FAMILY

The manor of Temple Newsam was granted in 1337 to John Darcy (D'Arcie), Constable of the Tower of London. Sir John was the founder of the Darcy line at Temple Newsam and in 1344 he was allowed to empark his woods and was granted "free warren" in 1345 with the park used for country pursuits. Sir John Darcy died in May 1347 and the estate was inherited by his son who fought at Crecy in 1346. In 1488/89 40 more acres of park were enclosed with the eviction of eight households and the changing of land from arable to pasture. The folk may have been re-housed at the medieval village of Colton: ridges and furrows still remain which showed cultivation by the peasants. The village was subjected to an archaeological dig in 1980 with the outline of huts/post holes revealed. The important remains discovered were in the field west of the track to the park from the gate at the south end of Park Road Colton: this path is an extension of the medieval village street. On the east side opposite Park Farm was possibly the village green and north of the farm there were remains of three terraced platforms, medieval housing and building platforms. The boundary bank was traced around much of the perimeter while the field systems to the east of the present village are marked with parallel lines: the strip ploughing method. The lack of stone/brick buildings proved that the medieval village was abandoned by 1650, probably due to the Darcy emparking. In 1820 the open fields of Colton were subject to the Enclosure Act.
John Darcy died in 1411 holding the manor: his son Philip died in 1418. The manor of Temple Newsam then passed to John Darcy who died in 1454. The last of the Temple Newsam Darcy line was Thomas Lord Darcy, who in about 1520 built the first Temple Newsam House on the present site. He took part in the Pilgrimage of Grace and in 1537 was found guilty of high treason and executed on Tower Hill and his Temple Newsam lands were confiscated. Most of Darcy's original four square

mansion was demolished following the purchase in 1622 by Sir Arthur Ingram. The first reference to the gardens was made in 1535 when George Darcy wrote in a letter to his father: *"The garthens at Temple Newsam could not be more out of frame. Pray send me some good garthener who has skill of the hop garth".*
The Tudor garden was on the south side of the mansion and the only remaining feature is the mound which served as a look-out post-by the site of the old gibbet. The Temple Newsam estate was given to the Earl of Lennox: the Earl married Margaret Douglas and their son became Lord Darnley who married Mary Queen of Scots in 1565.

THE INGRAM FAMILY AND VISCOUNTS IRWIN

In 1603 Temple Newsam was inherited by the 2nd Duke of Lennox who enclosed a further 285 acres at Temple Newsam for use as a deer park and pasture. His extravagance forced him to sell both house and estate for £12,000 on June 14th 1622 to wealthy London merchant Sir Arthur Ingram, who was the Secretary to the Council in the North. Sir Arthur Ingram only left the west wing which remains today showing the distinctive brick pattern. Ingram employed the Frenchman Peter Monjoye to remodel the park and mansion gardens in a formal way: a south front parterre, topiary, gravel walks and geometric flower beds. Estate accounts detail money paid for *"work in the gardens and home farm 1619-1795".* He worked at Temple Newsam until 1639 when Sir Arthur gave him a £10 gift when he left service. The garden features included 20 stone beasts carved by Thomas Ventris Jnr of York in 1637: similar beasts made for Sir Arthur's other mansion at Sheriff Hutton near York are still a garden feature. In 1635/36 a banqueting house was built on a raised mound at the west end of the south terrace and a bowling green was completed to the west; the banqueting house was generally used for the service of the last course of a huge meal. In 1963 there was an archaeological exploration of the banqueting house: nothing conclusive was found of a building demolished by Etty in 1727 for replacement by another building.
There are records in 1684 of the dog kennels being rebuilt and again in 1697 when the cost was £73: on Dog Kennel Hill. When the 23 year old Arthur 3rd Viscount Irwin took over the estate in 1688, he preferred to manage the park to suit the needs of the forester, huntsman and game keeper. He was a sportsman who enjoyed fox hunting, deer stalking, pheasant shooting and attended the races at York and Ripon as well as those on Chapeltown Moor (1682). Arthur's portrait at the house shows him in sportsman's attire: he had nine sons and five succeeded to the Irwin title. The plan of Temple Newsam by Jan Kip (1653-1722) from a drawing by Leonard Knyff shows the formal gardens, avenues and the

buildings that once were a feature of the 18th century House and surrounds. The great barn of Home Farm dates from 1694 as shown on a main beam: the outside bears a stone plaque wrongly dated 1744: this was another project of the 3rd Viscount.

THE END OF AN ERA

Emily Charlotte Wood was the eighth and youngest child of Sir Charles Wood 1st Viscount Halifax (1800-1885) and his wife Lady Mary Grey, who he married in 1829: daughter of Charles 2nd Earl Grey (1764-1845) she died in 1884. Emily was born on July 19th 1840 at Hickleton Hall. Sir Charles was the son of Sir Francis Lindley Wood 2nd baronet and Anne Buck (married 1798): she died in 1841. He was the Liberal MP for Halifax for 33 years and in 1866 was raised to the peerage as 1st Viscount Halifax of Monk Bretton: the manor had been bought by George Wood (died 1589) in the early 16th century. Lord Halifax's career included serving as Chancellor of the Exchequer, First Lord of the Admiralty, President of the Indian Council and Lord Privy Seal.

One of Emily's brothers was Charles Lindley Wood 2nd Viscount Halifax who was born in 1839 and succeeded to the title on the death of his father in 1885: he married Lady Agnes Elizabeth Courtenay in 1869 who died in 1919. Charles and Agnes's child was Edward Frederick Lindley Wood 3rd Viscount Halifax and 1st Baron Irwin (second creation): he was born on April 16th 1881 and married Lady Dorothy Evelyn Augusta Onslow. He succeeded to the Halifax title on the death of his father at Hickleton Hall on January 19th 1934. He was the Parliamentary Under-Secretary for the Colonies (1921-22), President of the Board of Education (1922-24) and Foreign Secretary (1938-40) becoming the British Ambassador to Washington (1941-46). He had two sons of which one was killed in 1942 and a daughter; mother became the Dowager Countess Dorothy Evelyn Augusta Wood. She was born on February 7th 1885 and died at Bugthorpe near York on February 2nd 1976. Their son was Charles Ingram Courtenay Wood 2nd Earl of Halifax born on October 3rd 1912, married Ruth Primrose in 1936 and died on March 19th 1980: Ruth died in 1989. Their son was Charles Edward Peter Neil Wood 3rd Earl of Halifax of Garrowby Hall born 1944, who succeeded to the title on the death of his father in 1980: he married Camilla Younger in 1976.

Emily Meynell Ingram married Hugo Francis Meynell of Hoar Cross Hall Staffordshire at St.Paul's Church Knightsbridge on August 11th 1863. Hugo was the son of Hugo Charles Meynell-Ingram who married Georgiana Pigou, daughter of Frederick Pigou of Berkeley Square London. Hugo Charles was the son of Hugo Meynell of Bradley and Elizabeth Ingram Shepheard. She was the daughter of Charles Ingram 9th Viscount Irwin and Frances Gibson Shepheard, sister of Lady

Hertford and Frances Ingram Shepheard/Lady William Gordon. Hugo Charles inherited Temple Newsam on the death of Frances Ingram Shepheard in 1841. He held the estate until his death on February 25th 1869, when his eldest son Hugo Francis inherited the estates. He was born in 1821/22 and was MP for West Staffordshire. Georgiana who with her husband spent only two or three months at Temple Newsam every year, died at Hoar Cross on October 26th 1868. In February 1870 Hugo Francis sustained serious injuries in a riding accident on the Hoar Cross estate and he died on May 26th 1871. His body was taken to St Peter's Church at Yoxall until the completion of the Church of the Holy Angels. The tombs of the founder and her husband for which the church was completed are on either side of the altar.

The east window of the south chapel at Whitkirk Church was placed as a memorial to her husband by Emily Meynell Ingram, who also provided the stained glass coats of arms in the south aisle windows. These include the arms of Hugo Meynell, Emily Meynell Ingram, Hugo Charles Meynell Ingram, Hugo Francis Meynell Ingram and Sir Charles Wood.

Emily devoted much of her time to church affairs being patron of Hoar Cross, Altofts and Whitkirk, where she gave £1000 towards the chancel extension in 1901 by the architect of Hoar Cross Church George Bodley (1827-1907). She endowed St Edward's Church Holbeck with £30,000 employing George Bodley as architect and Lord Halifax laid the foundation stone in November 1903: it was dedicated a year later. Mrs Meynell Ingram gave the site and £800 to build Halton Institute: the foundation stone was laid by Mary Emily Wood, sister of the 3rd Viscount Halifax on January 21st 1904 and the Institute was opened later in the year. The Meynell Ingrams were great supporters and benefactors of the Halton National School (Temple Newsam Halton Primary) and the church: Emily purchased the advowson of Whitkirk Church from Trinity College Cambridge in 1898 and after her death the vicars have been appointed by the Meynell Trustees.

Emily Charlotte Meynell Ingram died of heart failure and Bright's Disease (chronic inflamation of the kidney) on Wednesday December 21st 1904. Her doctor Dr William Pogson of Seacroft had advised a visit to Dr Pavy Senior Physician Guy's Hospital London a year prior to her death. She died at 6.30pm and funeral arrangements were made at Hoar Cross for the Saturday. There was a short service at Temple Newsam Chapel prior to the coffin being taken by train to Hoar Cross. Tenants and friends on the Temple Newsam, Stanley and Altofts estates left Leeds Midland Station for Burton-on-Trent with two saloon carriages specially provided. The mourners journeyed to Hoar Cross where there was the main funeral service at Hoar Cross Church conducted by Rev Canon Knox Little. The coffin was of oak with silver mountings and a silver inscribed plate: the only flowers were a wreath from the Hall and a floral

cross. There were over 200 at the service which was attended by local people and tenants from all her estates.
The will left money for a scholarship at Lichfield Theological College, £5000 to the Meynell Ingram Cottage Hospital Yoxall. There were legacies for her Temple Newsam servants including the head gardener Robert Dawes, coachman Frederick Lycett and the maids and servants at the mansion. She left the Temple Newsam Estate together with her estates at Leeds, Halifax, Heath, Warmfield, Altofts, Stanley, Sheriff Hutton, Hatfield and Barton-le-Street to her nephew Hon Edward Frederick Lindley Wood. The estates at Hoar Cross and Laughton together with her London home at Eaton Square were bequeathed to her brother Lord Halifax. It was said that while at Temple Newsam she had led *"a very quiet retired life in the company of a few select friends and entertained on a large scale only when royalty or distinguished persons stayed with her. Her chief recreation was yachting and she spent a period every year cruising in the Mediterranean or elsewhere on her private yacht".* The yacht was the "Ariadne" built by Camper & Nicholson at Gosport in 1874 for Charles Sabine Augustus Thellusson of Brodsworth Hall: it was 380 tons and one of the largest schooners afloat. The value of her estates in 1871 was £180,000 and on her death in 1904 were valued at £2 ¼ million inclusive of rents and stocks & shares.
One of the first local projects that the Hon Edward FL Wood was involved with following his inheritance of the Temple Newsam estate was the provision of the Halton Parochial Hall. He provided the site near the old pinfold together with £500: the hall was opened in January 1909. In 1910 the north drive was realigned through four lines of newly planted trees when the 3rd Viscount Halifax bought a new car. In the Great War part of the mansion became a VAD hospital and was opened to the public on rare occasions.
On December 7th 1921 Leeds City Council accepted the offer made by Hon Edward Wood MP on November 17th to sell the Temple Newsam Estate comprising 917 acres, with the mansion and other buildings for £35, 000. Most of the contents were dispersed in a seven day sale and the house was initially shown to the public with few exhibits.

PUBLIC OWNERSHIP

The estate was officially handed over to the Council on September 19th 1922. The Chaplain to Lord Halifax was Canon Wylde Vicar of St Saviour's Church and with his choir and organist conducted a short service in the House chapel. Viscount Halifax was made a Freeman of Leeds on March 5th 1923. Following the sale a further 18 acres of land between the estate and Halton Moor Road were purchased for £1650 and the official opening of Temple Newsam House was by Sir Montague

Barlow Minister of Labour on October 19th 1923. The following day there were about 20,000 visitors to the mansion and a firework display was held in the evening. Prior to opening the ponds were cleaned out, bridges rebuilt and the walled kitchen garden was let to AR McGill of Thorner for use as a zoo: in a year he had gathered a vast collection of foreign birds and animals. The zoo closed on November 6th 1923 and the stock was sold at auction, much being bought on behalf of the Leeds Corporation with many animals taken to Canal Gardens Roundhay. Menagerie Woods is the area through which the disabled access road runs to the car parks by the upper pond and the rose gardens. A new road was constructed to Lawn Pond: this familiar feature was used for model yachts but was filled in by 1954 and is now used as a car park. An early drawing of the mansion and the gardens showed formal gardens on both south and north sides with avenues of trees towards Leeds and Whitkirk. One of these avenues was the old coach road which can still be followed for some of the way towards Leeds, along Sycamore Walk and across the golf course.
The Great Yorkshire Show was held at Temple Newsam in July 1932 covering 35 acres on The Lawn and the football pitches west of North Plantation.

<u>LIVING IN HALTON</u>

The Kingdom of Elmet was created following the departure of the Romans c410 and this extensive kingdom which included Halton was administered from Barwick in Elmet. It stretched from the Peak District to the headwaters of Wharfe and Nidd and from the western edge of the Plain of York to the Pennines: the old West Riding. The Anglo-Saxon invaders conquered Holderness, Wolds and Plain of York in the 6th century but westward invasion was prevented by the Kingdom of Elmet. The Saxon kingdoms of Deira and Bernicia united as Northumbria in 593AD but in 615AD the Saxon Hereric was poisoned in Elmet. Hereric was the nephew of Edwin who invaded Elmet in 617AD in retaliation for his murder: the kingdom was at an end by 637AD.
Edwin was baptised in a wooden church at York in 627AD by Paulinus and this was followed by the conversion of ordinary people by Paulinus and James the Deacon-Edwin was killed at Hatfield in 633AD. The subsequent heathen rule by the Mercians ended with the defeat of Penda at Whinmoor in 655AD. At the Synod of Whitby in 664AD the church adopted the Roman church. The Saxon settlement of Leeds could have been on Quarry Hill and there would have been a 7th century wooden church-burnt by Penda in 633AD and rebuilt in stone on the site of the present Parish Church. The church remained until the Normans rebuilt in the 11th century. The end of the 8th century saw raiders from Denmark

and Norway attacking the coast and the Norse Vikings reached Yorkshire from Ireland and built on their toft: a piece of land for a house. The stone cross in the Parish Church dates from the 9th/10th century.

Halton was in the Skyrack wapentake: the name is derived from Old Norse "vapnatak" meaning a flourish of weapons; a sword was raised to signify assent in a judicial assembly. The centre was at the Old Oak at Headingley where early meetings were convened. A wapentake was an administrative district in the former Danelaw shires and was the equivalent of the Hundred: a 10th century division of a shire where administration was by the shire reeve (sheriff). The Danelaw was the north eastern area of England occupied by the Danes in the 9th and 10th centuries which included the kingdoms of Bernicia, York and East Anglia together with the five boroughs (Derby, Lincoln, Nottingham, Leicester and Stamford). In 1894 the Local Government Act established District Councils which were the successors to the wapentakes.

Halton would have been a collection of rough huts with thatched roofs where a small number of folk made a meagre living from the soil. The Norman Conquest would have affected the area with the Harrying of the North and subsequent devaluation of the land for taxation as seen in the Domesday Book of 1086. The nearest corn mill was at Leeds powered by the river: Templar crosses were displayed on the houses of the Manor of Whitkirk to indicate their exemption from grinding their corn at the King's Mills on Swinegate. A re-sited cross is on the restored Pack Horse Inn and the cross once on the Old George public house Lower Briggate is now re-positioned high up on the adjoining property south of the railway bridge. There were originally six on Lower Head Row and Lady Lane with ten on Templar Street: there were at one period 19 Templar crosses in the city. Crosses exist today on two houses at Whitkirk on Colton Road and Selby Road.

In the subsequent centuries Halton continued being a mainly agricultural hamlet owing allegiance to the Templars and after their dissolution to the Knights of St John and then of course to the later owners of the Temple Newsam Estate. The aftermath of Bannockburn in 1314 may well have affected Halton with the Scots coming south to plunder the riches of the area. In 1349 an outbreak of plague passed through the county with many hundreds dying from the deadly disease. The 14th century also saw the extraction of coal around Leeds for the needs of the local communities and for the many forges. The following years would have seen a few clothiers living at Halton as their trade developed into an important industry in the West Riding. The first fulling mill in England was at Temple Newsam by 1185. The Poll Tax returns for the "Wappentagnum de Skyrak" for Newsam includes Johannes de Halton and the listings included *"Austwthorp, Seecroft, Gerforth and Ledes"*.

The Skyrack Wapentake musters for *"Tempyll Newson & Halton cum Colton"* listed 3 archers with horses, 22 archers with long bows, 8 men on horseback with bills (a scythe on a shaft) and 29 without horse. In Halton belonging to the town were 2 jacks (body cover), 2 sheaves (arrows) and a salade (steel head piece with neck cover).

The Bubonic Plague or Black Death devastated England in 1349 and would have affected the village; the priest at Thorner was killed by the outbreak as well as half his parishioners.

King Charles 1st granted Leeds a charter in July 1626 and during the Civil War the town fell eventually into Parliamentarian hands in 1644 and a year afterwards Bubonic plague struck the district once again. A second charter was granted to Leeds in 1661 with the first mayor being Thomas Danby.

The folk of Halton may have been attracted to the curative powers of the Waddington Spa, the stone built bath house on Gledhow Valley Road is inscribed with the name of Edward Waddington and the date 1671. The spa was mentioned by Leeds historian Ralph Thoresby in his Ducatus Leodiensis (1714).

Leeds and Halton were to benefit from better communications with the opening of the Aire and Calder Navigation Canal passed by Act of Parliament in 1699 with Leeds at the western end: the canal opened to Leeds Bridge in 1700. The first boats to use the Leeds canal basin entered on Friday November 17th 1700. The Leeds and Liverpool Canal is the longest in Britain with a total length of 127 miles linking Liverpool with the Aire & Calder Navigation Canal at Leeds. It was in Yorkshire that a canal was proposed in 1766 and the merchants were keen to improve the supply of lime and limestone from the Dales and to expand the cloth market via Liverpool to the developing colonies. In 1773 the canal opened from Bingley to Skipton and the next year from Skipton to Gargrave. By 1777 the canal opened from Liverpool to Wigan for coal transport and from Leeds to Gargrave; construction stopped due to a lack of available cash and it was started up again in 1791 from Gargrave westwards. The proposed route was altered and it was fully opened in 1816: every year there was over a million tons of coal carried with 50,000 tons of limestone although more economic were the carriage of other merchandise-grain, machinery, cotton, wool and cement. Trade declined after the Great War as road transport improved.

The people of Halton who worked with cloth benefitted with the opening of the cloth halls of Leeds during the 18th century. Halton derived great benefit from the turnpike roads from Halton Dial to both Tadcaster and to Selby. The muddy tracks were to be properly maintained: at least that was the idea. Turnpike roads were opened from Leeds to Birstall (1824), Leeds and Bradford & Halifax (1741), Leeds and Elland (1741), Leeds to Selby (1741), Harrogate (1752), Otley & Skipton (1755), Tadcaster from

Halton Dial (1751), Wakefield (1758), Wetherby by Roundhay (1808) & Collingham (1824) and Leeds and Whitehall (1826). The tolls were removed to Roundhay and Harrogate in 1867; to Elland in 1868; to Whitehall in 1870; to Otley in 1873. The turnpikes were the gated entries to walled town where travellers were originally checked by a sentry with a pike: he would lower his pike to prevent entry.

The villagers of Halton were tenants of the Temple Newsam Estate to whom applications were made for any change in leases, property and the environment. These later included the gift or sale of land at a moderate rate for village facilities, including the churches, halls and land for allotments and feasts. At one period every householder in Halton received a joint of beef and a large loaf of bread plus a ticket which enabled them to obtain a blanket and a sheet. This dole became extinct after serving the village for a number of years.

More recent events affecting the population of Halton including the effects of the Boer War and two World Wars. The advent of better communication made the villagers more mobile and visit the parks of the city including Roundhay Park opened in 1872. Visits to the many theatres and cinemas around the city and in the centre would have been made possible by the trams and buses connecting Halton to other parts of the city.

Archive material illustrates the many aspects of Halton life over the early years

1507 *"for a measure and oxgang now in the occupation of John Graveley".*

1544 A cottage and five acres to be transferred after the death of Alice Beverley to the use of John Estewood and his wife Alice.

1575 A lease from the Countess of Lennox to John Hartley of a tenement in the "*towne and fyeldes of Haulton*"; the rate was four shillings and sixpence a year.

1596 Lands in Halton to be passed to the Leeds Free School (Leeds Grammar School) by Lawrence Rawson included parts of Cross Green Lane and Wilfred Avenue.

1601 Lands in Halton were with John Heald, William Irish and other tenants.

1631 A lease of a cottage with ten acres of arable at £3 a year to Thomas Genebury of Halton labourer. He was instructed to enclose the moor and waste of Halton and to grind his corn at the lessor's mill.

1631 Sir Arthur Ingram granted to Roger Iveson a messuage and 15 acres arable and pasture in Hawton. He also had to agree to carry two loads of coal yearly from Halton Pit to the Grimston Marshe near Tadcaster.

1633 John Pease is mentioned as using wood on his land to repair his cottage at Halton.

1637 The year also saw an agreement with Thomas Thorpe for 9 acres of arable in Gillsykefield, Crossfield, Cawseyland, Garthland, Oxeclose and land in the Deane.

1641 Agreement with Sir Arthur Ingram to Roger Heald for two closes called Wikebridge in the township of Halton.

1643 A claim was made for a way from the Gillsykefield to the Willowes and Kirkleys of Halton.

1649 Sir Arthur Ingram made a lease agreement with Elizabeth Bootle for one tenement, a dovecote and 63 acres of arable land and meadow in Halton. The rent was to be £30 a year with two capons at Pentecost and a hen at Christmas to be taken to the mansion.

1653 John Pease applied for permission to cut wood to repair his Halton cottage.

1657 Gyllsyke in the occupancy of William Rawson and an acre of meadow between lands of Michael Graveley and John Rhodes.

1667 The division of Gillsyke Field into two parts: New Field to be hedged on dividing. Mention of wire-drawer Henry Barmby of Halton and Jane Hartley tenant of Lord Viscount Irwin with a house, barn and stable.

1669 and 1672 Collections were made in the village for William Turpin and for widow Elizabeth Wright who had three sick children.

1674 The will of Hellen Brooksbanke of Halton stated that her three grandchildren would receive £10 each together with her heifer with calf and a brass pot.

1675 The contents of Roger Heald's house: range, iron, tongs, iron cleaver and the rooms include the old parlour, old chamber and new chamber, low parlour, milkhouse, buttery, corn laith, barmby laith. The stock included 2 oxen, 3 cows, 2 calves, 2 heifer, 2 mares, 4 ewes, 20 sheep, 2 geese, 2 cockerels and 7 hens. There was a plough, harrow, coulter, shares, saddles with 3 acres of sown corn. The review was appraised by Michael Graveley.

1684 Jennet Cowper lived in Halton in a cottage, laith and garden, half acre of arable on Gill Syke Field between the lands of Henry Iveson and Michael Bywater.

1684 Alice Heald of Halton property "iron range, tongs, frying pans, spit, brass basin, brass mortar and pestle. The house had 39lb of pewter with a chest, ark, tables, chairs, feather bed, spade, fork, purse and apparel.

1685 Field between Ann Swinden and Elizabeth Rhodes and butts between George Pease and William Barmby and one rood of meadow in Halton Garth End Field next to Roger Judson's stone quarry. The will signed in presence of Robert and Edmond Graveley.

1686 Mention of Garthend, Smarlings, Stacks, Intake and Slackbank (Halton Hill) in the occupation of Mary Swinden. A lease from Viscount

Irwin for a house and close in Halton with a rent of £10.9.9d a year plus a capon at Pentecost and a hen to the Hall on January 1st. The lease also of Walter Rosse carpenter from Edward Viscount Irwin of a house for two, arable at £2.5.3d a year; mention of a cottage in Halton on wasteland and open ground called a deane.

1691 A cottage with an orchard, garth, gardenstead near to a laith or barn and orchard with meadow close to Little Moore adjoining Temple Newsam in Halton. Mention of a Halton cottage, orchard and garden at a rent of £3.5/- a year.

1693 A transfer of land from Robert Graveley to Henry Iveson.

1696 A lease to Thomas Dale of Halton of a tenement with a barn, laithe, foldstead, orchard and garth. The land was in Garth End Field, The Deane and Smarlings at a rate of £8.17.6d a year.

1697 A house in Halton with a barn, orchard, intake in Garthend, The Deane and land called The Smarlings.(Smarlings Road was the continuation of the present Cross Green Lane at The Leodis across open fields towards Hollyshaw Lane: then as continuation of Cross Field Road.

1703 In March historian of Leeds Ralph Thoresby rode by Halton and Whitkirk to visit Sir William Lowther at Preston.

1704 A cottage in Halton of Joseph Croswaite with a barn and orchard from Michael Graveley.

1708 A lease of cottage and land to William Irish Yeoman in Cross Field and Gilsyke Field. There was also a mention of a butcher called John Pickering and a cottage of Jane Prince at 5/- a year.

1717 A new enclosed piece of ground in Laine between Halton and Leeds: between the Dyall stone and Osmondthorpe Yates. The same year records mention William Broome gardener of Halton with a house, gardens, orchard, arable and pasture.

1719 Halton Crossfield has a house, barn, garth and an ox close, deane and arable.

1721 A mention of the Halton Otewell Pit Holes.

1724 Robert Graveley had a house, barn, stables on the New Close.

1742 To be sold an estate at Halton with house, outhouses, two messuages and 14 acres: apply to Edmund Graveley.

1749 Lease to James Nelthorpe of Seacroft of several cottages with folds, gardens, orchards, stock garths with orchards and loft where a cottage of Roger Judson smithy of Halton. His son William rebuilt the house including garthends, crossfield, new field, gillsykefield and the Ings.

1751 Joseph Croswaite yeoman surrendered Pinfold Garth in Halton Cross Field. This was the end of Pinfold Lane and shown on the earliest maps.

1765 Mention of a blacksmith called John Armitage.

1782 A mention of Halton Town Gate.

1793 On December 2nd Joseph Clarkson of Methley having visited his brother at Halton missed his way home and fell into the river opposite Temple Newsam. His hat was found the next day but no sign of the body.
1799 A conveyance between Viscountess Irwin widow of Charles IX Viscount and Thomas Morkill of Halton. This included an orchard in Gilsyke Field, barn, stable and lands in Cross Field and Stocking Roods.
1800 A conveyance between Frances Viscountess Irwin and William Graveley of land in Gilsyke Field with lands of the Leeds Free School in Shaigh's Close.

DIRECTORIES FROM 1822 TO 1899

The directories held in various reference libraries record the names, occupations and often the place of residence of Halton folk. The following lists only mention the first inclusion of the name in the directories.

Directories included Baines, Kelly, Parson & White, Pigot, Robinson and White

The first major listing for Halton was included in "History, Directory and Gazetteer of County York published in 1822/1823 by Edward Baines. He was born on February 5th 1774 and came to Leeds in 1795 being apprenticed to Binns & Brown, printers and proprietors of the Leeds Mercury. In 1797 he became a printer with John Fenwick and in July 1798 married Charlotte Talbot. In 1801 Edward Baines became the proprietor of the Leeds Mercury and later became an MP. He had started his book publishing career with hymn books for the Methodist New Connexion.
The complete entry for Halton in Baine's Yorkshire:
Halton (Dial) in the parish of Whitchurch, wap of Skyrack; 2½ m E of Leeds.
Atkinson and Co. manufacturing chemists, (oil of vitriol, aqua fortis, dyer's spirits, Epsom salts &c).
Atkinson John vict Old Engine, Atkinson Mary dress maker, Blackett M academy, Briggs Wm bricklayer, Clark Peter manufr of bunting for ships colours green gauze for window blinds & corn miller White Bridge mill, Clark Wm corn miller, Graveley Christopher attorney, Gott----- gentleman, Grubb Geo vict Dog and Gun, Hardwick John vict Cock & Coronet, Hebden Joseph blacksmith, Hemsworth Wm land surveyor &c, Hick Wm gentleman, Hoyle John plumber and glazier, King David baker, Kirby Matthew shovel manufacturer, Laycock John vict Union Inn, Lumley Richard bar keeper, Pearson John Beesom manufr, Rhodes Joseph vict White Horse, Scarr Ellen gentlewoman, Shirtcliffe Edward surveyor of taxes, Simpson Mrs gentlewoman, Simpson William

gentleman, Wainwright Christopher schoolmaster, Wrigglesworth Thomas wheelwright, Wrigglesworth George schoolmaster, Wright William carpenter.

Bricklayers: Grant William, Jackson Thomas *Butchers*: Laycock John, Swift William *Cabinet makers*: Atkinson John, Atkinson William *Farmers*: Armitage John, Graveley TM & W, Hardwick Matthew, Hardwick William, Phillips Edward, Scholefield Wm, Smith John, Smith Thomas, Swift William *Gardeners:* Pickersgill John, Tinker Joseph *Grocers*: Pickersgill George, Strickland Wm, Wilson Thomas *Hay-dealers*: Dickinson William, Pennington Joseph, Scott Christopher, Westerman Wm *Shoemakers*: Chippendale Law, Hare William, Hodgson John, Hoyle Samuel, Rollinson John *Shopkeepers:* Maude Betty, Teale Francis *Tailors:* Beaumont George, Kay Mark.

1828 *Cattle dealer* Emerson Pickering; *Chemist* Joseph Atkinson, Thomas Phillips ran the alum, copperas, aqua fortis, oil of vitriol, tin spirits works at Whitebridge: his residence was Wade Lane Leeds *Draper* Eleanor Strickland *Gardeners* John Neal, Joseph Rollison, George Tinker *Joiner* William Atkinson *Navigation works* undertaken by Richard Pearson. *Plumber/Glazier* James Keighley *Stonemason* Thomas Jackson *Tailor* Mary Kay.

1830/1834 *Boot & Shoe Makers* Thomas Carr, Samuel and William Hoyle, William Lumb, George Rawlinson, John Ripley, John Rollisson *Cabinet Maker* William Harrison *Carpenter* Haddock Atkinson, George Wrigglesworth *Colliery Viewer* William Hemsworth *Dress Maker* Alice Chippindale *Farmers* John Armitage, Edmund Connell, William Hardwick, Stephen Pearson, Christopher Scott, John Walker, J Westerman, William Westerman *Gardeners* John Neale, Joseph Rollisson, Arthur Taylor, Joseph Tinker who died aged 85 in 1853 and his wife Ann died aged 55 in 1824 with son Joseph Tinker dying aged 65 in 1853. The Tinker family are buried outside the west church door at Whitkirk *Grocers* John Barker, Mary Dawson, John Hargreave, Robert Shaw, Benjamin Smith and William Strickland *Haydealers* James Dawson, John Westerman *Horse Dealer* Stephen Pearson *Joiners* William Atkinson, William Harrison, Benjamin Robinson, George and Thomas Wrigglesworth *Plumber/Glazier* Samuel Hoyle *Shopkeepers* John Clifton, William Strickland, Francis Teale *Stonemason* George and William Briggs, Thomas Jackson *Wheelwright* Charles Hodgson.

Catherine Wade was a gentlewoman: she was the last surviving relative of the reformer John Wycliffe (1320-84) and she died “in great peace” on January 29th 1838 aged 75 and was buried in the churchyard at Whitkirk.

1835 The listing of Halton residents by Richard Roundell for the election held on May 11th/12th 1835 was Joseph Atkinson, Peter Clark, Thomas Clark, John Graveley, Thomas Matthews Graveley, William Swift, John Walker, George Wrigglesworth.

1837/38 *Cattle Dealer* William Wilson *Chemical Works* Joshua Bernard *Gardeners* John Neale, Arthur Taylor *Joiners* William Atkinson, William Harrison, Benjamin Robinson, Thomas Wrigglesworth, George Wrigglesworth *Shoemakers* Thomas Carr, Samuel Hoyle, William Hoyle, William Lumb *Stonemasons* George Briggs, William Briggs *Tailors* John Pashley and Henry Skelton.

1841 *Boot & Shoe Maker* John Rawlinson *Bricklayer* William Briggs *Grocers* John Clifford, John Clifton, John Hargreave, Richard Kay, Robert Shaw, Fanny Teal *Joiners* William Atkinson, George Winn *Plumber* John Hoyle *Whitesmith* Thomas Wrigglesworth.

1842 *Artist* Henry Andrews Taylor *Ironfounder* Samuel Lawson *Tailor* James Varley *Shop Keeper* William Simpson.

1843 *Boot & Shoe Maker* George Crosthwaite *Butcher* John Sheppard *Cattle dealer* John Swift, William Wilson *Chemist* Benjamin Robinson. *Cooper* George Smith *Draper* Abraham Craven *Farmers* Thomas Adkin, John Connell, John Jennings, William Mathers, Stephen Pearson, Thomas Shaw, William Shaw, Thomas Stevenson, Henry Vause, John Westerman, William Westerman *Gardener* John Dickinson *Grocer/Shop Keepers* John Clifton, Richard Kay, William Simpson *Horse Dealers* William Pearson, Henry Vause *Tailors* Henry Skelton, James Varley *Toll Collector* James Adams.

1846/47 *Currier* William Dove *Farmers* John Jennings, William Wilson. *Grocers* Isaac Parker, Robert Shaw *Plumber* Samuel Hoyle *Tailor* John Pashley *Tobacconist* John Carlisle *Wheelwright* William Briggs.

1848 *Miller* Peter Clark *Millwright* William Briggs.

1853 *Horse dealer* William Pearson *Gamekeeper* Thomas Phillips *Oil merchant* Edward Phillips *Hay dealers* Richard Shaw, William Westerman *Gardeners* George and John Tinker.

1855 *Butcher* John Shepherd *Flax Scutch Mills* Edward Lawson *Grocers* John Clifton, James Haigh and Hannah Pawson.

1861 *Butcher* Squire Swift *Carpenters* William Atkinson, William Briggs *Chemist* Thomas Robinson *Butcher* Joseph Swift *Farmers* Matthew Cheesman, Francis Morritt, William Pearson, Edward Phillips, Christopher Scott, Thomas Stevenson, Mary William Swift, Henry Vause, Thomas Walker *Florist* John Tinker *Greengrocer* James Dobson.

.**1863** *Toll Collector* B Atkinson *Farmer* John Jennings *Gamekeeper* Thomas Phillips *Joiner* Joseph Tinker jnr *Shop Keeper* Hannah Pawson.

1864 *Farmers* Thomas Bean, William Boothman, Samuel Jackson *Market Gardener* James Dobson *Tailor* James Bean.

1866 *Auctioneer* David Bartle *Brickmakers* E Arthur and George Briggs. *Brick & Tile Maker* William Wilby *Butcher* Joseph Swift *Farmers* Edward Birdsall, Caroline Jackson, William Mather, George Rollinson,

Robert Stevenson, Mark William Swift, John Walker, William Westerman. *Gardener* Arthur Taylor *Hay Dealers* Andrew Cowman, George Rollinson (died aged 61 March 3rd 1871), George Shaw, Robert Shaw, William Shaw *Oil Merchant* Edward Phillips *Plumbers* Samuel Hoyle, James Keighley. *Potato Dealer* John Dobson *Shopkeepers* John Clifton, John King, David Fryer, Thomas Stockdale (PO) *Tailors* John Pashley, Henry Skelton *Wheelwright/Joiner* William Smith.

1867 *Engineer* Joseph Scholes *Farmers* George Bell, Martha Elizabeth Bellshew, Joshua Kershaw, Thomas Stevenson *Saddler* Isaac Eels Anderson.

1870 *Auctioneer* William Hall *Bank Clerk* James Hadfield *Gamekeeper* John Eccles *Manufacturer* James Gurney *Merchant* John Phillips *Saddler* George Stephenson *Underground Steward* John Fryer *Waterworks Manager* Joseph Scholes.

1871 William Bartle, John Clapham, John Curtis, John Fox, John Graveley, John Hart, James Hatfield, Edward Tinsdale.

Blacksmith Jeremiah Hebden *Boot & Shoe dealers* George Crosthwaite, William Hoyle, William Lumb *Butcher* Luke Hoyle *Farmers* George Bell, Christopher Scott, Henry Skelton, Frederick Stevenson, Henry Stevenson, Mark William Swift, Thomas Walker *Greengrocer* Mary Dobson *Hay Dealer* John Rollisson *Saddler* Isaac Anderson, George Stevenson *Plumber* Sarah Hoyle *Shopkeepers* Samuel Ambler, Ann Clifton, David Fryer, John King *Wheelwright* John Smith

1875 *Brickmaker* John Clark *Farmers* George Bell, Joshua Kershaw, William Morton, John Phillips, George Shaw, Martha Walker *Gardeners* George Crosthwaite, Mary Dobson, John Tinker, Thomas Walker *Milliner* Louisa Atkinson *Registrar of Births & Deaths* John Fryer *Saddler* George Stevenson *Shoe & Boot Maker* Jesse Crossthwaite

Shopkeepers Samuel Ambler, William Bell (PO), John Watson *Threshing Machine Owner* James Atkinson

1877 *Farmers* Edmund Kirkby, John Walker *Fishmonger* John Heseltine *Saddler* Isaac Barker Atkinson

1881 *Agent for Prudential Insurance Co* Isaac Atkinson *Basket Maker* Thomas Atkinson *Boot Maker* Solomon Law *Builders/Bricklayers* Edwin Arthur and George Briggs, John Lindley, John Pawson *Butcher* Luke Hoyle. *Chapel Keeper* Gideon Lumb *Chemist* Astley Cooper *Cloth Finisher* JW Crosthwaite *Coal Owner* John Guest *Confectioner* William Hanson. *Farmers* Joseph Darnbrook, Edward Thomas Kirkby *Greengrocer* Joseph Scholes Lawton *Grocer* George Thompson Herbert *Joiner* John Senior. *Market Gardener & Pleasure Valley Gardens* George Jennings *Milliner* Margaret Macleod *Plumbers* Francis Johnson, Henry Meldrum *Road Surveyor* Joseph Groves *Sewing Machine Maker* Thomas Hallewell *Shoe Maker* Jesse Crossthwaite *Shopkeepers* John Carr, Juliette Fryer, John Malhain *Watchmaker/Tobacconist* Joseph Milburn.

1887 *Boot Maker* Alfred Whiting *Draper* Benjamin Smart *Engineer (consulting)* John Ward *Farmer* David Speight *Grocers* John Burton, James Dodsworth, Hannah Hoyle, William Peaker (born in 1828 a former farm labourer whose sons worked down the pits; he wife was Christiana and sons John William was a greengrocer and George was a signalman), Richard Walker *Hairdresser* Frederick Whiteley *Milliner* Amelia Wilby *Plumber* Benjamin Clifton. *Tailor* Samuel Wraith *Traveller* James Wilks Lowe.

1889 *Auctioneer* Edward William Batley *Boot & Shoe Maker* Alfred Whiting *Confectioner* Susannah Wright *Cowkeeper* George Bell *Draper* Benjamin Smart *Farmer* Edward Wilson *Greengrocers* Mary Dobson, Joseph Lawton *Grocer* Richard Killerby *Joiner/Builder* John Lindley *Market Gardener* William Elliot *Plumber/Painter* Nathan Hoyle.

1899 *Boot & Shoe Makers* William Ball, Benjamin Leadbetter, Thomas Stockdale *Bricklayers* George Langley and Stephen Pearson Briggs *Butchers* William Walker, Mark William Swift *Clerk to PCC* George Julian Sunter *Clothier* Kit Stevenson *Confectioners* Harriett Crampton, Grace Tyzack *Cowkeepers* James Crawley, George Benjamin Roberts, Squire Swift *Drapers* Louisa and Ellen Heaps *Dressmakers* Emma and Kate Ambler, Elizabeth Atkin *Farmers* Edward Hartley, John Kirby, Henry Stevenson, George Taylor, William Verity, Alfred Wilson *Fishmonger* John Earl *Gamekeepers* Thomas Barnes, William Day *Grocers* Frank Butler, William Gaunt *Haydealers* George Rollinson, John Walker *Hairdressers* Thomas Forbent, Frederick Whiteley *Insurance Agent* Robert Stevenson *Newsagent* John Clayton Schofield *Rate Collector/Clerk to Halton School Board* William John Green *Saddler* George Stevenson *Shopkeepers* John Ballance, Charles Crosby,

Hannah Hoyle, William Peaker, Richard Walker *Tinplate worker* James Dobson *Watchmaker* Arthur Botterill *Wheelwright* Thomas Shaw.

Census Records of Halton 1841-1901

The Census is taken every ten years and lists the inhabitants of Halton together with where they lived, ages and occupations. The census returns from 1841 show the population of Halton starting at 1324 and rising over 10 year periods to figures of 2316, 3358 and 4516. The records show that the village was mainly agricultural with a substantial number of miners working in the local pits.

1841 Henry Britton was an agricultural labourer and Patrick Barker was a 70 year old army officer. Jeremiah and Joseph Hebden were the Halton blacksmiths with the cooper George Smith. John Swift was the local butcher. James Keighley was a plumber/glazier and Samuel Lawson was an ironfounder in Leeds; he started The Hope Foundry in 1812 on Mabgate which closed in 1930. Joseph Holdsworth was the mason and George Briggs was an early member of this well known building family of Halton. Ann Pickersgill made straw bonnets and the surgeons were Edward Pateath, 35 year old Richard Dalby Pawson and Edward Windle Tinsdill who lived at Gillsyke House employing two servants. There was also a besom maker, shoemakers, cabinet maker, tailor, publicans, draper, wheelwright, grocers and the Graveley family represented by attorney Charles and wife Ann. The census shows 14 farmers, 42 working in agriculture and 41 miners.

1851 Christopher Graveley lived at Hawthorn House while Joseph and Matthew Britton continued the family line.

1861 The Ball family makes a first appearance in the records: Isaac was a miner and with wife Sarah and her nine children mainly born in Derbyshire. The farmers now included Robert Stevenson with his wife Betsey and five children with a servant at the farm which spread over 44 acres. Henry Vause farmed 50 acres, Thomas Greetham had 40 acres and William Mathers farmed 90 acres around the village. William Graveley was a "landed proprietor" and Joseph Swift ran a butcher's shop. Samuel Hoyle had a plumber's shop and the records mention houses on Chapel Yard, Graveley Yard, Amblers Fold, Atkinsons Yard, Shaws Yard and Back Lane.

1871 There were 107 houses in Halton with Samuel Townend living on Town Street as a 30 year old blacksmith and the Hebden family were still the local blacksmiths helped by 23 year old apprentice Samuel Spence. Town Street is also given as the residence of David Bartle who was an auctioneer and valuer. The family later lived in Garforth and Swillington and John Clapham Bartle opened the Whitkirk Auction Market at the top of Hollyshaw Lane in 1909: now Travel Inn. George Stevenson is listed as a saddler & harness maker while Sarah Hunt was a druggist & dry salter. Thomas Stockdale was a grocer, Alfred Briggs a builder and Ann Robshaw was the Halton gatekeeper.

1881 Stevenson's Farm was Beechwood Farm on Engine Lane (Irwin Approach today). There is mention of Groves Cottages and of Joseph Groves who was a 72 year old corn miller at Park View House. The census has the first mention of Graveleythorpe as an area of the village, developed by John Graveley of Hawthorn House with Woodman Row, Clifton Row, Clapham Terrace, Grove Terrace and Hermon Terrace. Squire Swift was at Laurel House farming 120 acres and there were houses on Rose Terrace, Mills Yard, Chapel Villas and Stocks Hill.

1891 William Bell was at the Post Office and grocer's shop with George Osmond and his brothers and sisters. David Daniel lived at Laurel House with Thomas Schofield being the village newsagent on Chapel Street. Grocer Richard Killerby was on the High Street with wife Maria and children. Frederick Pogson was a medical student living at Rose Terrace and wheelwright Tom Shaw was on the High Street. Dr Arthur Thomas Wills was at Gilsyke House with wife Judith and a son and daughter: there were two servants working at this large house.

1891/1901 The records continue to show a large number of Halton residents working at the pits with an increasing population. In 1901 there were 60 miners with 1050 residents in the village. The information in these census returns has been used to shape this book.

In the 2001 Census for Leeds MD the population was 715,402 being an increase of 1.2% from 1991. The population of England and Wales in 2001 was 52,041,916.

AN A TO Z OF HALTON

ACTORS

Halton had many opportunities for amateur acting mainly through the churches and societies. There was one famous actor who had a temporary link with the village and he was ***Henry Ainley***. Henry Hinchliffe Ainley was born on 21st August 1879 at Belle Vue Terrace Leeds as the son of Richard & Ada (Hinchliffe) Ainley and christened at St George's Church near the LGI. The family moved to live at Victoria Road Morley and on Rooms Lane; Henry attended St Peter's School and Bundle's College. At first Henry worked for his father at the mill but soon became a Leeds bank clerk and then moved to a bank at Sheffield and afterwards worked at a firm of stockbrokers. He loved acting in his spare moments and was attracted to Birmingham to be with Benson's Shakespearean Company. He toured the country and was to make his first London appearance in 1900 and went to the USA in 1903 followed by a visit to Paris. In 1909 he played Shylock in The Merchant of Venice at Stratford-on-Avon. He appeared in films prior to serving in the Great War as a gunner; he obtained a commission and served in France and in Italy.

It was while serving in the army during the Great War that he was posted to command the anti aircraft post at Whitkirk and Temple Newsam. He was a good swordsman and he gave a demonstration of the art at the Parochial Hall Auxiliary Hospital where Nurse Bell was the matron. Christabel Burniston remembers in her book "Life in a Liberty Bodice" that her mother recognized Henry Ainley. *"In Halton a collection of army huts had been made into an improvised hospital where disabled soldiers could convalesce after the horrors of shell shock, trench frostbite or war wounds".*

It was in 1932 that Henry Ainley was taken ill but recovered to celebrate his 60th birthday in Ilkley. He died aged 65 on October 31st 1945: Laurence Olivier and Lewis Casson read the lessons at his funeral service. He left a legacy of memorable acting; his London appearances ranged from 1900 to 1945 and he appeared in a total of 24 films from 1911 to 1941.

ALLOTMENTS

Allotments were derived from the early enclosures initially of the 18th/19th centuries where an area of land was allotted to an individual. The 1845 General Inclosure Act made provision for the landless poor to have a quarter acre field garden. The site of the Old School House in Selby Road was such an area from this act. In 1908 it was required that the local authority provided the allotments. In 1922 an allotment was

defined as *"a garden area used for the cultivation of crops for consumption by the occupier or his family."*
In the Great War there was a general growth of allotments from 600,000 to 1.5 million and afterwards these plots reverted to their original use. In the Second World War allotments were used again to grow essential food with the Dig for Victory campaign seeing the annual food production rise to 1,300,000 tonnes a year from 1.4 million allotment plots. In 2003 there were 330,000 allotments in Britain with the local authorities owning 89% with an average plot size of 298 square yards and an average annual rent of £25.
There were allotments in Halton on Green Lane (Bye Law Men's Field), Green Lane (north) from The Croft to Greenway, Field Terrace, Field End Grove, Selby Road (Temple Moor School site) and Primrose Lane (Leodis and housing site)-pegged out in September 1940. The largest of the Halton allotments was on Primrose Lane to the north of Morritt Drive and was once suggested to become the site of corporation housing. In 1950 the plots were sold by Lord Halifax and tenants were able to buy them. In 1917 there were 17 allotments available in a field secured from JP Hartley.
After a few attempts to secure the site for building it was announced in 1979 that a 10 acre site which included the allotments and the sports field was to become the site of 400 houses with 30,000 tons of coal to be removed at the start. The plans were finally abandoned in 1980. The most historic of the allotments in Halton is the Bye Law Men's Field on Green Lane: shown on a map of 1834 and allotted to the workers on the Temple Newsam estate by means of a bye law. The land is a green area and no building is allowed on the allotments (Green Lane Allotments & Gardens Association). The Soldier's Field on Selby Road had 100 plots which were allotted to servicemen from the Great War by Lord Halifax. The secretary of the local ex-servicemen's association was Richard Thomas of the Council School who was concerned with the acquisition. It was Coun Brooksbank who suggested that the land be used for a new school, although this did not mature until 1956. The Soldier's Field was sold to the Education Committee in 1939 for £6250. There was once a wooden gate at Field End Grove off Selby Road which became the main entrance into the new school grounds. These allotments were run by the Temple Newsam & District Soldiers and Sailors Garden Holding Association. In 1919 the Discharged Soldiers & Sailors Smallholders Association was founded with Richard Thomas as President. A Challenge Cup was presented in 1918 by Major Edward Wood of Temple Newsam to the Temple Newsam Parish Council for competition amongst allotment holders of Halton and Colton. The first presentation was made in September 1918 by Lady Dorothy Wood. In 1921 the 7th annual show of the Temple Newsam Allotment Association was held in the Halton

Parochial Hall with Reg Knight opening the event; in 1931 they held their 23rd annual meeting at Halton School. The President was Richard Thomas, Secretary Albert Scarfe and Treasurer Alfred E Baron.
In 1923 Leeds City Council reaffirmed the 1908-1922 Allotment Acts and stated that *"Any man or woman who is resident in the city shall be eligible to become a tenant of an allotment garden subject to the statutary provision that one person shall not hold allotments acquired under the Acts exceeding five acres".*

ARTISTS

Arthur Terry Blamires was born in 1930 and was educated at Batley Grammar School where he won the Sixth Form Art prize. He obtained an honours degree in Geography from Leeds University 1951-55. He taught at Bingley Grammar School from 1955 and was appointed Head of Geography at Temple Moor School from Easter 1961 until he retired in July 1984. He had art tuition from Ronald Pawson who died aged 60 in 1977. Arthur turned professional in 1984 being inspired artistically from the many Geography field trips he led from school. He works mainly in oils and specialises in paintings of the English Lake District, where he sells his paintings. He has exhibited at Ilkley and undertakes demonstrations of his craft. Arthur lives in Whitkirk with his wife Joan: they have two boys Mark and Michael.
William Gilbert Foster was born on May 9th 1855 in Birkenhead being the son of a portrait painter and at first worked under his father. He was educated at Leeds Grammar School and exhibited annually at the Royal Academy Exhibition from 1874, as well as the exhibitions at Leeds, Bradford and at the Paris Salon. He lived at 4 Winstanley Terrace Victoria Road Headingley from 1885 to 1893 and by 1892 was a photographer at 14 Tower Buildings. He was elected RBA (Royal Society of British Artists) in 1893 and Vice President of the Yorkshire Union of Artists. He lived at Beechwood on Chapel Street Halton with his wife Nora Mary who was born in 1857 at Thorp Arch. Their family were Amelia (1878), Dorothea (1881) who was born in Headingley and also became an artist, Hermione (1895) and son Gilbert Lancelot. His shop in Tower Buildings Woodhouse Lane also had an entrance on Albion Street: the address was 35 Woodhouse Lane and 132 Albion Street. The triangle of shops at the junction of Woodhouse Lane and Albion Street was the site of Marsden's monument now on Woodhouse Moor. Other businesses in that area included Edmund Bogg at 3 Woodhouse Lane: he lived at 2 St James Square with a later shop at Wade Lane mainly selling picture frames.
Gilbert Foster exhibited his paintings at the RA and these included: Lane near Chapeltown 1876, Woodlands Cottage Otley Road 1882 and

The Reaper 1906. His other paintings included Lingering Light, A Garden of Lilies, The Last Faint Pulse of Quivering Light, Summer Pageant, Azure Meadow (bought by Leeds City Council), Hush of Night (Paris Salon), Garden of Lyonesse (bought by RH Barran MP), In the glow of Autumn (bought by Bradford City Council), Be the day weary or be the day long-at last it ringeth to evensong; this was the subject of his last painting completed on his death bed in Halton. While he was bedridden he also completed several pastels for the Leeds & Bradford Spring Exhibitions. His painting A Life of Shadows was presented to the Leeds City Art Gallery by TP Reay of Weetwood. He exhibited his paintings at art galleries in the London, Liverpool and Manchester.

Gilbert Foster became the second art master at Leeds Grammar School soon after leaving the school as a pupil and was promoted to principal art master. One of his pupils at the school was Sir Charles Holroyd who became the curator of the National Gallery in London. He also taught at Leeds Art College and was a founder member of the Staithes Group of artists. The movement formed in the 1890's when a group of artists started painting at Staithes. The members were known as English Impressionists and included Mark Senior and Owen Bowen.

William Foster died on Tuesday July 3rd 1906 at the age of 51. He had been ill for some time having never recovered from the death of his son Gilbert Lancelot Foster born May 6th 1895 and died on February 24th 1901. Gilbert Foster was buried on Saturday July 7th with the long cortege leaving Beechwood at 2pm: he was buried with his son at Whitkirk Cemetery with the occasion attended by the headmaster of Leeds Grammar School Rev Canon JR Wynne Edwards. There were wreaths from the Leeds Artists Club, Leeds & Cross Gates Camera Club and from his pupils at the school. There were many fellow artists at the funeral including his pupil Owen Bowen who was to be buried at Collingham Church. Owen Bowen was one of the artists illustrating Edmund Bogg's book The Old Kingdom of Elmet (1902) and 15 of Gilbert Foster's watercolours were also reproduced in the book-available from 1987 as a facsimile reprint. There were also 25 watercolours reproduced for Bogg's Lower Wharfeland (1904), 15 watercolours and two pen/ink sketches in Bogg's Upper Wharfeland (1904) and more sketches in From Edenvale to the Plains of York and other volumes. The grave of the artist and his young son is marked by a large Celtic cross in Whitkirk Cemetery. On the death of Gilbert Foster his widow spent time away from Beechwood and applied for a reduction of water rent in 1909 which was refused by Hunslet RDC.

Henry Andrews Taylor also lived in Halton and worked about the middle of the 19th century. He was born on July 16th 1809 and died in Halton on August 6th 1892. His wife Rose Anna was born on March 10th 1816 and she died on February 6th 1903. They are buried in Whitkirk churchyard by the west door; the grave slab also remembers their children Edward who died in 1849 aged 13 months and Harry who died aged 11 on November 3rd 1851. Henry and Rose also had a daughter Mary born in 1839. Henry's brother Arthur died aged 69 in May 1891 and his wife Elizabeth died aged 60 in April 1878.

AUTHORS AND WRITERS

Christabel Burniston MBE recalled her early life in Halton (Morritt Avenue) in the book "Life in a Liberty Bodice" published in 1991 at the age of 82 and reprinted in 2004. Christabel was one of four daughters (the youngest member of the family was a son) of Fred and Annie Hyde of Fraisthorpe The Avenue. She was born on September 12th 1909 and christened Sarah Elizabeth Christabel Hyde at Whitkirk Church. Christabel was seen by Dr Bean at Christmas 1914 when she had measles; she was educated at Halton Council School and at Chapel Allerton High School. Her mother was Annie Wainwright from Sherburn-in-Elmet whose father was a farmer and butcher; Annie married Fred Hyde in 1900. Fred was the manager for the Bradford branch of the Commercial Union. Frederick Thomas Hyde died aged 73 and was buried at Whitkirk cemetery on May 4th 1946. Christabel Burniston founded the English Speaking Board in 1953 and became the director and life president. In 1946-50 she was County Drama Organiser for Lancashire and for 18 years was the Principal of the North West School of Speech and Drama. She published the novel The Brass and the Velvet in 1999: Christabel Burniston lives in Cheltenham.

Andrew Morton was born in Dewsbury in December 1953: his father Alec Morton (1925-2002) was a printer who turned to picture framing and later graphic design. In 1954 Alec & Kathleen Morton with their young son Andrew David moved to Morley and then to Halton at Whitsuntide 1956.

Andrew's younger brothers are Ian born 1962 and Alistair born 1956 with sister Caroline born in 1959. Andrew attended Halton Moor Primary School and then Temple Moor School from 1964 to 1971: he obtained a BA in History at Sussex University. He married Lynne whose family came from Burley in Wharfedale and they have two daughters: Alexandra born 1984 and Lydia born 1986.

Andrew joined the Mirror Group Training Scheme in 1974 and then joined The Star becoming the Royal Correspondent after James Whittaker:

he lived in Muswell Hill London. In 1988 he left newspapers to concentrate on writing books which have included Diana Her True Story, Diana A Princess Alone and Diana Her New Life. His other books are Inside Kensington Palace (1987), The Playboy Prince (Prince Andrew) (1983), The Wealth of the Windsors Theirs is the Kingdom (1989), The Royal Yacht Britannia, Fodor's Royalty Watching, Inside Buckingham Palace (1991), Moi (Daniel Arap Moi), Monica's Story (Monica Lewinsky) 1999, Duchess (Duchess of York), Diana's Diary, Posh & Becks, Madonna (2001), Nine for Nine (The Pensylvannia Mine rescue (2002).
Andrew David Morton opened the new west wing of Temple Moor High School on October 1st 1993.
Pamela M Pennock was born in Redcar and lived in Norfolk from 1954 moving to Leeds in 1963. Pam trained at James Graham College and taught at Kippax North JS, St Augustine's RC and Halton Middle School from 1976 to 1982. Pam is a member of the East Leeds Writer's Group and her publications have included "The Evolution of St James's" for the Thoresby Society: 1848-94 Leeds Moral and Industrial Training School, Leeds Union Workhouse and Leeds Union Infirmary, "Tales out of School" being an account of the Leeds Workhouse on Beckett Street published for Macmillan Nurses, "Reaching the Beach" which includes Pam's childhood memories in Redcar and published by the Yorkshire Arts Circus and "I am a tree" which contains reflections by Pam and friends for St Gemma's Hospice and endorsed by Jane Tomlinson MBE.

BALL FAMILY

The Ball family established a greengrocery business in Halton in 1893. The family lived at Dial House and had shops adjacent to Dial House, Premier Fruit Stores on the corner of Cross Street & Chapel Street and Whitkirk View. In the 1901 census Dial House was the home of Cheshire born shoemaker *William Ball* (57) & Margaret Ball (39) with children William (19), Frank (18), Harold (1892-1941), Gerald (7) and Lawrence (2) together with daughters Elsie (16), Ethel (12), Annie (5) and stepdaughter Florence Thompson. William ran the Dial House fruiterers and hardware shop; a notice from 1904 states that butter and fresh eggs are available every Thursday. Ethel married 18 year old Thomas Elliott Chadwick of Moor Drive on May 6th 1908.
Lawrence Ball lived with father William Ball who died aged 64 on September 21st 1907 at Dial House. Lawrence was a POW during the Great War at the age of 18 and a member of the North Staffordshire Regiment. He married Ida Tinker of Woodland Road on October 26th 1925 and lived at 9 Temple Walk: he died in February 1943 aged 46. Ida Tinker worked for Isaac J Dewhirst who attended their wedding: they had their honeymoon in Blackpool. The last of the houses on Whitkirk

View was once Ball's greengrocer's shop. Gerald, Dorothy & Harold Ball who died aged 49 in May 1941 lived at the house/shop which had been converted into a greengrocer's shop in May 1928 by Gerald Ball. *Gerald Ball* of Dial House married Dorothy Muriel Johnson of Colton Mill on October 12th 1918: her father was Andrew Johnson. Gerald's daughter Esther Muriel Ball married Arthur Cowper on December 29th 1941. The shop was run in later years by CW Murgatroyd and in April 1978 was again converted into a private house.

Noah Ball was a respected cricketer being a member of Halton CC first team and bowled many times on the old Rec ground on Primrose Lane. Noah & Florrie Ball lived at 4 Hermon Street, 20 Wilfred Avenue and later at 10 Wilfred Avenue. Florrie worked for many years for the Gilleghan family at The Halton Pharmacy. Their son was Elias Llwellyn Ball who married Mary Chadwick Mortimer of Station View Cross Gates on January 13th 1923. When Noah died in 1961 Florrie moved to live at Seacroft. Enoch Ball married Edith Collis in 1909 but was killed during the Great War while on active service. Their daughter was Evelyn who at the age of 24 married Frederick Gamble in July 1934. Isaac Ball married Sarah and their children were Sarah, Sam, John, Elizabeth, Thomas, James, Matilda, Charles and Sarah.

BANKS AND BUILDING SOCIETIES

The Halton Penny Savings Bank opened in the village on October 17th 1859 and met for business on Monday evenings in Halton School; the president was John Graveley of Hawthorn House. The only other bank in Halton village was ***The Midland*** which opened on Halton Parade in 1963 and closed in late August 1983. When the Midland announced the closure there was a petition from customers with over 1000 signatures objecting to the proposal. Halton's Midland Bank was one of 150 Midland bank closures nationwide. Prior to the opening of the bank there was a banking service available in a hut on Primrose Lane. *The bank had started in Birmingham in 1836 amalgamating with the Leeds & County Bank and Exchange & Discount Leeds in 1890; in 1891 it became the London & Midland and in 1923 The Midland Bank. The HSBC bought the Midland Bank in 1987 and changed the name a year later.* The Halton bank managers included Jim Gregory and Edward Leach, who came from the North Street branch of The Midland; the accountant at Halton was L Kitson

Building Societies have included ***Halifax*** as a part of the Halton Centre: the premises became Godson's Travel in 1995. *The Halifax granted its first mortgage on May 30th 1853 and the site is now part of the current Halifax offices. The society was launched in the Oak Room above the Old Cock Inn Halifax with 584 members joining the Halifax Permanent*

Benefit Building & Investment Society. In 1928 the Halifax Permanent merged with the Halifax Equitable to form the Halifax Building Society. The Halifax merged with the Leeds Permanent in August 1995 and in December 1996 Clerical Medical became part of the Group. In June 1997 the Halifax converted to plc status and became a bank. In September 2001 the Halifax merged with the Bank of Scotland to become HBOS.

Leeds & Holbeck Building Society had an office on Chapel Street; the office moved to Grandways Parade. *The Leeds Union Operative Building Society opened in the old schoolroom Marshall Street Holbeck in 1845 followed by four other terminating societies. The sixth society was founded in 1875 on a permanent basis in Holbeck Mechanics Institute with bankers William Williams Brown of Park Row. The Albion Street premises were bought in 1886 and the head office of the Leeds & Holbeck Building Society was formed. New premises were opened on Albion Street/Headrow in 1930 which were extended in 1970.*

Leeds Permanent Building Society had their office in what is now the car park for the Chapel Street Social Club. The office was first planned on the High Street but a wooden hut was used on Chapel Street by February 1928; the premises were to be used at first for only five years. *The Leeds Permanent was opened on November 8th 1848 as the Leeds Permanent Second Building & Investment Society on the site of WH Smith Lands Lane. They moved to Park Row in 1858 and to Park Lane/Calverley Street in 1878. Permanent House was opened on The Headrow on May 15th 1930 and closed on merging with the Halifax: the building is now the Radisson SAS Hotel and Brown's Bar.*

BARKSTON ASH LAUNDRY

The plans for the laundry were passed by Hunslet RDC on February 22nd 1905 and it was opened three years later on Wilfred Avenue; it was named after the adjacent wapentake. The first owners were John Procter Scott and son Allan S Scott who built Rose Lea in 1915: John Procter Scott died on April 9th 1919 aged 76 and his wife Mary died November 17th 1916 aged 72; their daughters Mary Isabella died in 1913 aged 32 and Mary Sheela died on March 6th 1913 aged 42; the family came from Oakworth near Keighley.

Ronald Wheater was the next owner and his wife was Dorothy Ballance; their daughters were Ethel, Dorothy Mary born in May 1925 and Lillian Rachel born in April 1928. The family lived at Rosella/Roselea on the corner of Selby Road/Wilfred Avenue and former home of John William Preston: demolished in 1991 for new houses. Ronald married Mary Steel of Grove Road in April 1942: following Dorothy's death in June 1940. When he married Mary Steel they moved to 27 Grove Road.

Allan Scott had a van shed erected at the Laundry in 1911 and the same year there was a temporary dining room, which lasted until the end of the Great War. The laundry started in a small way and the temporary wooden building erected on March 14th 1912 was ordered to be taken away by the Hunslet RDC. The factory was extended in 1914 with factory space and a fuel store and further extensions took place in 1923. In March 1928 the laundry applied for permission to build an underground petrol tank with pumps. Application for an extension to the laundry was placed in April 1937. The manager following ginger haired Ronald Wheater was Laurence Lightwood (1957-70): he was succeeded by Mr Martin. Margaret and Laurie Lightwood celebrated 40 years of marriage in 1982. During Laurence Lightwood's time workers at the Laundry included Lily Alcock and Mr Carroll vandrivers who delivered the laundry in large baskets to places such as Barkston Ash and Bardsey; Ada Lee was the manageress, Irene Childerson ran the washhouse, Mrs Almond from Primrose Valley Farm was a stoker, Mr Blakeborough was the boiler and furnace man and Danny was the engineer. There were between 40 and 50 workers at the laundry and they were employed in the sections including unloading, sorting, washing and spinning, drying, rolling and pressing, folding, sorting and packing, the office and canteen staff: the canteen with Alicia Taylor in charge was upstairs.

The staff at the Laundry were annually treated to a dance and entertainment at the Halton Parochial Hall and the manager cooked two 25 lb turkeys for the staff at Christmas. In the 1960's Barkston Ash Laundry was owned by the Initial Services Ltd who in June 1969 built an extension: in 1967 they had put in new machinery and in 1976/77 applied unsuccessfully for an extension on more land. The owners indicated that if the Council planners did not allow the front extension the Laundry would possibly close with the loss of 20 jobs. Prior to being taken over by Initial the Laundry was known as "Dependable". The laundry was closed on August 31st 1984 as the result of a merger of Initial and Advance Services: both companies being part of BET plc; BET was later taken over by Rentokil plc and today the company trades as Initial Textile Services. The premises were taken by Terry Haddock in 1987 for the manufacture of Haddock Ranges for fish shops and takeaways: he moved from Swincar Works Kirk Lane Yeadon. The business moved to Unit 3 Cross Green Close and the old laundry buildings were demolished in 1989 with housing replacing the laundry buildings soon afterwards.

Prior to the completion of Wilfred Avenue as a through route the main entrance to the Laundry was from Selby Road. Wilfred Avenue was surfaced in 1930/36 and the Laundry Field opposite the factory once had drying lines strung across and an air raid shelter in the war years.

BARNBOW LASSES

The war memorial at Queensway includes two young girls killed in an explosion at the Barnbow Munitions Factory during the Great War. They were Ethel Jackson and Maria Rowley; Ethel Agnes Jackson lived at New Row Colton and her family received £125 compensation: she was buried aged 20 at Whitkirk Church on December 10th 1916. Maria Evelyn Rowley lived at 19 Newsam Square Halton and was one of the 35 women killed at the explosion at the No 1 Shell Filling Factory at Barnbow at 10.27pm on December 5th 1916. The explosion occurred in Room 42 killing the women and injuring many more; a shell burst in the underground fusing room. There were two other explosions at Barnbow Factory: March 21st 1917 and May 31st 1918.

Production started at Barnbow in December 1915 with 17,000 workers; 16,000 of these were women who filled a total of 24 million shells and 36 million cartridges, using 61,000 tons of propellant. The women worked three shifts a day and were fed in one of three canteens which held 2000. The workers were taken from Leeds by 38 special daily trains and 15 ordinary service trains.

The girls are remembered in the restoration of the Five Sisters Window in York Minster and on the screen there are 970 names with 240 munition workers of which 37 were killed at Barnbow. The Barnbow Lasses were remembered at a ceremony at the Royal Armouries and in the laying of the wreath at the Queensway Memorial on Remembrance Sunday in November 2002.

BELL FAMILY

The off licence on the corner of Chapel Street and Woodman Street was once George Osmond Bell's grocery shop. His father William was born in Wakefield on December 15th 1841 and became the Halton sub-postmaster for many years from 1880. *William & Ellen Bell's* family were Clarence born in January 1874 living for 5 weeks, Clarence born in August 1877, Mary Emma Bell born in June 1875 and died aged 65 in April 1940, Harold born in December 1878, Victor born December 1880, George Osmond Bell born in 1881, Camilla born in October 1887 and died in February 1889.

William Bell of Vine House died aged 66 on January 9th 1908; Ellen died aged 81 on Saturday February 7th 1925 at Hopewell House Woodman Street: there was a service at the Halton Methodist Church and interment at Whitkirk. Victor Bell married 21 year old Lena Short on October 12th 1905.

In the Great War his son *George Osmond (Ozzie) Bell* worked at the Barnbow Munitions Factory and his bakery on Chapel Street provided for the Temple Newsam estate during the last War. He retired to live at the house adjacent to the shop, although he had intended to live at Morecambe. GO Bell was a keen cricketer and played in the Barkston Ash League until he was nearly 50. By 1960 the shop was run by H & R Parker.

George O Bell married 28 year old Beatrice Taylor on August 11th 1908; she was the daughter of Jonathan Taylor a builder of Cross Street. Mary Emma lived at Hopewell House. George Osmond Bell died aged 82 in 1963 and his wife Beatrice May Bell died in April 1970: she left £27,000 in her will which included a trust fund which was to finance the GO Bell award for cricket at Temple Moor School in memory of her husband.

BIRCH AVENUE

The row of the first five houses from Cross Green Lane on the west side was first known as *Stanley Terrace* and built by John Graveley c1878. The street was then known as *Graveley Road* and the north end of the street built by John Graveley in 1880. 1 Stanley Terrace was the shop of confectioner Charles Bumby in 1908 and later was Bennett's shop; 5 Stanley Terrace (end house of the original row) was once the Halton Boy's Club and Halton Girl's Club prior to their transfer to the Parish Hall in 1909. In 1927 there was a complaint to the Hunslet RDC from FW & AE Baron who objected to the money to be spent on the road surface of Graveley Road as "only two cars a day used the street and the private street went nowhere". The street was surfaced by JA Sutcliffe under the Private Street Works Act 1892, together with Graveley Street/Sycamore Avenue.

The mattress factory and Thorpe House were also on Birch Avenue, owned by the Baron family. The site of both factory and house was developed into six town houses in 2002. In 1940 Thorpe House was home to Frederick William Baron of Alfred Henry Baron & Sons Bedding Manufacturers. These were known as the Excella Works. Albert Baron lived on Cross Street and the family sold the business in 1946, by 1947 Thorpe House was the home of Ernest Smith.

In 1958 was reported the death of Fred Wellock who at 92 was possibly the oldest Halton resident; his funeral service was held at Garforth Methodist Church.

BIRCH CRESCENT

The street was created in 1938/39 on the site of the drive to Chestnut Grove: later The Grove and home of both Crosthwaite and Sandy families. The plans were finally passed for the new street in March 1938 for the Property Management & Investment Co (Leeds) Ltd for 42 houses. There are 36 in nine blocks of 4 through houses built by William Airey.

In 1954 was reported the death of William Henry Bowers who died aged 71 in March. He was a school crossing warden at Cross Gates at the railway station bridge. He worked at Micklefield Colliery, enlisted in 1914 and served with the Royal Engineers. In the Second World War he helped to run the First Aid Post at Halton Methodist Church.

BLACKSMITHS OF HALTON

The first recorded mention of a Halton blacksmith was in 1770 when *John Armitage* worked in the village: he had written his will in 1765. In September 1878 John King applied to the Council to build a new blacksmith's shop and house at Halton. Brooks and Pickup had their plans passed by Hunslet RDC for a "blacksmith's shop on the Halton brickfields" in October 1900.

The blacksmiths of the village were based at the corner of Grove Road and the High Street. There were mainly two families concerned with the business over the centuries: Hebden and Townsend. *Joseph Hebden* was the Halton blacksmith in 1820's-1850's with son *Jeremiah Hebden* in the 1860's and *George Hebden* was the blacksmith from the 1870's. George

& Anne Hebden's daughter Harriet was born in February 1874, Annie in August 1875 and Lucy was born in February 1902. Charles Hebden and

Grove Road, High Street corner

Benjamin Hebden were also the family blacksmiths in Halton and Charles & Jane's son James was born in April 1868; Benjamin & Margaret's son Harry was born in 1868.

Blacksmith John Townend of Garforth died aged 45 in 1826 and his wife Elizabeth died aged 55 in 1840 and were buried in Whitkirk churchyard. Samuel & Mary Townsend lived at one time at Waterworks/Reservoir Cottage: he was born in 1841 and his wife was born in 1842. Samuel was the waterworks manager: their children were Samuel Joseph born May 19th 1867, Thomas born 1870: both were Halton blacksmiths, Albert born March 1878; daughters were Mary Elizabeth born 1874 and Lily Stella born December 1881 and Florence; Samuel Joseph Townend married Annie Speight. The smithy's detached house was adjacent to the workshop: *Samuel & Annie Townend* came to live here with their four children. Annie was the daughter of David Speight and she died in January 1941 aged 76. Their daughter Elsie was born in July 1893 and daughter dressmaker Amy Speight Townend was born in June 1895, married 44 year old corporation gardener of School Lane Herbert Skinn (Edgar Skinn's brother) in January 1943 and moved to live in the bungalow built on the site of the Whitkirk Water Tower. Clifford Townsend was born in September 1897 and Harold in May 1904. Their other daughters were Violet Hannah born in February 1899 and married William Tranfield of Beeston on June 8th 1924, Stella who married William Henry Dixon of Grove Road on February 17th 1926 and Lillie Stella who married 47 year old widower Robert Verity in February 1920.

The blacksmith at Field End was *Frank Dodsworth*: he and his wife Jane lived later at Graveley Street. Their children were Edna, Arthur and Enid Grace born in 1905 and married Harry Facer on April 19th 1930. The family were also the Halton chimney sweeps living in a cottage adjacent to the Irwin Arms public house on the High Street. Frank Dodsworth died aged 81 in May 1945 and *George Henry Dodsworth* died aged 82 in June 1930.

BOTTERILL FAMILY

Matthew Botterill was the youngest son of John and Mary Ann Botterill who changed his name to Bradbury and back again to Botterill. Matthew was a wholesale clothier in the family firm, which was run by two of his sons.

Matthew was born in 1849 and he married Charlotte Smith (1850-1908) having eight children. He lived at 35 Marsh Lane, 44 Well Close Mount, 27 Lyddon Terrace and 19 Springfield Mount adjacent to the Community of the Resurrection. Matthew Botterill died in 1902 leaving the wholesale clothiers Botterill & Seanor of Victoria Mills Hunslet to his sons Frederick and Matthew. The sale of the property and assets covered three days and included a Hansom cab.

The firm had started as Seanor & Co at 24/26 East Street Leeds and by 1892 6 York Place Leeds. Samuel Seanor was a hackle (comb for flax or hemp) and wool comb manufacturer who lived at 36 Springfield Place. In 1893 the firm became Botterill, Seanor & Co of Old Crown Yard Kirkgate. By 1901 the business had moved to Crown Factory Carlton Cross Mills Exeter Place Woodhouse Lane taking over from woollen merchants Brigg & Sons. They later moved to larger premises on Goodman Street/Atkinson Street Hunslet, where their telegram address was "Value Leeds". The factory was close by the river and canal and South Accommodation Road. The business was later run by wholesale clothier Frank and son Albert Clough with Botterill, Seanor & Co going into liquidation by c1989. Part of Victoria Mills on Atkinson Street/Goodman Street became nut and bolt manufacturers RH Bruce. Robert Herbert Bruce started his business in 1865 supplying mills with their essential tools: at first Dodgson & Hargreaves blanket mill, where the book keeper started his son RH Bruce up in business. Brass founders and sheet metal workers RH Bruce were in Hunslet Road and moved in 1967 to Atkinson Street. This ironmongers business moved in 1993 to The Idas Pontefract Road. The now disused mills became a listed property including the Atkinson Street frontage.

The children of Matthew and Charlotte Botterill/Bradbury were:

Walter Botterill who died as an infant in 1868. Herbert who was born in 1869.

Arthur Botterill (1871-1943) was a Leeds watchmaker and jeweller with premises at 33 Woodhouse Lane (13 Tower Buildings) and 10 County Arcade. In 1897 he lived at High Street Halton and then at 11 Bagby Square Woodhouse Lane. Arthur was married to Ellen (1874-1943) and

was a respected rock climber with his younger brother Fred; his later address in 1920 was 13 Archery Terrace Woodhouse Lane. He lectured on alpine climbing at Halton Institute in 1904.
Charlotte Botterill lived on Brudenell Mount and was married to Harold Carr: their son was Philip born in 1908.
George Henry Botterill (1875-1937) was the second son following the early deaths of two of his elder brothers. He was at first a clothier's assistant and lived at 15 Bagby Street Woodhouse by 1900 and moved to Roseville (Rose Villa) High Street Halton: Matthew is listed here in 1897. George Henry married Lizzie Palmer (1879-1941) on September 24th 1900 at Halton Methodist Chapel. Lizzie was the daughter of Charles and Mary Ann Palmer of High Street Halton.

George Henry and Lizzie Botterill with son Charley

George Henry Botterill bought the land on Chapel Street/Woodman Street from the Halifax Estate in 1911 and in 1913 plans were produced for two houses on the site by architects John Preston. The family moved into the property at 1 Chapel Street: later 17 on completion of the row of shops in 1928/29. In June 1929 George Botterill applied successfully for the construction of a baker's oven in one of the new shops. The shops were built in the family garden and with the houses were compulsorily purchased by Leeds Corporation in 1966.
George & Lizzie Botterill moved to Seathwaite 41 Pinfold Lane which was a new house in the road by 1929. George died suddenly at Pinfold Lane on March 17th 1937. A service was held at Halton Methodist Church with interment at Whitkirk. The Pinfold Lane house was then home to his widow with his son Charley and wife Constance and their daughter Pauline. George & Lizzie's daughter was May who died in infancy in February 1903: she had been baptised on February 20th 1903. Lizzie died in April 1941 at her Pinfold Lane home.
Frederick (Fred) Botterill (1877-1920) worked in the family firm and became a much respected rock climber with a new route on Scafell in the Lake District. There is still a "Botterill Slab" today as part of this route. Fred lived at 16 Beechwood Mount off Cardigan Lane Headingley and 10 Consort Terrace in Leeds. There was a period when Fred's address was

Claridges Hotel London.
Matthew Botterill jnr (born 1880) married Sally Thornton living at 76 Kirkgate and later at 70 Belle Vue Road, 122 Hyde Park Road and 5 Kingston Grove. Their son was Dennis Botterill (1904-1969) who was a poet and the London sub-editor for the Yorkshire Post. Matthew worked in the family firm and retired to live at Ben Rhydding near Ilkley.
Charley Botterill was born on May 5th 1911 and died on June 21st 1969; he married Constance Mary Smith on October 11th 1941. Constance was born on July 17th 1911 and died on November 22nd 1983; they are buried at Whitkirk Church. There were two children: Pauline born in August

Wedding Pauline and Peter
(from left) Constance, Charley and Bryan Botterill

1943 when Charley was a vehicle builder and she married Peter McDonald (born 1938) and died in 2002. The youngest child was Bryan George Botterill born in March 1948 and married Andrea Dixon. Their children are Ian Martin and Karen Joanne.

BOY'S BRIGADE

Halton Methodist Church founded their 5th Leeds Boy's Brigade Company, which was started in 1969. The Brigade took the company number from Gipton Lady Lane Memorial Church Boy's Brigade. The Company with Douglas Keighley who died in 1981 as the first Captain followed by Peter Young, ended in 1995; the Juniors and Anchor Boys ended in July 2000. The Girl's Brigade started in 1974 and ended in 1995. The Boy's Brigade Band was started in 1971 and their last parade was in

1990 to mark the 150th Anniversary of the Methodist Church.
The Boy's Brigade Queen's Award has been awarded to Paul Grubb, Paul Keighley, Ian Cowie (1976), Nigel Pattison (1978), Craig Shipton, Paul Berry (1980), John Rudge (1981), John Firth, Andrew Pepper (1982), Dale Hackett (1983), Mark Stevenson, Alan Dean (1984), Simon Guy, Richard Dowling, Richard Staveley (1988), David Harris, David Schofield (1989), Robert Longden, Christopher Young, Richard Bacon, Stephen Bacon (1990) and Matthew Harris (1992).
The Boy's Brigade was founded in Glasgow by Sir William Alexander Smith on October 4th 1883. He was born at Pennyland House Thurso October 27th 1854 and at 15 years old he moved to Glasgow to work in his uncle's business. While in Glasgow he joined the volunteers and became a lance corporal. By 1883 William Smith became a lieutenant in the North Woodside Mission Sunday School and it was here that the Boy's Brigade was created and he worked for the movement both here and in the USA. The badge was to be an anchor and the motto "Sure and Stedfast" (from Hebrews VI). The 1st Glasgow Company was alone in the first year but three years later there were 2000 boys as members of what was to become Britain's largest Christian uniformed youth organisation. In 1903 the annual display at London's Royal Albert Hall proved significant; from this can be traced the start of the Boy Scout movement. Baden Powell back from Mafeking agreed to preside over the display and thus started a friendship with William Smith and BP saw the opportunity of teaching boys the art of scouting. In 1909 William Smith was knighted by King Edward VII. He died on May 10th 1914 after a Boy's Brigade meeting in London and he was buried in Glasgow.

BROOKSBANK FAMILY

Major Joseph Brooksbank was born in Leeds near the Parish Church in 1894 the son of James Brooksbank who died aged 85 in March 1940. He attended St Peter's School as did his six brothers and four sisters: he attended Cockburn School. His mother died when Joseph was 8 years old and in 1931 the family moved to Grove Road. Joseph's sister Polly looked after the young family for many years and married Charles Hayes living at 15 Grove Road. Charles Hayes died on February 1957 having lived in Halton for 25 years. Charles served as a regular with the King's Liverpool Regiment and was an Old Contemptible who founded the Leeds & District Old Contemptibles Association and was a founder member of the Halton Angling Club. He was the secretary of Halton Conservative Association and a member of the committee who maintained the war memorial on Selby Road. *The Old Contemptibles were those who had served in France with the British Expeditionary Force from August to November 1914.* After he was invalided out he joined his parent's firm of Thomas Hayes in Leeds Markets.

The Brooksbank family had their roots in the Tadcaster area: Stamp Brooksbank bought Healaugh Manor in 1715 from Lord Wharton.Stamp was a Governor of the Bank of England and MP for Colchester and Saltash. The family lived at Healaugh Old Hall and later at the new Healaugh Hall in Tadcaster, built in the 1770's by Benjamin Brooksbank. In the late 19th century it became home to Edward Brooksbank JP and was restored after a fire in 1901. The mansion was demolished in 1944 after failing to attract the reserve price at auction. In the family plot at Healaugh Church are buried Benjamin Brooksbank (1757-1842), Edward Brooksbank (1826-1916) and Sir Edward Clitherow Brooksbank (1858-1943). The Brooksbank connection with Healaugh ended in 1961 with the sale of the Old Hall to Major Gillam and it was sold again in 1991 to the Samuel Smith brewery estate.

After leaving school Joseph Brooksbank enlisted in the Royal Marines serving his country for nearly 40 years. In the Great War he saw action in the Balkans, Battle of Jutland and in the naval raids on Zeebrugge and Ostend in 1918. He was wounded on six occasions and awarded the Belgian Croix de Guerre for gallantry. In the inter-war years duties took him on royal tours with Edward Prince of Wales, Duke & Duchess of York, Princess Elizabeth and Princess Margaret.

In the Second World War Major Brooksbank served in the Pacific, Australia, Mediterranean, North Africa, Italy and France-taking part in the Normandy landings. Following his retirement from service he was a Halton Conservative Councillor from 1950 to 1967 and eventually an Alderman of Leeds; he was also vice chairman of the Halton Ward Conservative Association. Councillor Major Brooksbank served on many committees including the Highways and Fire Brigade and always had a concern for the development of the Halton youngsters. In 1934 Major Brooksbank supported the acquisition of Soldier's Field allotments for a new school, which was not built until 1956 as Temple Moor Grammar School. Major Brooksbank was a governor of Temple Moor School from 1956 until his death in October 1972. In 1964 he became Chairman of the Temple Moor Governing Body taking over from the Rev Walter Dillam Vicar of Manston St James. Major Joseph Brooksbank was also a Governor of St Kevin's RC School and is remembered in Halton today in the Brooksbank Home opened in Halton in 1974. Joseph Brooksbank was interred at Harehills Cemetery on October 27th 1972.

BROOKSBANK RESIDENTIAL HOME FOR THE ELDERLY

The Brooksbank home was named after Major Joseph Brooksbank of Grove Road, who was a well known local councillor. The property was built by Pickles Contractors and was started in 1972 and was nearly ready for occupation in early 1974. The home was built on the site of Graveley Square and Dial Row and cost £134,000. The home offers sheltered housing and was officially opened in June 1974 by Dr Hugo Droller who was the Senior Geriatrician at St James Hospital. The first officer in charge was Muriel Bryan who retired in September 1985.

BUILDERS OF HALTON

Airey Houses built some housing in Pinfold Court Halton and at Birch Crescent: the firm was based at Eldon House Woodhouse Lane Leeds. William Airey & Son were based on Claro Road at the start of the 20th century. William Airey died in 1905 aged 63 and his wife Elizabeth died in 1898 aged 53: they are buried at Lawnswood Cemetery. Sir Edwin Airey was the younger son of William who took over the business as governing director. He built for the government in the war years and devised a method of building houses using concrete slabs: 1600 were built for the Leeds Corporation. He was knighted in 1922 and was Lord Mayor of Leeds in 1923. He was Treasurer of Roundhay Methodist Church having been a member for 46 years. William Airey & Son were responsible for both the Brotherton Library and the Queen's Hotel in Leeds. Sir Edwin Airey died aged 77 years old on March 14th 1955, having been the High Sheriff of Yorkshire. The Cross Gates estate was built by William Airey Ltd from 1921 when plans were approved for 200 houses.

Edward Ashton built the houses on the north side of New Templegate: Northern Ideal Homesteads built to the south in the 1960's. Their headquarters were on Stonegate Road with a temporary site office on Templegate Drive. The houses on Templegate Drive were completed by 1961 being sold for c£2150: the land was originally pasture with underground coal workings. The houses were built on concrete platforms to prevent sinking. In the Great War this area had an ack-ack gun with a searchlight sited nearer to Whitkirk.

Norman C Ashton of Trafalgar Row Works Meadow Lane built the shops/flats on Irwin Approach on the site of Stevenson's Park View Farm. Norman was the younger brother to Edward Ashton and drove a Rolls-Royce: he lived in a bungalow at Adel.

Thomas Atkinson was a builder living at 1 Primrose Road in the 1940's.

Gertrude Bray was a builder of Halton and Cross Gates and a property owner. She was the daughter of Frederick & Alice Mary Park of 57 Grove

Road who were married at Roundhay Road Chapel on December 26th 1901.

They celebrated their Golden Wedding in 1951 and Alice died in September 1958. Gertrude Bray lived at 59 Grove Road before moving to the Manor House on Colton Road from 1954 which she bought from Lord Halifax. The building firm was initially Bray & Park and Park & Green (AV Green) who built two semi-detached houses on Grove Road (the family homes) in 1930: Gertrude's father helped his daughter to run the business. The firm completed the Willow Well estate in 1937-38 and converted the old farmhouse into two houses in early 1938. The plans for the 20 flats on Temple Court were passed in October 1937. The Bray firm built the row of houses on Chapel Street from the corner of Primrose Road in the gardens of Hawthorn House in 1936. The houses on Pinfold Grove, Hill, Mount and Road were built by the firm from 1936. Other projects included parts of Grove Road and Templegate, Alan Crescent, Jean Avenue, Primrose Garth in 1935 and Valley Drive from 1936.

Gertrude Bray was a councillor for Mill Hill ward in 1945 and for Holbeck ward from 1947 and a co-director of Gertrude Bray Ltd. She planned the Penda's Estate and railway station and became the President of the Garden Village Welfare Association and Community Centre. Gertrude Bray was the President of the Friends of Seacroft Hospital and was connected with the North East Gas Consultative Counncil and Leeds Music Festival. She was chairman of the Civic Catering Committee and the Music & Civic Theatre Committee, Library & Arts Committee and Town Planning Committee. She had become a member of the Council in November 1945 and retired from that position in May 1968, becoming an Honorary Alderman. She retired from her building firm in 1976. Gertrude Bray was Deputy Lord Mayor in 1964-65. Her husband Harry Bray died in May 1983 aged 76 and Gertrude Bray died in January 1992 aged 85 in a nursing home: the service and cremation were at Rawdon Crematorium. Their last home was at West Burton Wensleydale. There were three children: daughter Catherine, who was educated at Wennington School Wetherby and married Peter Darnell of Hasland Chesterfield at Whitkirk Church on July 6th 1957 at which a wedding guest was Lord Milner. They met while students at Leeds College of Art-Peter was art master at Temple Moor School from January 1967 having been a scholar of the Slade School of Art. The other children were Helen Bray who married John Armstrong and John Bray who is a doctor in the USA.

Briggs were Halton builders in the 19th century. *William Briggs* was born in 1793 and his wife Elizabeth was born in the same year; their children were Hannah (1827), William James (1827), Elizabeth (1831) and Maria born in 1833. *George Briggs* was born in 1807 and this bricklayer and his wife Maria had children Edwin (1831), Oscar (1833) and Alfred (1839). Oscar Bushby married Ann Hawkshaw and was a bricklayer: their daughter Edith Fanny was born in March 1867.

George L Briggs was a Halton builder born in 1849 and he and his wife Maria had children Maud (1877), Maria (1882), Frederick (1887) and Catherine born in 1894. George died on May 13th 1918 and Maria died in 1874. Charles Briggs died aged 72 at his home in Vitriol Yard Halton at the age of 72. John Walter Briggs was born in 1846 and died aged 76 in October 1922 at his home on Dial Row. *Alfred Spencer Briggs* was a bricklayer and Traveller's licensee (1839-78) who married Caroline: Annie was born in 1861 and Christopher George in 1864. *Edwin Briggs* married Eliza: Alice was born in March 1857, Stephen Pearson was born in 1859, George Edwin born in 1862 and twins Martha & William Frederick were born in June 1866. *George Briggs* of Halton was a builder and bricklayer married to Maria: their daughter Harriet Booth Briggs married David Scholes on August 6th 1866. Harriet was born in 1844 and died on November 22nd 1878; their son was Benjamin Charles born October 1851. *George Langley Briggs* born 1859 was a builder of 11 High Street: his wife was Louisa born in 1864. Their daughters Maud Elizabeth was born in March 1877, Maria was born in August 1881, Harriet was born in September 1883, Kathleen born in October 1893 married James Albert Parker of Sycamore Cottage in 1922 and their son Frederick was born in 1886. *George Edward Briggs* born in 1861 was a Halton builder and with his wife Emily born in 1867 had children Edwin Arthur (1890), Gertrude Ursula (1894), William Cyril (1899) and Charles Bernard (1908). They lived at one period on Grove Road. *Edward Arthur Briggs* (1832-1889) was a village builder and his daughter Martha married Thomas Waddington of Whitkirk in 1884 and daughter Henrietta Maria married wheelwright John William Brown on August 3rd 1889. His son George Edwin married 23 year old Emily Todd on June 17th 1890: she was the daughter of miner William Todd. George Edwin died aged 47 on December 22nd 1908 and Emily died aged 60 on December 14th 1926. *Walter Briggs* was a builder in the inter-war years and his daughter Muriel born in 1916 married Albert Tooley on September 28th 1940.

Britannia built the housing estate on the Congregational Church land: the first of the 44 houses completed was occupied in March 1993 and the last house was occupied on April 29th 1994. Britannia is a privately owned company by Paul Rider and David Firth; it was founded in 1981 and they have already built 3000 houses including the 65 units at Kippax. Their headquarters are at Lawns House Farnley once a teacher's training college. Britannia moved from Pudsey to Lawns House in March 1994.

Henry Carter built houses on Barwick Road and Green Lane, where he lived until his death on January 13th 1949 aged 77: he was buried at Manston Church. He worshipped at Joseph Street Methodist Chapel Hunslet and was a member of the Sons of Temperance Movement. His daughter Agnes married Arthur Brown on January 24th 1948.

Dunhill Bros started their joinery and undertaking business in 1870 at White Horse Works York Road near Sumrie's clothing firm and soon branched out into building. The business moved nearer to their development at Bridge Works in c1941, which was by the Wykebeck Arms and Whitebeck Farm. The business closed in c1951 and the site became Wykebeck Petrol Station using the old petrol pumps; this became Wykebeck Recovery Services.

It was William Dunhill's father (1861-1946) who started the firm and William was the builder of the business. *William Dunhill* was born in 1887 and he married Emma Crann (1889-1976) of The Drive whose father engineer Henry Crann died in late 1933 aged 80, on November 3rd 1917 living at 243 York Road. They moved to Firdale Grove Road and then Beech Villa Hollyshaw Grove: Emma died at Whitebridge Avenue in October 1967. Joseph and Herbert ran the firm until closure. Joseph was the joiner with his own undertaking business. Joseph and Gladys lived at The Gables Wetherby Road Bardsey where he died aged 62 in January 1960. Herbert was the firm's engineer whose job was to keep the lorries on the road. He and wife Emma lived at 389 York Road: he died aged 88 (he was born on September 28th 1890) in 1978 and Emma moved to 37 Dunhill Crescent with new housing being built on the York Road works site. William's other son was Alan Dunhill who married Elizabeth Waite on May 29th 1948 and lived in Shadwell.

One of the joinery foremen working for ten years for Dunhill Builders was William Foster who died in November 1933 at his Primrose Lane residence.

The firm was responsible for completing the semi-detached development on Halton Hill: Dunhill, Verity and Whitebridge streets in the 1930's. Dunhill Rise dates from 1934. These were named after both the builder and the farmer who leased the land from the Temple Newsam estate. In 1933 Dunhill Brothers bought 16 acres of land for £1500 on which to build their estate: they were the builders of the parade of shops and Crossways Hall on Halton Hill in 1936/37. Dunhill's were responsible for the building of Sherbrooke Avenue in the 1920's, Alexander Avenue, Broadway (Bull Lane), Howard Avenue, Oak Road, Portage Avenue in 1932 and Poplar Avenue in 1935. Dunhill Bros built the houses on The Crescent following the filling in of the water reservoir and the top houses on Temple Walk.

BC Dyson built The Halton Parade which opened in 1929.

Eastwood Builders built the shops at the end of Green Lane now Paws for

Thought and once Carter's greengrocers in 1938 with housing on Knightsway and Woodland Road in the same year

Fairweather & Longbottom built a few houses on Graveleythorpe Road from 1938. Fraser Fairweather and S Longbottom ran their joinery/building business at 394a Harehills Lane. Partner Fraser Fairweather lived at Somerville Green The Oval Seacroft. Other houses built by the firm are on Templestowe Crescent.

George William Fenwick and his son George Lockwood Fenwick were Halton builders. George Fenwick was responsible for the present post office in 1931 with a bakehouse added to the adjacent house in the same year. Other houses were on Plantation Avenue (1932), semi-bungalows on Grove Road (1932), row of five terrace houses on Sycamore Avenue (1934), Cross Green Lane from 1935, Pinfold Lane in 1930, Selby Road in 1930/31 and the southern row of Overdale Terrace in 1933-34. The semi-detached housing on Primrose Lane from Sycamore Avenue to Valley Drive date from 1937 with the firm also building houses in Rawdon and Cookridge.

George William Fenwick first lived at 4 Stowe Grove Osmondthorpe and later at 216 Selby Road to 1930, 304 Selby Road to 1937 and then 26 Primrose Road from 1939 and 2 Sycamore Avenue in the 1940's with his wife Annie (1882-1942). He died aged 70 on July 10th 1952 in St James Hospital, having been in Halton for 25 years (1927) and a builder for 30 years (1922). The funeral service was held at Halton Congregational Chapel. George Fenwick's daughters were Dorothy born 1903 and married Herbert Balmforth on October 14th 1931; Annie was married to Archibald Hill of Leeds on April 20th 1935.

George Lockwood Fenwick was born in 1906 and first lived at 22 Brown Hill Avenue Hudson Road and at 1 Overdale Terrace. He married Lucy Ann Longden on November 21st 1931 and they had a daughter Jean Fenwick born on April 21st 1933. Jean was a dancing teacher in Halton who married George Victor Gill in May 1955. Her sister Veronica Ann Fenwick was born on June 28th 1944 and married Philip Alexander on August 14th 1965. In 1989 a gift was made to Lucy Ann Fenwick to mark her strong links with Halton Congregational Church where she had been an elder: she had left the district to live with her daughter. George Lockwood Fenwick died aged 52 in February 1959 and was cremated at Lawnswood on Saturday February 14th following a service at Halton Congregational Church: he was a member of the Men's Fellowship.

Gaunt & Dalby built the housing on Oak Crescent in 1937-38. Bernard Gaunt and Arthur Dalby ran their joinery/building business from Back Harrogate Parade Moortown. Arthur Dalby lived on Temple Walk.

John Graveley lived at Hawthorn House with his family and when he died in 1909 his widow Elizabeth lived there until the sale to the Jones family. The concept of a small village within Halton was created by John Graveley and known as Graveleythorpe: the first application from John Graveley to the RSA was in September 1877 to build five houses. He was responsible for much housing in the area from Cross Street to Green Lane including Sycamore Avenue (Graveley Street) and Birch Avenue (Graveley Road). The first part of the row from Thorpe Street to Park Street, Chapel Street shops/houses on Cross Street corner, Whitkirk View (1879) and Park View Terrace are all John Graveley's buildings.

John Graveley died on Friday May 7th 1909 at his residence of Hawthorn House and the obituary read *"He had for many years taken a prominent part in the public life of Halton. He was a member of the Hunslet Rural District Council, on the Board of Guardians of Temple Newsam Parish Council and was for over 20 years a churchwarden at Whitkirk Church. He was a member of the executive committee of the Barkston Ash Conservative Association: his geniality and charm won friends among all parties and classes".*

Leonard Green lived at 51 Pinfold Lane and built houses in the 1930's on Graveley Road and Green Lane: for sale in 1937 at £595.

Mark William Haley of Ivy Grange and Ecclesburn Street built semi-detached houses on Woodland Hill, Cross Green Lane and a newly created street Templestowe Gardens. The other director of the building firm was George William Haley with his base at Bennett Road in Headingley. Mark Haley was also concerned with the building of much of the Halton Moor Estate for the Council in the 1920's and 1930's.

Headrow Housing Group Ltd is a non-profit making Housing Association established in 1974 and which completed the first housing development at Horsforth in 1976. The business has over 1100 properties throughout Yorkshire and is based at Ingots Building Cemetery Road Yeadon. Headrow Housing Group completed Wheaton Court in September 1980 which replaced the San Remo home of Reggie Knight. The architects were John Brunton & Partners and builders were Jack Lunn & Co Ltd of Bradford Road Stanningley. Prospect Gardens was completed in January 1978 on the site of Chestnut Grove. The architects were John Brunton & Partners and the builders were WA Bushell of Ossett and Spofforth.

George William Hemingborough built some housing on Woodland Hill from the end of 1937.

Holmes & Parsons built many houses on Valley Drive from 1936 alongside the Bray development as well as houses on Primrose Lane from 1936.

Frank Horsman of 62 Woodland Hill built houses in this area.

Hunter's Builders Ltd of Gipton Approach have their offices in the old

Gipton Police Station. The firm built new housing on Templegate Avenue and Templegate Road in 2000 replacing the original houses by Northern Ideal Homes which were demolished on the old infilled quarry site in 1965. David Hunter started the business in 1992 and moved to the Police Station in 1997.

William Jowitt was a builder who lived at 631 York Road on the corner of Harrison Crescent. He built houses on the Halton Moor Estate off Rookwood Avenue and on Harrison Crescent where he lived with wife Louisa and daughter Lily. William Jowitt bought some land on the Estate to erect shops/houses at Selby Avenue in 1927/29. He had a fish and chip shop built for his own management at 3 Selby Avenue and another on Neville Road. He bought the Halton Mission Room for £239 in December 1939 to be used as a builder's store.

Edward Humphrey Lawson was a builder who lived in a house he built on Woodland Hill. The firm was on Dewsbury Road: his brother worked at the Fireclay company of Whitehall Road. The houses he built included sections of Woodland Hill and Templestowe Hill.

Layton & Gath built houses in the mid-1920's on Woodland Road. George and Ethel Layton with Frederick and Florence Gath lived on Woodland Road.

Lazenby Bros built houses on Morritt Drive in 1925. Building contractors Lazenby Bros had their headquarters at Headingley Works on St Michael's Lane.

George Morritt came to Halton in 1897 starting his building business. The first houses built by George Morritt were on Halton Hill: four blocks on William Avenue, William View and Lucy Avenue and named after his two children William and Lucy Morritt in c1899. The Morritt works were based at 92 Jack Lane Hunslet. He built Morritt Avenue and Morritt Drive by 1905. Terrace housing was further developed on Gladstone Mount Cross Green Lane. George Morritt lived at the end house of Gladstone Mount (22) before moving to Sunshine Villa Morritt Avenue and The Bungalow at Austhorpe he built for himself in 1929. In 1924 George Morritt applied to have street lamps erected supplied by new gas pipes along Selby Road to Austhorpe: the Cross Gates Gas Co replied that they could only lay the pipes to Whitkirk Lane End.

Northern Ideal Homesteads built much of the Templegate estate with Templegate Close in 1962. The plans for a row of shops on Templegate Way/Templegate Avenue were passed in 1970 but never built.

John Pawson of Graveleythorpe lived from 1845 until September 23rd 1888: his wife Mary Ann died aged 82 on August 8th 1931. He was the son of the Halton surgeon Richard Dalby Pawson. John & Mary's daughters were Ethel Maude born May 1874, Florence born in August 1875, Maria (1877), Gertrude born in March 1878, Eveline (1883), Hilda

Mary (1885-1933), Jessie (1886) with son Arthur born in September 1880, Harry, Edmund Dalby born in July 1882, Frederick (1892) and George. Mary Ann was asked to sing at the home coming of Mrs Meynell Ingram at Temple Newsam Clock Court after her wedding in 1863. Edmund Pawson was the secretary of the Barkston Ash Cricket League from 1909, secretary of Whitkirk CC and involved in the transfer from the field by the Brown Cow to the present site. Edmund was also in the choir at Whitkirk Church and was the Treasurer of Halton Institute.

William Pickersgill was a Halton bricklayer born in 1811 and with wife Hannah born in 1817 had a son George Pickersgill born in 1839.

Purdy & Sons built the houses off Green Lane including a new bakehouse on the corner of Green Lane and Station Road in 1937. They also built the houses on Greenway in 1935: their base was off Ellerby Lane.

Paul Rhodes was a building contractor with a temporary yard at Halton Dial: his headquarters were Park View Works Cardigan Lane Burley. He built the tramway booster station at Halton Dial as well as schools, factories and banks including Lloyds Bank Vicar Lane. Paul Rhodes was born at Kippax and died aged 74 in January 1934: Paul Rhodes was the builder responsible for much of the Halton Moor Estate.

William Willans Schofield built Temple Rise, Temple Avenue, Temple Close and Greenway Close with parts of Green Lane, Woodland Road, Knightsway and Graveleythorpe Road with a bungalow on Hollyshaw Lane near the site of the disused Prince Arthur Pit. The works were on Gordon Road Hunslet and 54 Joseph Street Hunslet was the residence. The impetus for small firms to enter the building boom were the cheap loans and mortgages available in 1931-32. William Schofield died in 1960 and he was followed by his three sons William, Harry and Frederick. William went down to Somerset to seek the work for farm buildings and cottages. Harry and Fred Schofield were in partnership in building: the two sisters Mary and Hilda worked in the office. Gradually the business was wound down and Harry died aged 89 in 1998 and Fred died aged 61 in 1976; his son is the Halton councillor David Schofield.

Percy Sedgwick was a builder first based at 13 South View Church Lane Cross Gates moving to Craig y Don 13 Park Avenue (Austhorpe Grove) and then at 60 Austhorpe Road who built on Plantation Avenue in 1931-34, Grove Road (1930/31) and on Selby Road in 1934.

JW Shippen built the houses on Primrose Crescent, Gardens and Grove in 1935-36 and on Primrose Lane in 1934 (Valley Gardens Estate). The firm was based at Broomhill Works on York Road near the White Horse public house with Thomas Shippen in charge in the late 1930's who lived at 813 York Road Seacroft. For a few years Arthur Mannix worked for the firm as a joiner: he lived on Primrose Lane with his wife Emily. It was Daniel Mannix who came over from Ireland to work as a plasterer on the

Quarry Hill flats and his two sons were Arthur and William (Bill). Daniel and Annie Mannix lived on Primrose Lane. Arthur had two sons John and Michael and a daughter; Bill had a son Brian. The three men worked for the firm which moved from York Road near Pontefract Lane to Aberford. The firm ceased to operate by the 1970's.

Charles Smith was a Halton builder who died aged 70 on March 10th 1867: his wife Elizabeth died aged 75 in 1869.

Alfred Stevens & Sons built new houses on Grove Road (Peggy Lane) in 1928-29.

John Trant Building Contractors Ltd of Fountain Street Morley built the townhouses on Birch Avenue in 2002 on the site of the former premises of Baron's Excella Mattress Works. The extension to Irwin Approach was by Trant and together with the last shop unit was made into six flats in 2003.

Wheatley & Easton of Cross Gates built parts of Hollyshaw Lane in 1903, Green Lane, Clapham Dene Road and Wilfred Avenue. Frederick's family included WA Easton who was building on Green Lane in 1914. In October 1901 the firm applied to build ten through houses on Cross Green Lane on land which had already been bought from the Temple Newsam Estate. On March 20th 1902 the firm had their plans passed for five houses and an end shop on Wilfred Avenue and in the same year plans were passed for the seven through houses on Charlotte Grove. The plans also included a stable and workshop on Back Charlotte Grove.

Arthur Wilson lived at 375 Selby Road in one of the many houses he built in the 1920's on Templegate (Pit Gate Lane), Selby Road, Queensway, Kingsway and Knightsway. In 1929 he applied for permission to build 26 houses on Pinfold Lane and Pinfold Grove. Wilson houses were built on Pinfold Lane and Pinfold Grove from 1930. Builder George Wilson lived on Carter Avenue in the early 1920's and his architect was GW Atkinson.

George Wimpey built the 44 houses near the Halton Methodist Church by 1973.

CARROLL AND GODSON FAMILIES

The Carroll family lived for many years at Holly House on High Street and were involved in farming, haulage and a petrol station.

Charles Carroll was born in Ireland and married Catherine Waldron living at Holly House. Their children were Charles Joseph, Kate, John William, Thomas, Henry, Joseph Patrick and Richard.

Charles Joseph Carroll married Florence Mary McCauley from Ireland and they lived at Princess Farm Colton. Later they lived at the Coach House on Colton Road Whitkirk: their children are Mary, Jean and Peter.

Kate Carroll married James Mannion and they moved from Ireland to live in Woodlesford and then later lived at Clifford: their children are Mary and Eileen.

John William Carroll was born in 1898 at Wakefield and in 1920 married Beatrice Arundel who was born in 1896; they lived at Holly House. There were three children Walter, Catherine and Josie.

Walter Carroll married Kathleen Murphy both born in 1920 and he lived on Chapel Street, Selby Road and at South Milford. Their son Tony was born in 1943 and he ran the Holly House Shell/Fina petrol station; daughter Maureen was born in 1945 and she married Norman Potts: their son is Andrew.

Catherine Carroll was born in 1927 and she married *John David Godson* on September 21st 1959. Catherine died on September 10th 1995.

Josie Carroll was born in 1930 and in 1957 married Dennis Morritt born in 1928: their son is Christopher.

Thomas Carroll ran The Grove public house at Holbeck and was married to Kitty: Henry Carroll married Mary Morris and ran the Holly House haulage business: he died in 1985; their children were Kitty, Thomas and Charlie. Their daughters were Bernadette who married Thomas Swarbrick at St. Theresa's Church in September 1962 and Clare who married Michael Grant who run Whitkirk Produce and live at Easingwold.

Joseph Patrick Carroll was born in 1903 and he married Ella Stephenson: their son is Michael Carroll who married Maureen Riley in 1968 and they ran the Farm Shop at Princess Farm on Meynell Road Colton for many years before closure in 1997.

Richard Carroll died when he was 15 years of age.

William Godson (1768-1841) was from Brailes (Upper & Lower Brailes) east of Shipston-on-Stour Warwickshire. He married Sarah Crossley (1775-1853) and they had twelve children of whom the tenth was Richard Godson (1816-1877) who was a master tailor born at Brailes. He moved to Cherrington after his marriage to Anne Saunders (1815-1869) of Cherrington Shropshire west of Newport with the nearest church at Tibberton. Their seven children were all born from 1843 to 1858 at Cherrington and included William Godson.

William Godson (1848-1910) married Sarah Firth in 1877 at Wakefield: Sarah was from Monk Bretton where she was in service at Bretton Hall. Their children were Mary Ellen, Clara, Frank, Annie Mildred, William Henry, Elizabeth Gertrude and George.

Mary Ellen Godson was born at Sherburn-in-Elmet in 1878 and died unmarried in 1949: she worked as a market gardener.

Clara Godson was born at Sherburn-in-Elmet in 1880 and became a private nurse: she died unmarried in 1953.

Frank Godson was born at Sherburn-in-Elmet in 1882 and in 1910 he married Miss Strickland at Bramley: he died at Pontefract in 1947. Their children were Kenneth William (1912-71) and Frank Geoffrey (1917-90), who were both directors of Dunhill's Builders.

Annie Mildred Godson was born at Sherburn-in-Elmet in 1884 and she died at Tadcaster in 1907.

William Henry Godson (1887-1965) was born in Sherburn-in-Elmet and in 1925 he married Lucy Firth (1886-1975) at Selby. They came to Cross Gates where he lived at Sandbed Lane and was a haulage contractor. William died aged 78 on November 5th 1965 and Lucy died on March 24th 1975: both were buried at Manston. Their son John David Godson was born in 1926 and in 1959 he married Catherine Carroll living on Templestowe Drive from 1959 before moving to Sandbed Lane in 1976. David followed the family business of haulage and started a taxi service before the successful coaching firm today which started in 1966. Catherine died on September 10th 1995 aged 68 and was buried at Manston after a service at St Theresa's Church Cross Gates. David and Catherine's sons are Richard John born in 1962 who married Jennifer Jordan from Belfast and James Matthew Godson born in 1972. Richard trained as an accountant and with his brother runs the family coaching business from Sandbed Lane and from the travel office in the Halton District Centre, which opened in 1995. Richard and Jennifer's children are Harry Alexander born in 1993 and Lucy who was born in 1995.

Elizabeth Gertrude Godson was born at Sherburn-in-Elmet in 1891 and was a market gardener who married Priestley Jennings in 1922: Elizabeth died in 1986.

George Godson (1893-1968) was born in Sherburn-in-Elmet and was a haulage contractor: he died on June 15th 1968 and was buried at Manston Church. He married Lilian Maud Briggs (1897-1965) in 1922 and had two sons William born at Ossett in 1926 and Robert born in 1933. Lilian died on July 8th 1965 and was buried at Manston.

Bill Godson was a civil servant who in 1955 married Marjorie Scott at Whitkirk Church. Their son Christopher Charles was born in 1961 and trained as a civil engineer; he married Clare Lavinia Soden in 1988.

Robert Godson was born in 1933 and became a market gardener: he married Eunice Maffin in 1958 and their children are Susan Ann, Robert Bryan and Trevor John.

CHAPEL STREET

Chapel Street was a cobbled lane and was once Cross Field Lane (Road) and Green Lane to Cross Gates prior to the opening of Halton Methodist Chapel in 1840.

North Side

There was a row of five cottages which had been built in 1878/79 on the site of a demolished mistal for a farm in Graveley Square: shown on a picture from 1860. The site bordering both High Street and Chapel Street was sold by auction on June 27th 1878 and included old cottages, sheds, joiner's shop and a house/shop on the High Street with cottage gardens on the road side. The occupiers in 1878 included John Smith, Benjamin Wellock and Thomas Nicholson. The first of the new cottages was converted into a shop for James Schofield's newsagents. Jonathan Clayton Schofield was a miner who married Sarah Ann and their daughter Emily was born in September 1866. Halton miner Henry Clayton Schofield and his wife Elizabeth had a daughter Hannah born in September 1866. *James Clayton Schofield* was born at Osmondthorpe in 1850 and he and his wife Ann who was born in 1853 ran the shop on Chapel Street with Thomas Clayton Schofield. Their children were Walter (1875), George Henry (1876), Alvara (1883), Mariam (1884), Eveline (1885), Vernon (1889-1926) and James Hilton. James Clayton Schofield was a miner and later sold newspapers from his house and then with his son Alvara on Chapel Street opposite Pinfold Lane. He died on May 18th 1919 aged 70 and Ann died on February 16th 1929 aged 76. Vernon Schofield married Alice Thompson of Brownhill Terrace on September 28th 1918: Alice died aged 36 in November 1926.

James Hilton Alonzo Schofield (1894-1930) was wounded in the Great War when he was a Private. He died on December 23rd 1930: his wife

Minnie died February 12th 1965 aged 69. Minnie retired to live on Wilfred Avenue and died at a house on Temple Court. Jack (John James) Schofield served in the RAF and with his wife Joyce ran the shop for over 30 years from 1942; their daughter Julia was born in March 1955. They moved from the shop which was due for demolition, to live over Fred Hill's shop at Dial House and then opened their shop at Grandways Parade on Selby Road before the sale c1983 to the Sheppard family. Jack Schofield died in 2002. The Chapel Street row was mainly boarded up in 1974 when questions were being asked about the future: agreement to demolish was obtained in 1975. 6 Chapel Street was with motor driver David Speight and his wife Alice: she ran a draper's shop from c1916 and through the 1930's and 1940's.

8 Chapel Street was coal merchant Arnold Bedford who converted the house into an office in 1935. 10 Chapel Street was shoe repairer Mary Leadbeater and later hairdressers Helena Marsland and Sarah Hollander. In 1930 ***Graveley Square*** was the home to William Broadhead, William Scholes, George Tiffany and Edwin Wood: George William Byford lived at 2 Graveley Square and was a cartman who died aged 48 on August 12th 1929 and was buried at Harehills Cemetery. Nine years later residents were Alvara Hardisty Bulmer, Fred Dickinson, Mabel Edwards, Samuel Grant and John Prince. In 1954 there were Alvara Bulmer, Sidney Jackson, Norman Lee, Richard & Wilfred Pemberton and Arthur Prince. In 1965 Graveley Square included Alvara Bulmer, Sidney Jackson, Richard Pemberton and William Rogerson.

Dial House was to the right side of the entrance to Graveley Square and

the listed house was the home of Laurence Bentley (1928), John Chadwick Brown (1930/40) and Ida Ball. The added shop was run by Laurence Ball and later Frederick W Hill greengrocer and Raymond & Carol Bowen. Fred's daughter Brenda moved to Aberford to run The Arabian Horse Inn. Jack Stuart White had his dental surgery at Dial House from 1950. The Halton Methodist Church had a row of cottages known as Chapel Yard once the home of chapel caretaker William Todd born in 1840 and his wife Jane Todd born in 1842: daughter Sophia was a dressmaker born in 1882. Edward Cummings was the chapel keeper who died aged 44 on January 2nd 1934 and was buried at Harehills. In later years the caretaker's house was 3 Woodman Street; another resident of Chapel Yard was Mary Thompson nee Collinson who was the daughter of a local preacher: her brother was William Collinson. Mary died on October 16th 1933 having had a lifetime enjoying playing whist.

Holme Lea had an attractive iron railing at the front and was the home of Dr Frederick Pogson and from 1929 dentist Jack Stuart White who had his surgery opposite at 17 Chapel Street and later at Dial House. The last owners were the Ginns family of decorators.

Nicholls and Pickersgill ran a haulage business prior to their move to Gilsyke Farm. The firm was involved with road surfacing and other work for the Hunslet RDC. Contractor James Edward and Maude Ethel Speight had planning permission for a builder's yard known as Speight's Yard in 1946: he lived on Manor Street.

Laurel House Farm was set back from the street and had a high brick wall for the garden. This was the farm of the Daniel family, dairyman Joe and Alice Stevenson (1928/32) and the Spencer family. The Daniel family had three boys all of whom joined the Halton Templars Scouts run by Jack White in the 1920's. There were two branches of the Daniel family: *Frank Daniel* (1858-1937) farmed from Colton with his lands including the fields on either side of the drive to Temple Newsam north lodges. Frank and Mary Daniel lived at Chapel Yard Colton. The large field to the east included Whitehead Wood now grazing for the cattle at Home Farm and the field to the west is now used for sports. *David Daniel* was based in Halton and his fields included those north of North Plantation, fields south of Selby Road between the water tower (Wilfred Avenue) and Templegate, the land on which the Golf Course was built at Temple Newsam, fields north of Nursery Wood and a field between Primrose Lane and the Valley. David Daniel was born in 1848 at Stillingfleet and was a farm labourer who married Frances Ann born at Headingley in 1852. Their children were Annie born at Stillingfleet in 1874 and was a tailor, Edith Mary born at Headingley Leeds in 1879 and was a schoolteacher, Charles born at Halton in 1882 who worked at the Primrose Valley Jam Factory, John born in 1884 who was a painter and Ernest born in 1891.

There were two shops on the corner of Primrose Road: the first was a butcher's shop which was later absorbed by the corner shop. This was at first run by the Wilby family and then Albert Edward Molden who was a miller and son of fitter John Thomas Molden and later a confectioner. Charles Wilby died aged 32 on October 31st 1883 and his widow Amelia nee Bates then aged 48 married Thomas Goldthorpe of 48 High Street on December 20th 1902. Charles & Amelia's son Arthur died aged 5 months in April 1878; daughter Margaret was born in 1877 and she married John Thomas Powell on July 31st 1901: she died aged 32 on September 14th 1908. Amelia died aged 82 on July 2nd 1935. Albert E Molden married Charles & Amelia's youngest daughter Maud Wilby on August 27th 1902; Maud was born in 1880 and helped to run the tobacconist, wools and toy business. The family owned some land at Halton on Chapel Street near the Parochial Hall. Albert & Maud Molden's daughters were Ivy May born in October 1903 and Margaret born in October 1905. Ivy May married Charles Bevins of Colton Road who was born in 1898,on September 16th 1925. In September 1930 Albert Molden applied for permission to build a wooden garage behind the shop. The corner shop was sold to Alfred Tomlinson who continued as a confectioners from 1936: the family were Alfred and wife Edith with son Derek Tomlinson. The shop changed to sell radio, television sets, china, glass and fancy goods.

New cast iron street name signs made by Glover & Wood Ltd with raised letters painted black were placed on the Halton streets during 1931. The numbering of Chapel Street was changed in 1935 with 1 becoming 17 Chapel Street. This area of Chapel Street was partly designated a clearance area in 1966 except for Dial House: the original plans included the demolition of the Institute and the building of a new community centre. The clearance area was approved in February 1968 with 46 houses built on the site from December 1971 and the new houses (Primrose Road/Close) completed in December 1972. The building of 44 houses in the Methodist Church area was started in February 1973 by George Wimpey. In December 1973 it was suggested that Chapel Street could become part of a one-way system for the ease of congestion.

Barker's Row was behind the shop at 20 Chapel Street and a short row of eight terrace houses. This was the second row of houses following Barker's Terrace off Primrose Lane. In 1928 the occupants of Barker's Row were Ephraim & Elizabeth Weatherill, Harry Stevenson, William & Sarah Fletcher, Alfred & Sarah Goodall, Samuel & Sarah Lumb, James & Maud Cunningham, John Plows and at 8 Barker's Row Walter Mark Dobson who celebrated his Golden Wedding in January 1926 at the age of 72.

Primrose Road had Button's hairdressers, a former post office and the police house together with The Orchards, The Nookin, Primrose Hill and

Halton Drive. This was the private drive to Hawthorn House and the long stone walled garden of Hawthorn House on the corner of the main street was once resplendent with Lilac trees, replaced by the present row of houses in 1937 built by Gertrude Bray. Bray & Park had sought permission from the Council to widen the Primrose Road/Chapel Street junction in December 1936: to include a crossing to Primrose Walk.

Hawthorn House was the home of the Graveley family and the site is partly occupied by the two semi-detached houses on the left hand side of Primrose Drive. The large house stood at right angles to the main street and had numerous outhouses and stables. It was demolished in 1956 and the area was cleared to make room for the new development of Primrose Drive. The houses on the corner of Chapel Street were part of the buildings by William Brown of Barwick-in-Elmet. When the present owners added their porch to the house the foundations revealed a cellar floored with blue slate, part of the shops which once stood on the site nearer the main street.

Laurel Farm was once the home of the Swift family and later William & Mary Verity until 1935. The old mistal became the headquarters of the Halton Templars in 1937 with the added Templar signs on the building end gables. Lord Halifax let the scouts have this old building for just £100 and it is still the property of the scout movement. The farmhouse and land became the business of Harry Hemsley coal merchants prior to demolition in 1956. The site is now occupied by the four flats on the corner of Primrose Drive and Chapel Street.

The first cottage of two on Chapel Street divided by a track leading to the scout premises is ***Primrose Cottage***. Following the death of Mrs Meynell Ingram in 1904 the property passed to a Trust who let the house and outbuildings in 1921 to artist Nora Gilbert Foster. In 1926 it was again let to Allan and Ellen Simpson of the Empress Hotel Church Square Harrogate and by 1932 farm labourer Arthur Trowles was living at the house. On February 16th 1937 the property was sold to Miles Verity of Gilsyke Farm, who already had a nearby field. Primrose Cottage was sold by Miles Verity in 1947 and Nancy Parker lived here from 1970.

The larger of the two cottages is ***Beechwood*** which was once the home of artist Gilbert Foster and is dated to the 18th century. The later owners included the Sowry family. The two cottages once had iron railings on the stone wall which were removed during the Second World War.

Halton Congregational Church was opened in January 1931 and closed 60 years later with demolition during November 1992. The site became Chapel Fold with four houses out of a total of 42 houses built by Britannia and called The Heritage Collection in 1994; the planning application in October 1992 was for 45 houses. The development includes Barley Field Court and Longfield Drive accessed by Primrose Drive. The site for the Congregational Church once included wooden huts where Halton Templars cubs and scouts met before their barn conversion at Laurel Farm. The more recent housing adjacent to the Congregational Church was once the site of four cottages (30-36 Chapel Street). The residents were Harry & Ella Oxley, George & Sarah Simpson, John Lake and William & Mary Penrose. By 1963 the residents were Dorothy Cooke, Esther & Joyce Green, Walter & Mary Cawthorn and William Penrose. To the rear of these houses were the dry middens for the use of the residents as well as those living at 38 Chapel Street. The area once

included piggeries and George Brigg's brickyard. The housing that stands today was built in 1970 by the Council who bought the properties from the Cowell family: most of these houses are now privately owned.
The few cottages on Pinfold Square were demolished and the site is a care home for Leeds Social Services known as Pinfolds.
The two cottages before the shops were 38/40 Chapel Street and later 72/74 Chapel Street after the renumbering. The first mention of these two brick built houses was in 1898 being the property of the Temple Newsam Estate. In 1920/25 the two houses and land to the rear were sold by the Halifax Estate to Alice Cowell, wife of Thomas Cowell. The first house was leased by George & Emily Day: Councillor George Day married Emily Cowell in September 1924. In 1949 Alice sold it to her son Rowland Cowell and his wife Jessie. Jessie Cowell sold 74 Chapel Street to Kathleen after the death of her husband Alec: she lived there from 1960 to 1974. 74 Chapel Street was sold to Ernest Edmund & Hannah Stinton: he was the ex-innkeeper of The Lord Kitchener Inn in New Barnet Hertfordshire and he died on February 14th 1975. In 1976/77 it was sold to Jeffrey & June Hayes who were married on November 6th 1976.
The row of shops date to c1891 being built by John Graveley as a block of two rows of small houses with walled private gardens on the Chapel Street side. The row of houses was first known as Clapham Terrace with the numbering changing in 1935: water was supplied to Clapham Terrace in October 1882. There were both front entrances to a house with a lower room and staircase to the upper floor and attic; at the rear were the entrances to the back row again with staircases to the upper floors and outside toilets together with a community well. The houses on both sides were decorated with floral motifs above the windows. The houses at the front were converted into shops from 1919 and gardens removed explaining the unusually wide pavement.
The shops on Clapham Terrace are:
76 Isaac Stephenson's butchers until the early 1980's: now Chapel Street Mowers.
78 Halton Fisheries from the 1930's under the Atack family, Fred Hutchinson and Jackson Stephenson. In 2003 it became the Shanghai Chinese takeaway closing and then reopened in October 2003 as the New Leeds Garden.
80 Chapel Street was first taken by William Bell as a private house and in 1919 this was sold to Thomas Burn with Charles Henry Ainsworth of Budge's Terrace Shadwell buying the property in December 1921. Planning permission was given in 1929 to alter a window to the existing shop/house. Charles Ainsworth died on June 6th 1938 and the business was passed to the Longfellow family. John William Longfellow's daughter Audrey was married to Stanley Dow in September 1946. The

numbers were changed in 1935 with 46 becoming 80 Chapel Street.

The shop became Stephenson Bros electricians in 1968: the business was started in Harehills by Jackson Stephenson of Seaford Avenue and Dennis Pickles of Seaford Grove in April 1957. They moved to Halton over the fish and chip shop next door with Geoff Dawson starting there in 1966. The business was sold to Liz Jackson who died in April 2003 and who worked for the business and Peter Rhodes but it was Liz and Geoff who ran the business. In 2003 Geoff moved from the Pendas estate in Cross Gates to live in the restored flat over the shop. Jackson Stephenson also owned Tom Drake's fish and chip shop opposite the Ritz Cinema Cross Gates. Jackson Stephenson opened the Graveley frozen food shop on Grandways Parade Halton and later opened a business in the wholesale market.

82 Ethel Ward and then William & Ethel Broadley stationers and newsagents followed by William Bennett. The business was bought by David Sheppard who had the property for two years before concentrating on his newsagents shop on Grandways Parade. The shop is now the Village News.

84 Alvara & Minnie Schofield's shoe shop; later Flair for Hair and Village Orchard.

86 William Peaker born in 1828 & Christiana Peaker (1836-1927): their sons were miners John William born 1873 and George born 1876; Theresa Mary Baker and then Gerald Ball's fruit and greengrocery, altered from a private house in 1936. This shop was run by Robert Henry Smith, Gerald Ball, William Clegg and later also the business of CW Murgatroyd who took the other Ball shop next to Dial House. This was Premier Fruit Stores with assistant Mrs Emery from Wilfred Avenue. In the 1960's the shop was run by C & T Johnson as Paramount Fruit & Vegetable Stores who also had the old Ball greengrocery on Whitkirk View.

South Side

The Halton Institute was built in a small garden that once was part of Dial House. A branch of the Leeds Permanent Building Society was based in the Institute grounds in the 1920's: now the car park.

The row of three shops was built by George Henry Botterill in his garden. The plans for these shops were passed in July 1927 and at that time he asked the Hunslet RDC to pave the causeway. He had already given some land to the Council to widen this path to six feet. The first shop was added on to the house and in June 1929 George Botterill applied for permission to build a baker's oven in the lean-to which was extended to the rear and became a lock up butcher's shop. This shop is the only one of the row which has a chimney, although internal modifications and improvements have dispensed with the oven and fireplace.

7 Ernest Morris chemist and Leslie and Gwendolen Scott's Chippy DIY. The shop was opened in 1965 after the closure of the chemist's shop, which retained the old pharmacy storage drawers. The last day of trading of Chippy DIY was April 18th 1996. The Hair Company is now the occupant.

9 William Stone and later Maud Jennings bakery: she lived on Woodman Street. Later tenants were White Rose Stationers, MH Wood watch repairs, Vickers tailors later bakers and from 1990 was a Sandwich bar and café.

11 Thomas Edward Bethell's wet fish shop: he was the head of a shellfish business at the Retail Fish Market at Leeds Markets. He sold rabbits, poultry and oysters and after being retired for 10 years died aged 80 on April 25th 1959. The Bethell family lived at 109 Morritt Drive: Edith was the wife of Thomas and she died aged 60 in February 1944. Their daughter Annie Bethell married James Whittle who was a police constable on February 16th 1931. Norman Edward Bethell worked in the family business and lived on Morritt Drive in the 1920's with wife Edith: their daughter Joyce was born in February 1928. The shop was later run by Albert Bethell born in 1917 and his wife Doreen who was born in 1919 and by Archer Bethell. The shop closed as a fish shop in 1962 and c1970 became Gee Fashions which closed in 2004: now Pinfold Press Printers.

15 opened as Ernest Barber butcher who had traded in Halton from 1926, prior to his transfer to the other side of Woodman Street. Ernest & Elsie Barber lived at Barkers Terrace for a few years; Ernest Barber died aged 72 on November 30th 1964 and his wife Elsie died aged 85 on August 22nd 1978. Their son Ernest ran the shop and lived on Pinfold Lane died aged 65 on December 24th 1985. Later tenants were jeweller SE Williams, optician George Croydon Stephens prior to his transfer to the other side of Woodman Street. George C Stephens was born in 1915 and he married Bessie Wood on May 11th 1940: their son David was born in 1946 and daughter Carolyn was born in 1948. David was educated at Temple Moor School and in the 1961 Sports Day achieved excellence in Javelin. George Stephens and family lived at 60 Chapel Street and later 9 Primrose Road. The shop became greengrocer Norman Ripley and later Armitage greengrocers. The shop is now Cream Professional Beauty.

The shops remained in the ownership of the Botterill family until compulsory purchase by Leeds City Council in 1966.

17 was 1 Chapel Street and the home of the Botterill family. Plans for a new house were placed in 1910 with a condition that the basement walls were to be nine inches thick. In October 1929 George Botterill applied for planning permission for a WC and to alter the coalplace to the house. The house was the dental surgery of JR Stuart White from 1929 before he moved to Dial House in 1950. In later years it was a barber's shop and there were plans for a hot food takeaway in 1999.

The corner shop on Woodman Street (19 Chapel Street) was outfitter Charles Palmer who had the plans passed for a new house and shop in 1913. The shop was then run by Henry & Ida Storr and Thomas & Mary Dineen who later lived at 23 Grove Road. They were followed by photographer David Latto until 1988 and there was then a motor accessory business. The extended shop is now the Halton Carpet Centre started by Colin Smith on 204 Selby Road Grandways Parade in 1986. He moved to Chapel Street in 1993 and the premises were purchased from Leeds City Council. The extension took place in 1998 on the site of a garden. Colin Smith owned 17 and 19 Chapel Street and once rented from the LCC: in the 1960's 17 had a peppercorn rent of 10/- a month. 19 Chapel Street is now divided into flats: planning permission was granted in 2001.

Woodman Street links Chapel Street and Selby Road and has Hopewell House, Poplar House and Vine House.

The off licence was once George Osmond Bell's grocery shop; his father William was the Halton sub-postmaster for many years. In 1925-1928 planning permission was granted for a dairy by the house and a licence was issued to sell Grade A milk. William Bell started at the shop in 1880: he was born in 1842. In the Great War his son George Osmond (Ossie) Bell worked at the Barnbow Munitions Factory and his bakery on Chapel Street provided the Temple Newsam estate during the last War. He retired to live at the house adjacent to the shop.

GO Bell was a keen cricketer and played in the Barkston Ash League until he was nearly 50. By 1960 the shop was run by Henry & Dora Parker: daughter Joan was born in 1935 and she married 30 year old Peter Deighton of Thorner on March 21st 1960. By 1970 the shop was run by Brian and Helen Moxon and is now Halton KG Wine Stores.

In c1933 the four shops were built by George Fenwick for Beatrice (Beattie) Bell, wife of Ossie Bell. The businesses were:

25 Cecil Hardcastle pork butcher; Ernest Barber & son butchers; Sweeney butcher and now part of the premises of George Askham.

27 Leeds & Holbeck Building Society followed by George Stephens opticians in 1970 and now part of the premises of George Askham. George Askam is a working jeweller and started in a workshop in Angel Buildings off Briggate in 1977. He moved to Halton Parade in 1986 in the old Midland Bank building and in 1990 moved to the present premises on Chapel Street.

29 Harry Illingworth shoe repairers shop; Capel's bakers offices, Halton Antiques and Christine Nolan from 1994.

31 Ethel Cluderay ladies hairdresser who lived at Sycamore Avenue; Helen Jackson hair stylist, later a chiropodist and now Glammapuss.

A bakehouse was adjacent to the last shop and is now the entry to a surfaced car park. The original bakehouse was built by the Taylor family and Leslie Trewartha ran the bakery with his wife Gwyneth and daughter Gwendoline by 1928. The Trewartha family lived at 30 Austhorpe Avenue. GO Bell applied for permission to add an oven to this bakehouse in April 1931 and it was known as the L & G Bakery by 1932 and with Peter & Kathleen Bennett by 1939. The enlarged premises were built by Lindrew's Bakery who were wholesale bakers owning two vans and a Bridlington restaurant. The Halton site was taken by Capel's Bakery specialising in Jewish cuisine. N & C Capel were at 14 Stamford Street Leeds 7 and moved to Chapel Street by 1960: in 1980 their registered office was at 29 Chapel Street and they ran three shops. Capel's Bakers moved from Chapel Street in 1973 to their office at 4 Middleton Park Avenue Leeds 10: Marshall Capel was a director. The shop at 31 was the bakery office and in June 1983 there were plans to convert this into a joiner's office. The old bakery has been demolished in recent years becoming the property of the church.

The old chapel of St. Wilfrid was bought by funeral director William Pease as the Mission Joinery Works and approval for conversion was given on December 12th 1944. William Pease of 58 Woodland Road and 441 Selby Road died on August 3rd 1968 aged 61 having been a funeral director in Halton for 25 years. He was a worker for the Halton Congregational Chapel where he was a church deacon and a Sunday School teacher for 40 years. His workshop moved from Mission Works to Lane End in late January 1958 and was later at the Windsor Works at Thwaite Gate Leeds 10. When the Jones family had left Hawthorn House, William Pease made use of some of the buildings as a workshop. The business continued and in January 1973 became part of W Roberts Funeral Directors of 82 York Road. The building was G & D Merchants

"The Fireplace Firm" and then became the Kingdom Hall of the Jehovah's Witnesses in 1972. In 2003 the old chapel was demolished as a new building was built by the members of the church which was completed in November 2003. The

track to Selby Road was surfaced by Leeds City Council in November 2003. This once was adjacent to two cottages.

The properties from the old chapel to Pinfold Lane were demolished c1970: they included a row of 3 cottages with an adjacent ginnel ***Beech Cottage*** with the tree growing through the low roof of the porch/kitchen by the roadside. This was the home of George & Ada Roberts with their family Elise, Hardwick and Matthew; Herbert and Walter George Crosthwaite wife Isabella and son George Donald; afterwards William Arthur & Gertrude Fleming and Edith Hannah Fleming.

Clifton House was the home of the Pindar family demolished in 1971 becoming part of Temple Newsam Halton Primary School's playing field. The address was 33 Chapel Street although the drive was from Selby Road. There was a short row of cottages set at right angles to the main street, which included the later home of Milton Jones and at the end of Chapel Street was the garage and the Halton Parochial Hall. Milton Jones Halton Service Station also sold petrol from two pumps. The garage was demolished and the new houses were built as Chapel Court in 1994; planning permission was granted for the development in 1994 to local builders Terence William Young of Wilfred Avenue and Brian Holroyd of The Croft. The site of the houses which stand back from the street on the right hand side were sold in 1924 to confectioner Maud Molden by Hon Edward Wood/Lord Halifax and again were sold to Leeds City Council.

CHARLOTTE GROVE

Charlotte Grove is a row of seven cottages parallel to Cross Green Lane by the former grounds of San Remo now Wheaton Court. Charlotte Grove was built in 1903. The row was sold by the estate in 1920; built by William Charles Wheatley & Frederick Easton. The building opposite to the row was once a small cotton mill and in recent years was the workplace of clothing manufacturer Kenneth Thompson. The building was sold in 2003 demolished and planned to be re-developed as a block of flats.

Charlotte Grove was named after Emily Charlotte Meynell Ingram (1840-1904) who was the daughter of the 1st Viscount Halifax.

CHEMISTS

Ronald Blass bought the Halton Pharmacy as a partnership in 1957 following the illness of Jack Gilleghan. Ronald Blass was born in 1923 and on leaving school worked as a miner. During this time he took his examinations at Leeds College of Technology and then Leeds University School of Medicine. He passed the examination and qualified MPS on August 25th 1945: the last year before the course became a degree. Ronald first worked for Ernest Morris on Chapel Street and York Road and then at the LGI. In 1950 he entered the retail trade with his partners on Burley Lodge Road and bought the Gilleghan business, from where he left in 1963 to run a shop at Acomb York for 22 years. He retired in 1985 and became an actor with many successful parts offered in theatres.
Edward Broadley was born in 1920 served in the last War and qualified as an MPS on July 7th 1949 at Edinburgh. He became a manager of a chemist's shop at Gildersome and in 1965 worked for the Taylor Drug Co Ltd (Timothy Whites & Taylors) at 9 Upper Accommodation Road. Ted Broadley bought the Halton Pharmacy from Ronald Blass who had a manager in the shop since his move to Acomb in 1963. The purchase was completed by December 1965 and Ted Broadley started at 38 Cross Green Lane in January 1966. He

retired in 1987 and the shop ceased trading as a chemist: he received a certificate in August 1995 marking 50 years as a member of the Royal Pharmaceutical Society. The property was purchased by Robert and Dorothy Sidebottom of Garforth who opened the Past and Present shop in late 1987.

John Gilleghan attended Leeds Grammar School and Leeds College of Pharmacy on Clarendon Road where he qualified as an MPS on September 24th 1926 and met his wife Violet Hilda Wilton Castelow at the College. *Violet Castelow* qualified as an MPS on September 23rd 1926: she had been educated at Leeds Girls Modern School at Leeds Institute. John Gilleghan took over at The Halton Pharmacy on Herbert Rennard's sale of the business on August 30th 1927: the business was bought by his father Herbert Gilleghan who ran his own pharmacy at 129 Roundhay Road. Following the wedding of Jack Gilleghan and Violet Castelow on May 28th 1928 at Epiphany Church Woodhouse Lane the Halton Pharmacy at 1 Whitkirk View became the family home. Their sons Jim

and John were educated at Leeds Grammar School. Jack's first car was a Singer in 1928 (NW2784). During their time at The Halton Pharmacy two of their greatest friends and colleagues were Dr Jack Young and Nurse Elsie Dacre, who spent much time with the family and were a great help during difficult times. Dr Moody and Dr Shires were also frequent visitors and close friends. In 1957 Jack Gilleghan had increasing illness with lung cancer and moved with his wife to live at 186a Selby Road (Gilsyke House) with Dr Young. Jack Gilleghan died on October 17th 1958 at the house and Vi moved to Selby Road at Whitkirk in September 1960 where son John joined his Mum from Durham with a post teaching biology at Temple Moor Grammar School. Vi Gilleghan tried to keep in touch with pharmacy by taking locum work including Beck's Pharmacy at Cambridge where John had a vacation post at the National Institute of Agricultural Botany during the long summer holidays from Durham University. John also worked in the long vacations at United Photographers Leeds and at the Villa Esplanade Hotel South Cliff Scarborough, where the manager's wife was the manageress of Boot's Library on Bond Street Leeds. Vi Gilleghan worked on two occasions for Garforth chemist Frank Holroyd before deciding that locum work was no longer possible. Frank Holroyd was qualified in 1948 and bought the Garforth shop in 1955 having served for four years in the Royal Navy: he was a member of the West Riding Pharmaceutical Committee. He sold the shop to Irwin Goldstein in 1984 and it is now one of the Lloyd's Chemist chain of pharmacies.

Richard Gordon opened his shop on Crossways Parade 49 Selby Road in 1993 having taken the business from Mike Williams, who started there in 1985. The shop was opened in the 1930's by Harold Sharp when the parade was built by Dunhill Builders.

Ernest Morris was a chemist born in 1894 and qualified on April 14th 1916 and starting his business at 20 Temple View Road (in 1936 the shop was William Clegg greengrocer) and then by 1920 at 170 York Road on the corner of Chantrell Street taking the business of Edward Baines. Ernest Morris opened another shop in 1935 at 7 Chapel Street. From the 1920's Ernest lived with his wife Ethel at Kencliffe 9 Grove Road where their garden backed on to Gilsyke House. They had two sons Ernest Kenneth and Clifford Henry; Clifford Henry Morris was born in 1922 and lived on Dunhill Rise serving in the army and married Muriel Richardson Worsnop of Sherbrooke Avenue in September 1946. Clifford was not a qualified chemist and he employed Max Cohen who qualified in 1933 to dispense in the shop. Ernest Morris died in 1959 and his widow remained at Grove Road until her death in 1972. Clifford worked at the pharmacy at Middleton Co-operative store. The business on Chapel Street closed in 1965 and the shop became Leslie & Gwendolen Scott's Chippy's DIY.

Moss Chemists is adjacent to the Gilsyke Surgery on Selby Road and was opened by Irvine Robert (Bob) Bloom in 1968 as a joint business with Max Bloom. The presence of a Bloom Chemist in East Leeds started in 1946 on Ullswater Crescent Halton Moor. The first shop in Halton was in 1958 when the family opened at 1 Irwin Approach with manager Stanley Simons. The shop was moved to the new Grandways Parade to be nearer the surgery in 1968; it was the first shop to be occupied on the new row with Bernard Bloom in charge. Irvine Bloom's son Brian Bloom sold the business to Moss Chemists in 1998.

Edgar Moss was the founder of Moss Chemists and he was born in 1879 into a Staffordshire family. He qualified as a pharmacist from

Manchester College in 1902 and in 1915 bought a pharmacy business in Feltham Middlesex. More shops were added and he arranged for a central source of supply for his eight branches by 1934. Feltham became the headquarters although Edgar died in 1958. Moss Chemists were acquired by UniChem in 1991 which merged with Alliance Sante to become Alliance UniChem. Moss Chemists have over 700 branches including seven in Leeds and one at Kippax.

Herbert Rennard was born on April 17th 1880 at Swaine Hill Yeadon as the son of Benjamin Smith and Mary Jane Rennard (nee Lodge). Mary Rennard was a relative who was the Registrar of the Wharfedale District and signed the birth certificate on May 12th 1880: she lived at Springfield Guiseley with her father Marmaduke Rennard. Swaine Hill is west of the High Street and north of Kirk Lane. Benjamin worked as a railway clerk and son Herbert qualified as a chemist and druggist on July 17th 1902. In 1905 he lived at 9 Cross Flatts Drive off Town Street Beeston; his apprenticeship was with Herbert Waite 4 Cross Flatts Avenue by the park.

It was in October 1907 that Herbert Rennard bought a private house at 1 Whitkirk View in Halton. The original house name was Glencoe and in 1901 was the home of 47 year old Mary Davies and her son 18 year old Oswald Davies. It was the end house of a row of eight terrace houses built in 1878 by John Graveley. It was also the largest of the houses with gardens to the front and an unmade cul-de-sac to the rear and a ginnel linking Primrose Lane and Back Whitkirk View.

Herbert converted 1 Whitkirk View later 38 Cross Green Lane into his chemist's shop surfacing the front garden. There was a brick wall with wrought iron fencing separating the front house entrance which had a wooden porch and high privet hedge. The front lounge of the house had

the floor lowered thus creating the shop accessed by two steps from the frontage and by two steps down from the hallway. There is some evidence that the property was the last to be built as the adjacent house discovered a small window on the linking wall during alterations. The small enclosed garden to the rear had a few flower beds and a wooden garage.

The house had a dining room/lounge to the rear, kitchen with steps down to the large cellar. The cellar was in two sections with room for storage and a large stone slab in the centre for a table. The smaller section was a small coal storage space which was adapted in the Second World War years as an air raid shelter with bunk beds.

The first prescription book of Herbert Rennard (1907-1911) contains many well known Halton names including the Crosthwaites of San Remo and Chestnut Grove, Daniel who ran one of the Halton farms, Graveley and Morritt who represented two of the earlier builders of Halton village. The book also features the families of Palmer who had a fashion shop on Chapel Street; Pindar who lived at Clifton House; Shaw who were wheelwrights and later funeral directors, Todds who ran the garage on the High Street, Dr Patricius Ashmore of Gilsyke House High Street and Dr Frederick Pogson of Holme Lea.

Herbert Rennard became the Registrar for the Temple Newsam sub-district of the Hunslet Rural District Council in 1914 while working in Halton and was later in charge of the Blenheim sub-district. Herbert married his wife Louisa in August 1904: she had been born on October 7th 1881. They had two daughters: Muriel born in 1908 who in 1947 was the Registrar for the Leeds Central sub-district with an office at 11 Park Square. Muriel worked as a hairdresser and later lived at Brighton Avenue Thornton Cleveleys Blackpool in a flat above a cobbler's shop at the tram terminus. She moved back to Leeds in 1961 after Herbert's death to live at Redesdale Gardens Adel where she died unmarried in 2001 aged 93. Daughter Dorothy Mary Rennard was born in 1911 and was in the Land Army during the war; she married Tony Jones and with her two daughters moved away to live at Brookside Newent Gloucestershire a few miles east of Ross-on-Wye. Dorothy Tyler-Jones died on June 16th 2003 aged 92.

When Herbert Rennard retired from pharmacy in 1927 the family went to live at a newly built semi-detached house Moor Lynne 7 Temple Newsam Road. In 1927 their house was renumbered as 66 Temple Newsam Road; the war years saw the Rennard family move away from Leeds and their house was bought by Dr William Ronald Jackson whose surgery was 1 Dunhill Rise. Herbert Rennard sold the property and business of The Halton Pharmacy in 1927 to Herbert Gilleghan who had his chemist's shop at Roundhay Road and who later lived in Oakwood. Herbert Rennard died in Thornton Cleveleys in June 1961 after a life of public service both as a local chemist and as a registrar for the City of Leeds; his wife died on September 7th 1978 at Lawnswood.

Herbert George A Richardson was a chemist who opened his shop at 10 Woodland Hill in 1956 and closed four years later. The shop is now Julie's Hair Salon who started here in 1986.

Harold Sharp registered as a pharmacist on July 28th 1928 and commenced at 534 York Road Leeds and in the 1930's opened the shop on Crossways Parade Selby Road. Dr Harold Sharp was a GP with surgeries at Cherry Row and Rookwood Avenue and he lived at 846 York Road.

Vantage Chemists opened as Wright's Chemist in Halton District Centre in September 1987. This was run by Charles Wright. The business is known as The Halton Pharmacy and is a member of the Vantage Group of Chemists, the trading name for AH Holdings whose head office is at Field Street Shepshed Leicestershire.

CHIMNEY SWEEPS

The village chimney sweeps included George Henry Dodsworth and Clarence Catlow. They lived at 7 Milestone Yard off the High Street. George Dodsworth was born in 1851 and lived with his wife Martha (born 1850); their stepson was Alfred Catlow born in 1880. Clarence was born in 1896 and died on March 2nd 1966; his wife Agnes died aged 58 in January 1955. Clarence Catlow's daughter was Joyce who was born in 1927 and married Thomas Marshall in March 1948. In later years George lived in Irwin Cottages adjacent to the original Irwin Arms. When he moved to 34 Woodland Road the Irwin Cottage was the home of the chimney sweeps Capsticks and Holdsworth & Son by 1938.

CHURCHES AND CHAPELS

Corpus Christi Roman Catholic Church had its origins in 1932 when the Provincial of the Oblates of Mary Immaculate wrote to Father O'Ryan of St Mary's advising him to seek clarification on new parish boundaries. The first parish meeting was held in the Shaftesbury Cinema on October 9th 1932. The first church was a hut and the school and presbytery were opened in December 1934 by Bishop Joseph Cowgill: the masses were held in the school. More land was purchased for £70 from the LCC in November 1935. The new church was opened by Bishop Henry John Poskitt on May 27th 1937 which was the Feast of Corpus Christi. On Thursday night September 28th 1950 the church caught fire with the Blessed Sacrament and vestments rescued. The church was opened on December 17th 1950 and in 1959 Manchester based Reynolds & Scott were consulted about a new church building. The work was started by Matthews & Sons of Leeds on the old bowling green site next to the old church. The stone used came from Hollington quarries in Staffordshire. The new Corpus Christi Church was opened by Bishop George Patrick Dwyer on July 8th 1962. In the church is a bust of Blessed Eugene de Mazerod (1782-1861) who was the founder of the Oblates of Mary Immaculate.

The origins of the ***Halton Congregational Church*** was as a PSA (Pleasant Sunday Afternoon) at the Methodist Chapel. This was formed in 1925 by Richard R Thomas but they were eventually asked to leave the Methodist Chapel. The records of membership of the Halton Congregational Church has this foreword: *"A number of friends conducting an unsectarian PSA in Halton Wesleyan Chapel, finding it impossible to continue there without becoming merged into the Wesleyan denomination, were compelled to seek other premises for their meetings. Having tried with no success to obtain the Parochial Hall and the Co-operative Guild Room have accepted an offer of a disused barn. With about 120 people gathered on the first Sunday in March 1926, a hearty service was held. Next week a wooden building was bought and erected on land off Chapel Street. The movement enlarged itself into an Independent Church known as the Halton Free Church. A committee of the Leeds Congregational Council came to Halton seeking a site to erect a church, the committee sought the assistance of RR Thomas schoolmaster and in an interview with RR Thomas and George Coleman, secretary of the Halton Free Church suggested that Halton friends should affiliate themselves with the Leeds Congregational Council. A meeting was held on July 1st 1926 which decided to do this and the Church was received into the Council on September 14th 1926. A meeting held on September 14th 1927 under the Rev GW Seager serving as the Moderator of the Church, decided that a service shall be held on Wednesday October 26th 1927 for the formal and authoritative institution of the Church. The Church was conducted by RR Thomas Treasurer, George Coleman Secretary, RO Thomas, H Killerby, W Purdy, E Monkman, B Sunter, Mrs SM Coleman and Miss Emily Scarfe who were all the deacons of the Church."*

The Halton Free Church congregation met at Hawthorn House in a disused barn, prior to the opening of the wooden hut known as Thomas's Tabernacle on Sowry land behind Beechwood, which was once the site of a tennis court. The old army hut was bought at Tommy Wass on Dewsbury Road and was transported and erected by the members. Second hand chairs came from Yeadon Picture House and eventually gas replaced candles for illumination. The platform came from Barnbow Shell Filling Factory as did the hymn book cupboard. The Leeds Congregational Council applied for planning permission to erect a church and Sunday School in October 1929. The foundation stone for their new church was laid on April 12th 1930 with opening following on January 3rd 1931. The building was designed by architects Chorley Gribbon & Foggitt and had cost £5000. The Sunday School extension Sanctuary Memorial Hall at the rear was opened in 1938. The church was known for the Congregational Galas: in June 1950 the Gala attracted over 1000. There was a procession through the village headed by the Salvation Army Band along Chapel Street, Green Lane, Temple Walk and Selby Road before returning to the field at the church. The queen Hazel Fox was crowned by Mrs JW Barnett wife of the Chief Constable of Leeds. The Halton Gala Queen was crowned by footballer John Charles in the Congregational field in July 1955: John Charles MBE died in 2004.

It was agreed to sell the church and land in December 1989: the church land included the land to Primrose Lane. The Congregational Church united with the Presbyterian Church to become the United Reformed Church in October 1972. The Halton URC was closed in February 1991 and demolished in November 1992: the congregation merged with the Halton Methodist Chapel to become Christ Church whose first service was on Easter Sunday 1993. The sale of the site was agreed in March 1992 and it became a housing development in 1993 by Britannia Developments of Pudsey: planning permission was granted in October 1992.

The table dedicated in memory of Richard R Thomas and daughter Nellie Jones together with a chair in memory of Edna Thomas are now at Christ Church Halton. Richard R Thomas was for many years the treasurer of the Congregational and his son was RO "Dick" Thomas who was organist, choirmaster and one of the deacons of the church.

The first minister of Halton Congregational Church was William George Seager who served from 1932 to 1946: he died at Chester-le-Street on April 2nd 1952. He was born in Somerset and was at Queen's Street Chapel Leeds 1911-32. He was the vice president of the Halton & Temple Newsam Gardens Association and retired in 1946. He went to live at Chester-le-Street where his son Rev Cecil Seager was the minister. A memorial at Halton Congregational Church was in the form of a pulpit, communion table and servers.

The first services held in Halton from Whitkirk Church were on January 31st 1853 when assistant curate Rev Henry John Longsdon, who lived in Halton held services in the schoolroom.

Halton Mission Room Chapel Street Church work in Halton developed from 1853 with a Sunday evening service in the National School. This lapsed and was revived with cottage lecturers and in 1868 there was an idea for a new mission church. The site had been offered by Mrs Meynell-Ingram at a nominal rent and let to Whitkirk Church for 21 years. Mrs Meynell Ingram had given £50 towards the total cost of £190. The building committee included Vicar of Whitkirk Rev George Platt

(Vicar 1863-1898) and John Graveley. The site for the chapel had been cleared of some old cottages. Church records state: *"The cottages were recently taken down opposite Mr Graveley's garden wall"*. The plans for the Mission Room were passed by Hunslet RDC in May 1888 and the foundation stone for the Halton Mission Chapel was laid on May 23rd 1888 by the Vicar of Leeds Rev Canon Dr. Francis Jayne and the builder was John Tomlinson. The inscribed stone was uncovered in the old wall during the rebuilding of the Kingdom Hall: "Foundation Stone laid by Rev Canon Jayne Vicar of Leeds May 23 1888". In 2004 the foundation stone was removed to St Wilfrid's Church. The Mission Hall was dedicated on Thursday August 30th by the Bishop of Penrith Dr. JJ Pulleine. In his speech the Bishop said *"that since the closure of the local collieries the population had steadily declined but had taken a turn upwards from the recent figure of 1000 in the village."*
In 1892 there were regular Sunday services led by WD Hollis and in 1895 Rev Frank Henry Bromwich was in charge of the Mission Chapel: he was licensed on February 28th 1895 and lived on Temple View. The assistant curates at Whitkirk were soon in charge at Halton including Rev Joshua John Prentice who was the chaplain to Mrs Meynell Ingram at Temple Newsam from 1900. Rev John Groves (1877) and Rev Frank Bromwich (1895) were also chaplains at Temple Newsam House. There was a small library in the Mission Room and in 1901 the altar from Whitkirk Church was moved there and on February 4th 1917 it was dedicated as the Temporary Church of St Wilfrid. Hawthorn House became St. Wilfrid's Church House with the kitchen used as a scout room. The service times

at the Mission Church in 1912 were Sunday 6.30pm, Wednesday 7.30pm, Thursday Holy Communion 7.30am and the Sunday School held in the Parish Hall at 9.20am and at 2pm.

The Rev Walter Hugo Pitcher lived at Hawthorn House for 18 months when the house was used as a boy's club and scout depot. Rev Pitcher was the assistant curate from 1914 to 1918.

The last service was held in the Mission Chapel on Sunday May 7th 1939 and it was bought for £289 in December 1939 by builder William Jowitt who used it for storage. In June 1940 the Mission Room was used for soldiers returning from Dunkirk-the evacuation was completed on June 3rd 1940. It became William Pease's carpenter's shop and called The Mission Joinery Works: permission to convert was granted in 1944. By 1958 it was G & D Merchants who were builders merchants and agents including the sale of fireplaces. The old chapel was restored and opened in 1972 as the ***Kingdom Hall of the Jehovah's Witnesses***. The building was stone clad by Geoff Haley and plans were forwarded to build a new Mission Hall. Land was acquired in addition to the original site and work was started by members of the Jehovah's Witnesses in May 2003. The boundary wall and car parking area were completed first and members built the new Mission Hall as a result of a quick-build project over a few weekends. The first meeting in the new Kingdom Hall was held on November 9th 2003.

St Wilfrid's Church Viscount Halifax had given land on Halton Hill for a new church site and the Conventional District of Halton was formed on February 26th 1936. In 1937 Sunderland shipbuilder Sir John Priestman offered £20, 000 to the Church Forward Movement in the Ripon Diocese for church building. The Diocese offered half of this sum to Halton and A Randall Wells (1877-1942) was appointed architect: he was the son of

Hastings architect Arthur Wells. The ceremony of Breaking the Ground was held on July 5th 1937 and the foundation stone was laid by Sir John Priestman in the presence of the Bishop of Knaresborough. The stone set into the wall by the main door is inscribed: *"This stone was laid on Saturday November 6th 1937 by Sir John Priestman Bt. of Sunderland".* Sir John Priestman died in Harrogate aged 86 on August 6th 1941 having been a shipbuilder from 1882; he was knighted in 1923 and became a baronet in 1934. There was a bazaar and sale of work opened by Lady Priestman in November 1937 to support the building fund.

The church was built in Yorkshire stone costing £11,700 and was consecrated on Saturday May 13th 1939 by Bishop Geoffrey Lunt assisted by the Bishop of Knaresborough and the Dean of Westminster. The new Halton parish was formed from Whitkirk on July 28th 1939 and the new vicar was inducted on Saturday October 14th 1939. The church contains the font from Barton Church north of Scotch Corner; the silver gilt bowl is 18th century and was donated by the architect as were the choir stalls, pulpit and lectern. The statue of St Wilfrid is by Eric Gill and the statue of Christ offering the church to his Mother is by Irene Kelcey in memory of Mary Mennard who died in 1951. In the chancel is a memorial to Winifred Stapleton (1919-77). The Mystery Plaques were dedicated in November 1947 with the Transfiguration Plaque in August 1950. The chancel curtain is by Evelyn Ross (October 1989) and the church was reordered in 1980 including the dedication of the north transept Lady Chapel altar and installation of the Icon of the Blessed Virgin Mary in November 1987.

The rented vicarage was at 2 Oak Crescent which was built in 1937 with the new vicarage on the church site blessed by the Bishop of Ripon on April 14th 1956. The church hall was opened on February 13th 1938 and a new hall to replace the wooden hut was started in 1971: in 1975 the fund for the new hall stood at £10,000.

William Paul of Oak Road was the treasurer and churchwarden who died in January 1954 aged 69. He had been a member of the Ripon Diocesan Board of Finance, British Legion, organiser of the local Poppy Appeal and a member of the Halton & Temple Newsam Conservative Association.

The church has many activities including Sunday School, Cub Scouts, Brownies, Rainbows and Guides.

Vicars of St Wilfrid's Church

Charles Ian Pettitt was educated at St Chad's College Durham University and gained a BA (1927) and MA (1930). He gained a Diploma in Theology with Distinction (1928) and became a priest in 1930. He was assistant chaplain and junior tutor at St Chad's College (1929-33) before a curacy at St Wilfrid's Church Harrogate (1933-36). Ian Pettitt became the priest in charge of the new conventional district of St Wilfrid Halton in 1936 and vicar from 1939 to 1944. He moved to Newcastle to be at St John's Church and was the examining chaplain to the Bishop of Ripon from 1944. The vicar was the chaplain to the Seacroft Emergency Hospital and the chaplain to the C Company Home Guard. Charles Ian Pettitt died on February 19th 1982 aged 75.

Ernest William Southcott was born in 1913 in Canada and trained at the University of British Columbia. He further trained at Mirfield and became a priest in 1939. He was the curate at Shildon Co Durham (1938-40), St James Church Gateshead (1940-42) and the Vicar of St Wilfrid's Church Halton from 1944 to 1961. He was also the Rural Dean of Whitkirk from 1955 to 1961 and was inducted on Saturday February 12th 1944 by the Bishop of Knaresborough. Rev Ernest Southcott was married in June 1944 to Margaret Carpenter and their daughter Mary Caroline was born on January 16th 1946. He was appointed an Hon Canon of Ripon in 1955. On November 23rd 1958 a service from the church was televised. Ernest Southcott's last service at St Wilfrid's Church was on Sunday November 19th 1961 and he became Provost of Southwark Cathedral and Rector of St Saviours and All Hallows from 1961 to 1970. He was the Commissioner in Nyasa from 1962-64 and Malawi from 1964. In 1970 he came back to England and was the Vicar of Rishton in the Diocese of Blackburn from 1970. He was elected a Canon Emeritus of Southwark Cathedral from 1970. While at Halton Canon Southcott introduced the Holy Communion to the homes of the parishioners through House Churches. Rev Ernest Southcott died on Saturday January 17th 1976.

Kenneth Hargrave Stapleton was born in 1911 and educated at Leeds Grammar School and trained at St Peter's Hall Oxford becoming a priest in 1940. He became a curate at St Bartholomew's Church Armley (1939-43), priest-in-charge at Bramley (1943-45) and from 1946-47 was an army chaplain in Germany. He was Vicar of Holbeck St Edward's Church (1947-62), Vicar of New Wortley St John's Church (1952-57) and was appointed the Vicar of St Wilfrid's Church Halton in 1962. The induction service was held on June 15th 1962 conducted by the Bishop of Ripon and the Archdeacon of Leeds. He stayed at the church until Easter 1978: his wife Winifred Maude Stapleton died at the vicarage in September 1977. He was appointed an Honorary Canon of Ripon.

Robin Patrick Greenwood was born in 1947 and trained at St Chad's College Durham University: he became a priest in 1971. He was a curate at Adel (1970-73) and was a Minor Canon & Succentor at Ripon Cathedral (1973-78) and became the Vicar of St Wilfrid's Church in 1978 until 1986. He moved to be a residentiary canon at Gloucester Cathedral (1986-95), Director of Ministry at Chelmsford (1995-2000) and was also an Honorary Canon at Chelmsford Cathedral. From 2001 he became the Provincial Officer for the Mission Church in Wales.

Graham Bryson Atherton was born in 1947 training at Edinburgh Theological College. He became a priest in 1980 and was a curate at Orford St Mary Liverpool (1979-82), Vicar of Warrington St Barnabas (1982-88) and Vicar of St Wilfrid's Church from 1988 until 1995. He was the Rural Dean of Whitkirk (1992-95) and became the Team Rector at Guiseley with Esholt Bradford from 1995.

Nicholas George was born in 1958 and after training at St Stephen's House became a priest in 1990. He was a curate at St Aidan's Church Harehills (1989-92) and at Richmond Hill (1992-96) as well as being the chaplain to Agnes Stewart COE High School. He became the vicar of St Wilfrid's Church in 1996 and left in 2002.

Mark Duncan Grainger Heather who was born near London in 1962 and worked for ten years at the British Council in London and Manchester. He gained a BA (Leeds) in 1999 having attended the College of the Resurrection Mirfield. He became deacon in 1999 and priest the year afterwards having been appointed to St Aidan's Church Roundhay Road. He was inducted as the Halton vicar on Thursday May 15th 2003.

Methodist Church The first Halton Methodist Chapel was opened for worship on October 10th 1810 by Rev JS Pipe on land occupied by two cottages being granted by the Marquis of Hertford and Isabella Lady Hertford to the Methodist Trustees. Shopkeeper John Atkinson and his wife Ann surrendered their cottages and yards for the new chapel. There were 11 trustees which included Peter Clark of Halton Hill and farmer Edward Phillips.

Next to the new chapel were two cottages owned by John and Sarah Atkinson who sold them to the Trustees for £125 on May 18th 1840. These were demolished to make room for a new larger chapel opened on September 25th 1840 by William (Billy) Dawson of Barwick-in-Elmet. The preachers used a pulpit carved by Thomas Ventris Jnr which is now

at Temple Newsam House. The leaders of the Halton Wesleyan Chapel included members of the Crosthwaite family of Halton including cobbler George Crosthwaite (1828-84) who was Sunday School superintendent, trustee and class leader. His wife Mary Ann (1826-97) also played an important part in the life of the Chapel as did their sons Walter George of Beech Cottage, John William and Ernest Crosthwaite. In 1908 George Crosthwaite's three sons paid for a new vestibule at the front of the Chapel in memory of their father.

The agreement on May 23rd 1876 was between Mrs Meynell Ingram and James Keighley and a month later between William & Mary Shaw with Mark William Swift. The re-registration of the enfranchisement was on July 15th 1879 with signatories butcher Mark William Swift and plumber James Keighley.

In 1892 the Trustees of Halton Wesleyan Chapel included cattleman Squire Swift, miner Gideon Lumb, warehouseman Samuel Green, builder Thomas Smith, Colton shoemaker Alfred Crosthwaite, JW and WG Crosthwaite, grocer William Gaunt, cloth maker George Laycock and farmer Henry Stevenson.

The Sunday School had a children's library and the laying of the foundation stones for a new schoolroom was held on May 22nd 1877 and was opened on October 7th. The Primary Room was built in 1900 and in 1921 the will of John William Crosthwaite bequeathed £400 to the funds. A Sunday School extension was allowed to proceed on December 17th 1934 being built for £1206 by Dunhill Bros and opened on May 18th 1935.

The congregations of Halton Methodist Church and Halton United Reformed Church united to become a Local Ecumenical Project known as ***Christ Church Halton***. The first meeting of the Christ Church Council

was held on July 20th 1989 and a celebratory dedication service was held on October 1st 1989. On November 6th 1989 Halton URC agreed to ask their Trustees to offer the buildings and site for tender. Plans were made for a new £600,000 Christ Church Halton by JH Langtry-Langton and the builders were WV Patrick Ltd. The old chapel closed on October 14th 1990 and the start of building was on May 5th 1992: the URC was demolished by September 1992. The take over at the new church was on April 9th 1993 and the church opened on Easter Sunday 1993.
Christ Church is an active community church and amongst many activities are the Sunday School, Junior Church, Junior Youth Club, Youth Fellowship, Christ Church Guild, Women's Guild, Brownies, Rainbows and the singing group Concordia.

Ministers at Halton Methodist Church and Christ Church from 1840

1840 *St Peter's Circuit:* Revs E Walker, T Cutting, J Smetham; 1844 Rev T Harris
1845 Revs T Eastwood, R Jackson, H Smallwood; 1849 Revs JP Haswell, R Inglis
S Walker; 1852 Rev J Loulet; 1855 Rev G Taylor; 1857 Rev G Roebuck
1860 Rev P Cooper; 1863 Rev J Heaton;1866 Revs J Morton,J Hay,D Dickinson
1869 Revs John Tuidall, George Walker, W Unsworth; 1874 Rev Peter MacKenzie
1877 Rev John Crake; 1880 Rev David Solomon
1833 Revs George Sanderson, Josiah Whydale (Garforth)
1886 Revs Thomas Whitamore, James Critchison (Garforth)
1887 Revs J Wesley Genge, J Smith, M Westcombe (Garforth)
1890 Revs George Russell, J Smith, M Westcombe (Garforth)
1893 *Richmond Hill Circuit*
Revs Samuel Vincent, G Renton, Benjamin Crosby (Garforth)
1896 Rev Crawshaw Hargreaves, George Armitage (Garforth)
1899 Revs James Duff, Herbert Hines (Garforth)
1902 Revs Thomas Willis, Seth Swithenbank (Garforth)
1905 Revs Thomas Hitchon, Dyson Frater, James Fielding (Garforth)
1908 Revs Alfred Elvidge, T Grant Tylor (Garforth)
1911 Revs Owen Jones, Alfred Harey (Garforth)
1914 Revs George Searle, J Ernest Clague, Edwin Bell (Cross Gates)
1915 Revs John Gray, W Eastwood (Garforth), Anthony Baker (Cross Gates)
1919 Revs Herbert Haslam, Maddison Phillips (Cross Gates)
1925 Revs Alfred Bromwich, F Boynton (Cross Gates), R Arthur Jones (Garforth)

1926 Revs Thomas Freeman, W Palmer Morris (Cross Gates)
1930 Revs George Douthwaite, JW Grindell (Cross Gates), D Collier (Garforth),
A Easton
1932 *Methodist Union*
1935 Revs Herbert Godman, WW Cherry (Selby Road)
1940 Rev CT Bishell; 1947 Rev WH Baker; 1951 Rev Frederick Brock
1955 Rev Edward Prentice; 1957 Rev Ernest Sawyer; 1958 Rev G Whitfield Luty
1962 Rev George Diggle; 1967 Rev Donald Taylor; 1972 Rev John ES Twining
1977 Rev Arnos Edwards; 1980 Rev David Livingstone; 1985 Rev Darren Walker
1986 Rev Marlene Wilkinson; 1993 Rev Howard Smith; 1995 Rev Keith Hunt
1996 Rev Ruth Crofton; 2001 Rev Robert J Kitching

St John's Roman Catholic Mass Centre was opened on Monday December 22nd 1969 by the Bishop of Leeds Rt. Rev William Gordon Wheler and dedicated in memory of Canon John Comerford who had started a Mass Centre in Halton Institute in 1947. St John's Catholic Centre is a Chapel-of-Ease to St Theresa's Church Cross Gates. The negotiations with Leeds City Council for the land purchase started in 1966 including the clearance of houses on Selby Road with final approval granted in May 1967. The funds for the new centre included a social evening presented by the Halton branch of the St Theresa's Guild at Carroll's car showroom. Work started in July 1969 on the new centre: the Mass Centre was in Halton Institute for 20 years and for a year was held in Halton-Temple Newsam Primary School. The architect for the St John's Centre was James Corker.

CLAYPITS AND BRICKWORKS

There were claypits at Halton which supplied a growing brickmaking industry. There were two large pits between Templenewsam Road and Grove Road. The clay was laid down at the end of the last Ice Age being the material carried in fine form by the melting glaciers which covered the coal bearing rocks in Halton.
The area of open land was not only for the clay pits as shown on a 1908 map but for brick making. Bricks were made from crushed clay and other materials and fired in a kiln at a temperature of 1000/1800 deg C. The coal required to fire the kiln was extracted from Halton Colliery on the same site. An earlier map shows a group of buildings labelled Halton Brickworks on land that was leased by the Temple Newsam estate to the

Townend and Stevenson families.
There were many brickmakers and bricklayers in the village although the Briggs family was the most important in the 19th century. The pits were sited alongside Grove Road and there is a record in September 1867 of Halton brickmaker John Edward Hartley whose daughter Martha Ann died at four days old. Most of the village houses completed in the 19th century used locally made bricks.
There was an early brickworks at Newsam Green where the bricks were made for Temple Newsam House. There is a record in the 1630's for a supply of 70,000 bricks for £5.

CLINICS

The Child Welfare Centre and School Clinic started on June 29th 1921 at the Wesleyan Schoolroom with Dr Patricius Ashmore in charge with chairman Isaac Dewhirst JP and district Nurse Harrop. The Clinic was under the Halton Clinic Maternity and Child Welfare Committee carrying on the work of the Care of Children Committee, being a branch of the post-war public service. In 1925 the voluntary organisation was taken over by the West Riding County Council who provided rent for the premises together with both doctors and nurses fees. The attendance averaged 60 and in 1928 the enterprise became part of Leeds Babies Welcome Association. The clinic was held later in the Parochial Hall. The Association took over the Halton Infant Welfare Centre in 1928 and the equipment was bought from the WRCC for £40. Land on Pinfold Lane was donated by Lord Halifax in 1926 for a new Child Welfare Centre: the site is now the school playground. By 1928 a Trust was formed and a deed of assignment drawn up with a temporary building to be erected. In late 1933 the Halton Babies Welcome Building Fund with its President Mrs Haste Carr had raised £200 to *"save the lives of mothers and babies and to help to rear the young in good health."* During the 1930's garden parties supporting the Halton Clinic and Babies Welcome were held at Hawthorn House. The plan for the new clinic was abandoned at the outbreak of war.
There was a row of 19th century cottages at the top of Halton Hill demolished in the 1960's. The corner shop on Halton Hill/Primrose Lane was run by Albert Scarfe as Primrose Cash Store and later run by Alice Maria Bonsall. The shop and corner housing together with Newsam Square and Rock Terrace were demolished and became the site for the new Halton Clinic which was announced in March 1980. The clinic was started in January 1983 and opened on May 14th 1984 at a cost of £351,000 for the NHS Leeds Primary Care Trust. The clinic prior to the new site was held at Halton Methodist Church.

CLUBS AND SOCIETIES

The many clubs and societies in which Halton folk have participated were for many years mainly concerned with the churches of the area. The Institute and Parochial Hall as well as the church halls were used frequently for social occasions.

East Leeds History & Archaeological Society was formed in January 1998. The East Leeds Heritage Centre was opened in the reading room at Cross Gates Library in 2000. The Society publishes the Leeds History Journal.

Halton Action Committee held the first meeting in December 1950 having been formed by hairdresser Leopold V Button of Primrose Road as a liaison between the public and the elected councillors. The chairman was Ossie Bell and Treasurer was LV Button. One of the concerns in the early 1950's was the state of the pathway from the bottom of Valley Drive to Cross Gates School.

Halton Angling Club was active in the village for many years: one of the founders was Charles Hayes of Grove Road.

Halton Band of Hope was based at the Halton Methodist Church and started in 1878. In 1914 the President was Mr Jewell, Secretary Albert Scarfe and Treasurer C Scarfe.

Halton Boys Club was started in a rented house by Whitkirk Church in 1906. The boys were aged from 12 to 16 years old and paid 1d a week with a 6d entry charge. The house was at 5 Stanley Terrace and the meetings were held on four nights a week. When the Halton Parochial Hall was opened in 1909 the meetings were transferred from the house.

Halton Girls Club was held from 1908 in the summer months at 5 Stanley Terrace when the boys did not meet. The Club for working girls transferred to the Parochial Hall on opening the next year.

Halton Branch of the League of Nations Union was active in the 1930's and on January 24th 1931 produced a Pageant Play in Halton Parochial Hall at which admission was 2/- or a reduced price of 1/-.

Halton Branch of the National Playing Fields Association held their first meeting in 1927. The Chairman was R Steel, Vice-Chairman JW Chadwick and Secretary Richard Thomas.

Halton Branch of the United Nations Association met from 1946 at St. Wilfrid's Church Hall. The chair was taken by the vicar of St. Wilfrid's Church Canon Ernest Southcott.

Halton Combined Cadet Division of the St. John Ambulance Brigade met at Temple Newsam Halton School.

Halton Concert Party gave many hundreds of performances throughout the area and had four pianists, a conjuror, ventriloquist Edward Monkman and violinist Harold Arnold. The original Concert Party included Edward Monkman, Dick Thomas, Ted Herrington, Joe

Herrington, Herbert Eastwood, Harry Eastwood, Jack Farrow, Wilf Purdy, Christopher Arnold, Harold Arnold, Harry Scupham, John Barrat and Nellie Thomas. The Concert Party visited Normanton, Selby and Bradford as well as giving one of the first performances at St. Georges Crypt in Leeds. Their show was described as "bright, clean and humorous".

Halton and Cross Gates branch of the National British Women Total Abstinence Union met in the Methodist or Congregational Church from 1949. In the early years of the century they were called the Halton Branch of the British Women's Temperance Association.

Halton & District Aquarists Society met twice a month in the 1960's at Temple Newsam Halton School; the Secretary was AF Senior.

Halton & District Homing Society were tenants of the Veteran's Shelter at The Crescent Selby Road: their lease was terminated in October 1972 and the shelter was demolished due to vandalism.

Halton Evening Group was started in 1970 by John Gilleghan for the Leeds City Council Leisurecard Scheme and featured the scenery of the Yorkshire Dales. It first met at Temple Newsam Halton Junior School and in 1975 opened at Halton Middle School. The group became independent in 1989 and became Halton Yorkshire Group later Halton Evening Group.

Halton Good Companions Elderly Peoples Club was founded in 1946 under the Leeds Council of Social Services and one of the Forget Me Not Clubs. Their meetings were held at the Sutton Estate Bowling Association pavilion.

Halton Gun Club met in the early years of the 20th century and were based at the Irwin Arms. In 1916 a meeting was held behind the public house when there was a starling shoot with prizes for the best shots.

Halton Local History Society was founded in 1987 and published The Templar.

Halton & Temple Newsam Gardens Association held their 47th annual show in 1982: they were founded in 1935.

Halton Health & Strength Club met from 1946 in Carroll's Yard on the High Street and was affiliated to the Health & Strength League. The Club ceased meeting in 1947 and the remaining funds were given to the LGI.

Halton Red Rose Club held their meetings in the Institute and at Halton Methodist Church. The Club was opened in June 1957 by Lord Mayor of Leeds Ald Joseph Hiley for the Leeds Council of Social Services.

Halton Wine Circle was started c1969 and meets in Halton Primary School.

Halton Men's Co-operative Guild was meeting in 1932 in the room at the shop. In that year was also formed the Children's Co-operative Class.

Halton Afternoon Townswomens Guild was formed on July 13th1954. A meeting to form the Guild was held in Halton Methodist Schoolroom on Tuesday June 29th 1954. The TWG hold their meetings at Halton Primary School. In December 1954 there were over 200 registered members and a long waiting list. The TWG became Halton Afternoon TWG c1997 after the foundation as an evening guild.

Halton Women's Co-operative Guild met in the room at the Co-operative Store on High Street Halton and in May 1933 organised a ramble around the new developments at Cross Gates of recent years.

Halton Young Conservative Association was formed in 1958 and held their meetings at the Golf House.

Halton Young Men's Institute was run by Whitkirk Church and met at various places in the village including the school during the late 19th century.

Halton Young People's Branch of the National British Women's Total Abstinence Union was founded in the village in late 1931.

Holly House Motor Club run by the Carroll family was active in the late 1950's and 1960's. There was a monthly treasure hunt: one of these was over a 51 mile route ending for tea at Boroughbridge. The 6th annual dinner was held in 1967 and trophies were presented including the Holly House Trophy and the Woodman Trophy.

The Leeds 15 Community Association became independent from the Leeds Education Authority in April 1979, having been formed a few years earlier as the Leeds 15 Community Committee. The last meeting was on November 14th 1995.

Temple Newsam Area Linen League was led in the 1930's by Mrs Bladen Jones of Hawthorn House to help Leeds General Infirmary's special appeal: the Patroness was Viscountess Halifax.

Temple Newsam Branch of the Royal British Legion was formed in the inter-war years and ended in 1951. The Halton & District Branch was formed on May 16th 1963. The colours were re-dedicated at Whitkirk Church in October 1963.

Temple Newsam Imps (Young Conservatives) met at a few locations in Halton and Cross Gates including socials held at Halton Parochial Hall in the 1930's. The Imps were members of the Junior Imperial League. They were allowed to practice tennis on a private court at Beech House Colton. They also gave concerts to support Whitkirk & District Nursery.

Temple Newsam Habitation of the Primrose League met at the Halton Parochial Hall. *The League was an organisation for spreading Conservative principles: the primrose was associated with Lord Beaconsfield. Following his death and the unveiling of his statue in the House of Commons it was suggested that a Primrose League be formed with Lord Randolph Churchill. The Habitations were groups meeting through the country. A Ladies Branch was formed by Lady Borthwick and the first meeting took place in 1885.*

Temple Newsam Women's Conservative Association met at Hawthorn House on Chapel Street with President Mrs Philip Marsden.

Temple Newsam Women's Institute was formed in 1926 and closed in December 1990. The Temple Newsam WI held their meetings at Halton Primary School.

Tufty Club at Halton opened in September 1964 at the Congregational Church and in March 1977 at the Methodist Church. The meeting places included the United Reformed Church, Scout hut and Christ Church before closure in 1998. The Tufty Clubs for young children were started by RoSPA throughout the country and were concerned with the teaching of road safety to under school age children. The Halton Tufty Club was financed and run by local folk and many helpers. The Tufty Club name originated with the Red Squirrel.

Voluntary Aided Detachment (VAD) of the St. John Ambulance Brigade was founded by Dr JA Young, Nurse Elsie Dacre and Mary Metcalfe. Jessie Blackburn had joined in 1926 and had 46 years of service gaining a long service medal in July 1974. She was a Sister of the Order of St. John and until 1971 was the Superintendent of the Halton Combined Division of the St. John Ambulance Brigade.

Women's Branch of the Royal British Legion was formed in September 1933 at a meeting in the Methodist Church schoolroom. The President was Lady Irwin, Vice-Presidents Mrs Marsden and Mrs Glazebrook with Chairman Mrs Dickinson.

COAL

The Ingrams at Temple Newsam were selling their estate coals from Halton Colliery to the Aire & Calder Navigation Co in 1794: the supply was delivered to the Thorp Hall coal staith.
Waterloo Main Colliery was opened in 1815 by William Fenton. There was an explosion at Waterloo Pit on January 31st 1840 which killed three miners. Kirkby Fenton took as his partner at Waterloo Colliery John Towlerton Leather. In 1901 it was proposed to sink a new shaft for Temple Pit Waterloo Main. The shaft was sunk and the pit head gear was restricted in height by Mrs Meynell-Ingram in order that she could not see it from the House. By 1917 the main contracts at Waterloo Main were with Leeds Corporation Gas Works and Monkbridge Iron Works.
There were local effects from the mining including subsidence at Colton Methodist Chapel in the late 1930's and in the 1960's. Colton Pit and shaft was sited at the end of Darnley Lane where there is a grassy area today. Waterloo Colliery closed in September 1965 and on November 23rd 1965 the last coal steam train carried folk in open wagons from Waterloo to Neville Hill sidings and return. In 1972 the plans for the site included removal of the pit buildings and the restoration of land affected by opencasting.

Coal mining at Halton

The main coal seams at Halton are the Blocking Bed Coal of the Lower Coal Measures which varied between 18 inches and two feet thickness and the Brown Metal and Middleton Little coal seams from the Middle Coal Measures with the Middleton Main seam in Primrose Valley. The beds are part of the Upper Carboniferous Rocks which include the Slack Bank rocks and are criss crossed by various fault lines.
In 1631 an agreement with Hawton (Halton) Pit ensured delivery of coals to Grimston near Tadcaster and in 1641 agreement was obtained for the Halton Pit to supply all necessary coals to Temple Newsam Hall. Most of the Halton house leases included a condition that coals underneath the properties were to be taken to the Hall if needed. In 1660 a lease agreement for three closes in Halton were with Launcelot Iveson and John Hargreaves in order to extract coal and build watercourses across land of the Ingrams of Temple Newsam. The lease stated that *"all coles and mines in Halton with full power to work same not in the park, build sough for drying mine through Ingram land by Wyke Beck and to build a smithy. Coals are to be provided for Temple Newsam Hall."*
In 1676 and 1686 Viscount Irwin passed a lease to Anthony Iveson of Black Bank and Henry Iveson all coals in Halton and Killingbeck until 1683: extended to 1693. In 1700 Richard Brooke sank coal pits and in 1730 Halton Colliery extracted the coal for use at the Temple Newsam mansion and estate. Temple Newsam estate records prove the existence

of coal pits in and around the Park in the 17th century and Halton Colliery was on the Gilsyke Field. There were also pits at Colton and Bell Wood to the south of the mansion would have had bell pits for coal extraction. By 1712/14 the pits were worked at Halton by Abraham Fenton (1673-1744) son of Thomas Fenton who died in 1705. In 1722 the wages at Halton Colliery were five shillings and fourpence for a pitman working for four days. In 1727 a boy working for five days got 2/8d, a boy loading coal got 1/6d, Richard Harrison got 6/- for pumping, Richard Webb got 12/- for a week's work. The total week's wages were £10/11/7d. In 1730/31 Edward Wilks obtained a 21 year lease to supply coal mainly to Temple Newsam House. The lease was for £200 a year for the first five years and £300 thereafter. He built his own house and enclosed the lands employing 18 miners at Halton Colliery also paving Allersher (Hollyshaw) Lane. In 1749 the lease transferred to James Nelthorpe of Seacroft with coal supplied to Temple Newsam House *"as needed"*. The clauses also included enclosure of Halton Moor and enclosure of a new house, use of a horse pump, appointment of a blacksmith, backfilling old pits and making a way from the pits to the river. In 1749 Henry Viscount Irwin sold the lease to James Nelthorpe of Seacroft with *"all mines of coal in fields in Halton except New Field for 21 years with coals to be delivered to the Hall on demand"*. Other restrictions on this lease included *"a fine of £100 for every man employed over 18 years and no sinking within two yards of any Halton house"*. There was a mention in the Leeds Intelligencer for 1749 when Hell Dike coal pit at Halton (late of John Wilks) was open again with steward John Webb. In 1763 it was further recorded that the pit was fully working with coals delivered to Halton Dial toll free at 4d per corf or delivered to Leeds at 6d a corf by steward John Procter. In 1770 there was a valuation at Halton Pit of the fire engine and utensils. In 1775 there were two Halton pits working and a third being sunk: sales in 1778 were 12,000 tons. In May 1775 the *"compting house of Lord Irwin at Halton Colliery was broken open and money was stolen"*. Between 1792 and 1795 there are estate accounts for *"felled trees for the colliery"*. In 1808 Temple Newsam records have an entry for *"works at the Engine and Gin Wheel at the Pit."*

The pit records in 1773-78 mention Townend, Thompson, Tifferey, Appleyard and Johnson Pits at Halton Colliery. Wage sheets are available for this colliery from March 31st 1722 until June 10th 1727 with the accounts in the 1770's. In coal operations during 1774 the balance which was given to Lord Irwin was £88 and the following year the operating profit was £195. In December 1775 a one month income was £186 and in January 1776 was £339. In August 1777 the coal sold amounted to £68 with about £40 being paid to the miners employed at the Halton Colliery. There is a reference to a *"coal mine at Halton commonly called Hell Dike"*.

Halton Colliery was first sited behind the present row of shops/flats on

Irwin Approach and on the field between Templenewsam Road and Grove Road. Engine Lane referred to the pumping engine probably designed by John Smeaton of Austhorpe Lodge; a map dating from 1771 shows the engine. The old buildings including a tall brick chimney once linked with the old colliery together with Stevenson's Park View Farm was demolished to make way for the shops.
The later *Halton Colliery* was in the area bounded by New Templegate, Temple Avenue and the North Plantation woodland. There was a site hut, service road and the two shafts to the east of the site with a pit hill in the centre. These pits were run by Arnold Bedford who had his office on Chapel Street and coal yard off Irwin Approach. These pits were operating during the 1930's and finished c1950 to be continued by Lindsay Parkinson as opencasting until c1953.
Garside's Killingbeck Colliery was operating for under a century, finally closing c1887. There were mine shafts, pit head wheels, cottages, stables and an ale house. In 1857/58 Richard & William Garside were also operating from the White Horse Colliery on York Road; in 1843 Robert & William Garside were corn millers at Garden Street Timble Bridge.

COAT OF ARMS OF LEEDS

The coat of arms of Leeds includes the three owls on the coat of arms of Sir John Savile, three mullets or spur rowels on the coat of arms of Thomas Danby and a fleece being the sign of a wool stapler.
Sir John Savile of Howley Hall (1556-1630) was the first Alderman of Leeds in 1626 when the new corporation adopted the arms of fleece and owls. King Charles II granted a new charter in 1661 appointing Thomas Danby as the first mayor and the revised coat of arms included his mullets.

In 1836 the motto Pro Rege et Lege meaning For King and Law was added following the Municipal Corporations Act of 1835. In 1921 the College of Arms confirmed and assigned the crest with supporters changed from *owls argent to owls proper.*
The coat of arms of Leeds is the signing of the *Leodis* public house on Green Lane Halton.

COMPULSORY PURCHASE ORDERS

The most important of the Council's Compulsory Purchase Orders (CPO) which affected the village of Halton was issued in 1966 as part of the Clearance Order for the intended redevelopment. The Council passed the CPO on March 2nd 1966 having declared the area for clearance on February 3rd 1965: official signing of the CPO was on April 26th 1966. The order was part of the Housing Act 1957. This was to clear several streets and main road houses in order to complete the Halton District Centre, Brooksbank and access road. The area was bounded by Rock Terrace, Primrose Lane, Selby Road, Chapel Street and Primrose Road.
The CPO for 1966 involved the rehousing and compensation claims for Rock Terrace, 195-217 Selby Road (row of cottages now the Halton Clinic), corner shop (219) once Bonsall's Corner and 4 Primrose Lane once part of Primrose Terrace, Barker's Terrace, Dial Row, Britton Terrace, Orchard Terrace, Shaw's Yard, Fryer's Yard, Dawson Square and Milestone Yard.
The CPO also included 36-38 Grove Road set at right angles to the road and including Grove House (40), 249 Selby Road: the Co-op shop, dairy distribution depot, Traveller's Rest eventually removed from the order, 261-267 Selby Road: the shops including Bower's Fisheries, Frame's Butchers, Vamplew's radio and Bedford's bakery. 269-273 Selby Road: the two storey houses/shops which once included FW White's grocers on the corner of Chapel Street. 206-208 Selby Road: two houses between Holly House Farm and Field End. 2-10 Chapel Street including Schofield's newsagents and Bedford's coal merchant office. 12a Chapel Street was a shop added to the side of Dial House and was a greengrocers run by the Ball family and by FW Hill. Chapel Yard: the four terrace houses, walls, toilets, coal sheds and gardens which included the home of the chapel caretaker. The Public Works Contractor's Yard adjoining the north side of the Chapel and Laurel House. Graveley Square and Dial Terrace adjacent and to the rear of Dial House. 2-4 Primrose Road: the one time post office and Button's hairdressers. 10-14 Primrose Road was demolished and a new house built on the site. 20 Chapel Street: Wilby's confectioners and later Tomlinson's electrical at the corner of Primrose Road. 35-39 Chapel Street: now part of the school playing field. Pinfold Square: now leading to Pinfolds Home. 64-68 Chapel Street with the

wash house, backyards, toilets and coal houses. 57-63 Chapel Street: a row of cottages at a right angle to the main street one being the home of the Jones family whose garage was adjacent.

CO-OPERATIVE SOCIETY

The Leeds Industrial Co-operative Society has had a presence in Halton for many years. The LICS butchers and grocers included stables and a dairy behind the shop on High Street opposite the end of Grove Road.
In June 1897 John Graveley offered another site in Halton, following the Co-op Board of Directors turning the original offer down. In January 1899 a Mr Strickland offered land with the cost labelled as "excessive and the Board was not justified in building at great expense in a place like Halton". The properties on High Street were bought from butcher Squire Swift of Halton at a cost of £850 in March 1899. The Co-op butcher's shop was opened on Thursday April 6th 1899 with alterations to form the grocery approved. The store was completed by November 1906 when a causeway to Fryer's Yard was relaid. William Sunderland was the manager and was followed by Fred Anderton as the manager of the Halton Co-op for 20 years: he had worked more than 40 years with LICS. He died in November 1933 aged 55 at his home on Overdale Terrace. The Halton Committee requested permission for the storage of paraffin in 1901 and the Food & Drugs Inspector called at the Halton Co-op store on January 22nd 1903 taking samples of butter, lard and ground ginger for analysis. On a brighter note the Halton Committee visited the Co-operative boot factory and bakery department in August 1907.
In 1964 the LICS owned the freehold of the Halton premises and they sought to have a presence as a supermarket in the proposed Halton District Centre. On January 14th 1967 Osmondthorpe Co-op butchery department was closed and business transferred to Wykebeck: they specialised in the sale of dripping to fish and chip shops.
By June 1968 the Halton store was losing £128 a week and the Board decided to close the

Halton Coop at left on High Street

Halton Co-op store on September 7th 1968 with Whitkirk Co-op closing at the same time. The butchers closed followed by the dairy in July 1968. It was proposed to lease the Halton building by the end of September although all the properties on the main road were earmarked for demolition. The Halton premises were under a Compulsory Purchase Order and the building was leased to EH Williams and Laverty & Sons Ltd who rented the grocers and butchers shops for £175 a year increasing to £260 a year. In October 1970 R Gott of Gottomatics Ltd offered to lease the vacant rear rooms and first floor of the old grocery at £260/year for the storage of vending machine ingredients. In 1971 Walter Ripley & Sons of West Street Leeds offered to rent the shop areas for £250 a year for the sale and stocking of hardware and for Do-It-Yourself materials; this was approved by the Board of the LICS. In 1972 there was an application from a Mr Sidebottom who was already the tenant of the other part to lease the rooms behind and over the former grocery at £520 a year. This was to commence on February 1st 1972 and the site used for the manufacture of mattresses. In 1977 an offer was made by estate agents Durgan & Dalby to purchase part of the property with an offer of £4500 which was refused. W Ripley & Sons ended their tenancy in 1977 and the agents eventually bought part of the building by 1978 and sublet the old butchers shop as well as the old Grocery & Dairy Departments. The lease was available from August 1979 at £1150 a year and was reassigned in August 1982 to Quality Carriers as a depot for three years. A new lease was agreed in March 1984 to Dr. Barnado's for three years. The Halton Co-op building was demolished in 1986.
The Halton District Centre was opened with the Halton Super C Store on October 27th 1987. The surveyors were Monaghan Partnership of Sheffield and the architects were Bowman & Riley of Skipton with consulting engineers Robert Adams & Associates of Otley; the contractors were Rush & Tompkins of the Grangefield estate. The Super C development included an in-store bakery, Blades Hairdressers, opticians, solarium and a travel agent; the first manager was Bill Marshall. A special visitor to the new store was Frazer Hines from Emmerdale Farm on November 18th 1987. The present Halton Village Co-op Store was opened on March 10th 2001 having transferred from the Halton Centre store. The old store was opened as Matalan on October 19th 2001 following extensive reconstruction. The Village Store was originally opened as Grandways and then became Netto who ceased trading in Halton in October 2001.
The *Wykebeck Village Store* on Selby Road/Selby Avenue junction at the bottom of Halton Hill dates from 1931/32. On February 2nd 1926 a conveyance was made between the site owners Leeds Fire Clay Company and the Leeds City Council. A second conveyance was signed on August20th 1931 between the Council and the Leeds Industrial Co-

operative Society for the sum of £838. The site of three shops on the Osmondthorpe Housing Estate had an area of 1677 square yards and were sold at the rate of ten shillings a square yard; the agreement was that the store was to be completed by May 1932. The store was opened by July 1932 when thousands passed or used the store during the Great Yorkshire Show at Temple Newsam Park. By 1968 the shop was taking £500 weekly and it was suggested that Wykebeck was to be turned into a one stop convenience store, particularly as the Halton and Whitkirk shops were closing that year. In 1972 negotiations started to acquire the former Gallon's shop adjacent to the Co-op shop. Gallons had paid an annual rent to the LCC of £10 and the lease expired in 1973. It was agreed that the Co-op would pay £7000 but there were many discussions on the Board and the price increased to £9000 by 1973. It was then agreed that the premises were to be sold to the LCC and leased back: the plans were passed by March 1974. It was after this acquisition that the whole store received a face lift and assumed the present appearance: plans to demolish and rebuild were passed in March 1976. The first phase was completed by builders Jack Lunn & Co on May 26th 1977 with the off licence opening on June 11th 1977. The new store was completed in October 1977 and there was an official opening afterwards.

The LICS started as the Leeds Flour Society at Benyon's Mill Holbeck in 1847: in 1853 this became the Leeds Co-operative Flour and Provision Society.

COUNCILLORS

The councillors representing Halton from 1928 as a part of the Roundhay, Seacroft, Shadwell and Cross Gates Ward were BT Graham, Arthur Lee and AE Ives. From 1930 to 1951 Halton was part of the Cross Gates & Temple Newsam Ward. Councillors representing included Wing Commander Charles A Goodall (1930-46) who married Constance Bennett, Frederick Leach of Fernlea Morritt Avenue (1930-44), Arthur Lee (1930-33), Ernest Steel (1933-38), Richard R Thomas (1945-47), Joseph Brooksbank (1950-67) and Colin Watson (1951-67).

In 1951 the Halton Ward was created with councillors including those already mentioned together with Percy Dodson (1950-57), John Dougary (1957-62, John Rhodes (1963-67), Richard Vaughan (1967-74), Martin Dodgson (1968-86), Mary Tomlinson (1967-73), Bill Hyde (1973-95 & from 2000), Doreen Wood (1973-87), David Schofield (1986-96), Don Townsley (1987-93), Lee Benson (from 1993), Doris McGee (from 1995) and Randolph Haggerty (1996-2000). The local elections held on May 1st 2003 elected David Schofield making the Halton Ward a Conservative gain. In 2004 the Halton Ward changed to become Temple Newsam ward to include Austhorpe, Colton, Halton, Halton Hill, Templegates and Whitkirk.

Doreen Wood

COWELL AND WOOD FAMILIES

Joseph Cowell was born in Scholes in 1837 and in the 1860's he married Ann born in Whinmoor in 1838; their family were Thomas, George, Benjamin and Alice.

Thomas Cowell was born in 1868 and he married Alice R Crosby in 1891 living in a terrace house on Grove Road. Thomas was a miner and when he was a boy worked at Prince Arthur Pit Hollyshaw Lane and later moved to the Waterloo Pit. When he was accidentally injured the severance money was used to buy an insurance round and he became a salesman. In November 1903 Alice Cowell became a teacher at Halton Council School for a few years. They later moved to live at 40 Chapel Street which they bought from the Halifax estate in the 1920's. Thomas Cowell died at 74 Chapel Street in December 1939.

George Cowell was born in 1869 and became a printer living at 10 High Street Halton: he married Hannah born in 1873. Hannah died aged 86 in

January 1959 as one of Halton's oldest residents having been a member of the Halton Red Rose Club for Elderly People and the Halton Congregational Church. Their children were *Frederick Hubert* who was working as a driver when in 1925 he married Clara Bulmer. Clara was born in 1901 and worked with her father as a gardener at Gledhow Hall Nurseries. Frederick and Clara were some of the first to register as members of Halton Congregational Church.

Ronald was born in 1897 and worked as a lithographic overseer and on December 26th 1929 married Agnes Bonsall born in 1907 whose parents ran the corner shop on Primrose Lane: after their marriage they lived with her parents for a short time. After the death of Agnes he married Sarah Mary and they lived on Grove Road; *Benjamin* was born at Stanks in 1876 and *Alice* was born in 1883.

Thomas & Alice's family were Edith Hannah, Harry, Alec, Cyril and Rowland.

Edith Hannah Cowell was born on May 8th 1892, baptised June 5th and on October 16th 1918 she married Wilfrid Wood of Waverley Fearnville Park and lived on Carter Mount. Edith worked at the Co-op shop in Halton for a few years. Wilfrid was the son of George and Celina Wood who lived at Wansford House Sunny Hill prior to their move to Waverley Fearnville Park. George & Celina's family were Ethel who married Loyce Moss and who lived to be 94, Clara who never married and died aged 92, Edith who married William Taylor, Wilfrid, Mabel who died unmarried aged 96, Lena who died as a teenager and Frank.

Wilfrid & Edith Hannah Wood's family were Colin who married Winifred Linley of 112 Green Lane: the family moved to York and Winifred died in October 2003, Marjory married Lawrence Powell of Glasshoughton, Denis married Doreen Cooper who became Lord Mayor of Leeds, Bryan who married Gwennie Cawthray who for many years worked as a conductress on both the Kippax & District "yellow bus" and later for Wallace Arnold, Alan who married Betty Fielding and Beryl who married Eric Beckwith who died in 2002.

George Wood lived at 3 Camberley Street Dewsbury Road and from 1884 ran a hairdresser/tobacconist's shop at 9 Domestic Street, taking over from Thomas Attrea. George ran three barber's shops in Dewsbury Road, Meadow Lane and the main shop at 50a Wellington Street at the corner of King Street with his brother Enoch Wood running barber's shops at 8 Eleventh Avenue and 4 Tong Road. It was at Wellington Street that George's daughters Ethel and Clara were lathers helping father in the busy morning period. Daughter Edith born in 1889 married William Arthur Taylor of Prospect House on October 14th 1914. In 1900 George sold the shops and opened a cutler & tool dealership at Stanton's Buildings Duncan Street. In 1932 the business moved to larger premises at 5 King Edward Street, becoming a limited company in 1955. G Wood

Wood family: George and Celina with (from left) Mabel, Clara, Ethel, Frank, Edith, Wilfred, Lena.

Tools moved in 1991 to 6 Eastgate when Bryan Wood retired and the Eastgate shop was closed in February 2004. The members of the family who worked at the shops were Clara, Wilfrid and Frank; Wilfrid's son Bryan continued with the business which was run by Bryan's son Paul Wood.

Wilfrid Wood was born on December 19th 1901 and died in 1955. Edith Hannah Cowell died at her daughter Marjory's house at Glasshoughton aged 74 on July 29th 1966.

Harry Cowell was baptised on February 3rd 1894 and married Doris Stringer at Halton Methodist Church on October 15th 1927 of 8 Sycamore Avenue: Harry and Doris lived at 18 Woodland Road by 1934. Doris was a children's nurse and was the daughter of a horseman at Gilsyke House and at her marriage the witness was Dr Herbert Eadie. They lived at 19 Sycamore Avenue and then moved across the road to live next door to her parents at 10 Sycamore Avenue. Harry worked as a joiner for Tom Shaw's funeral business and often helped Halton folk with odd jobs in the village. Their daughter Patricia Cowell was born in 1925 and on October 9th 1945 she married Raymond Holmes, a market gardener from Clifford born in 1928. Harry & Doris Cowell's son was Michael Thomas Cowell born in 1945 who married 33 year old Gloria Roddy in 1977. Doris Cowell continued to live at 10 Sycamore Avenue after Harry's death in 1965.

Alec Cowell was born in 1897 and on May 7th 1923 married Kathleen Weatherill. Alec served in the Great War and on returning took a job as a tram conductor and later driver. Kathleen was baptised on November

19th 1899 as the daughter of a colliery deputy Rayner & Harriett Hilda Weatherill of Fryer's Yard and later Temple Walk. When Alec and

Cowell family outside Grove Road house:
Thomas and Alice with (from left) Cyril, Alec, Edith, Harry, Rowland.

Kathleen were married they lived at 19 Sycamore Avenue and took over the grocer's shop at 2 Wilfred Avenue/15 Cross Green Lane from his wife's family John & Lilian Weatherill in 1932. John Weatherill married Lilian Craven on July 31st 1909 and they spent ten years in Montreal Canada before returning to Halton to open their shop in April 1923. The private house was converted into a shop having been bought from Emily Bean: John Weatherill died aged 46 in August 1931. Alec Cowell died on January 16th 1960 at the age of 63 and Kathleen moved to the Cowell property at 74 Chapel Street, having sold the shop and house to Alan Bradley. Recent shop owners have included Brian Garth proprietor of Brian Lesley Transport Services: they ran a video outlet and organised coach outings. The City Council had bought the property with the possibility of widening the road but the plans were abandoned. The present owners bought from the Council and are converting the shop area into a private dwelling.

Alec & Kathleen's family was *Kenneth Rowland Cowell* born in December 1924 and baptised on February 1st 1925. During the war he served in the RAF flying Spitfires. On July 15th 1948 he married Norma Frances Forshaw who had been born in 1928 and their home was on Pinfold Hill. Norma was the daughter of dentist Reynold Hampton Begbie Forshaw of 7 Pinfold Lane: her sister Pauline Marie married Hans Jakob Haffter at

Whitkirk Church on June 6th 1952. Kenneth Cowell became a dental surgeon and lives at Timble: they had two children Marilyn born in November 1949 and Ashley Robert. Walter Townend had rented 72 Chapel Street from the Cowell family for a few years: their son is Peter Townend. Sheila was married later to Peter Olsen. Kathleen Cowell was married again on October 24th 1974 to James William Bickerdyke.

Cyril Cowell was born in 1898 and married a Cross Gates girl: he worked in the grocery department at the Co-op store on Cross Gates Road where he became the manager. Cyril then became the manager of the grocery department at the head office on Albion Street from where he retired in 1963. He lived with his wife Gladys at 24 Hawkhill Drive and after retirement they moved to Filey for five years prior to returning to East Leeds.

Rowland Cowell was born in 1903 and he lived at 72 Chapel Street which he had bought from his mother in 1949. Rowland had married Kathleen's sister Jessie Weatherill born December 1903, on December 25th 1939 and worked for the Leeds Corporation Waterworks as an inspector. Jessie was born in 1903 and was a tailoress living at 25 Woodland Hill at the time of her wedding. Rowland Cowell died on November 5th 1957 aged 54. Jessie Cowell was married again to Benny Backhouse of Brooklands Crescent Seacroft on December 9th 1961; they lived at the Chapel Street house. Benny Backhouse was a trustee of the Halton Wesleyan Chapel. Jessie Backhouse served for 48 years in the St. John's Brigade and joined the Halton Division of the VAD in 1926 after the formation by Dr JA Young, Nurse Mary Metcalfe and Nurse Elsie Dacre. When the VAD was disbanded Jessie stayed in the St John Ambulance Brigade and until 1971 was the superintendent of the Halton Combined Division. Jessie Backhouse received the award of the Order of St John as a Serving Sister in July 1974 at a ceremony in London.

CRESCENT ESTATE

The Crescent Estate was started with the plans passed in May 1925 by Dunhills and covers Portage Avenue, Oak Crescent, Oak Road down Temple Newsam Road to Broadway, Howard Avenue and Temple Newsam View. In 1928 Oak Crescent and Oak Road were surfaced, together with Willow Crescent and the laying of electricity cables on Halton Hill. In early 1929 there was a report of *"a large number of houses have sprung up in the vicinity of Temple Newsam Golf Course. A few years ago there were green fields for as far as you could see and now there are modern houses with their own shopping centre"*. Later that same year a news article stated that *"there are now 300 houses and bungalows and a few shops serving the new Crescent estate. There are tennis courts available for residents and socials are held at the Golf*

House." The Crescent Residents Association was formed in the mid-1920's and catered for a few years for the needs of the increasing population. The Crescent Post Office was opened in 1931 and the corner shopping area on Temple Newsam Road and Oak Crescent also included Sydney Lees butcher, Stanley William Rowley greengrocer and James Dean confectioners. The first St Wilfrid's Vicarage was at 2 Oak Crescent where Canon Ernest Southcott once lived. Telephone boxes were sited at Oak Crescent, Halton tram terminus High Street and Wilfred Avenue in 1927.

Broadway is an ancient right of way indicated on early maps as Bull Lane. James E Speight was employed to make Broadway into a road: Temple Newsam Estate Tenants Association applied in November 1933 to have Broadway surfaced. The street was 36 feet wide by a bye-law but it was agreed to be 60 feet wide in 1936. The first houses were listed in 1930, along with Howard Avenue and Portage Avenue (1929). One of the Broadway residents was Arthur Thompson who received the MBE in the 1959 New Year Honours List. He started work in 1906 as a press photographer for the Leeds Mercury and then was with the Daily Mail for 33 years: he retired in 1959. The large plot of land north of Broadway northwards to Halton Hill was sold by the Temple Newsam Estate to William and Joseph Dunhill on August 24th 1925: a small area of land adjoining the main road was in the hands of Mary Swift. The first houses on *Temple Newsam New Road* were taken in September 1925.

CRICKETERS

John Brian Bolus was born in Halton on January 31st 1934: his father was the licensee of the Woodman Inn for 20 years. He was educated at St. Michael's College Leeds and made his first class debut in 1956. Brian learnt his cricket at Whitkirk Club where he was a junior member in 1948, moved to Leeds in 1953 and then to Bradford where he was opening bat. He was a right hand opener or middle order batsman and a left arm medium pace bowler. He made his debut for Yorkshire in 1956 and received his cap in 1960. Brian Bolus played 107 matches for the county between 1956 and 1962 and he played in 7 test matches for England in 1963-64. He moved to Nottinghamshire where he played 269 matches from 1963-72 and became Nottinghamshire captain in 1972. He then moved to Derbyshire where he played 64 matches and was their captain in 1973-75. He retired from first class cricket in 1975 and later played with Cleckheaton, Brighouse and Farsley which he led to victory in the Priestley Cup in 1983. Brian Bolus was made a Life Member of Whitkirk Cricket Club in 1964 and was a committee member of Nottinghamshire CCC. A display of his 6 caps and England sweater is at Whitkirk Club.

Geoffrey Alan Cope was born in Burmantofts on February 23rd 1947 and was educated at Manston School and at Temple Moor Boy's Grammar School, where he played for the school 1st XI. In 1962 Geoff Cope was the Captain of Yorkshire Schools and was selected to play for the England Schoolboys XI against a Public Schools XI in a 2 day match played on the county ground at Hastings. He left Temple Moor School in 1964 and played for Leeds (Yorkshire Council) and for the Yorkshire 2nd XI. He made his first class debut for Yorkshire on July 15th 1966 v Hampshire at Bradford Park Avenue and played 230 games for the county from 1966 to 1980. He played in three test matches for England: v Pakistan in 1977-78. His first class record was 2383 runs, 686 wickets and 71 catches. Geoff joined Yeadon in the Bradford League becoming president and was instrumental in having a new pavilion built in 1987. Geoff Cope was the Director of Cricket at Yorkshire CCC from 2002 to 2004, when he became Operations Director.

Another Halton boy who played for Yorkshire was *Anthony George Hatton* of Temple Lane. Tony was a bowler and in his first match for

First Cricket XI, 1963
Mr MB Cave, GA Cope, BK Sanderson, C Faulkner, A Hargreaves, D Prior, G Dawson S Baron, K Powell, R Burrow. D Bradbury (Capt), J Whitehead, F Fletcher, D Hall.

Yorkshire CCC took four wickets against Kent. He played for Castleford in the Yorkshire Council and also played for Colton and North Leeds. In the season 1960-61 he had one innings where he scored 4 runs and in bowling got 6 wickets with an average of 33.66.

David Bradbury was born in 1947 and attended Temple Moor School studying Geography and History. In 1960-61 he played for Yorkshire

Under 15 Cricket XI and was selected for the North of England Under 15 XI.

CROSS GREEN LANE

Cross Green Lane was named c1902 from Pinfold Lane to Green Lane. Originally part of Cross Field Lane it was developed with housing in groups known as Graveley Mount, Gladstone Mount, Whitkirk View and Sunny Hill.

North Side

Sycamore Avenue corner has two shops one of which was run by grocer Laurence Harry Taylor. The conversion of the original house to a shop was in 1922. This was where his daughter Kathleen was born before his move to 1 Cross Street which was Sharp's grocery and off licence. Plans were submitted by Gallons in 1938 to convert the properties to a store and it remained Gallons grocers until c1967. The firm originated in Yorkshire and became a part of Allied Suppliers. Gallons Ltd had their headquarters at Ingram Road Works and a bakery at Brown Lane Holbeck: in 1951 there were 45 Leeds shops. In more recent years there have been Netta's Fashions (Spencer family), Dales Stationery, a medical shoe shop (Vince Cowling) and Body & Sole (Ann Watt). At 4 Cross Green Lane was baker Patrick Dunbar, fruiterer Syd Walshaw and later Coombes Shoe Repairers and Pat's Hair Salon. The shop at the end of Birch Avenue was once confectioners Charles A Bumby and then J & A Fawcett, who lived on The Mount. The shop was bought by William Bennett when he came from Workington in 1935. His father was the Rev Edwin Cannington Bennett who became a priest in 1893 at Egremont Cumbria moving to Cockermouth (1894-98) and was the Vicar of Seaton from 1905. William & Mary Bennett ran the bakery while son William Frederick started in business at 9 Chapel Street as a sweetshop. He then moved to take over from Broadley's newsagents on Chapel Street where he stayed for 20 years: he died in January 2002. The shop on Cross Green Lane became Anne's Flower Box run by Anne Gargett and later a shop dealing in flags.

Thorp House on Birch Avenue in 1900 was the home of hay dealer William Atkinson who was born in 1849. A 51 year old Cross Gates born time keeper Benjamin Smart with wife Ann lived at Thorp House (1901) with their three children Sidney, Joseph & John Norman. Ann died aged 54 at Thorp House in May 1904 as did Edith Goodall in 1918 (aged 29). Thorp House was the Excella works of AH Baron & Sons who made mattresses. Plans for a storeroom and workshop were passed in 1903 and in the early 1920's ther was a temporary wooden shop at the works which the Hunslet RDC demanded it be removed.

The business was started by *Alfred Henry Baron* who lived at both The Orchards and Laurel Bank (Laureldene) at 26 Cross Green Lane (Gladstone Mount) prior to moving to Thorp House. The family at

Gladstone Mount were Alfred and wife Mary Ann with sons Frederick William born October 1904 and John Henry and daughters Ada and Lily. The business was taken by his two sons Frederick William and Albert Edward Baron. John Henry Baron married Florence Dacre on October 26th1903 and their son Frederick William was born on October 16th 1904 with daughters Edna May born in July 1906 and Mary born in February 1911. The brothers were working partners with Fred working on the upholstery on the top floor of the works while Albert dealt with the joinery and office work on the lower floor. There were only two other employees: Miss Roberts who worked the wire machine and the van driver. Albert Edward Baron celebrated his Golden Wedding in April 1943: he had been born in Morecambe in 1872 and married Elizabeth Eleanor at Heckmondwike where she was born in 1873. He was the treasurer of the Halton Allotments Association and Halton Cricket Club: wife Eleanor died on March 11th 1945 aged 72. Margaret Ann Baron died aged 33 in January 1949.

The firm finished in c1946 with Fred and family moving to 11 Cross Street. Albert and his wife Eleanor (Nellie) lived at 3 Cross Street. Frederick's son John Baron married Margaret Walker in October 1945. The business was sold and continued with new owners Ernest & Isobel Smith who applied for extensions to the factory in 1947. It was later with Alan & Frank Burley until 1970 and by 1973 became Excelsior Works of H Butcher haulage and removal contractors. In 1977 the store and office became a builder's office and storehouse and a year later plans were passed for a change of use to a service and car repair centre. This idea never matured and it was adapted as a Music Tuition Centre by July 1978. By June 1981 the Centre was being changed to a storage depot. In 1982 Jack Gahan Heating Engineers came to 12 Cross Green Lane and remained until 2001. The site was sold for new housing built by John Trant of Morley in 2002.

Thorp Street connects Cross Green Lane and Primrose Lane and in 1912 A Balance applied to have a wooden shoemaker's shop on the short street.

The row of housing from Thorp Street to Park Street was built by John Graveley and George Morritt in two separate sections. The style of the houses shows the date difference with the stone inscribed "Built by J Graveley 1898" and the other houses with a distinct letter M on the mouldings. The names of the two rows when first built were Graveley Mount and Gladstone Mount (22-36) after the Prime Minister William Ewart Gladstone (1809-98); Gladstone visited Leeds in October 1881. The plot of Gladstone Mount was sold by John Graveley to George Morritt in June 1898, who built the row to a new road called Park Street. The builder George Morritt lived with wife Ruth and children William, Maude, Lucy, Sarah and David for a time at the first house (22) prior to moving to Sunshine Villa and then the house he built for himself at Austhorpe "The Bungalow" in 1929: he died here in April 1931.

Graveley Mount

This row had no individual names and was numbered 1 to 7 Cross Green Lane in 1934 and 14 to 20 Cross Green Lane in 1935. Some of the earlier residents were:

18 Henry Alfred Massingberd born in 1847 at Derby, was a bank clerk; his wife Maude Mary (1860-1914) was born in India and they lived at 5 Stanley Terrace and Thelma Cottage; Henry died aged 67 on November 27th 1915. Their children were Vincent D'Arcy born in 1890 at Darlington and Charles born 1899 in the same town. Vincent became a locomotive fitter and at the age of 24 lived on Harehills Lane. Vincent D'Arcy and his wife Margaret Mary Christina lived at 5 Graveley Mount until 1936: their son was Donald Alfred Massingberd. Donald was born on June 7th 1914 and he married Constance Houghton Lockhard in July 1938: their son is Michael. Donald Alfred Massingberd died in 2000 having left Halton for Headingley and West Park.

The founder of the motor group Massingberd plc in 1963 was Donald's son Michael Massingberd who obtained the franchise for BMC, Wolseley, Riley and MG. In 1964 Killinghall opened and in 1966 a Standard Triumph dealership opened at Green Hammerton. In 1971 the Audi dealership was opened at Killinghall and the VW dealership at Ferrensby opened in 1973 followed by the main Ripon Road Harrogate branch in 1979 and the VW and Audi branch at Northallerton in 1982. Otley opened in the previous Eric Hunt dealership in 1986: refurbished in 2000 and Knaresborough opened in 1999.

Gladstone Mount

The houses had individual names and became 22 to 36 Cross Green Lane. 22 Hazeldene 24 Glengyle 26 Fernbank 28 Blairholme 30 Holmeleigh 32 Laurel Dene/Laurel Bank whose residents included Albert Edward & Mary Ann Baron with Frederick, Ada, James Henry and Lily, Percival Barran. Percival Barran's children were Olive born in 1920 who married George Forward on December 11th 1941; Robert born in 1923: who married Marjorie Varus in January 1944 and Edna Barran born in 1925 who married Douglas Westlake in August 1944.

34 Roslyn; 36 Southfield whose residents included Dr David Brook. For many years this was a doctor's surgery with Dr Leslie Walsh being senior in the practice.

Park Street was created by the early 20th century by John Graveley when he developed Graveleythorpe. The first house/shop on Whitkirk View was The Halton Pharmacy built as a private house and garden in 1878. This pharmacy was run by Herbert Rennard after conversion in 1907. In 1927 became the shop and home of the Gilleghan family-their name is still to be seen on the side wall indicating their sale of Kodak products. The family left the shop when Jack Gilleghan became ill in 1957 and the business was sold to Ronald Blass who was followed by Edward Broadley. It remained a chemist's shop until Ted Broadley retired in 1987 and it was sold to Robert Sidebottom.

The end property was converted into a greengrocer's shop in May 1928 by Gerald Ball, whose family also had the Premier Fruit Stores on the corner of Chapel Street and Cross Street and the greengrocery at Dial House. The shop was run in later years by William & RG Clegg who had a new shop front inserted in 1947 and CW Murgatroyd. In the 1960's the greengrocer's shop was run by R & R Perry. In April 1978 the shop was again converted into a private house. The four semi-detached houses were built by Frederick Horsman in 1937 (54-60 Cross Green Lane).

Sunny Hill is a row of nine terrace houses on the north side built in 1900 which were connected to the mains water in 1901. The houses had individual gardens to the rear and many of the houses were once owned by Gertrude Bray. The earliest reference in the deeds relating to the properties is dated August 3rd 1885 when an agreement was made between Mrs Meynell Ingram, John Gordon and William F Dean.

The allotments stretched down to Primrose Lane: the site became the Leodis public house in October 1967 and the town houses on Cross Green Lane and Primrose Lane. There were plans presented by John Smith Brewery of Tadcaster to develop the triangle of land between Cross Green Lane and Green Lane in May 1976. The plans for residential development were refused by the planners and the area remains as a green site.

South Side

1 Cross Green Lane was Scott's Bakery and then Henry & May Vinand's bakery/house from 1951 to 1973, when Henry died at the shop. Henry Vinand served in the RAF during the war as a chef serving the officer's mess. After the war Henry was a chef at The Queen's Hotel Leeds having moved from Manchester to Swinnow. They bought a shop at Yeadon and then bought the Halton property: son John was schooled at Pudsey and while living in Halton cycled to school daily. John Vinand met his future wife while studying at the Catering College Gower Street; Ann Wilson was the daughter of an army professional and lived at Strensall. She was born in Pontefract and married John Vinand at Strensall Garrison Church in 1960: John was a talented footballer playing for Leeds City Boys and for Whitkirk Wanderers. They both served apprenticeships and Ann had a catering job at a York shop prior to taking the shop on York Road opposite Seacroft Hospital. They ran this business for 21 years and their son Carl was educated at Temple Moor School. Ann was a partner in an outside catering business known as AnnDot which was sold in 2003. The property was sold to Barry and Celia Crocker's hardware business: Barry was a talented glider pilot. After a few different businesses it was divided into two shops: the original lounge of Vinand's and Crocker's house becoming Stainton's Estate Agents. The two shops later were Farm House Pine and Grade One Hair Studio.

Halton Post Office was opened in 1931 having been built by George Fenwick and moving from the demolished 1 Pinfold Lane.

Birch Crescent dates from 1938 and was completed on the driveway to Chestnut Grove, once home to both Crosthwaite and Sandy families. San Remo was a large house in its own extensive grounds surrounded by a high wall and large iron gates. This was another Crosthwaite home and later Reginald Knight lived in the house: it was demolished and is now the sheltered housing of Wheaton Court. Planning permission to demolish San Remo was approved in 1978.

Wheaton Avenue is to the rear of Wilfred Avenue and was the site of the Wellhouse Works of clothing manufacturer Ken Thomson. Charlotte Grove is a street with seven terrace properties dating from the early 20th century and once facing the open area towards Orchard Villa: gardens, orchards, tennis courts and bowling green.

Wilfred Avenue was developed from Cross Green Lane with the only building of size being the Barkston Ash Laundry with access from Selby Road prior to completion of the road from the original track in 1930.

The Thrift was opened by local Halton man Wright Popplewell of Pinfold Lane at the turn of the century. The Thrift Stores had two sections with grocery on the main street and the butcher's shop on Wilfred Avenue. The last butchers were Michael's Quality Butchers (JC & M Richardson) in the 1970's and A&H Butchers in 1978; it was then taken by Eric

Hazlegrave from October 1980 to March 1993 as Eric's Angling Stores which moved to the old Co-op building at Whitkirk. The old Thrift Grocery Store became Jim Windsor's bookmakers (Windsor Sporting Investments): other shops were on Primrose Lane and in the Arndale centre. Rod Keeligan and Derek Green started their bespoke tailoring business which occupies both shops. Vernon Bros tailors name comes from a forename of Rod Keeligan's grandfather. The business started in Halton in the late 1970's and they mainly make jackets for highland dress.

The grocer's shop at the corner of Wilfred Avenue and Cross Green Lane was run by Alec and Kathleen Cowell selling sweets and groceries. This was run by Emily Bean in 1904/05 and was later taken by John Weatherill. He was born in Halton but worked in Montreal until returning to the village in 1921: he died aged 46 on August 15th 1931.

The Halton Housing Estate was built from 1919/20: there were 121 houses on Cross Green Lane, Cricklegate, Temple Walk, Mayfield Road and Woodland Road. These street names were approved by Hunslet RDC in April 1921, along with The Crescent at Whitkirk. The route of Cross Green Lane from Wilfred Avenue to Cricklegate was widened by the Unemployed Relief in 1923 and they also were concerned with the straightening of Green Lane at the same period.

The original route of Cross Field Lane had a sharp right angled corner to Primrose Lane and then turned south at Mount Hermon to come out on Hollyshaw Lane; Hollyshaw Walk shows the original line as a footpath.

In December 1925 the vacant land on the corner of Cross Green Lane and Temple Walk was suggested for a row of shops but this proposal was turned down in favour of housing. The shops at the corner of Woodland Hill include a TV repair shop and 1st Sign. 67 Cross Green Lane was once Bell's Grocers and then Bennett's Grocers and is now General TV Services (Halton) Ltd specialising in TV repairs and HiFi being run by David Orange. They are part of the mid-1950's development by Mark Haley.

CROSS STREET

One of the original lanes of Halton leading from Chapel Street/Cross Green Lane to Back Lane (Primrose Lane).

Constone were founded in 1965 and provide building materials: they started in an old builder's yard. There was a large communal village well in this area at one period.

1 Cross Street. In the 1880's the shop was first with grocer Hannah Hoyle born in 1849: her husband Sam Hoyle was a plumber. Clara Hoyle born in 1874 was listed here in the 1901 census. By 1905 1 Cross Street was a grocer's shop run by Thomas Townend and later by William Peaker: Mrs Peaker applied in 1911 to the Hunslet RDC for compensation over a gas

leak on this "ancient highway" which was surfaced in that year, John & Mary Sharp, Ernest Appleyard and Reginald and Mary Sharp by 1929. John Sharp died aged 60 on October 12th 1925: the funeral was held at Killingbeck Cemetery. It was Harry & Minnie Taylor's grocery shop when he moved from 2 Cross Green Lane in 1935 and he also had the off-licence. The Penguin Bottling Co manufactured soft drinks; the firm started on Burley Road moving to Halton in 1950 from Dock Street. The business closed in Halton in late 1973 and the firm moved their operations to their mineral water depot on Chancellor Street Industrial estate. In 1979 Roman Construction operated from the site: involved in work on the Seacroft Estate for the Leeds City Council. AMK Maintenance (Leeds) Ltd bought the property in 1992. The firm had started in Cheshire and moved to Bramley in 1982: the name derives from Appleton, Megan and Keeling although the last two names were involved with the Cheshire operation only. The building maintenance specialist business is run by Neil Appleton and is dedicated to immediate response to repairs at high street shops and businesses.

3 Albert Edward and Elizabeth Eleanor (Nellie) Baron of the local mattress works.

5 John Hamilton Ballance died aged 85 in December 1923; Rowland and Edith Cousin with daughter Maud; their son Sam Cousin was killed in the Great War.

7 Frederick and Maud Akeroyd (1929); Eliza Ann Crawford; John Baron

9 John William & Florence Burdekin: Florence later lived on Woodland Road; Edwin and Edith Herrington; Albert and Ethel Hinsey; Robert & Edna May Noble

11 Ada Francis & Lily Baron; Frederick W Baron of the bedding firm who moved here from Thorpe House with his wife Hannah Alice Winifred Baron.

G Monkman was responsible for building some of the houses on Cross Street and Graveley Street for which Hunslet RDC approval was given in June 1923.

CROSTHWAITE FAMILY

The family had their local origins in Colton with James Crosthwaite a Colton grocer and farmer. *George Crosthwaite* was a boot and shoe maker of Colton who died aged 67 in 1860 and his wife Ann Smithies died in 1877 aged 80. Their son was *George Crosthwaite* (1828-84) following in the same trade as his father but moving to Halton after his marriage to Mary Ann Westerman in 1853. Mary Ann was born in 1826 and she died in 1897: they were both dedicated workers for the Halton Wesleyan Chapel. George Crosthwaite was a trustee, class leader and the Sunday School Superintendent. His three sons built the vestibule at the Chapel in 1908 in memory of their father.

Their son was *Walter George Crosthwaite* born in October 1854 and attended Halton School where in January 1867 he was awarded the prize for the recitation of poetry. He trained as a schoolmaster and became a council clerk prior to working for the firm in Leeds. He married Isabel Blair who was born in 1858 and they lived at Beech Cottage Chapel Street. Walter died on October 22nd 1909 and Isabel moved to live at Fairmont Pinfold Lane until her death on August 11th 1924: the service was held at Halton Methodist Chapel. He had been Society Steward and Sunday School Superintendent of Halton Wesleyan Chapel for many years. Their daughter was choir mistress at Halton Wesleyan Chapel: she had married Harold Bell who was Chapel Steward.

Walter and Isabel's children were Olive Isabel born in 1883 and *George Donald Crosthwaite* who was born on July 29th 1885 and lived at Brynmor Pinfold Lane with his wife Mary. George and Mary had three children: George Bryan born on September 21st 1911, Margaret Ruth born on October 27th 1912 and Isabel Clara born in December 1913.

George and Mary Ann second son was *John William Crosthwaite* born in April 1857 and married Mary Louise Smith (1860-1940). They lived at Chestnut Grove: he worked in the family business and was the chairman of the Cross Gates Gas Co. They had five children: Frederick who became a costumier living at Glengoyle Pinfold Lane, Maud, Horace Wilson, Wilson and Lily. In 1908 he moved to live at Rossett Green Harrogate and died on August 12th 1921. He had been choirmaster and the treasurer for the Trustees of Halton Wesleyan Chapel; he was also Chapel Steward, Sunday School treasurer, Circuit Quarterly Meeting Secretary and Circuit Overseas Missions treasurer. In 1897 he was elected a representative to the Wesleyan Conference held that year in Leeds and in 1916 he became the vice-president of the Leeds & Halifax Building Society.

George and Mary Ann's third son was *Alfred Ernest Crosthwaite* born in April 1859 and married Annie Hartley born in 1862. He worked for the family business in Leeds and they lived at San Remo Cross Green Lane: they later lived on Morritt Avenue with San Remo becoming home to the Knight family from Colton. Alfred died on June 5th 1907 and Annie moved to live at Oakdene Pinfold Lane with daughter Kathleen. Annie died at The Cottage Cridling Stubbs Knottingley on January 25th 1941 aged 79.

Alfred and Annie's children were *George Vernon Crosthwaite,* Emma (1888-1970), George born 1893, Dorothy born on January 28th 1894 and Kathleen Mary born on March 4th 1905. George Vernon Crosthwaite worked in the family business; Emma Hartley married Frederick Martin Walton (1890-1965) whose father was a founder of Mawson & Walton of Leeds. They were married on September 28th 1923 and lived at 100 Austhorpe Road Cross Gates moving to live at 21 Hollyshaw Terrace with Annie and Kathleen and then at 365 Selby Road Whitkirk. They had a son Michael Walton (1925-81) who married Jean Bolton Southworth (born

1929) on January 28th 1951. Their children were Martin Richard born in 1953 and Sally who was born in 1956.
Dorothy Crosthwaite married George Ingle Machell on July 12th 1922 when he was 29 years old: he was the son of lime burner George Alfred Machell. They lived at Northfield at Cridling Stubbs Knottingley and he died on the local estate after a shooting accident: Dorothy died in the mid-1960's.
Kathleen Crosthwaite was married in 1945 to Benjamin Bamber: they had a daughter Victoria. Kathleen lived at Oakdene Pinfold Lane with her widowed mother and moved to Buxton where she died.
The tall marble pillar memorial once surrounded by iron railings in Whitkirk Cemetery remembers several members of this Halton family.
The Crosthwaite family started their Leeds business in 1882 on York Street as The Crosthwaite Fire Bar Syndicate Ltd (iron founders) and were also woollen manufacturers. In 1898 Crosthwaite Brothers were listed as woollen manufacturers at 52 Wellington Street and in the former premises of Henry Wilson and Jacques & Rhodes at York Street: in 1900 they had offices at 3 Park Place. In 1907 they were listed as Crosthwaite Bros Woollen Manufacturers & Crosthwaite Fire Bar. In 1917 the firm was the Crosthwaite Engineering & Furnace Co Ltd at York Street Iron Works (Alfred, Edward and George Henry Crosthwaite). By 1947 the firm was known as Crosthwaite Furnaces & Scriven Machine Tools Ltd on the south side of York Street. In 1955 it was Crosthwaite Furnaces and the firm ceased trading in 1968.

DEANS (DENES)

Primrose Valley: Dene (denu) means a valley

Halton Deans were first mentioned in 1170-90 as Dena de Haleton and in 1323 was Haltondene. In 1715 Thoresby gave the following account of Halton Dens: *"A little north of Wyke Bridge are the Dens as they are corruptly called from den vallis. The natural situation of the place being a deep valley between pretty steep hills on each side. That this was a woody tract is not only attested by some aged persons yet living who remember it so, remaining slag of ironworks that I saw when I traversed the ground and its well known that those blasts or smelting furnaces were always set on woody places and now converted into gardens and enclosures"*
A map of 1821 shows a stream running along the valley to join with Wyke Beck near the bridge. A few of the old fields are labelled Deyn, Deyn Gardens and Deyn Closes. Those who held the Deyns from the Temple Newsam estate included Joseph Atkinson, members of the Graveley family, Thomas Morkill and William Swift. The land to Primrose Lane was known as the Intacks (intakes) and consisted of long rectangular

parcels of land. These lands were in the hands of the same people and also included Leeds Free School (Grammar School), Michael Scholefield of the Manor House at Whitkirk and Thomas Smith.
Maps of 1841 show Prospect Valley which included old quarries; this became the site of the 19th century Killingbeck Colliery run by Garside's of York Road. The valley is from the Halton Sewage Works to Almond's smallholding at Primrose Valley once an inn serving the miners. The Deans was landscaped with the old tip heaps and a stream which features some attractive wet lands and flowers. The area was later landscaped as a recreation park and by 1915 much of the land had been let by the Temple Newsam estate to the Temple Newsam Parish Council.
Halton Dene was once the site of a council rubbish tip which covered 60 acres and was the largest site in Leeds. This had access from Lucy Avenue and was closed in May 1981 and the area landscaped as a part of the new park. In 1978 a 7 acre site on Halton Dene was proposed for coal extraction with 30,000 tons of coal removed in under a year with a maximum depth of ten metres.

DENTISTS

Dentists serving Halton started when Jack Stuart White moved from Cross Gates in 1921 to live at Holme Lea Chapel Street to start his dental practice in 1928. *John Rowarth Stuart White* was educated at Leeds Central High School and the University Dental School where he graduated as a Bachelor of Dental Surgery in 1928. Jack opened his Halton surgery at 1 Chapel Street later 17 Chapel Street and lived at Holme Lea 14 Chapel Street with his parents until his marriage to Mary Sandy on May 11th 1935. They lived in Scarcroft where their son David was born in 1936 and his parents John and Frances White moved to 17 Pinfold Lane in 1932. Jack White served in the War and he returned to his Halton practice after the War and the family moved to Thorner in 1946; his wife Mary died in 1979. There were plans presented in February 1975 to convert the dental surgery into offices but he retired from dentistry in 1976 and sold the business to dentist Peter Rider who continued at Dial House until the building of the new ***Halton Dental Practice*** on Selby Road in 1992. *Peter Rider* qualified BDS Sheffield on September 16th 1975. Peter also founded Barwick Developments which had an office at the new building. The lease was taken by Grahame Stowe Bateson Family Solicitors who bought the property in 1998. Peter Rider sold Dial House to Leeds City Council in 1993 and it is now a Crisis Centre. The Halton Dental Clinic was taken by JS Matharoo & Associates.
The ***Selby Road Dental Practice*** on Halton Hill is run by Simon Agabeg and Associates. Simon Paul Agabeg was educated at Temple Moor School and qualified at Leeds University in 1986. He started at 178

Woodhouse Lane and in 1989 commenced at the Selby Road practice.

DISTRICT NURSES

The Whitkirk & District Nursing Association was formed in 1904: on the committee were the wife of the Halton GP Dr Bertram Basket, Mrs Walter Crosthwaite and Mrs Frederick Pogson. In 1916 there were donations to the Association from the Irwin Arms Bowling Club, Halton Allotments Club and later from the Pinfold Tennis Club. In 1920 the funds from the closed VAD Hospital passed to the Association.

The first district nurse was *Nurse Cateaux* appointed on February 11th 1904 who left after a year and ten months. She was assisted by *Nurse Ashby* and *Nurse Purvis* who started on July 4th 1906. In 1907 the nurse's house was 19 Chapel Street; *Nurse Harrop* who was born in 1877 and started work in the district in January 1908 moved to a larger house on Gladstone Mount (Cross Green Lane): the furniture at the Chapel Street house was sold for £1/17. In 1910 Mrs Walter Crosthwaite was elected president with Philip Marsden as the treasurer. The salary for the nurse was £90 annually. In 1911 there were 89 cases and 3315 visits made by the district nurse who worked for the WRCC as a health visitor and school nurse for a few years. Donations to the association included those from the Irwin Arms Harmonic Society, LICS, Hon Edward & Lady Dorothy Wood, Lady Gordon Charity Trustees and chemist's daughter Miss Rennard. In 1919 the salary for the nurse was raised to £120 and in 1921 was £142. The following year the Hon Secretary was Miss Bell of Hopewell House Woodman Street; on the committee were doctor's wife Mrs Ashmore, Mrs Alfred Crosthwaite, Mrs Leach of Morritt Avenue, Mrs James Pickles, Mrs Thomas Piercy, Agnes Pindar of Clifton House and JA Popplewell whose family ran the Thrift Stores.

Nurse Harriet Hannah Kitson was a maternity nurse in the Halton area based at the Halton Welfare Clinic. She was born at Woodhouse on May 21st 1861 and worked for 50 years as a nurse: she came to Halton in 1891 and was certificated in 1905. Nurse Kitson died in 1933 at her home on School Lane: one of the Halton almshouses.

Nurse Florence Harrop resigned to marry John William Liversedge of Morritt Avenue on April 18th 1922. A presentation was made by Walter Bowden Pindar of Clifton House. John Liversedge was a civil engineer and the son of tailor Edwin Liversedge.

Nurse Elsie Dacre was appointed from January 1922 living at the newly built house at 8 Temple Walk where there was a plate on her door and a slate outside on which messages were left. There was a salary of £146 per year and an allowance for uniform: in 1923 the nurse made 4782 visits. In 1923 Mrs Crosthwaite resigned due to ill health and Mrs Joshua Popplewell resigned and left the district. Mrs Hazel Young wife of the

new doctor at Gilsyke House was elected to the committee and worked hard for the association.
Nurse Ibbotson was working as an assistant in 1925 from 19 Cross Green Lane. In 1930 donations were received from Leeds Workpeoples Hospital Fund, Halton Templars Scout Silver Band, Temple Newsam WI, Junior Imperial League, Halton Irwin Arms Angling Club, Whitkirk & District Amateur Operatic Society, JA Popplewell, Lord & Lady Irwin and Pinfold Tennis Club. In 1933 there had been nearly 5500 visits and 202 new cases: the President was Mrs Marsden, Vice President Mrs Leach, Treasurer Mrs Pindar, Secretary Mrs Livingston and Assistant Secretary Miss B Piercy. In 1931 Nurse Elizabeth Ibbotson worked as the district midwife for Whitkirk, Halton and Cross Gates areas: she retired on October 18th 1961. In 1934 Nurse Elsie Dacre moved from Temple Walk to Denison 19 Templegate where a telephone was installed in 1936. In 1935 the president was Philip Marsden of The Grange Whitkirk with the committee including Col Glazebrook, Mrs Pogson and Mrs Young; *Nurse Gilbert* assisted on the rounds. By 1939 there were 5907 visits and in 1942 there were 5234 visits in the year with a contribution of two pence for a visit. There were so called Fire Parties which raised cash locally and these were held at Alexander Avenue, Morritt Drive, Oak Crescent, Queensway and Woodland Road. The District Nurse had free transport on the Kippax Motor Co buses. The Whitkirk & District Nursing Assocation ceased to exist in 1947 when the government took over its work.
Elsie Dacre retired in 1955 having had a total of 33 years service to Halton folk. Elsie Dacre trained at Scalebar Park and became assistant matron at Batley Hospital prior to moving to Halton with her husband traveller George Dacre who died in 1969. Elsie moved from Temple Gate to a newly built bungalow at 30 Field End Gardens. She formed a close liaison with Dr Jack Young at Gilsyke Surgery and with the Baby Welcome. When Elsie retired in October 1955 a fund was launched for a presentation with house to house collections. The presentation took place at Halton Parochial Hall on July 6th 1956 when a silver teapot and a cheque for £150 was presented by Dr Young. There was also a presentation by Andrew Mattock who was the youngest son of Dr Robert & Helen Mattock of Pinfold Lane. Andrew made the presentation with Jean Campbell on behalf of the children of the district. There was also a donation from Elsie's brother C Kear Esq of Detroit USA. Elsie paid for a new pair of wrought iron gates to be placed at the Temple Newsam War Memorial together with a plaque seen to the right of the gates.
Nurse Elizabeth Ibbotson was the District Midwife for Cross Gates, Halton and Whitkirk for 30 years: she retired on October 18th 1961.
Nurse Jean Donald living at 5 Wilfred Avenue was the health visitor with special responsibilities for babies. *Nurse Ida Precious* was born Ida

Bruce in Smethwick Birmingham in September 1909. The family moved to Kidderminster and Ida married Harold Precious in 1936 after training at Hull Royal Infirmary from 1931 to 1935; they moved from Hull to live at Halton. Nurse Precious started for the Halton and Whitkirk districts in the 1940's and relieved Nurse Elsie Dacre on a few occasions but finished work in May 1970 at the age of 60. Harold died on July 21st 1994 and her sister Doris died in 2002 aged 96.

Nurse Vera Whaler worked at the Halton surgery: she trained at St. John Ambulance and qualified in 1939/40 working at The Hollies on Weetwood Lane where there were some cases from Killingbeck which included evacuees. Nurse Whaler worked in the munitions factory at Thorp Arch where she was involved in filling 2 ton bombs and was involved in nursing care. After her marriage Nurse Whaler moved to ICI Armley Road and afterwards became a district nurse based at Cross Gates using just one car provided by the Association for the nurses in the area. She lived on Cross Gates Ring Road and then moved to Morritt Drive. She started Willow Bank on Barwick Road and then bought the adjacent house and received a licence for 12 residents. Nurse Whaler retired in 1972. *Nurse May Rycroft* died aged 77 on October 17th 1988; she was the daughter of George Robert who died May 29th 1941 aged 86 and Emily Minshull Rycroft who died in 1925 aged 81. *Nurses Mavis King* and *Vera Maine* served the Halton area and *Anne Kellett* was the District Nurse from March 1978 to March 1997. In more recent years the surgery has been served by Polly Tapsell, Jane Hall and Cathy Thornton.

DOCTORS

Early Halton doctors were *Dr Richard Dalby Pawson* (1805-1851): Mary Pawson married Private HJ Green in 1943 and her father was the Temple Newsam estate joiner. *Dr Edward Pateath* was born in 1801 and he served the village in the mid-19th century and lived with his wife Catherine who was born in 1813.

Doctors serving the village of Halton were mainly based at Gilsyke House: the entrance to the surgery was at the front of the house facing the main road. *Dr Edward Windle Tinsdill* trained in London and he died at Gilsyke House on June 7th 1871 aged 74; his wife Elizabeth died aged 52 on May 12th 1861. The gravestone at Whitkirk Church records that three of their children died in infancy: Anne Windle on 12th October 1857 aged a year and eleven months with John and Eleanor. His son was killed in the American Civil War 1861-65. Dr Tinsdill visited his patients on horseback and later by a gig. *Dr Charles Edward Wikely* was an assistant to Dr Windle and served as a Brigade Surgeon with the Army Medical Department and in India with the 19th regiment of Foot from 1858. He married Dr Tinsdill's daughter and served over 40 years in

India. He was interred at Blackpool after his death on July 24th 1926 aged 93 and is remembered at Whitkirk. He was married twice: Mercy died aged 21 on March 29th 1858 and second wife Georgina died on October 30th 1900. Dr Tinsdill was followed by *Dr Samuel Joseph Noake* who was born in Staffordshire and qualified at London and Edinburgh: he was married to Rachael and they had five children born at Seacroft. Birch Avenue was called Noakes Terrace for a few years as the doctor had bought the land from John Graveley. The children included Clara Evelyn born in February 1870, James Bertram born September 1870, Minnie born in March 1871 and Cedric Edgar born June 5th 1876. In December 1878 Dr SJ Noake applied to the local authority to build a house and stables on his Gilsyke site.

Dr Arthur Thomas Wills was at Gilsyke Surgery in the late 19th century. He was born in Staffordshire in 1858 and wife Judith Sarah had a family with daughter Helen Frances born in July 1888 and son Arthur born in 1890. *Dr Bertram George Mortimer Basket* was born in 1863 at Salford Lancashire qualifying at Oxford and London. In the early 20th century he was at Gilsyke House with wife Gertrude born at Plymouth in 1864; father George Crooks Baskett born at Newcastle-upon-Tyne in 1821 was a retired journalist and author. Bertram and Gertrude Baskett's children were Mildred born at Hampstead in 1894, Roger Mortimer born at Halton in 1895 and Aline born in 1901. George Crooks Baskett was the 27th to be cremated at Lawnswood Crematorium after he died aged 86 on July 20th 1906: cremation was on July 24th. Charles Edward Goodall was in service as a horseman for Dr Baskett for many years and became a market gardener. He was the president of the Temple Newsam Allotment Holders Association and died in March 1919 aged 62: his son was killed in the Great War.

Dr Patricius Wallace Ashmore followed Dr Baskett and his sons were William Barrett who died 2 months old in October 1910 and his other son was killed in the Second World War; his wife was the aunt of the Leeds surgeon David Feather. Dr Ashmore's partner was Dr Haygarth. It was in October 1898 that *Dr Rhodes Haygarth* came to Cross Gates at 15 Austhorpe Road and joined Dr Baskett as a partner in the practice. Dr Haygarth was born in Keighley and trained at Edinburgh: his son was John Rhodes Haygarth who was at Leeds Grammar School from 1911 to 1919, leaving school aged 17. In 1909 Dr Baskett left and he joined Dr Ashmore. During the Great War Dr Haygarth was in charge at the Halton Parochial Hall VAD Hospital from 1915 to 1919; he bought an AJS motorcycle from Jack Stuart White Snr and used it to get around the practice. Dr Haygarth retired from Austhorpe Road to live at Grange over Sands in 1934. The surgery later became that of Dr James Alfred Smorfitt and Dr William Ernest Smith.

Dr George Dean Compston was the GP on the retirement of Dr Ashmore in 1924. Dr Compston was the son of JA Compston Recorder of Leeds and was at Cambridge University. He was the cox in the University Boat Race of 1909 and his boat was beaten by three lengths. He served in the Great War as a Captain in the RAMC and served in Mesopotamia. He served with the Women and Children Hospital Leeds. Dr Compston died of leukaemia in 1928 after retiring to the South of England with ill health. He was cremated at Golders Green London.

Dr John Alexander Young was born and qualified in Toronto but when he emigrated he had to take a further course at St. Mary's Hospital London as his original degrees were not recognised in this country. He came to Halton with his wife Hazel to take over the Gilsyke practice in 1920; he qualified LRCP in 1922. He was a popular village doctor and was active in many aspects of village life with surgeries at 4a Temple View Road, 49 Chantrell Street, 426 York Road and Main Street Seacroft. Dr Young retired on Saturday March 7th 1962 and had for a few years commuted from Filey to Halton to take the occasional surgeries: he owned 44a The Crescent Filey. Jack & Hazel Young also bought a cottage on the green at Rosedale Abbey: their son John William Young who was in the Royal Navy and his wife Beatrice ran the Milburn Arms Hotel for a few years before moving to Scarborough: they were living at 186a Selby Road in 1954/56. Their daughter Joan Young was born on August 24th 1924 and she married Tony Merchant.

A presentation of a silver owl pepper pot was made to Dr Young in June 1962 at St. Wilfrid's Church Hall by Councillor Joseph Brooksbank. There was also a gift from the staff and patients of the Chantrell Street Surgery on York Road and from the Halton Childrens Welfare Clinic. The surgery's secretary for many years was Dorothy Holmes who lived at 9 Oak Road with her husband Clement Holmes: she retired in 1970. Dr Jack Young died on June 2nd 1975 and was buried at Scarborough.

Dr Herbert Arnott Eadie became a partner in 1924: he had been working at Leeds Public Dispensary for six months. Dr Eadie was killed while riding as a passenger on a 6 ton caterpillar tractor on Post Hill on Sunday September 27th 1931 aged 30. The tractor driver was Arthur Waterman who was the President of the Leeds Motor Club of which Dr Eadie was the medical officer. He was born in Edinburgh and became a Captain in the Royal Army Medical Corps and was a keen rider and golfer, living at Kelvedon Oakwood Lane. In 1928 he married Poppy Wingate who was the sister of the Temple Newsam golf professional Syd Wingate of Selby Road; they lived at Greylands Austhorpe Road Cross Gates with his mother Hannah Sophia Eadie.

Dr HA Eadie

Dr Albert Lawson Light joined Dr Young after Dr Eadie's death and left to work as a surgeon at Pinderfields Hospital Wakefield.

Dr Trevor Lynn Owen was at Gilsyke House in the early 1930's as Dr Young's assistant. He qualified at Leeds and London and was the resident surgery officer at Beckett Hospital Barnsley and a House Surgeon and Surgery Receiving Officer at the LGI. He was later in partnership as Hilary & Owen and later was the Hon Surgeon at the Selby War Memorial Hospital and a member of the York Medical Society.

Dr Edward Francis Phillips who joined Dr Young as an assistant leaving in 1955: he died in late 1980. *Dr David Arthur Kidd* (1955-59) lived at the Blacksmith's Cottage near the corner of Grove Road with his wife Stefania; he moved in March 1959 to become a partner in a Castleford surgery. Dr Kidd qualified in Leeds and later was a house surgeon and physician at Pontefract General Infirmary.

Dr Robert Pickard Mattock (1946-71) lived at Gilsyke House in a specially built flat from October 1946 before moving to 7 Pinfold Lane with his wife Helen and two boys Andrew and Ian. Helen was a nurse and became the Girl Guides Commissioner. Dr Mattock qualified at Leeds and was a house physician at St Luke's Hospital Bradford. He was also a Medical Officer RAMC and a surgeon at the Leeds Public Dispensary and Hospital. He left the practice in March 1971 and a year later worked in Silsden. He died on May 15th 2002 at Bridlington at the age of 86: they lived at East Court Mansions Lime Kiln Lane on the north side of the resort near Sewerby from 1986: from 1971 he also lived at Settle. He married for the second time to Constance (Connie) Scott of Halton: her son was Richard from her first marriage.

Dr Laurie Ramsay qualified in Leeds and was a resident Medical Officer and House Physician at St James Hospital Leeds. He joined the Gilsyke practice on April 1st 1959 living at Gilsyke House from 1961 to 1966. Soon afterwards the old house was demolished and was re-developed with Grandways Parade, the present Village Co-op store and Gilsyke Medical Centre. Dr Ramsay retired on September 4th 1993.

Dr Mabel Yates was appointed as an assistant to Dr Mattock and Dr Ramsay from July 2nd 1962 and left in summer 1967. Dr Yates qualified at Leeds and was the Primary Clinic Medical Officer Leeds East Health Authority; House Physician Geriatric and House Surgeon at St James Hospital.

Dr Ronald Johnson was appointed as an assistant in October 1967 and became a partner with Dr Ramsay on April 1st 1971: he retired on November 6th 1994. Dr Johnson was born in Birkenhead and qualified at Leeds: he worked at the Leeds General Infirmary and at Seacroft. *Dr Susan Grace Pearson* commenced as an assistant to Dr Ramsay and Dr Johnson on August 16th 1971 and left the Gilsyke practice in September 1972. Dr Pearson qualified at Leeds and was a House Surgeon at Seacroft Hospital and House Physician at St James Hospital. *Dr Arnold Geoffrey Zermansky* commenced as an assistant on November 1st 1972 and left the practice on January 31st 1973. He went into partnership with Dr Austin Duthie at the surgery on Dib Lane. Dr Zermansky qualified at Leeds and became a Tutor in General Practice at Leeds University and was an ex-chairman of East Leeds Primary Care Trust.

Dr Malcolm Addlestone commenced as an assistant on August 27th 1973 and became a partner on April 8th 1974 and later senior partner. Dr Addlestone qualified at Leeds and was a Senior House Surgeon at Leeds Maternity Hospital; House Physician & Surgeon at Leeds General Infirmary and House Physician at Chapel Allerton Hospital.

Dr Jane Renwick joined the Gilsyke practice in 1992. Dr Renwick qualified at Manchester and was a Clinical Assistant at Leeds General Infirmary. *Dr Adrian Smith* joined the practice on September 6th 1993: he qualified at Manchester. *Dr Mohammad Ilyas* commenced at Gilsyke Surgery on November 7th 1994: he qualified at Manchester.

Dr William Pogson qualified at Edinburgh and had a surgery at 4 Rose Terrace followed by his son *Dr Frederick William Pogson* who qualified at Edinburgh and Glasgow. Dr William Pogson lived at Seacroft Grange, north of The Green, with his wife Sarah and had two surgeries at Seacroft and Halton: he was the doctor who attended Mrs Meynell Ingram until she died of Bright's Disease in 1904. His son was born on January 18th 1868, entered Leeds Grammar School in 1879 and qualified c1892. He was the Medical Officer for the Hunslet Union with a surgery on Station Road Cross Gates and later lived at Holme Lea Chapel Street. Dr FW Pogson was married on January 6th 1897 to Louisa Fawthrop whose father opened a chemist's shop in Cross Gates in 1897. Dr Pogson had an accident on his bicycle in 1907 while on his way to see a patient: his application for compensation from Hunslet RDC was refused. He died on February 4th 1913; his father had died aged 75 on November 9th 1912. Frederick & Louisa Pogson's sons were William Frederick baptised on January 21st 1898 and Martin who was born in October 1902 at Holme Lea and was to

live at 2 The Crescent with his wife Louise. Both William and Martin Pogson attended Leeds Grammar School: the eldest son William F Pogson was a 2nd Lieutenant/Acting Captain RFA in the Kings Own Yorkshire Light Infantry during the Great War and suffered severe gunshot wounds; he recovered in a London hospital. He married Kathleen Bingham on Saturday February 19th 1925 at Wrangthorne Church Hyde Park and was an electrical engineer living on Dominion Avenue Chapel Allerton.
The house which was once between Todd's Garage (Troy) and Park View Farm (Irwin Approach) was also a doctor's surgery:
Dr William Harold Bean (died 1976) was qualified at Leeds and was a GP for 35 years and lived at Swiss Cottage Austhorpe Road converted into a surgery in 1939. The house was later demolished and was the site for the present post office. Dr Bean retired to Torquay and he was appointed an Officer Brother of the Order of St. John for which he had been a lecturer and examiner for 45 years. *Dr Edward Leake Brittain* was a partner with Dr Bean at Scholes. He qualified at Leeds and was a House Surgeon at Leeds General Infirmary and House Physician at St James Hospital. He was also the Resident Medical Officer at St Mary's Infirmary Armley. *Dr Robert Charles Neville Shires* first worked from 32 Morris Lane Kirkstall and then had a surgery in Scholes where he lived on Main Street with his family prior to moving to live at Traquair on Selby Road Whitkirk. Robert Charles Neville Shires was born in 1906 and attended Leeds Grammar School from 1916 to 1923. He qualified at London and became the Assistant Medical Officer Leeds Public Dispensary and was Medical Officer at St James Hospital. Dr Neville Shires retired in 1970 and went to live with his wife Betty in Highcliffe-on-Sea: he died in 1982 aged 76 and Betty died near the home of her eldest son Martin and his wife Carol in 1997. Martin and Carol were married on June 30th 1962; the youngest son is Alan born in 1941 who lived in Canada before moving to California. *Dr Harold Ernest Moody* qualified at London Guy's Hospital and became the House Surgeon at Royal Victoria Hospital Folkestone and was a Medical Officer with the RAF Volunteer Reserve (1940-46) and was an Acting Squadron Leader. Dr Hal Moody became a partner in Dr Bean's practice and lived on Manston Gardens Cross Gates. Dr Moody was born in 1915 in South London and was educated at Dulwich College; he died on Monday July 13th 1998 at St James Hospital and his wife Nancy died on December 24th 1998 at Seacroft Hospital aged 82. They had three children Anthea, Christopher and Julia.
The Halton surgery was closed and demolished in 1991 to be replaced with a new dental surgery for Peter Rider.
Dr Leslie Walsh qualified at Leeds and he had a surgery at 36 Cross Green Lane living at 2 The Drive Cross Gates. His two sons Marcus and John attended Temple Moor School: Marcus went to Exeter College Oxford and John was at Merton College. Dr Walsh retired after 36 years in October

1978 having started at Cross Green Lane in 1942. He was a Labour Councillor for Osmondthorpe Ward (1951-64) and his brother was Hon Ald JS Walsh and Lord Mayor of Leeds 1966/67. Dr Walsh died on January 17th 1979. *Dr Harold Moses Feldman* had surgeries at 48 Malvern Road Leeds 11 and at 45 Meadow Road Leeds 11. He qualified at London and was at the Cross Green Lane surgery in the 1930's, later at 48 Malvern Road Beeston. *Dr David Brooke* qualified at Leeds and had a surgery at 106 Cross Gates Road as well as being at Cross Green Lane. Dr Brooke was educated at Roundhay High School and Leeds Medical School; he died aged 33 in 1942 having lived at 36 Cross Green Lane from 1939.
Dr Harold Sharp who was also a qualified pharmacist had surgeries on Rookwood Avenue and York Road Seacroft. He qualified at London and at first had surgeries at 9 Park Lane and 40 Cross Gates Lane.
Dr Edward Tempany had his surgeries at 6 Selby Road and 65 Beckett Street. He lived at Red Lodge Roundhay and qualified at University College Dublin. He was Senior House Surgeon at a Dublin hospital and then Senior Resident Medical Officer at Sheffield City Hospital. Dr Tempany was a Lieutenant in the RAMC.
Dr Francis Robin Beetham was at 1 Dunhill Rise from 1935; he qualified at London. *Dr Herbert Arthur Beetham* qualified at Leeds and London; he had a surgery at 64 Harehills Road and later on Beckett Street. Dr HA Beetham was on the Leeds Pensions Committee and a Deputy Coroner North Riding Yorkshire. By 1936 Dr Francis Robin Beetham has surgeries at 2 Upland Road and 1 Dunhill Rise, where there were the surgery and waiting room on the ground floor and a flat upstairs. *Dr Oswald Dennis Beetham* of Upland Lodge Roundhay qualified at Edinburgh and Glasgow. He later lived at The Gables at Thorner having practiced at 115a Beckett Street, 462 York Road and 1 Easterly Road. *Dr William Ronald Jackson* qualified at Leeds and started at the Beetham surgery at 2 Upland Road before moving to live at 66 Templenewsam Road. The surgery opened at 1 Dunhill Rise by 1952. He retired in 1973: he was at Dunkirk and was for four years a Prisoner of War in the Far East prior to practising in Halton. His wife Margaret died in 2004 aged 86 having moved from Templenewsam Road to live at Clifton Brighouse: their daughter is Sheelagh. *Dr Geoffrey Martyn Welham* who qualified at Leeds was an assistant with Dr Jackson and when Dr Jackson retired he took the practice over. Dr Welham retired to live on the island of Mallorca. *Dr Arthur Walter Allen* of the Shaftesbury Clinic took over the Dunhill Rise practice and closed it down. Dr Allen qualified at Leeds and retired in 2004.

ELECTRICITY SERVICES

Electricity was first displayed in Leeds in 1880 and a year later part of Boar Lane was lit by electricity. A permanent electric supply was started from Whitehall Road in May 1893. The Crown Point Power Station was opened in 1897 and Whitehall Road Generating Station was built in 1902. Crown Point was closed on March 31st 1932. Leeds took over the electricity supply from the

Yorkshire Electric Power Co in June 1929.

Electric cables were laid to Halton and Whitkirk in mid-1924 and up Halton Hill by 1928. Electric street lighting replaced the old gas lamps over an extended period: Chapel Street was lit by forty three 60 watt Sodium lights replacing the twenty six gas lamps.

ELMET

Halton was one of a great number of villages in the Kingdom of Elmet

The Kingdom of Elmet was created following the departure of the Romans c410 and this extensive kingdom was administered from Barwick-in-Elmet. It stretched from the Peak District to the headwaters of Wharfe and Nidd and from the western edge of the Plain of York to the Pennines: the old West Riding including Leeds and district. The Anglo-Saxon invaders conquered Holderness, Wolds and Plain of York in the 6th century but westward invasion was prevented by the Kingdom of Elmet. The Saxon kingdoms of Deira and Bernicia united as Northumbria in 593AD but in 615AD the Saxon Hereric was poisoned in Elmet. Hereric was the nephew of Edwin who invaded Elmet in 617AD in retaliation for his murder: the kingdom was at an end by 637AD. King Edwin was converted and baptised at York in 627AD: the date of the commencement of the first Minster. Edwin was the King of Northumbria until 632AD and by then most of "Yorkshire" was under Saxon rule.

ENCLOSURES

The origins of the enclosures date to medieval times and are linked with the growing of crops, the land being in the hands of the Lord of the Manor. The early enclosures in the 13th/14th centuries introduced the hedgerows and field walls. There was much activity in enclosure awards between 1750 and 1845 and the enclosures of the Manor of Temple Newsam which included the village of Halton date from these times. A commissioner and surveyor/valuer were appointed by the parish. The fields were mapped and lines drawn for the enclosures with necessary fencing, hedges and quite often ditches. The cost of administration fell to the recipients of the awards: it was once calculated that in England 7 million acres of common land were enclosed as a result of 5400 acts passed between 1700 and 1914. Over 200,000 miles of hawthorn hedge were planted on a fifth of England's land with straight roads taking over from the earlier angular roads in previous enclosures.

The Enclosure Act of 1777 was concerned *with "enclosing common or waste called Halton Moor in the Township of Halton in the Manor of Temple Newsam, parish of Whitkirk in the West Riding of Yorkshire".* There were 95 acres in the hands of Rt Hon Charles Lord Viscount Irwin, William Judson, William Graveley and two of the owners of *"all messuages, cottages and land held for the Lord of the Manor".* The Commissioners were Mordecai Cutts, Richard Warner and William Leake.

The Enclosure Act for the Manor of Temple Newsam received the royal assent on June 22nd 1820 with the commissioner Nicholas Brown and surveyor/valuer Alfred Smith of Little Preston. A letter from Thomas Morkill to Alfred Smith asks him for a meeting to sort out the details of the award in Halton. A letter from Alfred Smith in 1822 asks for a meeting with local dignatories including William Schofield, William Graveley and Thomas Graveley in the Cock and Coronet public house (Irwin Arms). Maps by J Dickinson (1730) were used for the enclosures of Halton with a new map drawn in 1821 (Open Fields, Ings & Frontages) and the final maps and awards were published on November 24th 1834. The early maps refer to "Halton Town" with the north of Halton Hill referred to as The Deyns with Low Slacks and Slack Bank.

The 1821 map shows a few houses at the start of Back Lane (Primrose Lane) and scattered dwellings along Chapel Street and High Street to a group of cottages at Field End. This map shows Gillsyke House, the three existing public houses and farms of the old village. Pinfold Lane is shown as Pinfold Road which was continued across Selby Road (signed to Ferrybridge) as Baynes Intake Road and to the north across Back Lane as "Morkill's Road" into the valley.

ENTERTAINMENT

Most family entertainment was either created at home, listening to the radio or centred on the church and chapel

Cinemas A cinema was proposed for Primrose Road Halton by Harry T Jones in 1933 but the plans were rejected in January 1934. The site was to be on the corner of Chapel Street where Gertrude Bray built the row of houses in 1936: she led the opposition to the plans. In October 1938 Yorkshire Industrial Development Corporation submitted plans for a cinema on Chapel Street and in the same year Donald Alfred & Ronald Burnand submitted other plans for a cinema on a different site on Selby Road which would include three shops: the plans were rejected. In 1944 plans by the Roxy Cinema Co were submitted to build a cinema in the village: plans included a car park but they were rejected by the planners.

The Ritz Cinema

The Picture House Cross Gates was opened on August 5th 1920 and the name changed to The Ritz on October 5th 1938; the cinema closed on May 16th 1965. The Regal Super Cinema Cross Gates was opened on November 16th 1936 and closed on January 11th 1964.

Radio included the Home and Light programmes with the Third as a later alternative. A BBC Radio relay station was opened on Claypit Lane and the Leeds & Bradford Relay Station on Basinghall Street opened on July 9th 1924.

Galaxy 105 opened on September 29th 1997. *Aire FM* started broadcasting from their Leeds studios on September 1st 1981. *Magic 828* is based in Leeds at Aire FM and was opened on July 17th 1990.
Radio Leeds broadcast from studios in the Merrion Centre on June 24th 1968. Radio Leeds moved to the old Friends Meeting House on Woodhouse Lane in 1980. BBC TV and Radio Leeds relocated to a new purpose built building on Quarry Hill in 2004.

Television Many Halton villagers would have either seen the 1953 Coronation on a neighbour's set or on a newly purchased set. The *BBC* opened their first temporary interview studio in All Souls Church parish hall in 1968, prior to the move to a small studio at the rear of the Friends Meeting House. The new studios to the west of the Friends Meeting House on Woodhouse Lane were opened in 1974: this involved the demolition of a garage and workshop where Louis Le Prince worked. *Yorkshire Television* studios on Kirkstall Road were officially opened by the Duchess of Kent on July 29th 1968.
Cable TV/telephone cables were laid through the village and along Selby Road from 1995. The franchise was awarded to the Jones Cable Group of Seacroft after their application in September 1989; the business became part of the US/Canadian group Bell Cable Media in 1994. This became part of Cable & Wireless in 1998: C&W was a merger of smaller companies including Mercury and they sold their cable interests including BellCM to NTL Home (National Telecommunications Ltd) from 2000 who operate from the same Ring Road premises. The first cable customer in East Leeds was on Ramshead Drive Seacroft.

EXPRESSWAY

The Halton Expressway was being planned in the late 1960's and early 1970's. The scheme to divert traffic away from Halton village was abandoned in October 1973. This reprieved the top row of houses on Grove Road from demolition. The scheme was due to be started in 1968 thus creating a traffic free shopping area. The plan entailed closing part of Selby Road, stretching from Primrose Lane to Chapel Street and a diversion built enabling a pedestrian way to be formed.
The Halton bypass was planned in early 1936 being three miles of new road from Broadway, Temple Newsam Road and across to Austhorpe. The plans were shelved with the onset of war and by the 1960's the Templegate estate covered the proposed route.
In more recent times the main roads serving Halton have been enhanced with the opening of the London-Leeds M1 Motorway in August 1968 and the A1/M1 Linkroad east of Halton opened in 1999. The East Leeds Radial Road will link Cross Green with the A1/M1 linkroad.

FARMS

Halton has always been based on farms mainly in the Cross Field and Gillsyke Field.

In the survey of farms by John Dickinson on Lord Irwin's lands carried out in 1730 the following were the main farmers: Peter Atkinson of Garth End Field, Richard Auty, William Broadbent, Mrs Brook (Wike Bridge), Robert Close, Mr Dawson, Richard Dixon, John Goodall, Mr Hanson, John Hudson, Robert Kidd, Thomas Jepson, Mary Lee of Slack Bank, John Pickering, James Sedgwick, John Walker, Joseph Waite.

Field End Farm was a smallholding on Field End Road (Keighley Lane) near to Prospect House. The Farrell family ran the farm leased from the Temple Newsam estate at the start of the 20th century; Elizabeth Farrell died aged 22 on April 22nd 1907.

Gilsyke (Gillsyke) Farm at 204 Selby Road was run by David Speight by 1906 and he was followed by the Heworth family from Manor Farm Whitkirk. William and Ruth Heworth had two children Jim and Dorothy who was born in 1916: the family later moved to Lane End.

The next occupiers were Percy Thomas & Maud Nicholls with son Robert with partner Arthur Pickersgill by 1927; the farm was registered with the Milk and Dairies Act under William Verity's name in 1927. Nicholls & Pickersgill moved from Chapel Street to Gilsyke Farm until 1934 when Miles Verity came to the farm and lived with mother Annie after her husband's death in 1929 until she died in 1957. Thomas and Maud Pickersgill with Arthur Pickersgill moved to 5 Woodman Street. Gilsyke Farm was adjacent to Holly House opposite The Woodman and the cottages by Field End Road. Miles was a partner in farming at both Gilsyke and Laurel Farms in Halton with his younger brother William. When Miles was diagnosed by Dr Young as having a heart condition, he took the advice and retired from farming and his new home was a nearby house on Selby Road.

When the Verity family left Gilsyke Farm it became Fenwick's builders yard and then Lawrence & Kathleen Eshelby took over until the property was demolished in 1969. Lawrence came from a farm in Rothwell where there was a dairy business and Kathleen Parkin came from Sherburn-in-Elmet. Their daughter was Alice and sons were Christopher, Donald and John D Eshelby (Jack) who ran Gilsyke Farm as a manager for Billy Chapman but soon left for Whitby, where he lived at Fryup Hall and worked for the Bouvet family. After Lawrence died in 1968 Kathleen lived at Gilsyke Farm on her own; she moved to her son's home near Whitby where she died. Gilsyke Farm was a rented farm with the Chapman family of Austhorpe Hall using the land: William Chapman had a horse at Gilsyke Farm stables called John More: the builder of Austhorpe Hall in 1694.

Holly House Farm was on the site of Temple Motors with a large house and a smallholding which was converted into a garage, Burmah petrol station and haulage business. John Rollinson was a 49 year old farmer with 104 acres (1881) who died aged 61 in 1892 and his father George Rollinson who died the same age in 1871. John and Mary Anne Rollinson's children were George, Hannah, Ann, Clara, Benjamin, Hettie, Blanche, John, William and Herbert who were at Holly House at the start of the 20th century. Edward Bickerdyke then lived at Holly House until his death aged 64 in 1910. By 1915 the Carroll family had come to Holly House Farm taking over from William Dunwell Goodall. He also had farmland north of Primrose Lane near Valley Drive and in the area of Selby Road now occupied by 1920's housing of Knightsway, Kingsway and Queensway. This Selby Road land ran northwards to Green Lane on what is the west side of Knightsway. Goodall's lands included the fields south of the Whitkirk Cemetery (by Whitkirk Club) to the east side of Templegate and fields south of New Templegate (Pit Gate Lane). Charles Carroll lived at Holly House with his wife and son John following on from the previous tenant: they continued to run their milk business on nearby rented land. In the late 1920's they converted to a haulage business and Holly House Farm held a sale of surplus stock in late 1936. In 1922 Holly House Farm applied for consent to open a slaughterhouse although this was refused. The Halton Slaughterhouse was "not being used properly" in 1927 and the local butcher was ordered by Hunslet RDC to discontinue the slaughtering of sheep on the premises. Bulk Builders Merchants started in 1982.
Laurel Farm was on Chapel Street and was run by the Swift family: a stable, loose box and cow shed were erected by the Temple Newsam Estate in 1907. In later years it was run by partner brothers William and Miles Verity who lived at Gilsyke Farm with Laurel Farm being run by his workers. The mistal at Laurel Farm was used by the Halton Templars Scouts who placed Templar crosses on the end of the restored building in 1936. The farm produced milk which was taken around the village on a horse and cart by Harry Taylor: he died aged 101 in 1989. The milk was also taken by ponies to Leeds for sale. Laurel Farm was sold to the Hemsley family who were garden requirements and coal merchants: Harry & Nellie Hemsley 1939/56.
Laurel House Farm on Chapel Street was adjacent to Holme Lea and for many years run by the Daniel family. David Daniel died aged 75 in July 1923 and Frances Ann Daniel died aged 70 in August 1921. The Stevensons lived there running a milk delivery business and in later years the house was the home of the Spencer family.
Park View Farm was on Engine Lane (Temple Newsam Road) at the junction with High Street Halton. The farm was part of the Temple Newsam estate and was tenanted by the staunchly Methodist Stevenson

family for many years. The farm was also known in earlier days as Beechwood Farm and Engine Lane Farm. The land used by the farm was widespread and included fields on Keighley Lane (Field End Road), fields west of Peggy Lane (Grove Road) and the land east of Wilfred Avenue including The Crescent. Robert Stevenson born in 1805 farmed 44 acres with wife Betsey who was born in 1805: their children were Thomas, Christopher who became a tobacconist and married Hannah Thompson in November 1867, Henry, George and Frederick. Henry and Frederick inherited the business and by 1881 were farming 45 acres with elder brother Christopher. Frederick born in 1848 and wife Hannah had two children Mary born in 1871 and Joe born in 1877. Henry and Anne Stevenson ran the farm in the late 19th century: in December 1891 a new cow house with 14 stalls was allowed to be built at the farm. Henry Stevenson died aged 54 in 1896 and Anne died aged 75 in 1917: she was the oldest tenant farmer on the estate. Their children were Robert born in 1868, Ethel born in 1870, Harry who was born in 1871 and died in 1887, Ella born in 1873: she married James Dixon and died in 1921; Ben born in 1874, William Edgar born 1877 who married Lily (1879-1946) and their daughter Ella who was born at the farm on October 4th 1905. Robert Stevenson applied for a slaughterhouse at the farm in 1909 which was granted by Hunslet RDC. In the 1930's the farm was run by William Edgar Stevenson with wife Lily and children Henry, Albert, Nellie and Blanche born in January 1913. Henry delivered the milk in the area with a horse and cart: he later moved to live in Colton. The farm was a smallholding with a few milking cows, pigs, hens; the yard later became the site for a few small businesses. On September 10th 1935 22 year old Blanche Stevenson married Albert Lionel Moxon and 28 year old Nellie married Charles Briggs of the grocer's shop on Hollyshaw Lane on March 28th 1937. Joe and Alice Ann Stevenson ran a milk delivery business from Laurel House Farm. They lived initially at Park View Farm and their daughter Edna who was born in 1908 married tram driver Herbert Middleton on December 11th 1926. Joe died aged 58 on April 16th 1935 and his wife Alice Ann died aged 55 on February 3rd 1941.

White Beck Farm was on the east of Wyke Beck and was originally the site of Joseph Atkinson's Vitriol, Aqua Fortis and Epsom Salts Works in the mid-19th century. Joseph Atkinson lived at Austhorpe Lodge and had land in the Halton area. A new farm was built on this part of the Temple Newsam Estate c1845 and was run by George Colt Taylor who was born at Howden in 1861: he married Margaret in 1880. Margaret was born in 1847 at Northallerton and their children were Henrietta born in Foggathorpe in 1881 and married Edmund Atkinson on November 8th 1915, George born in 1882, Charlotte born in 1884 and Edward born in December 1885 and died March 1918.

In 1919 the Elam family took over at this farm which they rented from Lord Halifax having moved from Broom Hill Farm near the Shaftesbury Cinema. The Elams had already farmed from Osmondthorpe Farm: Herbert was living here with his sister Amelia and brother James Arthur prior to his marriage in 1906, the farm was on the site of the Co-op. White Beck farmhouse was of two storeys and had five bedrooms; there was a stable and barn for the cows and hay attached to the farmhouse which faced the main Selby Road. Their fields spread down to the Black Road, the land of the Sutton estate.

An odd occurrence was in 1929 when a chick with four legs was born at this farm; Alfred Herbert Elam provided stables for four elephants during their week's show at the Shaftesbury Cinema from March 30th 1936. The presentation was by Powers Brothers: Lena, Julia, Roxie and Jennie danced, played cricket, baseball and fenced on a strengthened stage. Before and after the shows the elephants were led along the main road to the farm on Halton Hill with cars protecting front and rear.

Elam's farm provided milk and there was a round with three floats supplying both Halton village and the Sutton estate as well as the Rookwoods. The carts were inscribed AH Elam White Beck Farm Halton. The farm had cows and pigs as well as horses to pull the milk carts and shire horses to pull the ploughs. One of the workers at the farm was Harry Bouskill who was born in Burmantofts in 1911 and educated at Victoria School. He had an early job delivering milk in the Dawlishes and afterwards worked at the farm. He started work at 5am to milk the cows and then took them out to the fields. Alfred Elam was forced out of his tenancy in February 1938 by Leeds City Council after a short but determined fight. The Elam family moved to Well Green Farm at Garforth Bridge until 1941 and later to a smallholding at Birkin. Alfred Herbert Elam was born on March 28th 1879 and died at Birkin on October 24th 1946. Their sons were Alfred (1907-1988), William (1912-1986) who was a poultry farmer at Garforth and later moved to Norfolk and Frank (1914-1972). Their daughter Mary married John Sampson of Burton Salmon in 1920; John died on October 25th 1985. The farm complex on Halton Hill was demolished and is now the site of housing and a small green area with car parking.

Whitebeck (Wykebeck) was built near the mill and some of the first tenants were John Green and Henry & Maria Bauze (1850's), William & Martha Pearson and then William Scott who died on November 24th 1874 aged 44. His wife Hannah died aged 85 on March 13th 1919 at Park Road Farm at Colton. Their sons George died aged 10 on December 9th 1879 and John died aged 59 on February 11th 1919; daughters Mary died on May 5th 1897 and Sallie died on June 15th 1927 at Burley-in-Wharfedale; son Christopher was married in October 1916 to Ethel Walton of Carter Mount Whitkirk. The tenant following the Scotts was Joshua Kershaw who died on March 18th 1883 aged 70; his wife Elizabeth died on January 28th 1870 aged 66; their daughter Annie died aged 89 on September 10th 1933.

This became Verity's Farm from c1883 with part of the old farmhouse being used today as the premises of Wykebeck Recovery Services. A Temple Newsam estate farmland distribution map of 1915 showed that the Verity family was using fields at Wykebeck as well as fields east of Field End Road (Keighley Lane) and south of Templegate. There were also fields to the south of Grove Road which were later to become the site of a Halton colliery. Wykebeck or Whitebridge Cottages were also part of the farm site by the Wyke Beck and were once the home of the Stubbs family: it was often known as Stubb's Farm. In 1928 there were Walter and Annie Stubbs living in the property. In 1935 George & Margaret Thomas; in 1938 John & Mary Barlow lived at this farm with children Joseph and John.

Willow Well Farm is represented by the large white building on the corner of Willow Well Road and the farm dates from the early 19th century. This was once *Paxton's* farm and was run by William Wilson in the 1841 census; Ann Dixon in 1851 who died aged 28 in November 1858 with cattle dealer John Jennings and then Francis Morritt.

Francis Morritt was born in Wortley in 1852 and he married Emma Graveley (1827-52) and their son was William Graveley Morritt (1851-95) who died on the Isle of Wight having lived at Dial House Halton. On Emma's death in 1852 Francis married Anne Warrington of Lead Mill Farm Saxton. Anne died aged 28 in November 1858 and Francis married Mary Ann (1823-63): there were two children William born on July 19th 1862 and Sarah Anne born on April 18th 1862. Francis and his three wives are buried at Whitkirk Church.

JW Morkill agreed to allow the farm to be further tenanted in December 1891. The next tenants of Willow Well Farm were William Heworth born in 1860 and Mary Elizabeth born in 1861 with their family William born

1884 and daughter Edith born in 1890.
Frederick & Wilhelmina Jowitt moved into the farm on their marriage on January 19th 1916. Frederick Jowitt died aged 78 on November 26th 1968: he had been a cattleman and dairy farmer in Halton for 53 years. He retired in 1955 and they moved to 30 Cross Green Lane. Wilhelmina died aged 75 on April 26th 1969 when the family had moved to Park View Terrace. Their daughter Hilda Alice married Percy Horner in May 1942.
Willow Well Farm was owned by his father Joseph and the family appeared at cattle markets in York, Wetherby and at Whitkirk. Joseph Jowitt's daughter May was married to Frank Miller in September 1925: she was 28 years old.
Willow Well Farm with the outbuildings were sold at auction in 1937 for £1100 and bought by developer Gertrude Bray. The old farmhouse was converted by G Bray Ltd into two dwellings and the firm built the housing on Willow Well Road from 1936.

FEAST

Halton Feast Sunday was held on the first Sunday after August 26th and for a few days afterwards the feast was held along the roads from the Golden Cock Inn on Kirkgate, along York Road and up the hill to the village. It may have had its origins as a commemoration of the consecration of St Mary's Church at Whitkirk. A news item from August 1738 commented that Ald Cookson's garden had its fruit trees raided by those coming from Halton Feast. Halton Feast is recorded as being held on Sunday September 8th 1782.
Halton Feast was held in September 1905 and as reported by the short lived East Leeds Weekly Echo *"the Feast was moved to a new site and there were swings, cocoanut shies, shooting galleries, hot pea stalls, boxing booths and classical exhibitions"*. The feast was held at various locations on a smaller scale including the site of The Parade; in June 1932 the Feast was held at the tram terminus field. This was an almost circular field with a stone wall and in the 1920's was visited by roundabouts, swings, cocoanut shies, fortune teller, hoop-la and hot pie & peas. In June 1934 the Halton Spring Feast was held on the Soldier's Field while there was another Halton Feast held in August 1934 on Savile Road: in that year it was described as "dying". The same year saw the Halton Carnival held at the Halton Congregational Church on Chapel Street: this was always much enjoyed and featured a Carnival Queen. On August 25th 1939 the Feast was again held on Savile Green York Road. After the War the Congregational Church revived the Annual Gala with the crowning of the Queen from 1946. In April 1948 Halton Feast was held at Carroll's Holly House Farm and for the next years was held in the field to the rear of the Congregational Church. In later years it was the Atha family of

Halton who provided entertainment at Halton Feast with their fairground stalls, roundabouts and music. One of the last sites for the Feast was by The Ritz Cinema in Cross Gates.

FIELD END

Originally the end of the village with a road towards the Temple Newsam Park known as Barrow Nooks Road which became Field End Road. The 1834 map shows the farm (Gilsyke) and a corner house on the north side. The 1881 census lists 18 dwellings at Field End. Albert and Mary Scarfe with their family lived at Field End by 1901. Maps from the enclosure award show a group of cottages at Field End and Field End Road south towards Temple Newsam. It was at Field End that Charlie Frame started his butcher's shop in 1900 and Walter Johnson ran a fruit & vegetable shop known as Field End Stores: the conversion of a house to a bakery was refused in 1910. Elizabeth Guest was based at Field End and in 1905 was advertising cab and waggonettes for hire. The map of 1908 shows Prospect House with nearby allotments and Field End with housing concentrated near the junction with the main road. In 1900 Walter Briggs was involved in legal proceedings due to the overcrowding of his small cottage and a demolition order was placed on 9 and 11 Field End in 1911. The row of six cottages on the main Selby Road was demolished and is now the site of the St John's Centre and a bungalow.
Field End Road was the main road in the early 20th century adjacent to open fields with Field End Mount from the 1920's. On Field End Road was Prospect House, home of the Fox family. Thomas Fox married Dorothy Brown in July 1927: he was the son of wool merchant Francis Fox. The younger son Harold Fox married Alice Baron: daughter of Frederick Baron of Excella Works in September 1939. There were also allotment gardens near Field End Farm where Elizabeth Farrell died aged 22 on April 22nd 1907.
Field End House was set back from Field End Road with access by a wide driveway between two cottages and the mistal. The L shaped main house had a north facing porched doorway with outside toilet, lean-to greenhouse and mistal to the east. There was a brick archway which led to the front garden, lawn and orchard with a field for the donkeys. The boundary was a hedge on the north side and a high brick wall to the south separating the property from Prospect House.
Field End House was built in 1914 by Thomas and Christiana Burn, who came from 40 Osmondthorpe Villas Osmondthorpe Lane to their newly built house. Thomas Burn was born in 1844 as the son of waterman William Burn; he married Christiana Bray on April 1st 1866 at St Saviour's Church Richmond Hill. Thomas Burn was a mechanic living on Richmond Street on his marriage: Christiana was the daughter of James

Bray of East Street and Beckett Street. Thomas Burn and his sons traded as Burn Bros being boot & shoe and patent leather ankle strap manufacturers on The Bank at Wesley Place from 1899. In 1892 Thomas Burn made slippers at 2 Macauley Street near Mabgate while living at Spen Street. Two years later he had moved to 35 Cromwell Street where he started making boots and shoes, later moving to the works on Wesley Place. This factory closed in 1930 and Thomas Burn retired: he died aged 87 on January 3rd 1932.

Their family were Henrietta Burn born in 1867 who married brass finisher Thomas Peel, son of flax spinner Edward Peel on April 15th 1895. His early death caused Henrietta to marry William Watson Ladley on January 24th 1903: their daughter Maud married Frank Noble who was living at Field End in the 1930's. William Ladley died aged 64 on August 23rd 1926 and was buried at Harehills Cemetery. The eldest son of Thomas & Henrietta was Thomas Burn who died unmarried aged 90 on May 25th 1961. William Henry Burn once lived at 3 Osmondthorpe Terrace with wife Elizabeth: daughters Edna and Louise emigrated to Canada. Edward Burn and his wife Amy and their family lived at 2 The Drive Cross Gates: he was in practice as a dentist at 115 Beckett Street. His son Edward was also a dentist with his father: he lived on Easterly Road. The youngest daughter Ada married Harry Horsman whose son Frank Horsman was a Halton builder and who was also responsible for removing the stained glass in 1939 at York Minster for safe keeping during the war years. His brothers were Harry and Bernard who with wife Maizie lived at 10 Field End Road in 1960.

There was a row of cottages on the east side of Field End Road which included Floramont, home of George William Wilson manager of the Leeds Greyhound track on Elland Road. He was an amateur comedian who performed at the Parochial Hall and at the Congregational Church. At the bottom of Field End Road was a smallholding run by James Bulmer who was a coal merchant of Temple Walk. The end of the road led to Field End Lane which connected Whitkirk with the Park and Bedford's coal pits. East of Field End Road were the allotments of Soldier's Field where Temple Moor School was proposed in the 1930's but due to the war was delayed until 1956. Part of the area used by allotments was the Melbourne Field used by local children to play both cricket and football. The cottages of Raoul Dene home of Thomas Foster and haulage contractor Thomas Chapman with Nature Cottage, home of Walter Wood were also on Field End Road.

The area around Field End Road and High Street Halton was widened when land was conveyed in 1931 by builder Arthur Wilson to the LCC. Field End Grove was once the site of allotments proposed for building bungalows for the elderly in 1970/1971. The demolition of many properties on Field End Road was complete by the 1970's. Field End

Mount and Field End Road became a Council development with 39 houses and a site for private building by the Yorkie Trust in 1935. Field End Close, Crescent, Gardens and Garth were completed by 1964/65.

FIELD TERRACE

Field Terrace is a row of eight houses on Cross Street built by John Field in 1878/79 and was declared to be a highway in 1911. John Field of Stamford Street Leeds had his housing completed and the first occupants moved in by July 1879. Early occupiers of the first house included Percy Gould of the Freehold Hotel on Freehold Street York Road and Harry & Annie Plews. In 1901 the 39 year old coal miner Arthur Bedford lived on Field Terrace with his 35 year old wife Martha and children Mary (8), Squire (4), May (2) and 3 month old Alice. In January 1939 Flora Elisabeth Hardwick died aged 86 at 3 Field Terrace; she was one of the village's oldest residents although she had been born at Swillington Common. The bottom of the street had the LC Highways Depot from c1906 with the 1.32 acre site being sold by the Temple Newsam Estate in December 1904 for £200. The area is now housing with the Field Terrace allotment area still under cultivation: there are only four allotments and one resident on Primrose Drive has had his allotment here for more than 40 years. The access to Pinfolds is from Field Terrace.

FIRE IN HALTON

One of the worst fires in Halton occurred in the early hours of Monday April 25th 1932 in a shop/house on the High Street in between the grocery shop of Fred Killerby and the Halton Co-op shop. Joseph Connell was a grocer, confectioner and automatic machine traveller and his wife Ellen usually looked after the shop when he was away. He opened his shop as normal on Sunday morning and closed at 9.30pm. He said that he remembered turning off the electric fire in the shop and made sure the children were fed and safe in bed. He and his wife made their way by car at 10pm to Staincross near Barnsley to show a nurse that their three month old baby Keith "had been shortened". The car broke down but they managed to continue by bus to their destination. They talked with the nurse until 1am and decided to stay until daylight before leaving for Halton where they arrived home at 8am.

Their three young children Elizabeth Ellen aged 11, Margaret Annie aged 8 and Alfred aged 3 were left alone in the house. Some clothes caught fire on the radiator in the closed shop and the fire took hold quickly at 2.30am. Dr Jack Young at Gilsyke House was woken by screams and he ran across in his dressing gown to try to enter the burning house. His wife Hazel telephoned for the police and fire brigade who arrived in six minutes: the doctor saw a child in the front bedroom crying "Save Me" and then the shop window exploded and the child disappeared. Dr Young managed to smash the back door down but was beaten back by dense smoke. The fire brigade managed to enter and found that the eldest girl was laying across the bed with the other two on the floor. When the fireman was carrying the children down the ladder flames were still shooting out from the shop window and dense smoke was coming from the rear. The fire was extinguished in a few minutes: the window frames and sunblind were destroyed with the staircase burnt away and the ceiling plaster collapsed. The three children were taken to Leeds General Infirmary where the two girls died in the receiving room and Alfred died the following morning.

There was an inquest on Tuesday afternoon at Leeds Town Hall at which Dr Jack Young and blacksmith Samuel Townsend whose house was opposite the shop gave evidence in front of coroner JH Milner and a jury. Evidence was also provided by their next door neighbour Fred Killerby who had a grocer's shop. He said that his sister was roused by children screaming "Mamma" and that "We ran out of the house to find that the shop was blazing so furiously that we could not get anywhere near it from the front. Just as I came out of my house Dr Young came across the road and made straight for the back part of the premises. After smashing the back door I believe that he actually got into the back downstairs room but he undertook a hopeless task for the staircase was blazing." Fred Killerby's shop is separated by a comparitively thin wall and as a precaution he removed some of his stock. He said that but for the prompt action by the fire service the entire block of property would have been involved. Another neighbour said at the inquest that she heard a child screaming "I want my mammy", "Fire" and "Murder". PC Edward Busfield examined the shop after the fire: the house and attic were gutted.

The coroner gave a verdict of Accidental Death through shock following severe burns. He also said that the parents Joseph and Ellen Connell were guilty of negligence. There was much discussion concerning the fact that the parents had left their children for too long a period. The coroner told the jury that *"this accident had shocked everybody who had come into contact with it and I can understand why some witnesses were so upset"*. There was no evidence to suggest that the property owner had been negligent with regard to the electric system in the property.

The funeral took place at Harehills Cemetery on Thursday April 28th with over 2000 people lining the route: the cortege had left Sandhurst Avenue Harehills. The service was conducted by Rev A Murray of St Agnes Church Burmantofts; the three children were buried in one grave. There were flowers from their schoolfriends at Halton School: Joe Connell collapsed at the graveside.

Other fires included that following a gas blast at 2 Primrose Road which was once the local post office. The blast also severely affected 4 Primrose Road which was Button's hairdressers shop. The blast occurred on December 3rd 1971 and injured the hairdresser LV Button and Walter Kirk whose house was affected. The council rehoused 84 year old Leopold Button and his wife on Cricklegate for a period before he moved to a ground floor flat at 14 Primrose Road.

FIRE SERVICES

Leeds City Fire Service had their first station on Fenton Street with their later headquarters on Park Street from 1883 as the Central Fire Station used by Leeds Police and Fire Service until 1941.
Halton is covered from the fire station on Gipton Approach: opened by Lord Mayor of Leeds Tom Coombs on October 7th 1937 and the architect was WH Thorp. The decision to erect a new station was taken in 1934 to ease the workload at Park Street. Gipton was one of the most advanced stations in the country including the fire station houses. In the last War changes were made to the administration and on August 18th 1941 the fire brigades were embodied in the National Fire Service. This was based on 12 Civil Defence regions with a Chief Regional Fire Officer in charge of each region. After the War the fire fighting functions were passed to the local authority's control. On April 1st 1948 the Leeds City Fire Brigade resumed responsibility for the service operating as a separate command and not as previously part of the police force.

FOOTBALLERS IN HALTON

Billy Bremner (William John) was born in Stirling on December 9th 1942 and lived at 2 Plantation Avenue with his wife Veronica and family: he was Leeds United's most capped player (54). He made 773 appearances with Leeds United and scored 115 goals: he played with LUFC from December 1959 to September 1976 when he was sold for £35,000 and he moved to Hull City until 1977 and to Doncaster Rovers from September 1979 with just two appearances. He was the manager of Leeds United from 1985 to 1988. Billy Bremner died on December 7th 1997 at the age of 54.

Jackie Charlton was born on May 8th 1935 and lived at the detached house 37 Primrose Drive in Halton: his first house was on Cross Heath Grove which he bought in 1959 prior to his wedding: their three children were born there. In 1966 he moved to a new house in Halton for a few years. He played for Leeds United Juniors and was signed professionally in May 1952 and was with the team until 1972: he appeared 628 times and scored 70 goals.

Mike O'Grady played for Leeds United from 1965 to 1969: he had 90 appearances and scored 12 goals in the League with 5 appearances and 1 goal in the FA Cup. He was born in Leeds on October 11th 1942 being the son of Ralph & Edna who lived on Temple Avenue Halton. He played for Huddersfield Town (1959-65) with Leeds UFC buying him for £30,000 in 1965; he played for Wolves from 1969-1971, Birmingham City (1971-72) and Rotherham from 1971-72.

G.O. BELL CRICKET AWARD

The *GO Bell Cricket Award* was first presented to Darrell McManus in 1971 by Donald Taylor. The award remembers George Osmond Bell who lived at the family shop on Chapel Street. Ossie Bell was born at the shop and with his brothers was soon playing cricket for Halton. He was a talented cricketer and always interested in the development of the sport. A trust fund was established in the will of Mrs BM Bell and discussions started with the Yorkshire CCC. At first the most promising cricketers of 1970 spent Friday evenings between January and March in the nets at Headingley coached by Barrie Leadbetter. The award was worth £100 spent attending the Scarborough Summer Coaching School, a credit to pay for clothing and equipment and a sum to be used at the discretion of the boy and his parents to further a future cricket career.

The award winners from 1971 were: SR Smith, AJ Ricketts, TJ Tomlinson, GD Lodge, DC Heselwood, AG Clark, R Jackson, A Coulthard,

K Rich, T Hegarty, S Dolan, R Sullivan, S Dixon, R Francis, M Freeman, M O'Brien, D Pawson, J Robson, R Virdee, P Farrer, A Watson, N Talbot, TC Glover, MFW Casling and in 2003 MW Gilroy.

GARAGES IN HALTON

Halton Garage The Halton Motor Co on Chapel Street was run by F Bevin in 1924 who applied for a licence to erect a petrol pump together with a tank storing 500 gallons. He was followed by Milton Jones who lived at 3 Pinfold Lane with his family in the 1920's and later on Chapel Street. In 1964 Thomas Curry Chapman followed at the garage: he was a haulage contractor who lived at 13 Sycamore Avenue and on Woodland Hill and at first worked from home. The demolition of the garage followed the occupancy of SJB & RJB cranes and steel erectors in the early 1990's: RJ Barratt. The Barratt family now live in Pocklington. The site became Chapel Court with housing from 1994.
Holly House Garage followed the farming concern of the Carroll family: in 1946 there were plans for a petrol station, tanks and pumps at Holly House. The plans included the demolition of the old garage together with a stable and mistal from the farm. It is now the site of Temple Motors who still use part of the old garage buildings. The Holly House Motor Club met on the premises for a few years. In 1967 there were plans to develop the premises with an office and extension.
Temple Motors started in Leeds in 1965 and in Halton in 1973 based in Carroll's Yard and included the demolition of the old house. Leeds chartered accountant Richard Boston opened as Mitsu Motors with a Burmah petrol station on the forecourt and Carroll's hauliers at the rear. The firm at first sold Mitsubishi cars but later sold Reliant Robins, becoming Temple Motors in 1978. Bulk Builders Merchants started in 1982 with the purchase of two tippers from the Carroll business. David

Gale is the owner of the merchants business started in 1982 and this is now the landlord of the Temple Motors car sales business. Brian Gouldsborough took over Temple Motors from Richard Boston in October 2000.

Todd's Garage on the High Street was also the residence 180 Selby Road of Louis Edwin Todd (1897-1952) & Emily Todd (1879-1975) from the inter-war years. Edwin Todd applied to the Hunslet RDC for a licence to store petrol in 1910. Louis Edwin was the son of Frederick & Mary Ellen Todd of Chapel Street and 16 High Street and was baptised on July 4th 1897 and after he married they lived on Orchard Terrace. Their daughter was Sophia Todd who was baptised on December 24th 1899. Son George Dennis Todd ran the business after his father's death: at one time the Dominion petrol sold for 1/5 a gallon.

He served with the RAOC in the War and married Mabel Atkinson in November 1939. Dennis Todd retired in 1969 and went south to live in Highcliffe-on-Sea where he died on the golf course in 1984 aged 68 and his wife Mabel moved to live in Bristol. They once lived near Betty Shires who had left Whitkirk to live near her eldest son Martin; Dr & Mrs Neville Shires are buried at Highcliffe-on-Sea Church. The garage then became the business of Frank Martin with son David taking over c1971: the family left in 1974 and the house was demolished. Frank Martin and family lived at 2 Templegate, joined by son David by 1974. The garage became Troy Motors who have served Leeds from 1965 and opened in Halton in June 1984.

Wykebeck Filling Station at the bottom of Halton Hill was on the site of a farm and Dunhill's Builders and is now Wykebeck Recovery Services. This was the Victoria Garage Ltd in the late war years and in the 1960's the garage was run by JW & D Blades. John William Blades married Mary Edwards Clark at St Wilfrid's Church on November 5th 1960. John W Blades was born in 1936 as the only son and was a road racing motorcyclist. The station was later run by Robert Hardy in the 1960's until closure by 1986 when plans were passed for Wykebeck Recovery Services.

GAS SERVICES

Gas was supplied for homes and street lights and there was a regular lamplighter in Halton who turned on the street lights using a long pole. Halton lamplighters included Harold and Albert Marrows of Primrose Road in 1919. Gas was manufactured at Cross Gates by the Cross Gates, Halton & Seacroft Gas Co in the area now part of the Cross Gates Centre south car park. Halton was supplied with gas street lighting from 1889 following numerous requests for a few years. Halton Hill was lit with gas lamps by 1896. The gas making ceased in 1928 and the gas supply came from Meadow Lane. There was a meeting of creditors of the Cross Gates, Halton & Seacroft Gas Company on December 17th 1927: Halton became part of Leeds on April 1st 1928. The company went into liquidation in 1928 and the site became the sidings for the NER in 1929/30. Gas pipes were laid on Selby Road to Whitkirk in 1930. There were four gas holders at Cross Gates with two being demolished soon after closure and in November 1965 the smaller of the remaining two gas holders was dismantled and removed to be rebuilt near Doncaster. The goods yard was closed in June 1964.

The conversion of the street gas lamps to electricity was started in Halton in 1954: the Templegate estate had electric street lighting from 1963. The number of gas lamps on Leeds streets was 16,439 in 1958 and 11,410 in 1962: electric lights numbered 14,162 in 1958 and 25,822 in 1962.

GILLEGHAN FAMILY

It is likely that the Gilleghan family arrived to seek work in Barnsley as a result of the difficulties due to the Irish potato famine of 1846-1851: over 1.5 million emigrated mostly to the USA. The spelling was different at the time of arrival in England-Gilligan. The records show that the name changed in the 1870's and that it was Thomas Gilligan who was the originator of the Barnsley branch. *Thomas Gilligan* lived at Somerset Street in Barnsley and found work as a labourer and he married Anne who was born at Monk Bretton in 1834: he died c1860. After his death Anne a washerwoman and later working as a linen yarn winder, married James Cawthrow who had been born in Portsmouth Hampshire in 1816. They lived in Barnsley where James was a boot and shoe manufacturer. Living at home with James and Anne were his son Thomas was born in 1858 together with his stepsons John Gilleghan born in 1856 and Frederick born in 1859: they became a colliery engine stoker and a boot & shoe rivettor.

Thomas and Anne Gilligan had three children: Martin who was responsible for the change of spelling; John and Frederick Thomas.

Martin Gilligan was born in 1854 soon after the arrival of his father in

Barnsley and his marriage in 1853: his father died when Martin was only three and his mother was to look after three boys. Martin's first paid job was when at 7 years old he was at Charles Mallinson's rope walk; at 8 years old he became a trapper at Willow Bank Pit and later at Swaithe Main Pit where he became a deputy and then in charge of the district until the pit was closed. Martin became a commission and insurance agent and then worked for a Friendly Society as well as being a staunch supporter of the Barnsley British Co-operative Society. He was elected as a director in 1900 and was a manager of St George's Day Schools and a member of the Education Committee. There are several foundation stones in the Barnsley area laid by *Martin Gilleghan*. including one on the old Co-operative store on Dodsworth Road. Martin married Eva Garner at St John's Church Wortley in 1876 when he changed the spelling of his name from Gilligan to Gilleghan: the marriage produced six children: Herbert, Arthur, Emma, Eva, Florence and Elsie.

Herbert Gilleghan was born on January 18th 1879 and he married Annie Dickinson (1875-1942); Arthur (1881-1947) married Ethel (1883-1967); Emma (1883-1958) married Frederick Winter in 1904; Eva was born in 1886 and married James Millward in 1914; Florence was born in 1889 and married George Edward Utley in 1915: their son is Rev Edward Utley who retired as chaplain to the Birmingham hospitals in 1989; Elsie was born in 1891 and married Charles Stanley Greaves.

Martin Gilleghan's younger brothers were John Gilleghan born in 1856 and Frederick Thomas (1859-1921) who married Lucy Ebden on December 24th 1883.

Herbert Gilleghan attended the church school near his house in Barnsley and at the age of 22 qualified at the London College of Pharmacy on April 19th 1901, when he was registered as a chemist and druggist. He obtained his first job in Darlington and married Annie at the St John the Baptist Church Barnsley on May 28th 1903. They lived in Darlington where their only son *John (Jack) Gilleghan* was born on April 7th 1905.

Herbert applied for a job in Leeds and they moved in 1907 to live in Burley; he worked for Frederick William Sutcliffe at 128 Roundhay Road. Frederick Sutcliffe retired and Herbert bought the house and shop in 1911; the family lived in the flat above the shop until 1934. Herbert became President of the Leeds Branch of the National Pharmaceutical Union and was a member of the Leeds Branch of the Pharmaceutical Society; from 1913 he was the Secretary of the Leeds Committee.

On May 28th 1928 Jack Gilleghan married Violet Hilda Wilton Castelow eldest child of Walter Thomas and Elizabeth Castelow of Woodhouse Lane Leeds at Epiphany Church. They had both qualified at the Leeds College of Pharmacy and became registered chemists and druggists in September 1926. Jack helped at his father's shop until the move to 1 Whitkirk View Halton, which was Herbert Rennard's Halton Pharmacy.

Herbert Rennard retired in 1927 and sold to Herbert Gilleghan who passed it to his son Jack. Herbert Gilleghan died on Thursday December 31st 1936 aged 57 and was buried at Harehills. In 1937 Herbert's wife Annie lived in Whitkirk for a year and then moved to live with her widowed sister in law in Barnsley where she died on May 1st 1942 aged 63. On Herbert's death the Roundhay Road shop became the property of Jack and Vi Gilleghan who in January 1937 appointed a manager Harry Thorpe. There were then two Gilleghan chemist's shops until Harry left Leeds for Nottingham in 1948: he died in 1971.

Jack Gilleghan died on October 17th 1958 and his wife Vi died aged 97 on Boxing Day 2001: they are buried at St Mary's Church at Whitkirk. Jack and Vi Gilleghan had two sons: *Jim Gilleghan* born in 1932 and educated at Leeds Grammar School. He qualified at Edinburgh and was in general practice in Scotland from 1963 until retirement in 2000; daughter Dr Shona Gilleghan, married Dr Neil Jenkins and they have a son Tom. Shona is in General Practice and Neil is a Consultant Radiologist.

Vi Gilleghan

John Anthony Gilleghan was born on July 28th 1936 with the same initials as Dr John Alexander Young of Gilsyke House Halton; he was educated at Cross Gates Boys School and Leeds Grammar School from 1945 to 1955, when he went to Bede College Durham University. He gained an Honours degree in Botany and Zoology together with an Education Diploma before starting his teaching career in 1960 as a Biology master at Temple Moor Grammar School. John was involved in many school trips both at home and abroad and was an ASM in the school scout troop. Many boys were introduced to the Yorkshire Dales; in 1970 John started an adult evening group in Halton featuring the Dales. This was followed by a group at Roundhay in 1977 and today the two leisure groups have a large membership with outings, theatre visits and visiting speakers enhancing the programmes through the year.

In 1974 John was appointed head of science at Halton Middle School from where he took early retirement in July 1991. He was involved with the Natural History Club which exhibited at Leeds University and for the Association of School Natural History Societies at the Natural History

Museum in London. The children collected for the Animals in Danger Appeal and many were presented with certificates for their efforts. There were occasional visits by Cyril Littlewood MBE the founder-director of the Wildlife Youth Service, which held their monthly meetings at Leeds City Art Gallery on Saturday mornings. There was a large number of rambles, coach outings to the Yorkshire Dales and to Safari Parks and Zoos. John was involved with weekends in the Yorkshire Dales especially at Airton and Kettlewell. The four day holidays in Bristol were popular with visits to the SS Great Britain, Bristol Zoo, Cheddar Caves and Slimbridge Wildfowl Trust. He was involved with showing feature films on Friday evenings and shorter programmes during lunchtimes, when there was also the school shop which supported school funds and the Animals in Danger scheme. He was concerned with the school table tennis team which became city champions on two occasions.

John developed his interest in local history writing a weekly column in The Skyrack Express from June 1982 to the last issue in November 2002. An occasional series started in the Leeds Weekly News in January 2003. John has written and published four local history books, is a regular contributor on local history with BBC Radio Leeds and presents illustrated lectures to groups throughout the county. He has written a regular monthly feature on Yorkshire churches for the magazine Down Your Way from early 2000 and has written the guides for Aberford, Garforth and Saxton parish churches. John has contributed various articles to a number of magazines including the quarterly Yorkshire. He recorded two programmes about his life for BBC Radio Leeds and was involved with the presentation of a TV programme concerning the life of John Smeaton and advised for BBCTV's "Local Heroes".

John Gilleghan was invited to a Buckingham Palace Garden Party in July 1998 and was awarded the MBE for services to local history, natural history, education and the community in Leeds in the Millennium New Year Honours List 2000. He was presented with this prestigious award at Buckingham Palace by HRH Prince Charles on March 21st 2000. John was invited by George Mudie MP to visit 10 Downing Street with two friends in November 2003. John has

always had an interest in lecturing, photography and world travel which combine in the many holidays he has undertaken over many years. These included a series of cruise holidays, safaris in East and South Africa, educational cruises and more recently a holiday in New Zealand.

GRAVELEY FAMILY

The first mention of the Graveley family in Halton was in 1507 when the rental records of the Manor of Temple Newsam included 18 tenants with John Graveley. There were mentions of the family in 1572 with William Graveley and Robert Graveley in 1588. Another of the same name was living in the village and was buried at Whitkirk Church in June 1604. William's son Robert of Graveley Hall died in 1630 and he had five children. Robert was the eldest and he had seven sons, many of whom lived in the village.

The eldest son was Michael Graveley (1622-84) who had five sons and three daughters. His second son was Michael Graveley who married Ann Bywater in 1689; he was a churchwarden at Whitkirk and they had five children. It was his younger brother Edmond who had three sons and three daughters. The eldest was Edmond who married twice and lived at Graveley Hall while his younger brother Christopher married Anne Judson of Halton.

Christopher & Ann Graveley's eldest son was William who married Mary Matthews of York: her father was the Lord Mayor in 1755. William's brother was Christopher Graveley (1743) and his three sisters were Mary who married John Batley, Ann who married Benjamin Atkinson of Austhorpe Hall and Elizabeth who married Thomas Morkill of Halton in 1768.

William & Mary's son was *Thomas Matthews Graveley* (1766-1817) of Graveley Hall who married Ann Hutchinson of Wakefield (1773-1850) and had a family of four sons and two daughters. They were Anne who married Rev William Lindley curate at Whitkirk Church and Emma Isabella who married Thomas Wainwright of Potternewton. They had four sons:*Christopher Graveley* (1795-1855) who was a solicitor and died unmarried, *Thomas Matthews Graveley* (1796-1860) who married Maria Cowlam (1802-69). *John Graveley* (1798-1865) who married Maria Torrens Payne: John lived in South Carolina, died at Leamington and was buried at Whitkirk on April 4th 1865. Their daughter Emma married Francis Morritt of Willow Well Farm Halton Hill: she died in 1852. Francis then married Ann Warrington (died 1858) and Mary Ann. Mary Ann Morritt died in 1863 following the births of William and Sarah Anne in 1862; Francis Morritt died aged 68 in 1885. *William Graveley* (1798-1861) who married Harriet Farrer: their daughter Anne Isabella married William Morritt of Harehills and Petropolis Brazil; she died in August

1878 at Palmeiras Rio de Janeiro and was buried in the British Cemetery. William & Anne Morritt had three children: William Graveley Morritt, John Matthews Morritt and Mary Isabella who married Ernest Morant of London. William Graveley Morritt was admitted as a pupil to Leeds Grammar School on January 25th 1864 while living at Dial House Chapel Street: he died on the Isle of Wight aged 44 on March 14th 1895.

Thomas Matthews and Maria Graveley had two sons: Cowlam Graveley who married Sarah Rivers, *John Graveley* who lived at Graveley Hall then renamed Hawthorn House. John married Elizabeth Tinsdill whose father was Dr Edward W Tinsdill of Gilsyke House. John Graveley was born in Halton on September 19th 1828, educated at Leeds Grammar School from 1841 and died aged 80 on May 7th 1909: Elizabeth died on March 30th 1917 aged 78. John's younger sisters were Maria, Emma and Isabella. It was said of John Graveley that "he was the only man in Halton who could write gentleman after his name". John Graveley lived at Hawthorn House: he was a Whitkirk churchwarden with a tablet to his memory in the church.

John and Elizabeth Graveley's children were Ralfe born 1875, Wynefrid Henry born 1879 and died 1953 being interred at Yardley Birmingham, Beatrice (1873-1931) with Agnes Maud (1877-1883) and Marie Millicent being an infant death. Wynefrid Graveley was married to ML Murgatroyd in June 1917: she lived at one time at Dial House and later at Highthorne House Shadwell. Ralfe married Maud Marion Davy on August 16th 1905 at All Saints Church Hartley Kent and their son was John Edward Graveley who was baptised in October 1909: he was educated at Leeds Grammar School.

After the death of John's wife Elizabeth in 1917 and when daughter Beatrice had moved away by 1922, Hawthorn House passed into the ownership of John and Catherine Blaydon Jones.

GRAVELEYTHORPE

This was the grand plan of John Graveley who built a few streets in his "garden village" from 1871 to 1898. There is a stone plaque on the last house on Sycamore Avenue inscribed Graveleythorpe 1878: the street was Graveley Street. Birch Avenue was once Stanley Terrace and the Graveley firm built houses on Field Terrace, Park View Terrace, Cross Green Lane from Thorpe Street to Park Street and Whitkirk View. The Council bought parts of Graveleythorpe in 1937 and the Halton Housing Estate with the intention of resale.

GREAT HOUSES OF HALTON

Beechwood is an extended detached house on the north of Chapel

Street (62) once a part of the Temple Newsam estate and adjacent to Laurel Farm and Primrose Cottage. It was built in the early 19th century and at the end of that century was the home of Herbert Greaves (1887/1908) followed by the artist William Gilbert Foster RBA, wife Nora Mary and their daughter Nora Amelia born in 1877 was also an artist who died aged 37 on July 11th 1914. William Gilbert & Nora Mary's eldest daughter was Dorothea born in 1881 who became an artist and their youngest daughter was Hermione born in April 1895: Nora Mary was born in 1858. In the 1920's the Sowry family were living at Beechwood: Harold, Jane Elizabeth and William Bolton Sowry. Gerald Pearce died here in April 1925 aged 17. RCT Prest lived here from 1937-39 with his wife Jane Elizabeth Prest. Leslie & Margaret Allen lived at Beechwood and their daughter Frances was born in May 1964 and baptised at Whitkirk Church.

Chestnut Grove (The Grove) stood at the end of a drive which is now Birch Crescent. The house was built a few years earlier than nearby San Remo for the Crosthwaite family: in the 1891 census Chestnut Grove was home to cloth finisher John William Crosthwaite and his wife Mary. They had two servants and in 1901 mother in law Mary Smith (aged 71) lived with the family.

Chestnut Grove became the family home of Henry & Elizabeth Sandy with their daughters Mary Barrand and Pat in 1923: they moved from their previous home of Iveridge Hall Oulton. Elsie Bowes was employed to look after the Sandy children and went to a cottage at Flamborough which the family took for August. Elsie was born in Seacroft in 1907 and married Aubrey Bowes of Foundry Mill Farm in April 1929. The Grove had a tennis court, rose garden, fruit & vegetable garden and orchard. Henry Sandy bought the field from the house towards Selby Road and sold most of it for housing. The family moved to Thorner after the death of Henry Sandy in 1938: Elizabeth died in 1964. In 1938/39 the houses were built on the original driveway to the house as Birch Crescent. Chestnut Grove was converted into six flats but was eventually demolished. Headrow Housing Group opened their development of Prospect Gardens in January 1978. There are 9 one bed flats and 7 two bed flats for the elderly. The architects were John Brunton & Partners and the builders were WA Bushell (Contracts) Ltd. The latest Leeds development by Headrow Housing Group is Queenswood Drive completed in 2002.

Clifton House stood between Chapel Street and Selby Road with its own private driveway opposite Field End. The large house was L shaped and had stables, coach house from 1893 and outhouses: trees which once were part of the estate are still on the present site. In 1871 the census shows Clifton House to be the home of sheriff's officer William Hall (46) and wife Mary with children Florence, Frederick, Edward and Catherine:

they also employed a residential nurse Mary Dodgson. The 1893 listing has Andrew McClure at Clifton House. In 1901 it was the home of Derbyshire born provision merchant Herbert Greaves (57) with wife Sarah (56) and children Vernon, Edith Annie, Eleanor & Gerty: they had a servant in their house at this time. It became the home of Walter Bowden Pindar who died on January 15th 1929 aged 63 and wife Agnes who died on January 3rd 1949. He worked at the Registry Office by 1905 at 61 Woodhouse Lane Leeds; he was the clerk to the Hunslet Rural District Council and Secretary of the War Agricultural Committee with the Hunslet RDC; he had moved from Hollyshaw Lane and he left £1144 in his will. Agnes Pindar died on January 3rd 1949 aged 78: she was a supporter of St. Wilfrid's Church and was Chairman of the Temple Newsam and Halton Women's Conservative Association. She worked for the old Mission Church prior to the opening of St. Wilfrid's Church in 1939 and allowed her house to be used for a variety of meetings and functions. The family offered a half acre of Clifton House grounds free of charge in 1917 for the children of the adjacent school to build a school garden during the Great War and they also provided a gate which gave access to the school from the south.

Their family were Arthur Pindar (1886-1950), Arthur Finlay Bowden Pindar born in August 1900 and educated at Leeds Grammar School, Florence, Margaret Edith Ellen born in March 1903 and Dorothy Agnes Joyce Pindar. Dorothy was born in October 1905 and was married to Frank Alan Todd of Liverpool on August 24th 1940. Arthur Pindar married Florence Sloman in late 1939: he died on November 14th 1946. Their son was Graeme Bowden Pindar who died on January 27th 1950 aged 6 years at the then family home Sandringham Crescent. The meetings of the Temple Newsam Women's Conservative Association took place at Clifton House and at Hawthorn House. In 1956 Clifton House was the home of Margaret Pindar with the rest of the house divided into two flats. When Margaret Pindar left Clifton House her home became that of Harry Facer with his wife Enid and Colin: Harry was the caretaker of the Primary School. The land and house had been bought by Leeds City Council Education Committee who used the house as homes for employees including Maureen Quin a teacher at the Primary School. The house was demolished in 1971 and the site became part of the playing fields: the only reminders are the trees and a seasonal display of crocuses.

Craigmona is the large detached house on Park Street to the rear of Whitkirk View and was built by John Graveley in 1892 on land which was a part of the Temple Newsam estate. The land had been the subject of an agreed tenancy by John Graveley's mother Maria in c1860. This was a feature of Graveleythorpe with the last of the developments being Graveley Mount in 1898. The sale plan of 1877 shows the area known as Graveleythorpe stretching from Green Lane to Garden Field Lane and

from Green Lane to Occupation Lane (now Primrose Lane). The land on which the house was built in 1892 was known as the Martinmas Lands: it stretched over 2.5 acres and was soon to be the site of Graveley Road, Graveley Street, Park View Terrace, Whitkirk View, Graveley Mount and Gladstone Terrace. The plot was passed to the builder contractor Joseph Speight in July 1877 and in July 1892 the house now completed was sold to the first occupier James Yates who was a public librarian of Leeds. One of the conditions of sale was to be a brick wall built on the Primrose Lane side with suitable fencing on Park Street. James Yates sold the property to Richard Haste Carr a Leeds engineer in late 1899; he was born in Bramley in 1865 and married to Ann Jane who had been born on the Isle of Man in 1861. Plans for a stable and coach house were passed by the Hunslet RDC in October 1900. During the Great War the family organised many activities: one was a concert at the Wesleyan Schoolroom for Blind Soldiers and Sailors raising the sum of £14. Richard and Annie shared their house with her mother Margaret and his 34 year old son in law. Richard Haste Carr trained as a mechanical engineer and qualified AMIMechE; in the early 20th century he was working from 5 Crown Point Road and later his office was on the second floor of Greek Street Chambers. He was a worker for Halton Methodist Church being trustee, secretary and circuit steward. He died suddenly at his Halton home on March 6th 1934 aged 67 and was cremated at Lawnswood on March 9th. Annie Haste Carr was a member of the Hunslet RDC Local War Pensions Sub-Committee which also included Philip S Marsden of Whitkirk.
Craigmona became the home of Thomas Horatio Ramsden from 1936 to 1945, followed by Samuel Terence Palmer. The garden facing Primrose Lane was sold for the building of a new house and in more recent years Craigmona was converted into flats and from 2000 it has been converted again to a single private house.
Dial House was built in 1720 and restored in 1755 as a plaque at the rear indicates. The house has the original timbers in the roof which may have come from a sailing ship. It was the property of Temple Newsam estate and once was the home of the farm bailiff. Dial House was also one of the homes in Halton of the Graveley family with William Graveley in the mid-19th century; William's daughter Anne married John Morritt. In the 1891 census Dial House was the home to Elizabeth Mills (born 1843) with her sister Charlotte Issott. Dial House had many tenants including Mary Proctor with son Herbert; Mrs Ball (later Mrs Brown) ran a fruit and vegetable business from the house. She built a double fronted shop on the right hand side for her son's fruit shop which was later taken by Fred W Hill. John Chadwick Brown lived here: his wife Margaret Brown died in August 1941 after 47 years at Dial House and after three marriages: she was 79 years old. Margaret Brown applied for permission in January 1931 to alter part of Dial House to a shop and sought for

permission to complete a WC and stable. Harold Ball died in 1941 and was one of the sons of William & Margaret Ball of Dial House. The shop was demolished during the preparations for the building of Brooksbank Home.

Dial House and the area were remembered by Halton dentist Jack Stuart White in 1988: *My family moved from Cross Gates to Halton about 1921: that was the year that father started the Halton troop of Scouts as an extension to the Cross Gates 13th NE Leeds and which soon became a troop in its own right, the 18th NE Leeds. We had moved to live at*

Holme Lea on Chapel Street next to the chapel. Holme Lea had once been the home and surgery of Dr Frederick Pogson, son of Dr William Pogson of Seacroft Grange. Dr William Pogson died in 1912 and his son died a year afterwards. Holme Lea could have been a farmhouse at one time as it had a mistal and stables which we converted to a garage and workshop serving as the first Scouts headquarters. On the other side of us away from the Chapel was Laurel House occupied by the Daniels family who had a girl and three boys who became members of the Scout troop. To the rear of their house was a haulage firm Nicholls & Pickersgill who had a collection of ex-wartime lorries. When their site was cleared they moved across Selby Road to Holly House Farm. The death occurred in 1936 of TPW Nicholls who was the first man in Yorkshire to beat the 5 hour record for a paced 100 miles in 1902-TP was a fine racing cyclist. *Dial House used to belong to the Temple Newsam estate and was occupied for many years by a succession of Graveleys. Dial House was originally built in 1720 and remodelled in 1755*

according to the date on the rear of the house and there were many more alterations over the years. There is a unique loft with the original king posts and curiously shaped oak beams, the access is up a steep stair entered through a cupboard in the bathroom. These roof timbers were said to have come from sailing ships and could well have done so as they show signs of many old dovetails where they have been joined onto other timbers and the deep marks where ropes have been pulled over them for many years. The downstairs floorboards were ten inches wide and badly worn: when we thought of turning them over to use the other side we found that they had already been turned. Dial House was built with locally made bricks and there had been three back doors in various places. Before I moved my surgery to Dial House in 1950 it had been occupied by a Mrs Ball, later Mrs Brown after remarriage and her family. Her ex-husband was said to have been a seafaring man whose ghost haunted the house as he stomped around on a wooden leg. We all heard it from time to time. She had two sons from the Ball marriage: Alec and Gerald. She set up Alec with a milk round which was operated from a shed in the back yard. A fruit and veg shop operated in one of the front rooms and I can remember walking over from Cross Gates with my Mother during the First World War to buy our fruit there. Later when Gerald married his Mother built on a shop with living accommodation for them. When they sold up it was bought by Fred Hill and his wife who carried on their greengrocers business. Thomas Frederick Hill's daughter was Brenda who married John Rimington at Whitkirk Church in June 1952. *Leeds Corporation decided that Dial House was a building of architectural importance and should be restored to its previous appearance. They removed the shop/house from the side thus preparing the way for future development. Halton Institute was built on land that had once been the orchard for Dial House and there used to be a few apple trees remaining between the Institute and Morris's chemist shop. Alongside Dial House was the opening to Graveley Square which led to Dial Terrace and Dial Row leading in turn to Primrose Lane and Morritt Drive.*

The listed Dial House was the dental surgery of Jack R Stuart White and became Peter Rider dentist from May 1976; afterwards it became the home of a few different small businesses who rented the property.

In February 1995 a user based crisis centre was proposed and in January 1997 a service was run with Leeds Social Services. On March 16th 1999 Dial House was bought for the new service, run by a committee of users and survivors of the mental health system. The Leeds User Led Crisis Service opened its doors on November 26th 1999. From June 2001 the service became known as The Leeds Survivor Led Crisis Service.

Alvara Bulmer and family with his dalmatian lived at the top end of Graveley Square in a group that appeared to have been coach houses.

He was an ex-Corporation cleaner, dustman and roadman. In later years prior to demolition only one of the cottages was lived in by the Pemberton family. On the other side of the opening to the square was a short terrace of shops and offices and behind them were the remains of a building known as Banty Cock Hall where joiner and undertaker Tom Shaw had his workshop before moving to Rose Cottage on Selby Road. Tom Shaw's workmate was Harry Cowell who was a good carpenter.

Gilsyke House was first built on the High Street in 1800 and was originally a farmhouse on the Temple Newsam estate. It had extensive gardens, stables, greenhouses and vegetable gardens. There was a brick wall surrounding the property with a short drive to the rear. The house was the home of many Halton doctors including the first doctor for the village Dr Edward Tinsdill. The surgery was at the front of the large house.

Vi Gilleghan and John in Gilsyke House gardens 1959

In 1947 plans were passed to alter the house and to develop the former servant's quarters into a separate dwelling: home to Dr Robert & Helen Mattock and when Dr Young's son John David married he also lived at this house. From 1957 to September 1960 186a Selby Road was the home of the Gilleghan family following the sale of the Halton Pharmacy. The last doctor to live at Gilsyke House was Dr Ramsay and his wife Marion: they moved out in March 1966. Dr Young sold Gilsyke House to the developers William Airey and it was demolished in June 1966 with Grandways and a shopping parade built on the site. The present surgery and Co-operative Village Store are in a building which dates from May 1966 and was built on the site of Springfield Place and Greenfield's cobbler's shop. The demolition of the houses prior to Gilsyke House allowed the surgery to continue without a break.

Hawthorn House on Chapel Street was the home of the Graveley family. The house dated from c1620, known as Graveley Hall and was built by Robert Graveley. It stood amidst pleasant surroundings with a large lawn, extensive grounds, stables and outbuildings and was later known as The Hawthorns. There was a small whitewashed gardener's cottage known as Rose Cottage on Primrose Road. The last tenant was gardener Smith and in July 1929 the cottage was demolished. The gardens extended along Chapel Street where there was a display of lilac trees where the row of 1930's housing was built. The main driveway was to the rear of this row and still called Halton Drive.
John & Elizabeth Graveley lived at Hawthorn House with their servant Florence Scarfe. When John died in 1909 his widow and daughter Beatrice continued to live at the House. Elizabeth died in 1917 and Hawthorn House became St Wilfrid's Church House with the kitchen used as a scout room. The Rev Walter Pitcher who was the curate from 1914 to 1918 lived there for 18 months when the house was also used as a boy's club and scout depot.
The family moved away and were followed at Hawthorn House by John & Catherine Broad Blaydon Jones, who worked hard for the community in the wartime. John Blaydon Jones was born in 1865 and became a wholesale grocer and provision dealer who started business in 1884. By 1905 he ran a shop at 29 Trinity Street Leeds and lived at 76 Markham Avenue Harehills and in the following years was living at 44 Cowper

Hawthorn House

Street, 5 Spence Lane and 114 Beeston Road. By 1921 he was running the Leeds Economic Stores at 78a Waterloo Road Hunslet and lived at 84 Francis Street. The family moved to Hawthorn House Halton in 1922 where he was declared bankrupt in 1923 having invested in a limited company of theatre fitters which was wound up. In 1928 another resident of Hawthorn House was Frederick Hodges and the Jones family stayed in the village until the outbreak of war. The family helped the villagers with the organising of events and allowing groups to use parts of their property for meetings. The house was numbered 22 Chapel Street prior to the later renumbering when the Bray houses were built in 1936. The building was used for ARP meetings and a workroom/storeroom for William Pease. The property became derelict and was demolished in 1956.

Holme Lea at 14 Chapel Street was adjacent to the Methodist Chapel with Laurel House on the other side. It had been built in the early 19th century and had an extensive garden, paddock and tennis court: a restoration date on the chimney was 1870. Annie Squires was at Holme Lea 1891/1908 and Dr Frederick Pogson lived at Holme Lea having his surgery in the house until 1913. Dr Pogson was a 30 year old medical student in 1891 living at Rose Terrace; in the 1901 census was FW Pogson and Louisa with son William Frederick (3). The dispensary and surgery were adjacent to the pantry and wash house. In 1921 it was the home of the Stuart White family until they moved to Pinfold Lane in 1931. Jack Stuart White had a wireless room at the back of the first floor and he set up two aerial masts on the chimneys: he had some early wireless crystal sets and used to listen to Morse code from Paris and other places. In August 1931 there was an agreement of tenancy between Halton Methodist Chapel, engineer Cyril Stephenson and cinema manager Herbert Sedgwick. The Ginns family moved into Holme Lea in May 1936 (the day of the cup final): William Henry & Nellie Ginns had lived at 99 Morritt Drive and 5 Primrose Road. Sydney Ginns took over his father's decorating business in 1948 at the age of 24 and for a few months was Ginns & Preston. William Henry Ginns was born in Nottingham in 1874 and started work as a picture framer employing a few folk during the 1920's; he died aged 96 in 1970. The house was demolished in 1969.

Laurel House Farm was adjacent to Holme Lea at 16 Chapel Street and it was the home of the Daniel Family. David Daniel was the Halton farmer who died at Laurel House aged 75 on July 25th 1923. Following the Daniel family were Joe & Alice Ann Stevenson who had a milk delivery business and once lived with the family at Park View Farm. Edgar Stevenson married Ada Medd (daughter of signalman Herbert William Medd) in June 1936; Hannah Stevenson married Harold Williamson in February 1936. Joe Stevenson died aged 58 on April 16th 1935: his wife Alice died aged 65 on February 3rd 1941.

Rose & Harry Spencer had a shop on Shaftesbury Parade and a shop at the end of Sycamore Avenue selling ladies clothing. Rose, Harry, Jack and Maretta Spencer were living at the house in the wartime with Harry previously at 74 Cross Green Lane.

Orchard Villa was built in October 1913 by George Morritt for the owner of Barkston Ash Laundry John Procter Scott, who then lived at Laurelbank. John's wife died in 1916 leaving son Allan and two daughters Elizabeth and Eliza. John died in 1919 and son Allan sold the laundry to Ronald Wheater. The next occupants of the house were confectioners Peter & Catherine Bligh who changed the name to Tralee. In 1928 the Blighs were made bankrupt and the house stood empty for a few years. Joseph Thomas of The Crescent bought the property as an investment together with the gardens and land on Wilfred Avenue. Joseph Thomas was the owner of a stone breaking machine company on Holbeck Lane: he died aged 80 in October 1949 and his wife Esther died aged 79 in the same month and year. It was while Ginns decorators were painting the exterior that Henry and Hannah Pease who were butchers in Beeston decided to purchase the property in 1934: Joseph Thomas gave the flowering cherry which still grows. The family were once resident in Colton: John and Caroline Pease were farmers and their son William married Ann Moore in Leeds Parish Church; Anne was the daughter of a servant at Temple Newsam. They had nine children including Eleanor born in February 1884, Thomas born in June 1887, Emma born in April 1889, John William born in August 1891 and Henry Pease (1877-1956) who married Hannah Jane Myatt (1878-1967) from Staffordshire in 1903 at Leeds Parish Church and they bought a shop in Beeston to which they added two more shops. Hannah died aged 88 in July 1967. They had four daughters and sons Oliver (died 1978), John and Abraham. The eldest daughter was Mabel born in January 1904, Eleanor born 1906 and died July 1945, Margaret Ann in 1910 and Eileen born 1911: father Henry died at Orchard Villa at the age of 79 in 1956.

Pickering (Pickrin) Lodge was built in 1821 and later extended: this large house has had 12 different owners and most of them made interior alterations. The house was probably built originally as a lodge for the Temple Newsam estate and maybe the home of the Temple Newsam estate surveyor. It was named after John Pickering who owned land in the village in 1732. The house passed to Thomas Smith who in 1832 left it to his grand-daughter and it was then purchased from the estate. The house was sold by collier/clerk/gardener Charles born 1828 & Ann Teale for £30 to William Smith. Charles & Ann Teale had four children: Henry, George, Sarah and Louise. In 1890 the local Crosthwaite family bought the Lodge and had plans passed for alterations in August 1893. They sold it in 1909 to schoolmaster William Wallbank born in Bingley 1867: his wife was Mary and son Alec. Seven years later he sold it to Robert & Carrie Shaw: Carrie married Claude Pybus in June 1930. John & Mary Farrow bought the property in 1933 and remained there until 1966. John Arthur Farrow died in September 1961 aged 75 having been a member of the Halton Congregational Chapel from the foundation. There were several owners until 1985 when Tony & Hilary Sheppard bought the derelict dwelling from the Robinson family and restored Pickering Lodge. Pickering Lodge is on Primrose Lane and Long Field Drive.

Prospect House was to the rear of the St. John's Centre on Field End Road: demolished for the housing estate. The house stood in extensive grounds and plans for a coal house and privy were passed in June 1886. Prospect House was the home of JE Brown & George William Brown, Frederick Jeffreys (1887), Daniel Crowther (1897), Marshall Porritt (1899) and the Taylor family.

William & Emily Taylor had four children: William (born 1889), Arnold (born 1891), Alicia (born 1894) and Herbert (born 1899). William Arthur Taylor was born in August 1889 to parents Arnold and Eva Taylor: he married Edith Wood in 1914. William Taylor was a leather worker and then a financial secretary; he later lived on Orchard Terrace and was a cashier with WC Jackson of Buslingthorpe for 34 years and was also the private secretary to Lord Allerton. He died aged 78 in January 1939. It was later the home of rag merchant Fraser Fox and later Francis & Alice Fox with children Harold, John, Marie Amy and Hilda. In 1936 the address was 16 Field End Road. Francis Fox was a director of Fox & Rutherford who were rag merchants on Mabgate. Harold Fox was born in 1907 and married Alice Baron in September 1939: she was the daughter of mattress manufacturer Frederick W Baron. Harold was a mechanic and lived at 17 Dunhill Crescent prior to his marriage. John Fox who was born in 1911 married Sheila Gascoigne in May 1936: Sheila died aged 33 on February 18th 1947 and their daughter Sheila Wendy Fox died aged 2 months in June 1944. Marie Amy Fox born in 1914 was married in August 1940 to engineer Thomas Kirkby of Glebe Cottage Whitkirk; Hilda Fox was born in 1917 and married Thomas Peel in

December 1941. Robert David Fox died at Prospect House aged 78 in August 1936.

San Remo The late 19th century house of San Remo stood behind a high brick wall in its own grounds: the main gates were opposite Birch Avenue. This was first built for the Crosthwaite family: in 1899 Ernest Crosthwaite was living here and in 1901 it was the home of wool manufacturer Alfred Crosthwaite and wife Annie with their three children. In 1916 San Remo became the home of Reginald Knight (Reggie) and his second wife Thirza Foss Knight: their Rolls Royce was often seen in the village. Thirza Bottomley was the sister of Horatio Bottomley MP and editor of the magazine John Bull. Their chauffeur and friend Ernest Pickersgill drove the Rolls Royce around the village wearing a pair of leather gaiters, plus fours and a flat cap. Reg Knight had a daughter during marriage to his first wife Alice Georgina: Mrs Parke who lived in London. Reggie and Alice lived at Colton for many years: she was killed in an accident while in London on April 5th 1910 aged 51: her maiden name was Smallpage. Alice was interred at Whitkirk cemetery on Wednesday April 13th .

Reggie was born in Chapeltown and his family intended that he should train for the church: he was a student at Bramham College. Reggie was a churchwarden at Whitkirk, a frequent judge at dog shows, chairman of the Tuberculosis Association, magistrate and chairman of the Hunslet Rural District Council from 1907. Reggie lived at Ivy Cottage Colton for 25 years and for 18 years lived at San Remo. Reginald Henry Knight was a member of the family who founded the Leeds printing firm of Knight & Forster.

James Young Knight was a bookseller and a publisher in Leeds in 1821; his son John Catlow Knight joined the firm in 1841 with premises in Leeds, Bradford and London. The London manager was Thomas Forster who was taken into partnership. The firm was well known for the manufacture of steel nibs for pens and won the prize medal at the 1851 Great Exhibition. In 1864 James died and four years later the firm bought lithographers Jonathan & Edward Pulleyn's business in Basinghall Street. Knight & Forster (Arthur Langford Knight & Edward Eustace Forster) moved their headquarters to Basinghall Street: John Catlow Knight died in 1885. In 1897 they bought land on Water Lane and moved to new premises (Water Lane Printing Works) in January 1899: the retail outlet was at 18 Basinghall Street. Reggie was the son of master printer Arthur Knight who lived at Woodbank Harden Bingley. His brother was Henry A Knight who lived at Colton: he was born in 1860 and was a printer in the family firm. His wife was born in 1860 and their daughter Isabella was born in 1887.

Reggie Knight died aged 74 at San Remo on Wednesday March 13th 1935: his funeral took place at Whitkirk Church on SaturdayMarch 16th. There

were no flowers but a cross of red roses was placed on top of the oak coffin.
Ernest Pickersgill lived in a flat in San Remo and continued to live there after the sudden death of Mrs Knight at the age of 78 on May 4th 1966: there was a service and cremation at Lawnswood on May 6th. Ernest lived at San Remo alone until he died at Wakefield in 1976 aged 73. There was considerable interest in the property by the Sue Ryder Homes who obtained planning permission for conversion and additions. The plans were abandoned and San Remo was demolished in 1977. Headrow Housing Group opened Wheaton Court in September 1980. There are 18 one bed flats and 12 two-bed flats for the elderly. The architects were John Brunton & Partners and builders Jack Lunn & Co Ltd.

GREEN LANE

This follows the old route of Cross Field Lane from the junction with Cross Green Lane/Primrose Lane

Prior to the realignment Green Lane was once alongside the edge of the Bye Law Men's Field allotments and across the present Woodland Road and Knightsway to Hollyshaw Grove. The Bye Law Men's Field existed on an 1843 map which also shows Primrose Lane as Back Lane and Garth Ends Road (after Garth End Field on the north west side), while Cross Field Road continued as Smarlings Road (Occupation Road) towards Hollyshaw Lane although not reaching as far as this. The route is now occupied by housing on what was known as Cross Field. The only through road was Cross Field Road (Lane) from High Street Halton to Cross Gates.
The semi-detached houses on Green Lane before The Mount were built in 1930 with John Hulse Atha living at Langdale 52 Green Lane. He was a retired schoolmaster and conducted the Temple Newsam Ladies Choir and was a Sunday School superintendent at Cross Gates Methodist Church; he celebrated his golden wedding in 1943.
The Green Lane Improvement Scheme was a development by Hunslet RDC in 1922-23 who used it as relief work for the unemployed. This entailed the making of a road from Morritt Avenue and from Hollyshaw Lane to the new junction complete with surfacing and sewerage.
The Mount was first mentioned as a named street approved by Hunslet RDC in December 1922. The land was acquired by builder George Alfred Ellison who built the houses in differing styles. The builder and his wife Sarah were to live at Nunthorpe and then they moved to Fraisthorpe. One of the first houses to be sold was 14 on February 2nd 1926 to Edward Braithwaite who died in 1937. Two of the houses opposite 14 were built on former tennis courts. The Mount development was also in the hands of T Cox builders by 1925. In 1930 5 The Mount was the home of Harold

and Alice Isabel Garrood nee Elliott who was born on January 1st 1894 with son David and daughter Fiona. Harold taught at Cross Gates School while his wife trained at City of Leeds Training College (1912-14) and taught at Green Lane CC School for Boys, Victoria School and then joined the staff at Cross Gates Boy's School in February 1943; she taught for 3 months from April 11th 1927 at Halton School. The house was later to become 13 The Mount. David was educated at Leeds Grammar School from 1945 and left at the age of 18 in 1953 having won a Leeds Senior City Scholarship and a State Scholarship having studied Classics. David moved to live at Epsom Surrey and became a Computer Consultant. Fiona emigrated to Australia.
The first houses on Green Lane came by the mid-19th century with houses bordered by Hermon Street built in 1865/67 on land owned by Edward Waud of Manston Hall from the Temple Newsam Estate.
The row of terrace houses known as "Dolly Houses", "Cuckoo Clock Houses" or "Bird Cage Walk" was built by George Morritt in 1902-04: his

plans were passed for the nine houses in mid-1900. The early story of 76 Green Lane is typical of the attractive row. The first date is October 4th 1904 when the land was sold by John Aysgough Rickards to builder George Morritt. In 1954 Rushford estates of Burton Leonard sold to the Ritz Cinema Cross Gates as a home for the manager.
72 Green Lane was the home of butcher Harry & Agnes Verity and son Joseph Eric Verity in 1914. Later the home of the Yelland family: Charley Yelland who died in October 1952 and wife Nellie Fawcett lived there in the 1930's and their children were George Stanley, Frank Edmund, Charley Yelland Jnr and Annie Fawcett. Charles & Dulcie Yelland later lived at Gipton and he wrote a local history book "The Gipton Story". The end house of the row is 80 and was once the home of the landlady of the Albion public house on Grape Street Hunslet.
The only housing beyond this row on the 1908 map were the four houses

on Hermon Road, houses on Green Lane and seven houses on Hermon Terrace. Clapham Dene Road did not exist and with the still unadopted road The Croft not even existing as a footpath. This area was known as ***Hermon Mount*** or Mount Hermon referring to the 9232 feet high mountain on the Syria-Lebanon border where according to tradition Jesus was transfigured.

Hermon Road has two older buildings with new housing nearer the railway. To the rear of the Dolly Houses was Field Terrace with the large square house facing both this street, Hermon Road and Clapham Dene. The Dene is a narrow steep sided short valley which once had a stream from Field Terrace to the railway. The gardens of houses on The Mount and Hermon Road use the slopes of Clapham Dene. On a map dated 1821 (revised 1850) this was described as "Hell Dyke Deyn".

The large house was built c1898 on land bought from Mrs Meynell Ingram for hearth rug manufacturer Charles Powell when it was known as Clapham Dene. There are some who remember the house being used as a small private school run by nuns: the present owners have kept the bracket from the school bell. When they moved into the house in 1955 they discovered a hidden cache of old stone bottles many in wicker baskers. By 1930 there were four dwellings: Walter Lister, Florence Taylor, George Taylor and Grace Bywater. The bungalow next to this large house is now called Clapham Dene being built about the start of the Great War. For many years this was the home of insurance inspector Arthur Coltman and his wife Mabel and is now two flats.

Clapham Dene Road area is mentioned on a 1793 map of Halton as Clapham Dean bounded by Lord Irwin's land on the west and by land held by Arthur Turner to the west; the northern limit belonged to the Township of Seacroft. The street was originally called Hermon Road but changed by December 1904. The land on which the terrace houses on the west side were built was bought in 1897 from Mrs Meynell Ingram and in 1934 was sold to builder William Jowitt in partnership with Leeds jeweller Samuel Isaac of Lands Lane. In April 1936 William Jowitt sold to Robert George Smith of Grove Road who was given permission to build by the planners in June 1936. The first house to be built on the east side was 1 Clapham Dene Road. The conveyance of the land was completed in April 1908 by the builder George Backhouse Marshall and WA Easton applied for permission to build four through houses.

The houses on the corner of Clapham Dene Road and Green Lane (90/94) were built in two stages with the first two connected houses built in 1907 with 94 added on a few years later.

One of the old houses is 96 Green Lane and the deeds show that in 1865 Edward Waud of Manston Hall held the land known as Far Deans from the Temple Newsam estate. The land was bought by Manston builder George Backhouse Marshall who erected the dwelling known as

Hollyshaw House. The house was bought by Joseph Hawkins who was the first owner in 1869 and he was followed by Joseph Lilley in 1872 and Thomas Townend in 1875. It was Margaret Mason, widow of George Mason who held the property in 1891 and after her daughter Mary Ellis Mason's marriage to 28 year old colliery manager Alvara Chadwick in 1892 they moved in to Hollyshaw House. Margaret Mason died aged 72 on July 12th 1893. In 1947 music teacher Ivy de Boer and her husband Betting de Boer were the new owners until 1974 when the property was sold to Dennis & June Lee. Ivy Louise de Boer sold her husband's Ballestrieri violin to help the Leeds Youth Orchestra make a trip to America. She was a past-president of Temple Newsam Women's Institute and died aged 81 in August 1979.

Hermon Street was known as ***Hermon Terrace*** and a grave in Whitkirk cemetery records the death of Thomas Townend of Hermon Terrace who died aged 85 on March 20th 1920: his wife Clara died aged 81 in December 1918. The row of seven dwellings date from c1872/76. This area was surrounded by a brick wall and had gates at the Green Lane end making it a private zone. The wall exists today on the east side complete with stone capping to the remaining corner pillar. The hand made bricks used for the row of houses are seen in the wall, which is also found on the railway embankment: built on the old railway stone wall from the 1830's. The houses were built by the Temple Newsam Estate for their workers and two of the rows have wells which are now filled in. The row was built in three sections: Hill House was the first seen with a different height to the roof level, followed by a block of two houses and the last four were built as a unit using decoration with different coloured bricks. The end house (7) had the original entrance on the side (north) of the house at basement level and the Yorkshire stone interior floors have been retained. When the houses were numbered Hill House was separate and the present 2 Hermon Street was 1 Hermon Terrace: renumbering took place in 1931. Hill House was the home of Edgar Glover in the 1930's.

The Croft is an unadopted street leading to the railway embankment and on a 1834 map of Halton is described as glebe land belonging to Whitkirk Church with the area to the north in the hands of a Miss Bold. Most of the other surrounding land was in the hands of the Temple Newsam Estate. A plan of farms administered by the Temple Newsam Estate in 1915 showed this area to be a part of Ernest Rawson's farmland. He also held lands in Primrose Valley, Pinfold Lane (site of Halton School), Green Lane (site of the former allotments/Leodis public house) and Field End on Selby Road corner. In 1929 the residents of The Croft were George Knowles (Kenwyn), Henry Gwillan (Ravenscroft), John Bride (Kirkdene), William Bramham (Lynwood) and John Hill (Dunholme). The semi-detached houses were built c1925 with Dunholme named after the owners Frederick & Minnie Dunhill and rented by James Frederick & Marion Smith in 1939. The house was purchased following the death of Mrs Dunhill in 1960: James Smith (1885-1958) worked as an inspector at the Wellington Street Goods Depot in Leeds while their daughter Doris born in 1914 worked in the Information Office at Leeds Railway Station. The family had come from Harrogate in March 1939 and Doris worked at Starbeck Station. Marion Smith was born in Glasshoughton in 1887: she died on May 3rd 1974.

The two semi-detached houses (106/112 Green Lane) were built in 1924 and the first residents at Lyngarth (112) were insurance agent Edward Linley and his wife Beatrice Mary nee Murgatroyd. Their family were Roger Allan, Marjorie Mary, Betsy Gertrude and James Edward Linley. Ted Linley was the founder of the Halton Racing Pigeons Society and kept a loft for the birds to the side of the house: now the access to the new bungalows. In those early days the area was fields down to the railway.

The electricity sub-station is adjacent to The Croft and the site of the former filter beds has now been landscaped. The three detached bungalows were built on former railway land with plans submitted for the first (112a) in May 1988 and March 1989 following sale of the land in 1986. The first bungalow was occupied in 1990 and the last one occupied by the developer in 2001. The first built house includes the preserved beech trees on the slope to the railway. Plans for a further bungalow were presented in November 1990.

Greenway Close was built in 1959 by the builder Fred Schofield on previous allotments between The Croft and Greenway Close: the factory was based in the old Hunslet Ragged Sunday School.

Builder Fred Purdy developed Greenway following the restart of the business after the Great War in 1924. The Purdy family included three bricklayer brothers: George, Ben and Joseph. George's son was Fred who was a keen cross country runner. Fred was a member of the Leeds Harriers who met at the old Irwin Arms Inn on High Street and won medals for his races. Purdy's also built on Cross Gates Lane, Barwick Road and Foundry Lane. The houses on Greenway were built on deep foundations as a shallow depth of soil covered an amount of rubble placed there by the workmen making the railway cutting in the 1830's; the site was originally a cornfield. Purdy Builders also built Tom Drake's fish shop and the few detached buildings, later filled in by a different builder. Tom Drake's shop was opened in 1939 prior to the outbreak of War: he came from a business opposite Victoria School on York Road. The row on Green Lane on the right now occupied by Paws for Thought once included Carter's greengrocery and was built by Parsons & Holmes in 1938/39.

The houses on the south side of Green Lane to Woodland Road junction were built by Eastwood in the late 1940's. The houses adjacent to the

allotments was built by 1979. The houses on the north side date from the 1950's.
Green Lane ends at the corner shops which include Hughes Funeral Services and Paws for Thought. Hughes Funeral Services started in 1983 when Madden's Funeral Services 92/94 Marsh Lane were bought by Hugh Peter Hughes: James Madden also had a business at 48 Sussex Street on Cavalier Hill. The York Road headquarters near the old swimming pool/library was opened in 1990. The firm took over Slack's bakery shop on Green Lane: it was opened by George Mudie MP on February 15th 1997 although trading started in December 1996. Slack's confectioners were established in the mid 19th century and they had shops at 152 Green Lane, 133 Cross Gates Road, 851 York Road and 99 Main Street Garforth. Slacks had a bakery on Lotherton Way Garforth which was closed by 1995. The first bakers in this shop were the Jowitt family followed by George H & Christina Wormleighton in the 1950's.
Paws For Thought was started by Dale Briggs when he bought the Halton Pet Stores on Templenewsam Road in 1979. They moved in 1994 to Green Lane corner taking over Field's drapers and an antiques shop with Carter's greengrocer's shop bought in 1997. Paws for Thought opened their present head office in 2002 in the former Victoria later Trotters public house: the property was bought in 1998 from Scottish & Newcastle Brewery. William H Carter opened his greengrocers shop in 1938 when the row was newly built: other businesses were Duncan's barbers and draper Amy Bargate who left to live at Goathland. Billy Carter retired in the 1970's: he married Marjorie Dennis and they had two daughters. Jill married Brian Britland and Shirley married David Nelmes. Dale Briggs married David & Shirley's daughter Virginia. Billy Carter died aged 78 in 1987. The shop was taken by C Varley by 1966 who also had shops on Swarcliffe Parade and Haslewood Drive.

GROVE ROAD

This was first known as Gillsyke & New Field Road - later Peggy Lane and one of the early streets of the old village.

The houses on the east side were built mainly by Dunhills and Brays during the 1920's. At meetings of the Temple Newsam Ratepayers Association in June 1922 and January 1925, Coun Reginald Knight requested that Grove Road would be better when paved by Dunhill Bros: one resident at this meeting said that the road is all right in width as it is "a road to nowhere". In 1928 proposals were being made for the road to be properly surfaced and Dunhill Bros complained about the state of the road when they were building six bungalows; the road was "unmade" at the bottom. There was a Council refuse tip in this part of Grove Road which was the subject of many complaints to the Hunslet RDC. In 1910 the road was to be made up using 40 loads of material from the York Road furnaces. At one time the lane was called Grove Road at the top and Peggy Lane towards Temple Newsam. The housing on Jean Avenue and Alan Crescent was approved for Dunhill's builders in 1924-25 with Bray and Park involved in 1936.

West side

The terrace houses were built in two phases on land that was once part of the Temple Newsam estate. The first row of four houses (6-12) was built in 1931 by William Verity: the building caused the renumbering of the odd numbers. William Verity was granted permission in October 1930 to demolish old cottages on this site. The second row (14-32) was known as Grove's Cottages built in 1866, being the year of disenfranchisement between Hugo Charles Meynell Ingram of Temple Newsam and Joseph Groves of Halton. He lived at Park View House and was a corn miller born
in 1809. The properties were all bought by the Verity family in 1930 who rented them out at 2/6d a week to their farm workers at Whitebeck, Gilsyke and Laurel House Farms. One of the second row was sold to Arthur & Winifred Wraith of Carter Terrace Whitkirk on March 2nd 1945. The cottages were probably earlier linked with the nearby Halton Colliery. The houses were the subject of a compulsory purchase order in 1966 as the land was being suggested as a car park for a new supermarket: this was overturned in the courts. 6-12 Grove Road had been earmarked for demolition for the Halton Expressway which was abandoned in October 1973. The plans for the Halton Neighbourhood Centre in 1967 included the blocking of Grove Road at the Selby Road end and the making of a cul-de-sac.
At the south end of the rows was a large house standing at right angles to the street. The north section was a three storey building with three houses, the street end house having a side door: numbered 34-38. On the south side of the building was the two storey Grove House (40) home of the Cookson family: Hilda Cookson daughter of Edward Cookson was born in

1903 was married to Harold Winpenny on April 18th 1927. In the 1930's Grove House was the home of Alfred Leach whose son Kenneth died aged 2 in August 1931; followed by Charles Robinson and Edward Winter. The whole building was subject to a compulsory purchase order and demolished c1970 being replaced in recent years.
The detached house at 42 Grove Road with an open view of the fields and bowling green is Grove Lea. The first mention of the plot of land was in May 1866 when the land was acquired from Hugo Charles Meynell Ingram by Joseph Groves of Halton then living at Aberford. In March 1885 Joseph Groves sold the land: agreed on August 18th 1885 to Joseph Smith and John Henry Robinson. Three years later these two owners sold to William Verity of Wyke Beck Farm Halton Hill. In 1929 William Verity had Grove Lea built for his family by Dunhill's Builders although his premature death prevented the family from moving in. Planning permission for the new house was granted on May 15th 1928. The house remained Verity property until 1962 having been passed to William in 1931 and his son William Edward Verity of Hollinthorpe Farm Swillington in 1951. Grove Lea was let to Leonard Arthur and Constance Rout by 1930, Crawford and Gladys Bryson and then was the home of Albert & Edwina Rex from 1938 to 1962. Grove Lea was bought from the Verity family by Major Jack Kenneth & Joyce Nixon on November 1st 1962. It was sold again on December 24th 1964 to Stephen & Christine Frazer who ran a children's nursery. On August 31st 1966 Grove Lea was sold to the present family.

East side

Some of the early residents were: 3 Brentwood: Wilfred Henry (drysalter) & Edith Corless. 5 Nanthorpe: Frederick & Doris Corless: he was also a drysalter. Fred Corless died aged 52 in 1954 having been a partner in grocers Wilfred Henry Corless. The firm of drysalters were based at 21a St Matthew's Street Holbeck. Geoffrey Corless was their son born in 1927 who married Jean Mary Buckley of Templegate on September 15th 1951; 7 Roydene Alfred Parker and George Woodcock.; 9 Kencliffe: *Ernest & Ethel Morris* with Clifford and Muriel: Ernest was a Halton chemist on Chapel Street.
11 Dorothy Dene: Polly Cuthbert; 15 Belvedere: Edwin & Elizabeth Stead and in 1933 Charles & Polly Hayes; James Brooksbank & *Ald Major Joseph Brooksbank.*
23 The Rowans: draper Reynolds & Elsie Steel whose daughter Mary became the second wife of Ronald Wheater of the Barkston Ash Laundry. *Reynolds Steel* was the Vice Chairman of Hunslet Rural District Council and was involved with the complex negotiations in 1925-28 involving the absorbtion of Halton into Leeds. In 1927 he was a member of the Hunslet RDC Finance Committee together with Reggie Knight, TH

Killingbeck, W Schofield and clerk to the council Walter Pindar.
27 Dungeven *Ronald & Mary Wheater:* Dorothy Wheater died in 1940 and Ronald was married in April 1942 to Mary Steel. She was the daughter of Captain and Mrs Reynolds S Steel and for a few years was a teacher at Victoria Primary School on York Road. Mary's uncle Ald EW Steel was a Mayor of Harrogate. Ronald Wheater had retired from being the manager of Barkston Ash Laundry.
33 Firdale: builder William & Emma Dunhill; William & Mary Sleight with their sons Peter and Malcolm. Firdale became a hostel for folk with learning disabilities in 1993: they had been moved from Hillcrest House Harehills. The home is a part of the East Leeds Supportive Living Scheme and has five beds. Hillcrest was originally for ladies with nervous troubles and marital difficulties in the late 1960's. In 1975 it became a home for adults with learning difficulties and in 1993 it was closed and the 36 adults were dispersed to homes including Grove Road and Seacroft.
35 Fairholme: Stanley and Joyce Stocks with sons Stephen and David. In 1928 Fred Stocks set up a block making business on sites at Easy Road and later on York Road. Increased production of the breeze blocks for building was handled at a new site on Thorpe Lane Robin Hood. In 1952 the Stourton site was acquired and a move was made in 1963 to Ninelands Lane at Garforth. Stocks Bros (Buildings) was founded in 1955 by Stanley Stocks making precast garages for homes; it developed into building car showrooms and then churches in the 1970's. Stocks Bros celebrated their golden jubilee in 1988.
37 Mayfield:Walter George Lappage: his daughter Heather married Robert Matthewson on January 8th 1983; son Martin married Helen Battley on July 12th 1986 and daughter Amanda married Jonathan Stocks son of builder Stanley Stocks.
39 Lyndhurst: built by Joseph & William Dunhill in 1925 and first occupied by Harry Whillance & Louise Sedgwick; in 1928 the house was with Ernest Lawson Crump; Ronald & Sarah Mary Cowell/Royal National Pension Fund for Nurses.
43: Newlands Tom and Vi Marsden; Tom Marsden died aged 58 in April 1931 and his wife Vi died aged 76 in May 1965. Mark & Dorothy Marsden: their son Michael Peter was christened at Whitkirk Church on October 16th 1955.
45 Sundown *Charles Percy & Hilda Price*: Charles was a well known Leeds photographer. He had a studio at 24 New Briggate and was known as simply "Charles". Charles Price was born in 1893 and married Hilda Fryer from the Irwin Arms Inn on June 12th 1923; his father was Charles Price who was a gardener living at Springwood Cottage Rawdon.
55 *Arthur Brining* celebrated his Golden Wedding in October 1953 having been married at Bourne Chapel in October 1903; he retired in

1945 having worked for Jowett & Sowry for 26 years; he and his wife were both 75 years old in 1953. *Barbara Wilks* who was born in 1929 married Arnold David Morritt the son of builder David Morritt of Austhorpe on October 24th 1953.
57 Rowark *Frederick & Alice (nee Rawling) Park* were married on December 26th 1901 at Roundhay Road Chapel.
59 *Gertrude & Harry Bray*: Bray's building firm was originally Park & Bray as her father helped his daughter in the building firm. Gertrude & Harry Bray moved to The Manor House Colton Road and afterwards lived at West Burton.

HALTON DISTRICT CENTRE

In 1962 the Buchanan report included the advice for a shopping centre at Halton. These plans involved the replacement of the Halton Institute with a new Community Centre, the opening out of Temple Court onto Grove Road and some demolition of property. There were plans in 1969/72 for a Halton Neighbourhood Centre which would include a clinic and a radical realignment of the main road. In December 1972 the plans for the Centre were shelved following a public inquiry in 1967 when the scheme was labelled as a "white elephant".
The Centre occupies a large tract of land which had been compulsorily purchased: Fryer's Yard, Shaw's Yard, Graveley Square, Milestone Yard, Dial Terrace and Dial Row were all cleared. The plans included the bowling green at the rear of the Traveller's public house.
The Centre was a £1 million development by architects Peter Kilmartin & Partners and contractors Rush & Tompkins of Pudsey for Moorfield Estates plc. In September 1980 plans were approved for the new Centre with a supermarket, 15 shop units, library, clinic and a car park for 250. Building started in February 1987 and was finished in November of that year. The first shop was opened in September 1987 and all the shops were let by that month including the chemist's shop. The 3 mile stone was resited ten feet from the original position after removal: this was completed by Peter Kilmartin & Partners. The new library was opened on Monday August 10th 1987 by Lord Mayor Doreen Wood. All the shop units were let by February 1988: a few of the shops included in the Centre have been Cinema 625, Wright's Vantage Chemists now Halton Pharmacy, B Harrison Florist and the Halifax Building Society; this became a cobbler's shop and is now Godson's Travel.
String's Diner was opened in the Centre in 1983 which was bought by Adrian Massarella in 1987: his uncle was in the ice cream trade. In 1998 Max Jones bought the business and now Maxwell's is a popular Halton restaurant serving the finest Italian and European dishes.
The Co-op Super C Store was opened on October 27th 1987 with a fuel

station opened in 1995. Following the abandoned plans by Morrisons Supermarkets, SuperC closed in 2000 and was structurally altered. Matalan opened on the Co-op site on October 19th 2001 with the Co-op Halton Village Store having opened in the old Netto/Grandways building on High Street on March 10th 2001.

Matalan plc was founded in 1985 by John Hargreaves who was the son of a Liverpool docker. Following a visit to the USA he opened the first Matalan Discount Club in Preston and by 1995 there were 50 stores. There were 163 stores in April 2003 with over 9 million members. Hargreaves was Chairman of Matalan with Angus Monro appointed as Chief Executive in 1996: he resigned in April 2001 to become the head of Leeds based Brown & Jackson (Poundstretcher). The business moved to their new headquarters at Skelmersdale in 1997 and in July 2001 Matalan bought the Lee Cooper Group and Paul Mason was appointed the new Chief Executive in August 2001. He left the company in March 2003 and John King became the new MD.

HALTON DIAL AND HALTON HILL

Halton Hill started at the Wyke Beck and ended at Rock Terrace. On June 26th 1934 all sections of the road from Halton Dial became known as Selby Road.

The Leeds/Selby Turnpike Trust was formed in 1740/41 in the hope of increasing the business between the two centres. Tolls were collected at a cottage which operated as a weigh house for both wood and coal. The cottage was later converted into a shop when tolls were lifted in 1874 and it was demolished in 1929. The bar house (Dial House) was run by John

Barber (1849), George Jordan (1850) who died aged 61 in May 1851, James & Ann Adams (1852), Samuel Thorp (1861), William Dancer (1871), John West (1881) and the Waite family.
Thomas and Elizabeth Waite had daughters Mary born in 1851, Ellen in 1845 and Elizabeth in 1847; Thomas was a labourer from Osmondthorpe. Thomas Waite was born in 1863 and wife Virginia with their three children ran the weigh house shop. Their son John and wife Emma ran the business by 1878 and they had two sons. Edward born in 1901 was killed with an accident at the factory where he worked aged 15; his brother John Edwin Waite (Jack) who was born on October 17th 1902 was the last shopkeeper before demolition. His son John was born in 1897 and he married Hilda Bulmer on December 1st 1920. His father had started Weigh House Garage on York Road in 1929 on the corner of Gipton Approach. In 1928 Leeds City Council bought the old weigh house following negotiations which started in 1926 and 390 square yards of land from John Edwin Waite for £1875.
The trams used the route of the original York Road by the side of Wild Wild West, once the City Lights public house until May 8th 1933 when the tracks crossed the filled in Killingbeck Pond. The realignment also meant the removal of the Killingbeck Motor Co run by the Waite family: in 1924 they successfully applied for a licence to erect a petrol pump and a storage tank for 300 gallons.
A Dial or dyal refers to a new turnpike which originally climbed Halton Hill on an unmade road often made into a worse condition by the many cartloads of coal using the road. Garside's Killingbeck Colliery paid an annual fee to the Trust whereas Gascoigne's Garforth collieries had free passage (Sir Edward Gascoigne was one of the trustees) until 1750. The Leeds-Selby railway opened on September 22nd 1834 and there was a short lived railway station at Halton Dial on Saturdays which was closed in 1864.
The land required for a new sub station measured 625 square yards and was bought at a rate of eight shillings per square yard. Construction started on a tramway booster station at Halton Dial erected by Paul Rhodes at a cost of £2187 in December 1931 and the building was opened on March 31st 1932. When the tramway system in Leeds was closed down in November 1959 the building was used as a storage depot for the Highways Lighting department. In 1987 when the Loveday family bought the site from Leeds Corporation, there was conversion to a public house called The City Lights and in 1991 the Weigh House restaurant was opened. The public house was closed and after a short while re-opened as a children's activity centre known as Wild Wild West in February 2000.
The reconstruction of the traffic routes at Halton Dial was started in September 1972 with further alterations in later years: the road was

resurfaced and signed in late 2003. The present traffic lights system and a one way road under the mid-19th century bridge dates from 1991-92. The trams at first had a double track through the railway bridge and then became a single track ascending Halton Hill with a double track from Willow Well Farm. Trams terminated at the Chapel Street/High Street junction on April 30th 1915 and this was moved to behind the Irwin Arms public house on November 8th 1936. This was made possible with the completion of the Halton Hill dual carriageway and the trams used a reserved track in the centre by July 1936. The scheme announced in 1935 cost £32,000 and the road was widened from 45 feet to 100 feet across; the carriageways were 25 feet in width and the trams used a 23 feet wide reserved track. The tram service ceased in November 1959 and by September 1963 the reserved carriageway up Halton Hill was grassed over and landscaped. The old lines were revealed again when the East Leeds Elite Bus Initiative guided bus route was being completed in late 2000.

North side

There was a large reservoir on the land after the railway bridge used for water stored from Wyke Beck. This reservoir was used from c1859 and the water was pumped up the hill by a water wheel to a large circular reservoir at The Crescent. This fed water to the water tower which was demolished about 1921 and replaced with a bungalow. The tower ensured there was a head of water to be distributed to Temple Newsam House and later to houses in Halton.

Whitebridge Mill used water from Killingbeck Pond north of the railway and was run by James Berkenhout of Dutch descent and Thomas Clark from 1779. *"Parliament had granted them £5000 on the condition that they would make known to the public their newly discovered method of dyeing linen and cotton cloth in scarlet, crimson and other variegated colours. The secret was attempted to be divulged but no hues could ever be produced like the specimens which in all probability were the effect of accident rather than skill."* The business made bunting for ships using one of the first power looms in England and it is said that Queen Victoria saw a flag made by the Halton firm while she was inspecting the fleet and asked for more to be made. Unfortunately the firm could not make the exact colours and the contract was lost; it was here that the first Union Flag was made in one piece. By 1822 Peter Clark was making bunting and green gauze for window blinds. In 1838 Whitebridge Mill and bunting works were run by Peter & Thomas Clark who were the sons of Peter Clark who died on January 23rd 1851 aged 75. Son Thomas died in 1845 aged 45 and Peter died on April 14th 1865 aged 67: the firm finished trading in 1857. In 1850 land on Trinity Street in Leeds was conveyed by Peter Clark. By 1859 the mill was converted into two dwellings and later demolished. The area of the reservoir and Whitebridge Mill and farm is now occupied by housing, Crossway Parade, Wykebeck Recovery Services and the Wykebeck public house. Killingbeck Colliery and associated housing dated from the early 19th century and was closed down in 1887. The spoilheaps from the workings were landscaped as part of a public recreation area known as Halton Dene.

It was Dunhill Brothers who bought 16 acres of land for £1500 in 1933 to build their new estate: they had their Bridge Works adjacent to the pawnbroker Herbert Brown. The Dunhill estate took two years to build and Dunhill Rise/ Crescent was completed by 1934/35: Crossway Hall was opened in 1937 together with the row of shops on the parade. Facilities included a library, confectioners and a dance hall with manager Arthur Jagger. The Hall was later altered to become flat accommodation. William Dunhill received Council approval for a music and dancing licence in the ballroom at Crossway Hall in December 1937.

The shops on the parade were: 43 Selby Road Tobacconist Arthur Jagger. This became a confectioners. 45 Jacob Goldberg hair dresser and later Crossways Hair Saloon; later Hair Express: the flats above date from 1993. 47 RJ & A Field drapers. This became Box Car Audio for a short period. 49 Sharp's Chemists: now Richard Gordon. 51 Ernest Almond greengrocers, later Ada Almond. Almond's lived at Primrose Valley Farm and Harry Almond's daughter Pearl Mary Almond was born in 1926 and she married Harry Teale on April 1st 1950. The younger son Wilfred Almond was born in 1934 and he married Shirley Balmforth in January 1958. The Selby Road shop became the Tan Express and Pretty Panache.

53 William Herbert Newsam butcher, later Fred Hardy and Denis Mapplebeck. The shop was converted into a flat. 55 Herbert Brown: Herbert Brown's business started in 1840 with the present main Leeds

office now on Eastgate. The Selby Road shop opened in 1937 and closed in 1961 being sold to a betting shop. *John Brown was born in 1793 in Hull and soon came to live in Leeds widening his outfitter's business to become a pawnbroker. His son Charles Hood Brown joined his father in the business and soon changed to become a jeweller and pawnbroker with shops by 1870 on Burley Road and Christopher Street. Charles son was Herbert Brown born in 1863 and he had eight children. Herbert was a Leeds alderman and stood against TW Stamford (Labour) as the Liberal candidate for Leeds West in the 1924 General Election: Stamford was elected. His youngest brother was also Herbert born in 1909 and his son was Colin who was born in 1936 joined the firm in 1953. Colin is the present chairman of Herbert Brown Ltd who is assisted by four of his five sons.* The shop was closed by 1983 with plans for a building society but it was converted into flats.

Whitebeck or Wykebeck Farm was built in c1820 near the mill and one of the first tenants of the estate farm was William Scott. The tenants following the Scotts were Joshua Kershaw and his wife Elizabeth. This became Miles and son William Verity's Farm with part of the old farmhouse and stables being used today as the premises of Wykebeck Recovery Services. Wykebeck Farm Cottages were also part of the farm site by the Wyke Beck and were once the home of the Stubbs family. In the 1950's Wykebeck Farm Cottage was the home of John W and Dorothy Blades who ran the filling station which was extended with new workshops in 1975. The business closed with plans for a recovery centre passed in August 1986. The Wykebeck Arms public house was opened on April 21st 1939 on the site of Whitebridge Mill. The licence had been transferred from The Greyhound Inn on the corner of Bath Street and York Road.

On the north side of Halton Hill beyond Wyke Beck was open land to Willow Well Farm, except for the four blocks of three houses. William Avenue, William View (Back William Avenue to 1933) and Lucy Avenue which date from 1903/05: this was known as the Halton Hill Estate built by George Morritt. He also had plans for a brush factory near the site of his housing although this was never completed. The seven semi-detached houses on William View were completed in 1934 with the road made in 1936; William and Lucy were the children of George Morritt. There is a gated road from Lucy Avenue which was once the access to the Halton Dean tip: it is now a public footpath to the recreation land once the site of the sewage works. The fish & chip shop was altered from a house in 1933 and the newsagent for many years was Thomas Sleightholme who lived on Harehills Lane: the shop is now Shokar Newsagents. Thomas Sleightholme first had 105 and 107 Selby Road but by 1942 occupied three shops: he applied for permission to build a house and shop on the Halton Moor Estate (York & Selby Road Housing Estate) in December

1928.
Willow Well Farm was the large white building on the corner of Willow Well Road. The land of Willow Well Farm and up the slope to Morritt

Drive was sold by the Temple Newsam estate to John William Morkill who died in 1881. An indenture dated 1883 includes the lands: farmhouse and outhouses, Low Croft, Old Heads, The Dean, Garden Field and Tuftlands or Tuftings.
At the end of Willow Well Road is the old Sewerage House: used by the supervisor until the sewage works closed in 1928. The caretaker by the end of the association with the works was Robert Adamson who died aged 71 on July 3rd 1929. The house is now called Willow Dene.
The horse drinking trough on Halton Hill was repaired by Hunslet RDC in 1909, when they also "*improved the Halton Hill causeway*".
St Wilfrid's Church was built on land belonging to the Temple Newsam estate and was consecrated on May 13th 1939.
The detached houses beyond Willow Well Road include 159 Ashlea and 161 Selby Road which Jim Windsor built for the family in 1936.
Jim Windsor was born at Kirkstall in 1897, educated at St Simon's School, fought in the Great War with the Royal Engineers and opened his own greengrocery on Kirkstall Road/Somerby Street by 1927. This small shop at the bottom of Hollis Street also served as a betting office and he had another place between North Hall Street and Angel Street (Alphabet streets). The North Hall entrance was for boxing and wrestling and Angel Street was the club known as The Stadium. He became a millionaire running the Commercial Club on Vicar Lane and selling his empire to Sears (Sir Charles Clore) for £3 million in 1972. Jim Windsor lived on Halton Hill from 1936 until 1946 when the house was bought by dentist William Denison Wood. Jim and Elizabeth Windsor moved to Broomhill Crescent and later West Park Crescent. His last dwelling was Cherry Dene on Wigton Lane Leeds 17. Jim Windsor died on December 21st 1984 aged 87.

The housing to the top of Halton Hill is 19th century and early 20th century development including the White House 171 Selby Road: now The David Latto Studio. David Latto started his business in the old Hardisty's bookshop on York Road Seacroft in 1963. He moved to Dodd's drapers shop on the corner of Woodman Street and Chapel Street Halton in 1971 keeping the Seacroft shop until 1975. David Latto moved from Chapel Street to Selby Road in February 1984 and added a purpose built studio in 1986. The White House was named by David Latto, although when it was in the hands of the Johnson and Goodhind families it was known as Sycamores or Sycamore House. In later years a market garden was run from the property.

The White House dates from 1841 and a document states: *"This copy of Frankpledge with Court Leet of our Sovereign Lady the Queen and Court Baron of Lady William Gordon Lady of the said manor held there for the said manor the third day of May 1841 before Michael Scholefield Steward. Be it remembered at this court it is witnessed by surrender John Atkinson of Austhorpe Lodge and his wife Naomi Rose Atkinson and Joseph Atkinson of Halton manufacturing chemist in consideration of the sum of 49 pounds, 19 shillings to them paid by George Briggs of Halton Bricklayer. That*

piece or parcel of land there staked out and containing by admeasurement one rood more or less situate in Halton and part and parcel of a close there surrendered and bounded by land there belonging to Lady Gordon on the north and west by the turnpike road on the south and by the said Slack Bank Close on the east and was then in the occupation of George Briggs together with the rights, liberties, privileges and appurtences......to the use and behoof of the said George Briggs his heirs and assigns for ever by rents and services according to the custom of the said manor upon which to this court came the said George Briggs and prayed to be admitted tenant to the said copyhold premises so surrendered to whom the lady of the Manor by her said steward hath granted and hereby grants admittance to have and to hold to him and his heirs for ever. By copy of Court Roll at the will of the Lady according to the custom of the said manor by the ancient rents and services therefore due and of right accustomed and he gave to the Lady for a fine (£1) for his admittance and having done his fealty is thereupon admitted tenant."

175 Selby Road was known as The Grange and was built in 1842 for chemist Benjamin Robinson having made an agreement for Slack Bank Close with Joseph Atkinson of Austhorpe Lodge. In 1868 Robinson left for Seacroft and the house was tenanted by draper John Sword of Brunswick Terrace. In February 1878 Mrs Meynell Ingram sold the land and house to John Sword for £140. In 1892 the house was the home of George Shaw and three years later was with butcher Ben Goodall. In

1920 Robert Morris had The Grange: he died in 1927. By 1946 the house was with the housekeeper Clara Livesley who had been willed the property but she sold to Joseph Fella, whose home it was between 1946 and 1962; it was also where Joseph Fell's Ice Cream was manufactured. The product was made in the old stables until 1962 when the property was sold. Prior to 1946 Joseph Fella had his factory at 36 Hill Street Leeds 9 and lived at Lincoln View.

Temple View is a row of five houses (177-185 Selby Road) built in two stages. The end block of two houses was built in 1899 on the site of the demolished Copperas works which existed in the early and mid 19th century. Copperas is the sulphate of copper and iron and the firm was run by Joshua Barnard c1830; during development several old glass bottles were discovered. The centre house was built a few years later. There are several wells at the rear of Temple View with one on the lane covered with bricks which shows a distinct dip: the wells were filled in and covered in recent years. Among the early residents were butcher Henry Charles Frame at 177 and shoe repairer Herbert Greenfield (179) who had a shop in the village.

South Side

Selby Avenue received a facelift costing £167,000 in 1974 to include the closing of the junction with the main road, a pedestrian area and parking scheme for the shops and the Co-op Wykebeck Village Store. Prior to the alteration of the 1931 store there was a Co-op butchers and general store as well as a Gallon's shop. In the early 1930's the parade on the other side of Selby Avenue included FW White, who had another shop on Halton High Street, butcher Bob Diggins, Habershaw's newsagents now Better Buy Provisions, Delaney confectioners, William Jowitt & John Martin fish & chips later Edith Hazelwood and Mary Boyes greengrocery. In later years they included Wykebeck Fisheries (Mr Phung Chinese take-away) and Launderama (AT Boxing).

The Selby Road and York Road Estate was built from December 1926 when plans for 800 houses were passed by the LCC and the notice to terminate tenancies on the required land was issued. In September 1927 houses, streets by D Speight & Sons and sewers were planned and a sanction was made for the LCC to borrow £58,000 for the housing on the new estate: street names were also approved. A Council minute indicates that 396 houses were to be built on Halton Moor from June 1936. The Halton Moor estate further developed in 1936 when 1236 houses and flats were built: the plans also included 12 shops and a doctor's house. In June 1939 the 20,000th municipal dwelling was opened on Coronation Parade. Builder Paul Rhodes was involved in the completion of many of the council houses: he was also concerned with the development of Brianside at Seacroft. WJ & R Turnbull were also builders concerned

with house building in 1927/28.
On the Halton Moor council estate is Corpus Christi Church: the first mass was said on December 24th 1932. A church was opened on May 27th 1937 which caught fire in September 1950. The new church was opened in January 1960. The Trustees of Mount St Mary's Church planned to build a new school in 1932. Corpus Christi School opened in 1935 and a new senior school opened in September 1968.
Wyke Beck has origins as Great Heads Beck and flows through Roundhay Park. Wyke Beck forms Waterloo Lake and flows beneath Easterly Road and Foundry Lane to Killingbeck Bridge. The beck flows under the railway embankment and Selby Road on the way to join the River Aire near Skelton and the site of Thorp Stapleton Hall. The main road bridge was widened by F Whittaker at a cost of £3710 and the road up Halton Hill was also widened which entailed much earth removal by the same firm. The works were sanctioned in Council on June 12th 1934 with a 60% grant from the Ministry of Transport. The works for the widening of the bridge and main road were in progress in June 1935.
White Beck Farm was on the east of Wyke Beck on the estate side: originally the site of Joseph Atkinson's Oil of Vitriol, Aqua Fortis, Dyer's Spirits and Epsom Salts Works in the 19th century: the firm was listed in 1822. In 1830 Thomas Phillips of Wade Lane was running the chemical firm. A new farm was built on this part of the Temple Newsam estate and was run by George Taylor who died aged 73 in April 1914. In 1919 the Elam family took over the farm having moved from Broomhill Farm near the old Shaftesbury Cinema. The Elams had already farmed from Osmondthorpe Farm on the site of the Co-op (now Dyron's Motorcycles) and Rowley Grange Farm Scarcroft.
Sutton Park on the south side of Halton Hill was started by Sutton Housing Trust in October 1932 "*in a field near the tram stop on Halton Hill*". The Trust was founded under the will of William Richard Sutton of London (1836-1900). When he died he left most of his fortune to found a

charitable trust providing low rent housing in London and other cities. In 1922 negotiations were started with Lord Halifax to buy 20 acres including the White Bridge Farm Estate but a lengthy delay meant purchase was not until 1931, despite plans being finalised in 1924. Architects Chorley Gribbon & Foggett (Harry Sutton Chorley) and builders William Thomson were concerned with this new estate of 265 houses, which was handed over to the trust in 1934. Planning permission was granted in May 1932 for the building of 46 semi-detached, 8 semi-detached flats, 132 through houses and 84 through flats. Collin Hall was opened in 1934 on Oak Road overlooking the estate. It was a brick built centre with stage used for a variety of shows, large kitchen, billiard room and committee rooms. Collin Hall was last used in 1999 and the Sutton Park Estate Office and Community Centre was opened in January 2000. The bowling green once stood by the new Centre and the site is now a children's playground and a landscaped garden financed by Frank Haslam Milan Co Ltd: it was opened on June 1st 2002.

Halton Hill was altered in 1923 to create the present Temple Newsam Road link thus making access to the newly opened public park easier for cars and trams. The road was at first called Temple Newsam New Road and part of the intended Halton By Pass Road. In late 1926 the LCC paid £200 to the Trustees of Robert Shaw of Pickering Lodge for land required for the new road and later 2072 square yards adjoining the route were also purchased. At this period the Halton tram terminus was at Chapel Street junction by the Institute, changing to the stand by the Irwin Arms on Templenewsam Road in 1936. The road up Halton Hill was made into a dual carriageway in 1936-38 as well as doubling the tram lines in a central reservation.

The triangle of open land at the junction of Selby Road (Halton Hill) and Templenewsam Road was a public park and administered in 1937 by the Parks, Allotments and Cemeteries Committee. There was a council agreement to turf and plant trees at a cost of £30 a year. A Park & Ride area on land adjoining the Irwin Arms public house was approved in August 2001 as part of the Unitary Development Plan proposals.

The retaining wall on the south side at Portage Avenue on The Crescent Estate was built by Dunhill Bros in 1933 at the same time that the Council had obtained land from the builders to widen Temple Newsam Road: there was a stone step access through this wall up the slope to the street.

HEALTH SERVICES IN EAST LEEDS

The *East Leeds Primary Care Trust* holds the budget for the local population of 146,000. The Trust has 26 General Practitioners, 25 dentists, 15 opticians and 36 pharmacists serving the area. There are five One Stop Centres at Garforth, Halton Moor, South/North Seacroft and

Osmondthorpe. There are also seven Health Centres and Clinics in East Leeds at Burmantofts, Halton, Harehills Lane, Garforth, Kippax, Seacroft and Swillington.

HIGH STREET

High Street Halton ran from Rock Terrace to Field End and in 1891 was called Town Street

North Side

There was a row of ten terrace cottages between Rock Terrace and the corner of Primrose Lane. There was a ginnel to the yards between the end of the row and the corner shop.

2 High Street became 201 Selby Road in the mid-1930's when renumbering took place. This was the home of plumber Nathan Hoyle and wife Fanny with William Henry, Mary Alice, William Andrew and George Henry. The Hoyle family were long time residents of the village: William Hoyle was a shoemaker who lived with his wife Hannah and John Hoyle was a plumber and glazier by 1830. Samuel Hoyle was born in 1822 and was a plumber: he and his wife Sarah had children Elizabeth (1852), Nathan & Eleanor (1859), George & Harriett (1860), Mary Jane (1862) and Luke Arthur 1864). William Hoyle died aged 63 on March 9th 1895 and his wife Rebecca died aged 40 in October 1871. Nathan Hoyle died in April 1929 and William Henry died aged 53 in March 1930.

6 John Towler Jones who was a coal merchant; 10 High Street was the home of George & Hannah Cowell with son Ronald who married Agnes Bonsall: they first lived with her parents. Hannah Cowell died at the house in 1959.

8 Ernest Johnson was born in 1888 and he lived in the cottage from 1928 with his family having Halton connection over two centuries. When the cottages were demolished the retired postal assistant inspector was

rehoused: the Council advised either a new house on Field End Road or on the Council estates at Swarcliffe or Whinmoor. Ernest's wife Clara died in the 1960's.

16 Charles Henry was the son of William born in 1806 and Ann Dunbar born in 1817: his brothers were Thomas, James, Charles, Henry, John and William; his sister was Elizabeth born in 1854 in Ambler's Fold Halton. William Henry Dunbar was born in 1885 as the son of machine shop labourer Charles Henry born in 1860 and Ann Elizabeth born in the same year as her husband: they lived on Cross Street. William's wife was Hannah (1886-1942). William Henry's brother was George born in 1893 and his sister was Mildred born in 1881. William Henry's son was Jack Dunbar who ran an off licence for only a few years in the shop on Cross Green Lane, which later became Bennett's shop. His father worked as a manager for FW White & Co on Selby Road near the Chapel Street junction. The other children were Janet who married and moved to Surrey,Stella married and lives in Halton and Arthur worked for the Co-op, joined the RAF and remained in the services until he died.

18 High Street was the home of James Edward Monkman (1896-1981) who was a confection salesman and ventriloquist: his brother William Parker Monkman died in April 1941 and was buried at Whitkirk Cemetery. Their parents were dressmaker Rose Annie Cawkwell-Monkman (1866-1941) and mining deputy Charles Edward Monkman. Charles was born at Hunslet in 1862 and was a porter at Barkston Ash Laundry; the family lived at Springfield Place. Rose's father James Reasbeck lived with his daughter at Halton for a time: he was born in 1827. On her husband's death Rose Annie lived in the almshouses on School Lane until she died in April 1941.The houses from 211 to 217 Selby

Road were set at an angle and the size of their small front gardens therefore varied in area.
20 High Street was the corner shop on Primrose Lane (219 Selby Road) and was run by Albert & Mary Elizabeth Scarfe as Primrose Cash Store by 1912. The shop was run by Thomas and Alice Maria Bonsall from 1930 to 1948: their daughter Agnes was born in 1907 and married Ronald Cowell on December 26th 1929: they lived with her parents at the shop for a few years before moving to Verity View. The shop was later run by Reginald & Winifred Cliff, Wilfred & Ida Pickering, Philip H & Edith Burhouse (1950's), Joseph & Olga Banner but with the nearby houses was demolished and became the site for the new Halton Clinic opened in May 1984.
The junction of Primrose Lane and the High Street was widened with traffic lights controlling the traffic. The proposal to widen this junction was suggested in 1952.
Halton Parade was built on one of the sites for Halton Feast and the area had been purchased from the Temple Newsam estate by Joseph Albert Bonner. In 1928 he conveyed 1080 square yards of his land to the Council for the widening of the High Street by the Irwin Arms. Joseph Bonner opened a hairdresser's shop in 1928 and by 1932 he had moved to Ebberton Selby Road Austhorpe. By 1938 this hairdresser turned builder had moved away from the area; he also had land on Hollyshaw Lane and on Harrogate Road. Building was started on the four shops and four shops/houses in 1929 with planning permission granted on July 17th 1928. The first shop was occupied in June 1929 and renumbering took effect in 1935. The first six businesses in 1928 were JA Bonner, Walter Eastwood, Francis Horsfall, Crockatt's Cleaners, Alec Martin and Minnie Cronk. The four house/shops and four shops in between were originally with walled gardens to the rear which were compulsorily purchased for the development of Halton Centre.
219a Selby Road/1 Primrose Lane. Kenneth Campbell Patterson plumber/ironmonger in 1937 a registered plumber & sanitary engineer, hardware, crockery and glassware; Monica's hair salon; Janet Macdonell/Janet Fraser hair salon, Jim Windsor bookmakers (at the rear) and William Hill bookmakers from 1992.
William Hill was born in Birmingham in 1903 and in 1920 opened a bookmakers; in 1934 he opened the first off track betting parlour for credit based bets. In 1939 the business was incorporated as William Hill (Park Lane) Ltd. In 1961 cash betting was legalised and William Hill died in 1971 and the firm was bought by Sears and in 1988 was acquired for £330 million by Grand Metropolitan. In 1989 Brent Walker acquired William Hill for £845 million and in 1997 the Japanese bank Nomura acquired the company for £700 million. In 1999 Nomura sold the business to CVC/Cinven for £825 million and in 2002 William Hill

went public with a value of £1 billion.

221/1 The Parade Hairdresser JA Bonner; Ladies fashion Christopher Charles Hayes, Mary Marker, Charles Roberts (1937), John P Vamplew radio shop (1955), Anne's Baby Shop which was closed by 1971, Two in One fashions and Tenbao Chinese Take Away and Restaurant opened November 2003.

223 Harry's Wedgwood Hygienic hair saloon opened June 1929, Joseph Ramsden, Mrs B Philips hair, Kathleen Walton hair, Anne's Baby Shop, Tenbao Restaurant.

225 John Glover hair, Emily Harker, Umpleby hair, William Bradshaw electrical who also had a shop at Lincoln Green Shopping Precinct, Midland Bank (1963-83), GR Askham traded from here in 1986 after the division of the Bank premises into two shops, Pizza take away (1990), Tenbao take away & restaurant.

227 Hopkinson's grocers, Eric Cook grocers, Midland Bank, Windows Centre, Cellar 5 wines and spirits, Tenbao Chinese takeaway. The restaurant was opened on November 1st 2003.

229 John Newhouse grocers, Eric Cook grocers, SW Kilburn grocer, Ladles, Kemp's store. ES Ladle self service became the mini-supermarket of Spencer & Cole. By 1970 this was Montgomery's off licence and in 1972 was with D & E Kemp.

231 Francis & Mary Horsfall confectioner/newsagent, Halton Video Club, Lees hair saloon.

233 Syd & John William Eastwood electrical: Syd & Alice lived at The Oval Seacroft, John W Eastwood lived at Seacroft Garage, Lavinia Monley hair, Crockatts dry cleaners, DorBo Chinese takeaway.

235 Crockatts dry cleaners, DorBo takeaway. The DorBo Chinese Takeaway was opened by FL Tse in 1972.

John Crockatt was a shipmaster of Tayport who married Anne Campbell in 1847. Their son John (1852-1927) joined Leeds based William Watson in 1873 and moved to Bradford and London. In 1875 he started his dyer and cleaners shop in Carlton Hill Leeds and opened a shop on Commercial Street. In 1910 Crockatt's works were on Stoney Rock Lane and in 1935 the firm merged with the Johnson Group of Dyers and Cleaners.

237 David & Mabel Wood, Alec Martin, Jack Smith greengrocer/fruiterer, Parade Fruit Stores, WH Wilson fruit, Kim's discount shop, Rudge's greengrocery; Halton Spice take away opened in December 2003.

239 The shop and house were also 6 The Parade and 9 Ingram Avenue. Bertram Lewis John & Minnie Cronk bakers, Ernest Rudge & Son and the present Upper Crust. In 1930 Bertram Cronk owned the bakery and they moved to live on Gledhow Avenue by 1939 and after his death his wife Minnie and Doreen ran the business. Minnie Cronk sold to Ernest Rudge in late 1943. *Ernest Reuben Rudge* was born on October 6th 1905 as the son of Thomas & Florence Rudge. Thomas worked at Carlton Colliery Barnsley: he died on January 3rd 1944 aged 64 at his house on William View - he formerly worshipped at Clark Lane Methodist Church. Ernest married Lottie in 1932 at Old Mill Chapel Barnsley. There were three children: John Barrie, Margaret and Rosemary Brenda. Ernest had shops at Stratford Terrace, Dewsbury Road and Kitson Street. His other properties on William View and 33 & 85 Selby Road (Halton Hill) were sold to pay for the new shop on The Parade where he lived with the family. During the war years Ernest was excused from call up being in a supply industry and he supplied bread to the Mount St Mary's Girls Orphanage at 3/6d a dozen loaves. When Ernest retired from the business in 1971 he passed the bakery to his son *John Barrie Rudge* and his sister Margaret Bowhill; he married Joyce Heesom on Easter Monday 1956. Ernest Rudge died on June 14th 2003 and there was a thanksgiving service held on Sunday June 22nd at Christ Church Halton: he lived on Selby Road. Barrie and Joyce Rudge retired from the bakery and sold the business after 60 years in the family to the Dunwell family of Upper Crust, to whom they sold the Pendas Way shop in May 2002 which they acquired in 1989. The shop changed hands on September 1st 2003. Sarah Dunwell lived in Cross Gates from 1978 having a career in customer service and

Ernest Rudge

retail management. Sarah runs the shop together with her mother Pat Meineck.
One of the first businesses on High Street following the site of The Parade was Alfred Baron's drapers shop: the family were to develop their mattress firm on Cross Green Lane based at Thorp House. The length of the main road from Engine Lane (Irwin Approach) to Chapel Street was paved in 1900, after many complaints about the poor quality of the road surface.
There were four small yards/squares with a group of 19th century brick built housing: Shaw's Yard (241 Selby Road), Fryer's Yard (243 Selby Road) demolished 1969, Milestone Yard (259 Selby Road) and Dawson Square (261 Selby Road) where the houses were demolished in 1968. Milestone Yard was demolished in the same year being named from the 3 mile stone by the main road.
In 1930 ***Shaw's Yard*** residents were Fred Collins, John Cundall, George Rollinson, Arthur Wadkin and John Wraith. In 1939 Shaw's Yard residents were Fred Collins, William Crawley, Clara Knighton and George Rollinson. Fred Collins died aged 71 in April 1942: he had been the manager at the Malvern Cinema. The Malvern was opened in 1912 and closed in 1971and was on Beeston Road Beeston Hill. Fred's wife Ada Collins died in December 1943. George Rollinson died aged 79 in 1943: he had been a hay and straw dealer and one of the village's oldest residents. In 1954 there were Albert Ashton, William Crawley, Harry Eden and Bernard Jordan; in 1965 there were Gaynor Glover, Walter Haines, Frank McNulty and Eileen Murphy.
In 1930 ***Fryer's Yard*** residents were William Briggs, Naomi Dacre, Sarah Dalby, Martha Kershaw, Florence McWilliams and Clara Tate. At one period one of the corner houses was used as a boarding school. In 1939 there were Ernest Dacre, Eva Marriott, George Payne, Mary Sharp and Clara Tate. In 1954 there were Ernest Dacre, Henrietta Hemsworth, Eva Marriott, Alec Staton and Clara Tate. By 1965 there were residents Raymond Chapman, John Greener, Ernest Hayton, Lilian Hodgson, George Kerr, Alfred Lester, Eric Marrows and Ronald Shaw. In November 1922 five houses on Fryer's Yard together with 24/26 High Street were sold by V Stanley Walker.
In 1930 residents of ***Milestone Yard*** were William Bowers, Walter Briggs, George Bulmer, Hugh Butler, Herbert Butler, Clarence & Agnes Catlow, Dorothy Cooke, George Henry Dodsworth and David Hall. Clarence Catlow and George Henry Dodsworth lived at 7 Milestone Yard and were village chimney sweeps. In 1954 there were James Keith and Doris Clark at 1 Milestone Yard: the parents of golfer Howard Clark who was born here; by 1965 only Mary Sykes remained. ***Dawson Square*** in 1930 had Sarah Barber, William Briggs, Arthur Dobson, George Mosby and Maurice Sunter. In 1954 Dawson Square had William Briggs, Eveline

Emery and Arthur Dobson.
The LICS butchers and grocers included stables and a dairy behind the shops: the shop opened in 1899. William Sunderland was one of the first managers; Fred Anderton was the manager of the Halton Co-op for 20 years who died in November 1933 aged 55 at his home on Overdale Terrace. The Co-op applied for permission to build four adjacent cottages to their new store but these were refused by the Hunslet RDC in 1900.
Joseph & Ellen Connell's grocery shop at 32 High Street was adjacent to the Co-op store: they had followed fruiterers Herbert & Emily Marshall and greengrocers William & Florence Broadhead. This shop was the scene of a tragic accident in 1932 when three children of the Connell family died as the result of a fierce fire. The shop remained empty for a few years until taken by William Street in 1938. At the time of the fire the property was owned by Joe's parents John and Elizabeth Connell.
34 High Street was Killerby's grocers at the end of the row before the Traveller's public house. Richard Killerby (1855-1931) opened his shop in 1877. John Killerby was one of his sons: he died aged 53 in 1945. The other children were Frederick William, George (1884), Beatrice (1886), Frank (1889) and Alfred Ernest (1896-1931) who played for Halton CC and
working for the clothiers Campbell Stewart McDonald and John Killerby. George & Edith Killerby's son was Albert Edward who died aged 21 in April 1932: he worked at Montague Burton's factory and played for Halton CC. Albert Edward Killerby died in April 1932 and George Killerby died in February 1956.

The Travellers public house was followed on the High Street by houses and by Rose Terrace. In an old cottage behind the public house was born Horace Sunter in 1875; he later lived at White Horse Farm and worked at Low Moor. He was a scorer for Halton Cricket Club and a Sunday School teacher at Halton Methodist Church. Horace had a family of four children, nine grandchildren and three great grandchildren.

There were three cottages set back from the road which were once the homes of the Smart family and Charles Palmer at 42 High Street. Charles Palmer (1848-1926) married Mary Ann Thompson of Halton (1851-1921): their children were Charles (1878), Ernest (1882), Morritt (1887) and George (1889). Charles worked as a domestic gardener at Beech Cottage Chapel Street for the Crosthwaite family. When Mary Palmer died Mary Spedding came to live with Charles as a companion until his death in 1926. His son Charles moved to live on Chapel Street by 1914 where he opened an outfitter's shop.

The first shop was Harold & Lily Bower's fish & chip shop altered in 1925; in 1936 Harry Bowers was living at 35 Chapel Street. Next door was butcher Charlie Frame. Henry Frame of Graveleythorpe Terrace was born in 1840 at Trowbridge and was a sergeant major with the Corps of Commissionaires. Henry's children were Henry Charles (Charlie) born at Windsor Berkshire in 1880, William Edward born at Hampstead in 1881: he was a tailor's cutter, Emily born at Windsor in 1883, George (1884), Helloise born at Sudbury in 1886 and Richard born at Camberwell in 1888.

The three shops were built in a row opposite Gilsyke House from October 1921. Charles Henry Frame's first shop was opened in 1900 at Field End when he was 20 years old: he married Marion in 1904. In December 1901 HC Frame had plans passed for a stable to be converted into a slaughterhouse in Pinfold Square. Charles died aged 60 on November 19th 1939 and Marion had died aged 28 on August 5th 1905. Their son Henry Charles Frame was baptised in September 1905, continued the business and lived at 177 Selby Road and on Morritt Drive: he married May Claughton on August 23rd 1930.

Their daughter was Ann born in 1935 who married Gordon Brookes at Whitkirk Church on February 5th 1958. Gerry Taylor worked for Charlie Frame from 1943 to 1963. The business was continued by Anthony & Joan O'Connor as Tony's Butchers until closure. This site became Halton Library replacing the original library opened on September 21st 1960.
The cycle shop was run by John Philips Vamplew: he was born in 1913 and he married Hilda Monks (born 1914) on June 29th 1940. JP Vamplew's father was book stall manager Harry English Vamplew and the family residence was at The Hawthorne Baronsmead. His eldest son was Harry English Vamplew born in 1912 when his father lived at Hounslow Middlesex: he married Naomi Isobel Brett on June 24th 1940. John Vamplew was running two shops in 1949: on the Parade and on the High Street.
The sandstone pillar once with painted black letters is set against the library wall and was once by the roadside being rescued by the developers of the Centre. This mid-18th century structure was inscribed Selby 17 miles/Leeds 3 miles and was measured from Leeds Parish Church ending at Gowthorpe Selby. The inscription was once on a metal plate and was later inscribed onto the stone itself: taken off in 1940 for security purposes.
There was a row of four houses known as Rose Terrace to the junction with Chapel Street. 44 High Street was 1 Rose Terrace and the home of Arnold and Doris Bedford who altered the house into a shop in 1935. Arnold was born in 1892 as the son of farmer David Bedford and he married 25 year old farmer's daughter Doris Bywater Heaps on February 2nd 1921: Arnold Bedford was an architect & surveyor. Doris's parents were Alfred Bywater Heaps and Hannah Heaps born in 1866; he was the Conservative Party agent for North Leeds and when he retired in 1927 had served for 47 years. He died aged 68 in 1928 when he was living at this house. Their children were Percival born in 1888, Frederick born in

1889 and Doris Bywater Heaps. The shop was later run by William H and Gertrude Bedford baker and later AW Scott.

46 High Street/2 Rose Terrace/269 Selby Road was the home of electrician Frederick (born 1870) & Paulina (nee Green) Battershill; their son was milk dealer William Albert Battershill (July 1894-May 1944) who married Dorothy Sarah Barr on June 7th 1922: she was the daughter of farmer Harry Barr. Paulina died aged 78 in May 1946 and William Albert died aged 49 in May 1944.

48 High Street/3 Rose Terrace/271 Selby Road was the home of the Goldthorpe family. Thomas Goldthorpe (1853-1936) worked down the pits and his children were Edith (1875), Polly (1877-1941), Sarah (1879), Louisa (1881), Robert (1883) and Lily (1887).

50 High Street/4 Rose Terrace/273 Selby Road was once William Pogson's surgery and the home of medical student Frederick William Pogson in 1891 and then it was taken by undertaker/joiner Tom & Sarah Shaw. Thomas Shaw (1850-1921) was a wheelwright and wife Sarah was born in Hunslet in 1851; having lived in Halton for more than 50 years she died in 1938 aged 87. They had three daughters Elizabeth, Ivy and Emily and sons Mark and Tom who was born in 1892. The business was founded in 1877 with a workshop in the old Banty Cock Hall in Graveley Square. The son Tommy Shaw moved to Rose Cottage by Woodman Street: his parent's house was converted into the shop of FW White grocers, later Alice's Flower Box run by Alice Fletcher. This shop was first suggested as a site for Gallon's Grocers who were to open at 2 Cross Green Lane. The offices and warehouse of FW White were at 6 Procter's Place Meanwood Road. Frederick William White started as a drysalter and the Leeds Vinegar Co in 1915 at 25 Meadow Lane. He lived at West Park Place and had opened 8 shops by 1940 including the Halton shop becoming a general grocer. FW White ceased trading in 1964 when their headquarters were at Oldfield Lane. This row of four High Street shops was the subject of much local concern after they became an eyesore in the mid-1970's.

The corner of Chapel Street/High Street is the Halton Institute with the foundation stone laid in January 1904. Rose Cottage was once the home of mining deputy Joseph Hewitt with his wife Elizabeth until it was bought by Tommy Shaw who was assisted by local carpenter Harry Cowell. Tommy Shaw's daughter Sadie was born in 1932 and she married Jack Beverley of Morritt Drive on January 5th 1952. Tom Shaw died aged 92 on November 12th 1984 and his wife Emily died aged 62 on June 14th 1962. Tom Shaw Funeral Directors was bought from Tommy Shaw's executors by Barry Jennings from Allerton Bywater in 1984 and a year later it was sold to House of Fraser; Jennings built the Chapel of Rest and lived at Rose Cottage. In 1985 House of Fraser bought Dodgson's Funeral Service established in 1842 and extended the name to the Jennings business in Halton. Dodgson's Funeral Service was started by joiner and undertaker William Dodgson who worked from a shop on Shannon Street. John Dodgson took over the firm and when he died in 1938 sons William and Lindley Dodgson (1885-1953) took over the running of the business. They moved to Cowper Grove where there was a Chapel of Rest. The firm was joined by William's son William Dodgson and in 1956 his son Martin joined the firm. They moved to Lupton Avenue and William Dodgson died in 1971. Martin Dodgson was the National President of the British Institute of Embalmers and left the firm in 1985. The Co-operative Wholesale Society bought "Dodgson's Funeral Service" in 1988 and it is now part of CWS and CRS Funeral Care based in Manchester with over 580 businesses under the banner. Wm Dodgson & Son is a trading style of the Co-operative Group (CWS) Ltd. Dodgson's Funeral Service have other branches at Harrogate Road, High Street Kippax and Middleton Park Circus.

Woodman Street has two of Halton's oldest buildings. The Woodman public house was originally built with stabling for the increasing turnpike traffic in the late 18th century. Woodman Row included two small shops as an integral part of the extended inn building. The residents in 1901 were grocer John Ballance, bricklayer John Walton and Charlotte Ibberson with her daughter Hannah who worked at the jam factory. In 1928 the shops were those of Horace Fell later A Dodgson plumber and Ezra and James William Rawling's sweet shop and in more recent years Halton Service Centre.

South Side

The old Irwin Arms which was demolished in 1936 stood adjacent to the later building which was built on the site of the bowling green. The inn had its own bowling team for many years and after the Great War was used by the Harehills Harriers as a changing room. There were two cottages with walled gardens attached to the two storey public house: the end one was a slightly higher elevation. The cottages were the home of the Taylor family and centenarian Harry Taylor was born there in 1888. The cottages were the home of chimney sweep George Henry Dodsworth (1848-1930) and Frank Dodsworth died aged 81 in May 1945. George Henry & Martha Dodsworth at first lived in Milestone Yard and their stepson was Alfred Catlow. Alfred and Sophia Catlow of 8 Milestone Yard had a daughter Connie in October 1913. Clarence Catlow who was their grandson lived at Woodland Road: he was born in September 1895 to mother Eliza Catlow of Milestone Yard. Holdsworth & Son were at Irwin Arms Cottages by 1938. Clarence Catlow's daughter was Joyce who was born in 1927 and married Thomas Marshall in March 1948. Clarence Catlow died in Leeds General Infirmary in March 1966 and his wife Agnes died aged 57 at their home on Woodland Road in January 1955.

Another member of the Dodsworth family was Charles Dodsworth who was a chimney sweep living at the junction of the Selby Road and the road to Kippax: still known as Charlie Sweep's Corner.

Halton police station was opened adjacent to the Irwin Arms in 1953 and was closed in 1965 and later was demolished.

Thrift Stores opened as a new building in July 1964; the founder of the Thrift was Wright Popplewell who lived on Pinfold Lane. On the closure of the Thrift in 1974 the building became the House of Holland. This was a general merchant retailer with shops at Kirkgate and 97 Vicar Lane: the Halton store closed by 1985. The store was converted into shop units which included Bedworld, Pizza Hut and Joyceramics. *Pizza Hut was founded in 1958 by Dan & Frank Carney in Wichita Kansas and entered the UK in 1973. The business merged with Pepsi Co Inc in 1977 and in 1986 the 5000th outlet opened in Dallas.* The Bedworld unit was converted into a dance studio by Nicola Hallard: the Northern Theatre Dance Studio founded in 1993 was opened in August 2003.

Park View Farm was a rented farm from the Temple Newsam estate on what is now a row of shops/flats on Irwin Approach (Engine Lane/Halton Moor Road). This was run by Henry & Ann Stevenson and demolished in 1954. Stevenson's farm occupied part of the low building and the Taylor family lived in the section towards Todd's garage from 1938 to 1947; the family previously lived at 24 Grove Road. Arnold Weber Taylor (1890-1942) and Eva (Edwards) Taylor had 10 children: Muriel (1915-80), William (1918-28), Eric, Brian (1923-84), Gerry, Tony (1928-79), Betty, John, David and Patricia.

Billy Byrne Taylor was killed on Wednesday June 20th 1928 after a six feet high wall guarding the Primary School on Selby Road fell on him. He had been watching a game of tug of war where the rope was tied around the end of the 20 year old wall. The wall suddenly collapsed at the base but when help arrived Billy Taylor was dead: an inquest the following day gave the verdict as "death by misadventure". A few days prior to his death 10 year old Billy had won first prize in the fancy dress section at

Halton Feast.
This area was also the site of Halton Colliery, Halton mortuary and a coal depot run by Arnold Bedford: his office was on Chapel Street and he lived in Colton.
The present building of dental surgery/solicitors was built on the site of a surgery of Dr William Harold Bean who died 1976: the practice was Drs Bean, Shires & Moody. Dr EL Brittain was Dr Bean's partner in the 1930's and 1940's. The surgery house was once the home of the David Crawley later Doris Wilson and John Pearce. The old surgery house was demolished in 1991 and a new building by Peter Rider's Barwick Developments was completed. On December 14th 1992 the lower floor became the dental surgery of Peter Rider who had transferred from Dial House on Chapel Street. Peter Rider left the dental business in 1995 to concentrate on Barwick Developments: it is still the Halton Dental Clinic. Grahame Stowe Bateson family solicitors own the building with their offices on the upper floor. They bought the property in June 1998 and transferred from the shop unit on Irwin Approach.
Troy Garages was opened in 1976 on the site of the garage run by Edwin & Son George Dennis Todd and later Frank Martin. The house where the Todd family lived for many years was demolished in early 1980 together with the old garage.
On the corner of Grove Road was the Halton smithy with Colton born blacksmith Samuel Joseph Townend born 1867 and his wife Annie born 1866. There was also the smithy's detached house adjacent to the workshop: in 1901 Samuel & Annie Townend lived here with their children Amy, Cliff, Violet & Stella. Annie was the daughter of David Speight and she died in January 1941 aged 76. Their daughter Amy Speight Townend was married to Herbert Skinn in January 1943 and moved to live in the bungalow built on the site of the Whitkirk Water Tower. Their daughter Stella married WH Dixon of Grove Road. The High Street house was the home of Dr David Kidd from 1955 to 1959 who had come to Halton from Moor Allerton.
Gilsyke House had a large walled garden, vegetable gardens, stables and garages and was built in 1800 as a farmhouse for the estate. The house was demolished for redevelopment in 1966 as a row of shops. The first store was opened as Grandways Store (owned by William Jackson) and became a Netto Store in 1990. The present Halton Village Co-op Store was opened in November 2001 having transferred from the Halton Centre store, which was later opened as Matalan.
184 Frying Machine fried fish & chip shop; 186 The original number for Gilsyke House: the unit was a betting office and a frozen food shop from 1981; 188 Rules Resaurant followed by Café Bengal; 190/192 Oddy's Hair Studio and Lady Intrim Beauty; 194 Dawson's Travel, Directours; 196 Halton Discounts and Naturel in 2002; 198 Leeds & Holbeck Building

Society opening in 1976; PSB Hi-Fi, 200 Launderette, Peter's Dry Cleaners; 202 Sheppard's newsagents run by David Sheppard until 1989: he died in 1991; 204 Top Girl Fashions and Halton Carpet Centre prior to their move to Chapel Street; 206 Thurston's Bakery later Gregg's Bakers: *Thurston's Bakers are based in Bramley while parent company Greggs are based in Newcastle on Tyne.The businesses adopted Greggs in 1998:there were 98 shops in 1998 and by 2003 there were 1200 Greggs and Bakers Oven shops;* 208 Deacon's Butchers; 210 Bloom's Chemists and now Moss Chemists who were the first occupiers of the new row of shops. Plans were placed by NMH Estates Ltd in 2003-04 to demolish the row and to replace it with 14 new shops and 24 two/three bedroom flats.

Rose Villa or Roseville was once the home of George Henry Botterill,son of Matthew Bradbury (Botterill). He married Lizzie Palmer and ran the clothing shop on Chapel Street which he built in 1914.

There were plans for a village public convenience in March 1887 although there was no action. Complaints in 1914 that the village did not have a public urinal led to one being built in iron for £94 by Walter MacFarlane Co in 1921 and was erected by Mason & Co for a sum of £52. This green painted structure had four stalls and a roof.

Springfield Place was adjacent to Gilsyke House drive and once was the site for Roseville Café and Confectioners run by Edward Monks (1885-1943) and Clara Rollinson. The shop was converted into a house and shop for JA Rollinson in 1915 with a bakehouse added the following year. The café hosted occasionally wedding receptions: there was also a tennis court in the area. The stables in Rollinson's Yard were used by Arnold Bedford and as another workshop for joiner Tom Shaw. In 1935 the shop at Springfield Place (192 Selby Road) became George Greenfield's shoe repairing business and after his death in October 1960

aged 71, the house was demolished having been condemned in April 1958. During this work a deep brick lined well was discovered near the shop front entrance. George Rollinson died in August 1943 in Shaw's Yard: he had spent his whole life in Halton as a hay and straw dealer. Springfield Place where John Rollinson lived was demolished in 1966 and is now Gilsyke Surgery and Halton Village Co-op Store. The passage between the chemist shop and the Co-op store was once the driveway to Gilsyke House.
Temple Motors and Bulk Builders Merchants are on the site of Carroll's Holly House Farm. The farmhouse was opposite the end of Woodman Street and was once a haulage business run by Nicholls & Pickersgill of Chapel Street. Holly House stood on land once tenanted by William Dunwell and became the home and haulage/petrol station run by the Carroll family. It was Charles Carroll who started at Holly House and he was followed by his son John William Carroll and his wife Beatrice Annie Carroll. Their daughter was Catherine Carroll who married David Godson of Sandbed Lane Cross Gates. John William died on March 28th 1962 aged 64 and Beatrice died aged 85 on January 16th 1981. The farmhouse was demolished in 1983.
East of Holly House Farm was Gilsyke Farm run by Miles Verity until he retired from farming due to ill health. There was a row of six cottages (206-216 Selby Road) and in the 1930's the occupiers were John Guest, Reg Thomas/John Rollinson (208); Albert Johnson/Harry Butcher (210); Benjamin Walker/James Walker Clark (212); Holdsworth/Barber (214) and GW Fenwick/Hudson (216). The site became a bungalow which stands adjacent to the St John Catholic Centre. This Centre was opened by the Bishop of Leeds on December 22nd 1969: the site had been the property of the RC Diocese from 1967.

INSTITUTE

Prior to the opening of the present Halton Institute in 1904 there was in existence the Albert Edward Institute. The Institute was founded following the visit of the Prince of Wales on Tuesday May 18th 1868. There was a Cricket Club formed which played at the Halton Gala. The Institute met in the Infants Schoolroom during winter from 7pm to 9.30pm when newspapers were available for reading. There were chess and draughts available and a library of 150 books brought from Whitkirk was available on Monday evenings. The Institute provided entertainment for the villagers in the schoolroom and there are many records between 1869 and 1904 of the use of this facility. In January 1904 the Institute was reported to be full of members every night and there were visits by lecturers including some from Leeds University.
The site of the Halton Institute was the orchard to Dial House and this

was given to build a new Institute by Mrs Meynell Ingram of Temple Newsam. The architect's drawings were available in September 1903 and were passed by Hunslet RDC on November 4th 1903. In June of that year a Grand Bazaar was held at Temple Newsam Park in aid of the new Institute; the event was opened by Mrs Meynell Ingram who gave some money for the building. The foundation stone was laid by Mrs George Lane Fox of Bramham Park on January 21st 1904. Mrs Lane Fox was the Hon Mary Agnes Emily Wood daughter of Charles Wood 2nd Viscount Halifax; she married George Lane Fox who was created Lord Bingley in 1933: he died in 1947. The architect for the Halton Institute was Sydney Kitson with the building cost being £1323. The Institute was officially opened by Sir James Kitson and the first president was Rev Gerald Sharpe Vicar of Whitkirk who became Archbishop of New Guinea and later Archbishop of Brisbane: he was vicar from June 1898 until February 1910. The other holders of positions at the new Institute included Vice Presidents James H Pickles, A White, F Whitfield; Treasurer H Stott; Secretary JW Thompson.

The Institute was opened with a sale of work and entertainment and the first members were enrolled on Friday September 23rd 1904 and included W Frame, Thomas Piercy, J Speight, H Killerby, Dr Frederick Pogson, Edwin Todd, Dr W Bean, Joseph Owrid, R & T Graveley,GO Bell, Dr Bertram Baskett and George Botterill. The trustees in 1928/29 were Lord Irwin, Rev Walter Warburton, JH Pickles, GO Bell, Vernon Schofield and the Hon Secretary was CE Sykes. By October 1906 there were 170 members enrolled who were required to be men over 16 years of age paying 6 shillings a year membership. There were two billiard tables available at two pence a game. The caretaker at the Institute was William

Oare who died aged 57 in February 1930: he had worked there for 20 years. A minute occurred in the Board of Directors records of meetings of the LICS during 1930 when JH Pickles applied to the Board for a donation for Halton Institute: it was turned down. Application to serve alcohol was granted by Lord Halifax in 1975 and the Halton & District Institute became the Chapel Street Social Club in 1977. The Club has had long associations with sporting activities. The Institute had a cricket team until wartime and a football team until 2001: the first season was in 1953 in the Red Triangle League. The Institute billiards team once played in the Riley Cup. Today the Social Club sponsor the Bowling Club meeting in Halton Deans and have teams for fishing, pigeon racing, darts and dominoes.

IRWIN APPROACH

This was originally the route of Halton Moor Road/Engine Lane through the farmlands of the Stevenson family of Park View Farm. The last mention of this farm was in 1954. The land to the rear of Park View Farm was the site of Halton Colliery with a map of 1771 showing an engine on this site: the road became Engine Lane. It is probable that it was Newcomen style atmospheric pumping engine designed by John Smeaton of Austhorpe Lodge. In 1775 it was reported that two pits were working and a third being sunk. To the rear of the present parade of shops the area was once cobbled and there was a chimney stack, perhaps being part of an old boiler house.

The second site for Halton Colliery was to the south of New Templegate which was operated by Arnold Bedford who had an office on Chapel Street and later lived at Colton; Bedford's coal yard was to the rear of Park View Farm. The small yard on the left of Temple Court included the business of joiner and undertaker Reg Kilburn, Oxley's decorators, plumber A Dodgson and shoe repairer Joseph Cunningham. Edward Oxley was a Halton decorator and his sons were Arthur who married Evelyn Bowman on July 11th 1923 and Edward born in 1902 and married to Jessie Hemingway on March 14th 1928. The family lived for many years on Morritt Drive.

The road was re-routed in 1936 to become a direct link with Halton Hill which had been made into a dual carriageway and to accommodate the new houses on Temple Newsam Road and Oak Crescent. To the rear of the Irwin Arms were the public conveniences opened in 1960, demolished in 1998 and nearby was a short row of cottages which was compulsorily purchased in c1962.

The businesses on Irwin Approach built by Norman Ashton: 1 IR Bloom chemist until 1973 when they moved to be nearer the surgery on Grandways Parade. Susan's Hair Fashions have been the business since the chemist moved, although there was a change in ownership. 3 Hobson's DIY Store have been the sole business since the shop was built with the family once living in the flat above. John Henry Hobson started his business at 4a Easy Road as a joiner on Nelson's Yard; his son Rodney opened in Halton in 1962. 5 N Hemingway sweet shop followed by Rite Price newsagents. Rite Price was bought by accountant Paul Millard in 2000. 7 Fitzpatrick Florists until 1970 when they moved to Compton Road; Don Giles menswear and later George G. Recent years has seen Lasertronics occupying the shop which closed in 2003. 9 William Bradshaw TV and electrical transferred from Halton Parade followed by Carousel Ladies Fashions. Trevor & Gerald Nabarro opened the Abbey National Estate Agency: it was officially opened on November 10th 1983 by the Lady Mayoress Vivienne Dodgson. The shop was also an agency for the Building Society. This was followed by Stainton's Estate Agency founded by David Stainton who opened in 1988. They closed the branch in March 1997 and moved to Ralph Batty's outfitters shop on Austhorpe Road Cross Gates. The business merged with Manning & Co in April 2000 to become Manning-Stainton. The Little Gem Café followed the occupancy of the estate agencies in 1997. 11 This unit opened as Smith's decorators and became Purdy's Quality Fruiterers and Fire & Brimstone selling wrought ironwork and fireplaces. 15 A baker's shop was followed by a Launderette and then opticians Hick & Webster. 17 Don Bullock shoe repairer and later Grahame Stowe Bateson family solicitors. Grahame Stowe Bateson was formed in 1981 and now has three senior partners: Grahame Stowe, Marilyn Stowe and Arthur Bateson. The firm opened on Irwin Approach in 1982 and closed in 1998. The shop has been converted into flats by Trant Construction in 2003 who extended the row in 2003 making a total of six flats.

JONES FAMILY

Milton Jones was a motor mechanic who ran the Chapel Street garage next to the Parochial Hall. The Jones family ran the garage on Church Lane in Cross Gates: the garage became Smart & Batty. In 1924 Milton Jones applied to run a bus service from Scholes to Leeds: the application was later withdrawn. In 1924 Milton Jones was advertising the hire of high class landaulettes.

The Jones family came from Carnarvon in Wales with Ebenezer born 1814 and his wife Catherine born 1812. Their children were Richard born 1841, Margaret born 1843, Ebenezer (1855-1926), Griffith born 1843, Anne born 1853 and Robert born 1855.

Ebenezer Jones married Mary Jane Howarth from Saddleworth in 1878 and their children were Seeva (1880-1948) and Milton Jones born in Saddleworth in 1882. Milton married Frances Anne Boddy from Pickering at Seaton Carew in October 1907 and their children were Roy

(1910-1980) who married Winifred Crowther of Templegate (1908-1986) in 1930; Edwin (1907-1988) who married Eva Ellen Thomas (1908-96) in 1933 at Halton Congregational Church and lived on Templegate; Sydney (1912-90) who married Gladys Williams of Ackworth in 1935 and lived on Templestowe Drive.

Roy and Winifred's children were Beryl who married Tony Cooling in 1965, Jennifer who married Anthony Mullins in 1964 and Barbara who married Graham Kerridge in 1966.

At the turn of the 20th century Ebenezer & Mary Jane and family were living at Ashfield Terrace Cross Gates and when Milton Jones married in 1907 he moved to live at Belle Vue Cottages. He worked as a grocer's assistant at the Co-op shop on Austhorpe Road where he became manager. Ebenezer with wife and daughter moved to Rose Cottage Shadwell and then moved away to Hull. Milton moved to live on Sandbed Lane and on South View in Cross Gates: he joined the Royal Flying Corps during the Great War. When he came back home they moved to 4 Church Lane where he was a cycle dealer in 1920. The business involved second hand cars, taxis and cycles and when the new garage on the opposite side of the road was completed in 1926 the business expanded becoming a dealer for Ford and Fordson. Milton became a garage proprietor while his wife ran the cycle business; the business had several small lorries and a warehouse in Hull. The poorly designed engines proved a disaster and the business was sold and the family moved to Halton. The family lived at Engadine 3 Pinfold Lane and Milton Jones ran the garage on Chapel Street. The business was based on

Roy and Winifred Jones wedding:
father Milton Jones is on the far left and his wife Frances Anne is next but one.

coal which the lorries picked up from the sidings for delivery and they also ran a domestic coal delivery service. Two of the lorries were driven by his brothers Edwin and Sydney: Roy set up Precision Motors on Joseph Street Hunslet. The business was proving hard to run and the family moved out of Engadine to live at 57 Chapel Street which was one of a short row of small cottages adjacent to the garage.

During the Second World War the family did much to help the local community and the war effort. There were cake bakes for the family, a knitting circle and many whist drives. Milton's health deteriorated and he died on April 6th 1960 aged 77 from heart failure and bronchitis. His wife moved to a flat on Field End and died in hospital on March 10th 1974 from heart failure.

In 1964 Thomas Curry Chapman followed at the garage: he was a haulage contractor who lived at 13 Sycamore Avenue and on Woodland Hill and at first worked from home. The demolition of the garage followed the occupancy of SJB & RJB cranes and steel erectors in the early 1990's. The site is now Chapel Court with housing from 1994.

KNIGHTS TEMPLARS

The Knights Templars were the Poor Knights of Christ and of the Temple of Solomon and received the gift of the Manor of Whitkirk which included all of Halton. In later times landholders of previous Templar lands marked their property with a Templar Cross to signify their exemption from grinding their corn at the manorial corn mill in Swinegate. There are two of these crosses on houses at Whitkirk and also displayed on the Halton Templars scouts headquarters on Chapel Street which were added to the barn in the 1930's. The Knights Templars had their origin in the Crusades which were wars undertaken between 1096 and 1291 to recover the Holy Land from the Moslems. The pilgrims on the road to Palestine were protected by the Templars which was an order instituted in 1118/19. The Templars had their home in Jerusalem on the east side of the Temple given by King Baldwin II of Jerusalem: members of the order were divided into Knights, Squires and Servitors and all the classes had their characters of piety and courage. In 1146 the Pope allowed the Knights Templars to wear a red cross on their white cloaks as a symbol of martyrdom to which they were being constantly exposed. The first Templar house was founded in 1128 and to raise money for their work they established preceptories. In England their centre was at The Temple London, where their round church survives. A preceptory was established at Neuhusum in 1155 by William de Villiers who gave the Manor together with Whitkirk Church to the Templars; the order had about 50 preceptories in Britain. Their preceptory near the river was archaeologically investigated in 1989 but was destroyed by opencasting at the Skelton site in 1991-92. In 1308 King Philip IV of France with papal authority suppressed the order. The Templars were abolished in England by 1312 although their estates had been confiscated in 1308; their lands were taken by the Knights Hospitallers.

LAND OWNERSHIP IN HALTON

Halton was part of the Temple Newsam estate and remained with this estate until parcels of land were sold to various owners which were to include Leeds City Council. On the death of Mrs Meynell Ingram in 1904 the estate was inherited through her will by her nephew Edward Frederick Lindley Wood who became the 3rd Viscount Halifax on the death of his father in 1934. The Halifax family continued the sale of the Halton lands until the mid-20th century.

The map of Halton drawn in 1834 shows the fields and their owners manyof whom were leasing the area from the estate. The principal people concerned with the Halton area were:

Joseph Atkinson who ran a chemical factory on Halton Hill:he died aged 55 in 1842.

The Graveley family who lived at Hawthorn House on Chapel Street and who were closely involved with the development of the village. The map indicates that there were three members of the Graveley family of Halton with land in the village. They were the four sons of Thomas Matthews Graveley (1766-1817): Christopher Graveley (1794-1855) who was an attorney; Thomas Matthews Graveley (1796-1860) who married Maria Cowlam (1801-69), John Graveley (1798-1865) who married Maria Torrans (1825-1901) and William Graveley (1798-1862) who married Harriet Farrer.

Leeds Grammar School or Leeds Free School whose lands were reviewed in 1837 and included rents from their estates totalling £1595 invested with the Committee of Pious Uses together with an income in reserve of £2000. The real estates consisted of 91 acres of land at Halton, Nether Green, Sheepscar and Wike. This was together with a number of shops, houses and warehouses let to 44 tenants in Call Lane, Vicar Lane, The Bank, Holbeck and Marsh Lane. The land and buildings in Halton and Marsh Lane were partly left by Lawrence Rawson between 1597 and 1603. The Halton lands included those south of Cross Green Lane including Wilfred Avenue, north of the lane in the region of Whitkirk View, part of Primrose Valley, part of the Soldier's Field now Temple Moor School and the lands on which were completed Clapham Dene Road and Hermon Road.

Rev William Lindley was the curate at Whitkirk from 1817 to 1843; he married Anne Graveley (1800-25) one of the two daughters of Thomas Matthews Graveley.

The Marchioness of Hertford who lived at Temple Newsam mansion and was the principal owner of the land which passed down through the family. Lady Hertford inherited the estate on the death of her mother Frances Gibson widow of Charles 9th Viscount Irwin in 1807. Lady Hertford had married Frances 2nd Marquis of Hertford in 1776 and owned Temple Newsam until her death in 1834. The estate was inherited by her younger sister Frances Ingram Shepheard who married Lord William Gordon.

Thomas Morkill who lived at Austhorpe Lodge and whose family were owners of the lands for many years. The Morkill family moved to Newfield Hall in Malhamdale.

Rev Charles Musgrave (1792-1875) who held the glebe land as vicar of Whitkirk from 1821 to 1837.

Thomas Phillips who ran a chemical factory at White Bridge and lived on Wade Lane Leeds: he died aged 52 in 1857.

Michael Scholefield who was the steward of the Manor of Temple Newsam and lived at the Manor House on Colton Road. The north chancel wall at Whitkirk Church has a memorial: he died aged 80 on May 17th 1842 and was buried on the south side of the church with his wife Elizabeth.

William Swift whose family were long time Halton residents and who were concerned with farming and running the butcher's shop in the village. The map indicates that he had bought the land from Thomas Matthews Graveley.

LIBRARIES

There was a library with 450 books available to parishioners of Whitkirk Church opened in the Old Reading Room during 1866. Books were available for public use in the Albert Edward Institute at the Infants Schoolroom. There was a library in the Halton Institute opened in 1904 and a few books were retained at George Greenfield's shoe repairers at Springfield Place and the Mission Chapel. The first purpose built public library opened on High Street adjacent to the Travellers on Tuesday September 20th 1960 by Lord Mayor of Leeds Coun Lillian Hammond. The new library building had cost £4200 and held 8000 books with Eileen Pratt of Garforth and Christine Glover of Pudsey as the librarians. It was the 32nd branch library to be opened in Leeds and as Coun Mrs Gertrude Bray said at the opening *"The new library is welcomed by all Halton residents"*. The chairman of the Libraries Committee Ald Arthur Adamson was also present at this official opening; in the first three weeks there were 900 members.

The present ***Halton Library*** was opened by Lord Mayor of Leeds Doreen Wood on August 10th 1987. Those attending included the Lady

Mayoress Mrs Sheila Staveley (Doreen Wood's daughter) and David Edelman the Director of Moorfield estates. The meeting room was opened on April 23rd 1997 by Councillor Lee Benson and author Frances Anne Bond

LISTED BUILDINGS IN HALTON

The listing of building of architectural and historic interest started in 1947 with the Town & Planning Act. There are nearly 400,000 listed buildings of which over 90% are Grade II. Grade II* are particularly important buildings of more than special interest.

There are three listed buildings in the village: Dial House Chapel Street dates from 1720 and was Listed Grade II on October 19th 1951. The listing states: *"Dated 1755. Flemish bond, stone dressing, stone slate roof. Moulded stone eaves cornice forming eaves gutter. Rusticated stone groins, three storeys, three bays. Central doorway with stone shoulders, architrave and pediment. Window of simple Venetian type on each side of doorway. Smaller windows above them. On first floor flanking a round arched window over doorway with moulded architrave, impost blocks and keystone. On second floor are three plain rectangular windows. All sashs, only second floor with glazing bars. Rebuilt brick end stacks."*

St Wilfrid's Church was consecrated in May 1939 and was Listed Grade II* on March 9th 1981. The listing states: *"Anglican church by A Randall Wells. Coursed thin gritstone rubble, flat roof of asbestos cement covered originally with Permanite. Timber tower and spire, shingle cladding. Plan: three bay nave and very narrow low aisle, crossing with polygonal tower and spire, transept, chancel and round apse. Exterior: Windows show early English Gothic influence in the groups of* *five straight sided pointed lancets in a relieving arch of stones set on edge and flush with wall face; side windows have large rectangular glazed panel centre. Aisles blind, apse has small pointed window on north and south sides. Single storey vestry and porch in re-entrant angles of nave, transepts and choir, plain mullioned windows. Timber tower gabled on each face, spire has louvred bell openings. Interior: Expressionist-style massive plastered quoined vaults rise from window sill level, square section piers support aisles, shallow pointed arches, round arched recesses between walls. Doors, choir stalls, screens of Columbian Pine, turned wood screens to lectern and pulpit, chairs of Ash. Original flooring was of rubber on asphalt, heated by gas boilers, hot water battery and electric fan, indirect electric lighting. Cost of structure was £11,700 excluding fees; furniture and fittings £800 including chairs. Seating was for 402 with 34 in choir".*

Temple Newsam-Halton Primary School Selby Road was Listed Grade II on August 5th 1976. The listing states: *"School dated 1842. Dressed stone slate roof. Single storey eight bays. End bays project left end with coped gable. Off centre a steep gable slightly projects with large ornate barge boards and datestone, stone bellcote over gable with square wooden bell turret behind. All stone mullioned windows some with drip moulds. Two large stone mullion-transom windows rise through eaves with hipped roofs. Three small buttresses at front. Stone chimney stacks".*

LOCAL GOVERNMENT FOR HALTON

Halton was in the Barkston Ash Division of the Skyrack Wapentake and part of the Township of Temple Newsam which was a part of the medieval Manor of Temple Newsam. Temple Newsam Township in the Parish of Whitkirk comprised Colton, Halton, Newsam Green, Osmondthorpe, Temple Thorp and Whitkirk. In 1894 the old Township of Temple Newsam was divided into two Townships of Temple Newsam and Osmondthorpe. The Temple Newsam Township in 1922 covered 3092 acres with a population in the 1911 census of 3346, compared to 1728 in 1871.

Halton was part of the Rural Sanitary Authority of the Hunslet Union whose first meeting under chairman John Graveley was held on August 29th 1872. One of the first inspections carried out by the RSA was based at *"The Irvine Arms in the Hamlet of Halton when the drainage will be inspected, including privies and poor water supply".* This meeting resulted in a drainage survey for Halton by a Mr Fox in 1873 and a tender was accepted for £200 from Silas Abbey under his superintendent Joseph Groves. It was Francis Johnson who dug the village trenches to lay water pipes in September 1875 *"as far as Squire Swift's butcher's shop".*

Changes in January 1895 saw their functions taken by Hunslet Rural District Council of which Reggie Knight of San Remo and Walter Pindar were members of the committee. Halton became part of Leeds on April 1st 1928.
Halton became a part of the Hunslet Union in 1869 as a part of Temple Newsam (Leeds County Court Division of Hunslet,Leeds and Tadcaster Unions). This came about as a result of the formation of the Boards of Guardians. Hunslet Union comprised Hunslet, Middleton, Oulton-with-Woodlesford, Temple Newsam and Thorp Stapleton. It was the 1834 Poor Law Amendment Act which gave rise to the Poor Law Unions. The main town had a Leeds Board of Guardians from 1844 and the Leeds Union Workhouse was built on Beckett Street by 1861, now the Medical Museum. The Public Vaccinator of the 5th District Hunslet Union was Dr FW Pogson of Holme Lea. It was through the many meetings of the Temple Newsam Ratepayers Association that the new boundaries were agreed with Leeds and the Temple Newsam Estate. One of these meetings in 1920 discussed the forthcoming incorporation and condemned the proposals but eventual agreement was reached. In May 1924 a meeting at Halton requested the Hunslet RDC to call a meeting in the village in order that the intended changes can be explained. In June 1924 the Leeds Corporation Bill was passed in the House of Commons and in the village most of the residents were in favour of the proposals. On November 30th 1926 Ald Sir Charles Wilson MP addressed a meeting of the Temple Newsam Ratepayers Association at the Parochial Hall to explain the proposals to a packed hall of electors. One of the outcomes of this meeting was that a postcard ballot was to be held on the subject. Sir Charles who once said "I am Leeds" always supported any extension of the City. In 1927 the Bill had run its course through the House of Commons and House of Lords and a rate was agreed for the village of 13 shillings in the pound which was guaranteed for 15 years. The inclusion of Halton into Leeds brought many advantages although the tram access had already been made in 1915 and to Temple Newsam in 1924. The Hunslet Board of Guardians and the Temple Newsam Rate Payers Association ceased to operate by January 1928. In 1937 the Hunslet RDC became part of the Rothwell UDC.

LORD MAYORS OF LEEDS

Doreen Elizabeth Wood was the 94th Lord Mayor of Leeds and lives in Halton. She was the daughter of a serving soldier Charles Arthur Cooper who married Winifred Light of Dorset in 1920. The family moved to York after Doreen's birth in 1921 and came to live in Halton in 1939, when her father was promoted in his job as a railway policeman. Doreen Wood was first elected to Leeds City Council in 1968 representing

Osmondthorpe Ward; she lost the seat in 1970 and in 1974 was elected to represent Halton Ward as a Conservative member. Doreen married Denis Wood and their children are Christine, Sheila and Peter. Her daughter Sheila Staveley was the Lady Mayoress: she was born in Halton and was educated at Roundhay High School and the Margaret McMillan Memorial College of Education Bradford. Sheila was a steward of Halton Methodist Church (Christ Church). Doreen Wood was elected to be the Lord Mayor of Leeds in 1987: she was also the chairman of the Leeds Licensing sub-committee and was shadow chairman of the Social Services Community Care sub-committee. She represented Leeds on the Yorks and Humberside Division of the National Society for Clean Air, Yorkshire Pollution Advisory Council, Yorks and Humberside Home Safety Council and the North Regional Association for the Deaf. In her mayoral year Doreen Wood visited Israel, Dortmund and Lille: she retired from the council in 1988.

Martin Dodgson JP was the Lord Mayor of Leeds in 1983/84 and was a partner of William Dodgson & Son Funeral Directors: he was the fifth generation of his family to be associated with the firm which was founded by his great-great-grandfather in 1842. Martin was first elected as a Leeds councillor in 1968 and represented Halton Ward until 1987. He served on many council committees including being the Chairman of the Environmental Health Committee, Schools sub-committee and the Education Committee; Design, Construction & Engineering; Licensing; Social Services, Leisure Services, Personnel and Finance & Policy Committee. Martin Dodgson is a magistrate and a member of Cross Gates Rotary Club. He is the Director of The Leeds Centre for Deaf and Blind People based at Centenary House Leeds. Martin Dodgson was the youngest Lord Mayor of Leeds and he resigned as a councillor in 1986.

MANORS AND THE MANOR COURT

A manor was a feudal estate and for 500 years after the Norman Conquest was the unit of local government. The manor was held of the king by a Lord of the Manor with the management in the hands of a reeve and the administration by the Steward.
The Steward of the Manor of Temple Newsam in the 19th century was Michael Scholefield who lived at the Manor House Whitkirk. In 1828 Michael Scholefield sent a letter which stated: "*The Manor of Temple Newsam comprises the Mansion, grounds and the villages of Halton, Colton, Whitkirk Lane End and Waterside, Newsam Green, Osmondthorpe and other minor places extending 3000 acres.*"
Michael Schofield has a memorial plaque in the chancel at Whitkirk Church and was buried on the south side of the church. He was born in

1762 and died on May 17th 1842. His wife's family had held the position of Steward for nearly a century; his wife Elizabeth died on December 23rd 1859 aged 86.
Halton was in the Manor of Temple Newsam: this was the way in which people were governed. The Lord of the Manor held land granted by the Crown and the Court was held twice a year at the Manor House and later at the Brown Cow Inn. The manor court was concerned with civil proceedings, transfer of lands, conduct of the agricultural system and petty offences. Many of the Manorial Records for Halton are held in the West Yorkshire Archives: they were originally written in Latin and many are available from 1702.
The Court Leet dealt with the petty offences such as trespass while the Court Baron dealt with land administration tenancy and the rights of the tenant and Lord of the Manor. The Lords of the Manor were the successive owners of Temple Newsam Park.

MAPS OF HALTON

One of the earliest maps of Halton appeared in 1731 which showed the four field systems and a small village with a winding high street with few houses and no sign of Chapel Street. This was a map drawn for the Manor of Temple Newsam by J Dickinson whose map was used in 1807 to show the property of the Marquis of Hertford; it was an endorsed plan of the intakes and low ings of Halton. A year prior to this map J Dickinson published a plan of the Temple Newsam estate in 1730.
The lands of Temple Newsam estate belonging to the Free Grammar School were published on a map in 1793 drawn by J Teal. The map was originally published in 1792 by the Committee of Pious Uses. Chapel Street is shown from Selby Road to Pinfold Lane and then a track across the Cross Field to
Seacroft; the street was to be known as Cross Field Lane. The land south of the turnpike road was known as Barrow Nooks Road while to the north were the Causey Lands.
Maps of Halton drawn between 1830 and 1834 included one drawn in 1834 by Alfred Smith for the Halton Enclosure Act. It is a very detailed look at the village with individual houses together with the fields and local folk who rented them from the Estate; Chapel Street is continued as Cross Field Road. Primrose Lane is drawn as Back Lane and Garth Ends Road to join with Cross Field Road. Field End is continued south as Barrow Nooks Road joining with New Templegate, then known as Gill Syke and New Field Road later Pit Gate Lane. This continued into Selby Road where Templegate enters the main road today. Most of the fields were in the hands of the Graveley family and the Marchioness of Hertford.

The first official survey map was published in 1850 although there are no street names except for the Selby & Leeds Trust Road. The only buildings on Halton Hill were the Old Vitriol Works and the Epsom Salts & Copperas Works together with Willow Well Farm. Back Lane was now continuous to Cross Gates and Green Lane enters Hollyshaw Lane at the present Hollyshaw Grove. Halton was concentrated around High Street, Chapel Street and east of Back Lane: it was mainly open land from Pinfold Lane and the School on the main turnpike road.

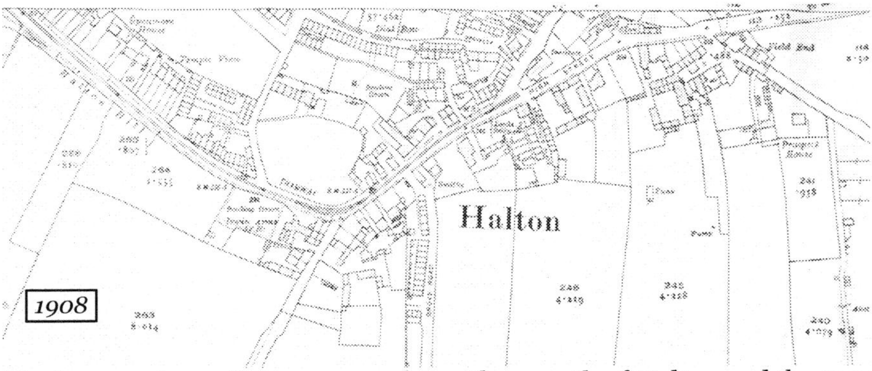

The large scale 1908 survey map shows the growth of Halton and the 1915 map of farms and their lands surveyed for the Hon Edward Wood's Temple Newsam Estate is an interesting insight into how the village was divided. The other survey maps of 1894, 1921 and 1933 blend into the OS maps of more recent date.

MEMBERS OF PARLIAMENT

Since Halton became a part of Leeds in April 1928 Halton has been represented by three members of parliament. *Osbert Peake* was elected for Leeds North (Conservative) in 1929 following Sir Gervase Beckett. He was the son of GH Peake of Bawtry Hall: Osbert was born on December 30th 1897 the great-great-grandson of Lord Grey, great-nephew of Mrs Meynell Ingram of Temple Newsam & Hoar Cross Hall and a cousin of Lord Halifax. He was educated at Eton and Sandhurst and then attended Christ Church College Oxford where he read Law. He married Lady Joan Rachel de Vere Capell on June 19th 1922: daughter of the Earl of Essex. For a few months in 1955 he represented North East Leeds prior to receiving a peerage on January 17th 1956. Lord Ingilby 1st Viscount of Smilesworth died on October 11th 1966 aged 68: his heir was Hon Martin Peake of Boston Spa born 1923. Osbert Peake was a major in the Nottinghamshire Yeomanry & Lieutenant Coldstream Guards in the Great War. He was a barrister of the Inner Temple (1923), Parliamentary Under-Secretary at the Home Office (1939-44), Financial Secretary to the

Treasury (1944-45) and Minister of Pensions and National Insurance (1951-55).

In 1955 Halton became part of Leeds East and was represented by *Dennis Healey* (Labour) until 1992. Dennis Winston Healey was born in 1917 educated at Bradford Grammar School and Oxford University. He was raised to the peerage in 1992 as Lord Healey of Riddlesden. He was MP for South-East Leeds from February 1952 to 1955 and a member of the Shadow Cabinet from 1959-64, 1970-74 and 1979-84.

The general election of 1992 elected *George Mudie* as the MP for Leeds East. He was born and educated in Dundee and coming to Leeds was the local councillor for Seacroft. In 1980 he became the Leader of Leeds City Council from which he resigned in 1989. In the 2001 election George Mudie obtained 18290 votes with Barry Anderson (Con 5647), Brian Jennings (LibDem 3923), Raymond Hargreaves (UK Indep 634), Mark King (Soc Lab 419) and Peter Socrates (Indep 142). There was a turnout of 29,055 being 51.5% of the electorate: in the 1997 election the turnout was 62.8%.

MILESTONES

The twenty miles from Leeds to Selby were marked in the mid-18th century by stone and metal milestones on the south side of the turnpike road. The stones were erected by the Leeds & Selby Turnpike Trust soon after the opening of the turnpike road in 1741. The stones had no relation to the turnpike bars and measured from the Leeds Parish Church to Gowthorpe which is a distance of 20 miles: the present distance is 20.5 miles. The stones were all the same in structure with the pillar made from sandstone and the metallic plate screwed to the base: the plate was flat on the top inscribed Leeds and Selby Turnpike Road and the triangular section at the base was inscribed with raised lettering and painted black for ease of viewing. The milestones were paid for by the turnpike trusts, public subscription, the landed gentry and the local authority. The milestones are listed structures and on the road now there are six remaining: Halton without the metal plate, Garforth by the traffic lights at Ninelands Lane, Monk Fryston prior to the railway bridge; Breck's Farm & Wood east of Monk Fryston; Thorp Willoughby by the inn and the entry into Selby by Mile Tree House.

The original stones were indicated on an OS map of 1857: York Road (1), Dog & Gun Inn (2), Halton High Street (3), Whitkirk Church east of Colton Road (4), east of Garforth Bridge opposite the inn (6), Dogcroft Road now Ninelands Lane (7), west of Peckfield House and Quarry (8), Ledsham Road by Boot & Shoe Inn (10), Red Hill Lane (11), Lumby Road at Mile Gap Quarry (12), west of Monk Fryston (13), east of Monk Fryston (14), Breck's Wood (15), west of Hambleton (16), east of Hambleton (17), Thorp Willoughby (18) and Mile Tree House Selby (19). The original measurements were from St Peter's Church in Leeds to a point by the present High School at Gowthorpe. There were two milestones not included on the old map and no stones were made for the extreme ends of the road. *The miles in brackets are those that were inscribed on the milestones from Leeds to Selby.*
The Halton milestone was rescued during the redevelopment of the area in the 1980's and there was no plate in living memory. The position of the hole through which the iron screw was placed in the stone is visible and in later years the measurements were inscribed into the stone and removed in 1940 with the fear of German invasion.
The first toll bar was at Halton Dial followed by those at Peckfield Bar, Hambleton (Bar Lane) and Gowthorpe.
The Milestones Society was founded in May 2001 and has logged over 1200 Yorkshire milestones: there are about 2000 in the county most in West Yorkshire which account for about a quarter of all those in Britain.

MORKILL FAMILY

The Morkill family held land in Halton including Low Slacks on Halton Hill, land north of Primrose Lane and at Primrose Garth (Primrose Road).

The Morkill family came from Springthorpe Lincolnshire where they were settled in the 17th century. Thomas Morkill of Halton died aged 71 in July 1810; his wife Elizabeth died aged 78 in October 1818 and their son William died aged 39 in February 1808. John Morkill of Halton died aged 95 in December 1822 and wife Mary Morkill died aged 92 in January 1822. Their daughters were Mary Ann Hargrove who died in December 1812 aged 41 and Margaret who died at Temple Newsam aged 68 in November 1841. Anne Morkill was the first wife of Sir James Falshaw: she died aged 49 in 1864.
John William Morkill was born on May 3rd 1861 and lived at Austhorpe Lodge which had been built by John Smeaton's grandfather. John Morkill's father John Morkill lived at Killingbeck Lodge and he married Mary Greenwood. John Morkill died on April 29th 1881 aged 64; his wife Mary died on Sunday July 24th 1904 aged 82 at Newfield Hall and their daughter Annie Louisa died aged 16 on April 14th 1881.
John William Morkill was the only son of John & Mary Morkill and was

educated at Radley College and Oriel College Oxford obtaining a law degree and MA. He had an illustrious career and was High Sheriff for Yorkshire 1929-30 following Sir John Harrowing, Deputy Lieutenant West Riding, Chairman WR Bench (Leeds), Deputy Chairman WR Quarter Sessions, JP for the West Riding from 1894 and in 1911 was the Chairman of the Skyrack Bench in Leeds following the death of WH Maude. John W Morkill moved to live at Newfield Hall Malhamdale in 1901 and was a Member of the Skipton Bench of Magistrates, Skipton RDC and Skipton Board of Guardians. He was the Chairman of the Yorkshire Fishery Board and from 1929 was the President of the Yorkshire Fishery Boards and Vice President of the Skyrack Division Conservative Association. He was a representative of the Bradford Diocese Conference in the House of Laity of the Church Assembly and was vice president of the Bradford Diocesan Board of Finance.

John William Morkill was the co-author with Rev George Moreton Platt of "Records of the Parish of Whitkirk" (1892) and author of "The Parish of Kirkby Malham in the West Riding of Yorkshire" which he completed just prior to his death. The book was published on the instructions of his widow by William Bellows of Gloucester. He also was the author of the book "The Manor of Roundhay".

Newfield Hall was built on the site of Newfield Grange and on the estate of James Morrison. The estate was sold to Bradford architect William Alcock and in 1856 Newfield Hall was built as a house for his son William Alcock. There is a stone emblem which includes this date and A on the original house. It was the same family who added on the front wing which includes the porch and entrance hall: a date of "1887 A" exists on the addition. In 1890 it was sold to William Illingworth of Bradford and in 1901 John William Morkill leased the Hall until he bought the whole estate in 1929. The present stained glass heraldry on the staircase windows includes the coat of arms of the Alcock family and those of John William Morkill and his wife Hannah Hobson. The Morkill shield comprises three vertical columns featuring three martins (birds) centrally flanked by "vair" represented by a bell design. The Hobson crest includes two hobbies (birds) and a representation of the sun. John William Morkill was Lord of the Manor and the principal landowner.

John William Morkill married Hannah Shaw Hobson on March 1st 1889 who was the youngest daughter of Peter Hobson of Castle Lodge Yorkshire. She was the niece and co-heiress of Sir James Falshaw. They had three sons and a daughter Frances Helena baptised April 6th 1895 who married Rev Hugh Lowthian Bell, son of Yorkshire ironmaster Sir Maurice Hugh Lowthian Bell born on March 29th 1871 and educated at Eton. He became the director of Bell Brothers and Dorman Long and died on November 17th 1944. He lived at Mount Grace Priory in the

manor house and then at John Carr's Arncliffe Hall. Rounton Grange designed by Philip Webb was used for war evacuees and for Italian POW's being demolished in the 1950's.
His father was Sir Thomas Hugh Bell of Rounton Grange Northallerton and Mount Grace Priory who was born on February 10th 1844 and educated at Merchiston Castle Edinburgh and Paris. He was a JP and High Sheriff and a Lord Lieutenant for the North Riding from 1906. He succeeded to the title on the death of his father Isaac in 1904: he died on June 29th 1931.
One of John William Morkill's sons Ronald Falshaw who was baptised on March 17th 1892 was killed in 1915 in the Great War; Alan Greenwood Morkill was born in July 1890 and he was in the Malay Civil Service and later Colonial Office and his other brother was Captain Hugh Bernard Morkill (born October 1896 & baptised November 11th 1896) of The Green Howards. St Michael's Church Kirkby Malham has a paten dish donated by JW Morkill and an almsdish given in memory of his son Ronald and dated June 25th 1915. There is also a chalice inscribed "*A mother's thank offering for the safe return of two sons from the War.Kirkby Malham (HSM) 1920.*"
John William Morkill died on April 27th 1932 at Newfield Hall. He held much land in Craven; the funeral was held at Kirkby Malham Church on April 30th 1932 and conducted by the Vicar of St Michael's Church Rev CH Pauling, the Archdeacon of Craven and the Rev Walter Warburton Vicar of St Mary's Whitkirk. The family mourners were Hannah Morkill, Mr & Mrs Alan Morkill and daughter Mrs Hugh Bell and included amongst the large congregation were PS Marsden of Whitkirk representing Lord Irwin and Mrs Eade of Seacroft Grange.
There are three Morkill graves on the east side of the churchyard at Kirkby Malham: John William and his wife Hannah who died on June 2nd 1937. The third grave is of one of their three sons Ronald Falshaw Morkill who was killed in a flying accident on June 23rd 1915 aged 23. Ronald was a Lieutenant with the 1st Battalion West Yorkshire Regiment Prince of Wales Own and a Flying Officer in the Royal Flying Corps (RAF). He was the husband of Ellen Mary (Wilkinson) whose family came from Neasham Abbey near Darlington and east of Croft on the River Tees. There is a stained glass window in the north nave of St Michael's Church remembering the young man.
Following his death the contents were sold by Hollis & Webb on October 5th/6th 1932 when few high prices were achieved. The property was then bought by All Soul's College Oxford and it was leased by the Holiday Fellowship from 1933. Hannah Morkill moved to live at Bucks Hill House near Kings Langley Hertfordshire. The grand two day sale had 713 lots and included an 1895 painting by Halton artist Gilbert Foster "The woods in spring". The large library included books by Harry Speight

"Lower Wharfedale", "Ralph Thoresby his town and times", "Adel and its Norman church", three copies of "Records of the Parish of Whitkirk", Dugdale's "Visitation of Yorkshire", Ralph Thoresby's "Ducatus Leodiensis" and Whitaker's "Loidis and Elmete".
The Holiday Fellowship had been founded in 1892 by TA Leonard a Congregational Minister from Colne who became a Quaker. Newfield Hall became a part of Holiday Fellowship Holdings being a non-profit making industrial and provident society.
The west wing of Newfield Hall was destroyed by a fire in January 1991 when it was being converted from a Youth Guest House to become a hotel specialising in outdoor type holidays. The Hall reopened in 1992 and later the walled garden was reclaimed from wilderness conditions. New building incorporated a swimming pool and dining room with rooms above opened in 1996.
The stained glass in St Mary's Church Whitkirk vestry dates from 1901 and represents the coat of arms of John William and wife Hannah Shaw together with those of Sir James Falshaw who had married Anne Morkill. In 1888 JW Morkill paid for the new marble tiling in the chancel and sanctuary at St Mary's Church Whitkirk, removed in 1980 on the re-ordering of the church. In 1926 he presented a silver alms dish bearing his coat of arms.
James Falshaw was born in Leeds on March 21st 1810 to William & Hannah Shaw Falshaw of East Street on The Bank: William was a Leeds wool merchant on Alfred Street and they had 14 children: his wife was the daughter of James Shaw, while the Falshaw family had come from Coverham where James's great grandfather was a farmer. James Falshaw was educated at Jonathan Lockwood's School on Brunswick Terrace Leeds. He was apprenticed to architect and surveyor Joseph Cusworth and later worked for G Leather of Leeds engineers of the Aire & Calder Canal. At the age of 33 James started on his own as a railway engineer and contractor. He worked for Robert Stevenson on the Lancaster & Carlisle Railway and then for Hamer & Pratt on the Leeds-Selby railway from 1831 until 1834 where he was the agent for a section of line between Marsh Lane and Cross Gates. In 1836 he was involved in the construction of the Whitby to Pickering Railway and a year later was involved with the construction of Eccup Reservoir, Weetwood and Woodhouse Moor holding reservoirs for Leeds Waterworks. Between 1837 and 1844 he worked on the Stockton & Hartlepool Railway and for Bradford Waterworks. In 1841 he married Anne Morkill daughter of Thomas Morkill of Astley. Anne died on April 23rd 1864 aged 49. James Falshaw moved to Stirling in 1845 and was in charge of 8000 men; in 1854 he moved from Perth to Nairn again involved with railway construction. He became a partner with Thomas Brassey & William Mackenzie in the building of the Scottish railways from Inverness and in

1858 moved to Edinburgh living at 14 Belgrave Crescent. He became a councillor in 1861 and a Bailie in 1864, magistrate until 1867. In 1862 he was in partnership with Morkill & Prodham in building the Berwickshire Railway and the Blaydon & Conside Railway. In 1867 he ended his railway career and visited Italy. He was present at the opening of the Suez Canal in 1869. In 1871 James Falshaw married Jane Gibbs of Upper Norwood (1824-1889), daughter of Thomas Gibbs of Spring Bank. In 1872 he was elected to represent St George's Ward Edinburgh. In 1874 became Lord Provost of Edinburgh involved in the widening of Princes Street and the West Princes Street Gardens, re-roofing Waverley Market, acquisition of the Arboretum and involved with the Edinburgh Waterworks. On August 17th 1876 he was created a baronet by Queen Victoria on the occasion of the unveiling of the statue of Prince Albert in Charlotte Square. In 1881 he was Deputy Chairman of the NBRC and a year later was elected the Chairman of the North British Railway Company following the death of Stirling of Kippendavie; he held this post until 1887. He opened the Exhibition of the Edinburgh Photographic Society on December 20th 1876: the Society was established in February 1861. Sir James Falshaw died on June 14th 1889 and had no children and the title became extinct. He was buried at the Dean Cemetery Edinburgh. Dean Cemetery is north west of the main city by the Waters of Leith and is split into two parts by a road. The main cemetery maintained by the Heritage Lottery Fund has hundreds of memorials and was opened in 1845 by the Edinburgh Western Cemetery Company on the site of Dean House on the Dean Estate which had been bought in 1609 by William Nesbitt.

MORRITT AVENUE AND MORRITT DRIVE

George Morritt built *Morritt Avenue* as a private street after a visit to Italy and it was once guarded by wrought iron gates across the road and had a gatekeeper. He vetted the horse drawn vehicles and allowed other folk by the side gate. There was a sign at the entrance which once read: "Private Street". The 24 houses were built in 1902/03 with the Morritt family living at Sunshine Villa: in 1907 his new house had a stable and coach house. These houses are decorated with a variety of stone figures and roses and feature balconies and turrets. The gates were removed in July 1911 when the street was surfaced by GL Briggs for £53.

Amongst the residents of The Avenue were the Hyde family. Sarah Elizabeth Christabel Hyde was born in 1909 as the fourth daughter of Anne (Wainwright) born 1873 and Fred Hyde, married in 1900. Christabel's sisters were Kathleen born 1901; Nancy Annie born September 4th 1905 who became a student teacher and taught at Halton School from October 1923 to September 1924 from where she trained at

Ripon College: Annie married Geoffrey Sheppard on August 1st 1932; Betsy born June 2nd 1907 was awarded a County Minor Scholarship in 1918 and later taught in both Infants and Mixed Departments at Halton School in 1926. The land which was to be The Mount was sold to Frederick Thomas Hyde of Fraisthorpe 17 Morritt Avenue on March 28th 1919. The house was named after the village of the family farm in the East Riding near Carnaby where the family are buried. Fred was the manager of the Bradford branch of the Commercial Union Assurance Co after the war: he became a City of Leeds Insurance Inspector. Fred Hyde died aged 73 in May 1946 and was buried at Whitkirk cemetery. Christabel was awarded a County Minor Scholarship at Halton School in 1921 and later she married and became the author Christabel Burniston who wrote "Life in a Liberty Bodice" in 1991.

Frederick & Mary Emma Leach lived at Fernlea 27 Morritt Avenue with son James Morton Leach, Marjorie Alexandra born in 1902 who married Thomas Bennett of Rosella on June 6th 1923; Elfreda Margaret was born in 1904 and she married Harold Bennett a 23 year old glass merchant on May 16th 1928. Alderman Frederick Leach was a councillor for the Halton ward and Chairman of the Leeds Transport Committee. His position lasted until November 1938 when he took over from Coun Donald Cowling. When Cowling joined the RAF in August 1940 Leach took over the chairmanship again until 1945 when Coun John Rafferty was elected to the position. Frank & Eileen Leach lived at the house: their daughter Hilary was baptised at Whitkirk Church on April 1st 1962. Ald Fred Leach was Deputy Lord Mayor of Leeds and died at Grange over Sands in December 1954.

Morritt Drive at the High Street end of Primrose Lane was built by George Morritt and was due to be two complete rows of terrace houses, although only one was completed in two sections. The land was bought from Mrs Meynell Ingram of Temple Newsam by John W Morkill whose estate sold it to George Morritt in 1883. Plans were passed for 61 through houses in 1903 later reduced to 47 and the two rows were completed and had private access guarded by large iron gates at the Primrose Lane end: these were refused at first by the Hunslet RDC. These were replaced during the war with the present railings, which limit the rough track from

the grassed section. The street was originally called Quarry Mount but changed to Morritt Drive by 1905. The first houses were occupied by April 1904 and there was much discussion between George Morritt and the Council regarding both drainage and water.
The semi-detached houses filled in the gaps left by the Morritt development: the houses at the far end were built on land sold to John Morkill on April 7th 1883 who sold it to George Morritt on June 6th 1904. The end house on Morritt Drive was once Clark's Stores (Quality Corner) selling boiled hams as a speciality. Charles & Elizabeth Edwards had a grocer's shop at the row end. The adjacent shop in 1908 was where Walter Scott ran a Fish & Chip shop; in the 1950's the shop was Morritt Drive Fisheries (Mary Bostock) and then Hilda Greenwood and Jean Moran from January 1958. In the 1960's Morritt Drive Fisheries was run by RG & LM Turner as The Fisherman's Cabin Café; the shop was then

taken by Harold Archdale. Plans were submitted to convert 1 Morritt Drive from a shop to a private house in November 2001.

MORRITT FAMILY

The Morritt family has roots in North Yorkshire where they bought Rokeby Hall from the Robinson family in 1720 and built a new hall by 1731 to replace Mortham Tower as residence. Members of the family are buried at Rokeby Church: John Sawrey Morritt (1815), John B Sawrey Morritt who was a friend of Sir Walter Scott (he wrote Rokeby in 1813) and died in 1843.
A branch of the Morritt family went to Cawood to farm the land. In Selby Abbey is the Morritt Chapel in the north west corner and now the site for

a historical video of the abbey. The memorials in the chapel include the Cawood family: Edward (1722) and wife Margaret (1711), Mary (1694), Isabel (1698), Catherine (1811) and Mary (1812). The wall memorials are to Bacon Morritt of Cawood who died aged 80 on November 28th 1773 and wife Anne Sawrey of Plumpton Lancashire: she married in 1723 and died in May 1769 aged 51. Their son Bacon died aged 18 on June 11th 1751. There is a memorial on the north wall to Robert Morritt the Rector of Ryther who died on November 22nd 1705 aged 40 and to his son Robert who died aged 12 in 1704. His eldest daughter was Anne Eliza who died aged 71 on December 1st 1795.

James Morritt (1747-1830) married Elizabeth (1748-1820) and had seven children including William Morritt (1788-1873). He married Ann Jolly at Cawood Church on December 2nd 1811 and they had seven children including the youngest son George Morritt. He was born on November 20th 1826 and married 22 year old Jane Lund of Leeds on April 1st 1854. Their family were Sarah Ann (1855), Thomas (1857), Martha (1862), Maude (1862), George (1864), Emma (1867) and John (1870).

George Morritt was born in Cawood on June 26th 1864 moving to Dewsbury Road Leeds in 1872. He married 18 year old Ruth Lund at Hunslet Parish Church on Christmas Day 1883. George bought some land near the Pottery Field as his first interest in building. Their children were William, Alfred, Maud, Lucy, Sarah, David and George.

William Morritt was born 1886 and lived at Sunshine Villa Morritt Avenue with his wife May Douglas. William View and William Avenue were named after him. They had a daughter Audrey born in 1911. *Alfred Morritt* was born in 1890. *Maud Morritt* was born in 1893 and she married Arthur Ernest Read who was born in 1878 on October 6th 1943. She carried on a repair business with David and George after the war for a few years. *Lucy Morritt* born 1895 married Harold Oswald Feyer on April 4th 1921 and lived on Park Drive Austhorpe. *Sarah Morritt* was born in 1897 and married Roland Simpson on January 27th 1923. *David Morritt* was born in 1900 and he married Nellie Sutcliffe and lived at the Austhorpe Bungalow; their son Arnold David Morritt was born in 1929 and he married Barbara Wilkes on October 24th 1953: he died in January 1938.

George Morritt was born in 1902 and became a joiner; he married launderess Annie Scott of 9 Chapel Street Halton on December 26th 1925. Annie was born in 1903 being the daughter of collier William Scott. George & Annie lived at Penrose 13 Austhorpe Avenue where he died in August 1951. George & Annie's son is *Dennis Morritt* who was born in 1928: he married Josie Carroll of Holly House Farm.

The builder George Morritt Snr died at Austhorpe on April 6th 1931. He was a member of the Society of Friends until coming to live at Halton where he attended the Methodist Chapel. The funeral service was conducted at the chapel by Rev WO Robinson with interment at Whitkirk Church. He was always remembered for his benevolence and never hesitated in helping the poor of the village.

NEWSAM SQUARE

Newsam Square was a cul-de-sac off Primrose Lane and by the side of Primrose Terrace-which became part of Primrose Lane in the 1930's. The entry to the square was between the low building of 4a and the short row of terrace housing (6-14 Primrose Lane). In the 1901 census Newsam Square included coal miners George Silverwood, Joseph Harrison, William Connor and Alfred Crossley.

Between 1928 and 1938 the residents of the 20 houses were: 1 Wilfred Jackson 2 George Horsman, Richard Lacey 3 Thomas Bartram 4 Mary Medley 5 Walter Masshedar 6 John Longdon, Albert Smith, Albert Broadley 7 Polly Shaw 8 Stanley Wall, Herbert Lacey 9 George Hunter 10 George Hardcastle, George Batey, Albert Ashmore *George Batey married Cecilia in 1924 and his brother John James Batey jnr lived at 2 Britton Terrace; George & Cecilia later moved to Coronation Parade on Halton Moor* 11 Robert Bowes, Joseph & Elizabeth Ellen Connell, John Goodall *It was Joseph & Ellen Connell who were involved with a fire at their shop on the High Street in 1932 when three of children died.* 12 Edward Wilson, Albert Broadley, John Bradbury 13 Frank Robshaw 14 Mary Wilson, Stanley Jackson 15 Timothy & Louisa Guest 16 Albert Smith, George Hunter 17 John Dawson 18 James Guest, William Lacey 19 Arthur Isles, Reuben Ashmore 20 Benjamin Hirst, Henry Wheatcroft.

There were three blocks of terrace houses on Newsam Square with a short block on Primrose Lane: a mixture of back-to-back and through houses. There was a row adjacent to 2-6 Rock Terrace, a row on the right side and a short row on the left backing on to the yards of the row of houses on High Street now demolished. In 1901 there was much concern over many old Halton houses regarding sewage disposal and they were often treated by Hunslet RDC as "nuisance" properties. Newsam Square

was connected to the main sewer in 1901/02.
A compulsory purchase order for Newsam Square was made by the Council in November 1956 which became a clearance area. The houses were demolished from 1957/58 and the site later became the new Halton clinic and car parking.

NEWSPAPERS COVERING HALTON

The *Leeds Skyrack Express* was a free weekly published by Johnston Press at the offices of the Yorkshire Weekly Newspaper Group in Southgate Wakefield with the editorial office was on Austhorpe Road Cross Gates. On April 10th 1886 the Roundhay Gazette was first published and incorporated the Shadwell, Seacroft, Thorner and Cross Gates Courier: the title soon became the Roundhay Gazette and Skyrack Courier. The Skyrack Courier was published on June 4th 1887 published in Albion Street Leeds and closed in 1923 to be followed by the Skyrack Express in mid-October 1923: printed in Wakefield. In January 1978 the title changed to Skyrack and East Leeds Express and became a free newspaper; 1982 saw the title changed to the Leeds Skyrack Express and in 1984 became a tabloid. When publication ceased on November 8th 2002 the title was the Leeds Express incorporating the Leeds Skyrack Express: changed in November 1996. The title was incorporated in the East Leeds edition of the Leeds Weekly News which was a part of the Yorkshire Post Newspapers (Johnston Press). Over the decades the Skyrack covered Halton village life and reported in detail the activities of the clubs, churches and the lives of village folk. The newspapers are on microfiche at Wakefield (from 1916) and Leeds Local History Library covering 1924 until closure.
The Yorkshire Post was founded in 1754 as The Leeds Intelligencer and in 1866 the title changed to become The Yorkshire Post. The paper incorporates The Leeds Mercury published from 1718 and was acquired by the Yorkshire Post in 1923.
The Yorkshire Evening News was first published in 1872 with the last issue in December 1963.
The Yorkshire Evening Post was first published in 1890 and *The Leeds Weekly News* is a free weekly first published in 1980: the paper includes an occasional local history series "Scenes from the Past".
All the issues of these newspapers are available to the public on microfiche at the Leeds Local History Library.

OVERDALE TERRACE

The north side of Overdale Terrace was built in 1906/07 and the south side was built by George Fenwick in the 1920's and the road was surfaced in

1936 by contractor JE Speight. George Lockwood Fenwick lived at 1 Overdale Terrace with his wife Lucy Ann Fenwick. He died in his house in February 1959 aged 52: he was a builder who worked in his father's business. Their daughters were Veronica and Jean Fenwick who married George Arthur Gill on May 21st 1955 and was a dancing teacher who met her future husband while on holiday on the Isle of Man.

One of the residents was Samuel Brooke Chadwick who died in July 1957. He had seen Halton grow from a village to a Leeds suburb; he had interests in politics and gardening being a committee member of the Halton & Temple Newsam Gardens Association and a member of the Leeds Paxton Society. His wife Gertrude Naylor Chadwick died aged 65 on August 15th 1954.

PALMER FAMILY

Charles Palmer (1849-1926) and his Seacroft born wife Mary Ann Thompson (1851-1921) lived at 42 High Street. Charles was born at East Bilney in Norfolk being the son of Edward & Elizabeth Palmer. He worked as a miner in the local pits and was a gardener to the Crosthwaite family at Beech Cottage Chapel Street, who gave him a good pension for his faithful service. They had been married in Hunslet on June 6th 1870 and celebrated their Golden Wedding in 1920. When Mary Ann died in 1921 Mary Spedding lived with Charles as his companion until his death in 1926. Their children were *William Edward Palmer* (1871-1950) married Edith (1886-1941) in 1920 living at 6 Park View Terrace Halton. Their children were Edith Mavis born in 1919 who married Leslie Atkins on October 13th 1945: they now live in Essex. They had three children: Bronwen who married Nick Adams, Anthea and Brian. Muriel Gertrude Palmer (1895-1959) lived in Chapel Allerton. Olive Anna Palmer (1922-1974) married Polish war hero Stanislav (Stan) Kondras at St Anne's Cathedral Leeds: they met when the Palmer family was on holiday in Blackpool and Stan was recovering from war injuries in the resort. Stan received the Polish VC from Major Wladyslaw Sikorski (1881-1943) for his bravery in a mine laying raid on German U Boats. His plane was shot down and crashed: he was transferred to a recuperation hospital in Blackpool. *Major Sikorski was the prime minister of the*

Charles and Mary Palmer

Polish government in exile during the Second World War who was killed in a plane crash off Gibraltar. Olive & Stan lived at 6 Park View Terrace and their children are Peter and Paul.

Anne Palmer was baptised on August 4th 1873. *Charles Palmer* (1877-1952) was a tea merchant's assistant when he was in his early 20's; he married Sophia Todd (1882-1967) who was the sister of garage owner Edwin Todd and daughter of William & Jane Todd. They ran their clothing /fashion shop on The Island later 19 Chapel Street in the house built by George Henry Botterill in 1914.

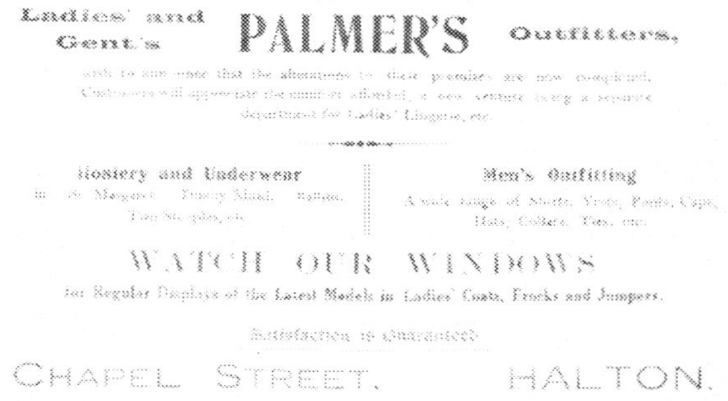

Lizzie Palmer (1876-1941) married George Henry Botterill (1875-1937) in 1900; she lived with her son Charley and his wife Constance on Pinfold Lane. *Ernest Palmer* was born in October 1881 and was a teenage butcher's apprentice; he married Eliza living at Rose Terrace and at 4 Wilfred Avenue. There five children were William Edward (1910-50), Mary (1913), Fred William (1915), Marion (1917) and Jack (1918). *Harriet Palmer* was born in 1887 and *George Palmer* was born in November 1888.

PARK STREET

This short street links Cross Green Lane with Primrose Lane, Park View Terrace and Craigmona built by John Graveley in 1892. The first owner was James Yates with Richard Haste Carr and Thomas Horatio Ramsden, Gertrude with daughters Jean and Isabella from 1936 to 1945. It was later converted into flats and is now being made into a family home again. The street was named in 1901 together with Cross Park Street which divides the rear of Cross Green Lane with Park View Terrace.

PARK VIEW TERRACE

The street has a reverse numbering compared to the other houses on Primrose Lane starting at 1 from Park Street. The first six houses were built by John Graveley in 1897 with the first residents in 1898: 1 was Charles William Lambert. The houses which front Primrose Lane were built prior to the other properties and had an uninterrupted view of New Manston Park. This was built in 1846 for the Waud family of coal owners who had moved from Manston. When the row was completed to the west by 1898, the unmade street was changed from Occupation Lane to Primrose Lane thus continuing the street from High Street to Green Lane. The plot for 11 Park View Terrace was bought by John Graveley in March 1877; he was a tenant of Mrs Meynell Ingram on the Martinmas Lands. In 1897 he sold the new house to the first occupier. One of the residents at 11 was "Mr John" Ladies Hairdresser: later manager of Marshall & Snelgrove Department Store in Leeds. The other six houses were built by John Graveley and sold to George Morritt who finished them with his characteristic style prior to selling in June 1904. 6 Park View Terrace was the home of William Edward and Edith Palmer whose daughter Olive Anna lived there after her marriage to Stan Kondras. Edward & Dorothy Bolus from the Woodman Inn lived at 10 and Frederick & Wilhelmina Jowitt from Willow Well Farm at 12 Park View Terrace.

PAROCHIAL HALL

Halton Parochial Hall was built near the site of the village pinfold by Whitkirk Church offering Halton parishioners a Recreation Hall and Sunday School. The site had been donated by the Hon Edward Wood who also donated £500 towards the cost estimated to be £950/£1100: the church authorities appointed Leeds architect Percy Robinson. Building commenced in June 1908 and it had the roof completed by October and was finished in December. The Parochial Hall was opened on Wednesday January 13th 1909 with a parish tea attended by over 200 parishioners. The Church Sunday School was transferred to the Hall.
The Hall became a VAD Hospital from June 1915 with a team of nurses looking after the soldiers. One of the many local people who helped to run the Hall was Alec Taylor of Graveley Street: this respected tennis player died aged 20 in 1925; the Halton VAD treasurer was Walter B Pindar. The Commandant of the VAD Auxiliary Military Hospital at

Halton was Edythe Mildrid Marsden who was awarded the Royal Red Cross in 1915; in 1916 Sister Dockray was in charge at Halton VAD. In April 1920 Whitkirk Amateur Operatic Society presented The Mikado in the Parochial Hall with prices at 3/- reserved and 1/3d at the back of the Hall. The wounded soldiers were given frequent concerts, outings and entertainments including a concert by the 13th NE Leeds BP Scouts. One such outing in January 1916 was to the Briggate Picture House in Leeds accompanied by the team of nurses and the sister.
The hall was granted a licence for music and dancing in 1928 and in 1948 was proposed as a licensed club. In 1933 there was a Christmas Day Dance with Gordon White's Band opening at midnight until 4am Boxing Day. The hall was compulsorily purchased by the City Council for road widening but the plans were abandoned. In later years the hall was used for scout meetings of the Temple Moor School troop and by the primary school. In 1974/1975 the Hall was used for lunches by the first children of Halton Middle School who were waiting for their new school to be opened. The hall was also used for their first school play Joseph & The Amazing Technicolour Dreamcoat. The Hall became derelict and there was a fire in 1987; in 1990 there were plans for a community centre. The old parochial hall was eventually sold to Excel Flooring (Leeds) Ltd with planning permission granted in February 1992. The alterations to the old Hall included the demolition of the stage area and building onto the side to compensate for the loss of floor space. Gerry Howdle made Excel House his new headquarters in 1993: he had started the business on Dolly Lane in 1983.

PICKLES FAMILY

William Pickles and his wife Elizabeth Wilson ran the Crown & Anchor public house on North Street: the site later occupied by the West Yorkshire Bus Station. Their son was James Pickles born on June 18th 1834 and married Sarah Jane Mountain (1831-91) and worked as an accountant for a Bedale brewery (later Tetleys) living at Aiskew Wensleydale. James died at Bedale in 1872; their children were *William Pickles* (1860-1945) and was buried at Manston Church. *James Henry Pickles* was born in 1861 and was brought up by his uncle. On May 26th 1885 he married Sarah Emily Hall of Bradford at St Peter's Church Leeds. This was two years after starting his 47 year career with Roberts Mart & Co of Bank Mills East Street. He followed his father by working for Tetley's Brewery Leeds from the age of 12, who had paid for a year schooling at the Leeds Middle Class School Vernon Street. He started at Roberts Mart & Co in 1883 aged 22 in the office as a book keeper. In 1915 he was paid a bonus of £20 which rose the next year to £26. He was waged at first and became salaried from February 6th 1928 until his retirement on January 31st 1930: it was in this period that he bought a car and took his family to the coast for holidays. When he retired he was presented with a wall clock inscribed *"Presented to James Henry Pickles on the occasion of his retirement after 47 years loyal service by the directors of Roberts Mart & Co as a small token of their appreciation and regard January 31st 1930";* the clock was made by Owen & Robinson of Leeds. He lived after his marriage on Graveley Mount prior to moving to Beechurst 7 Pinfold Lane. James Pickles was involved in village life in Halton and was a Trustee of the Halton Institute. James and Sarah's children were Emily Dorothy (1886-1966) who was a milliner's apprentice at 14 years old and later a District Nurse and worked for a time at the VAD Hospital at the Parochial Hall Halton; Mary Elizabeth (1887-94); James William (1888-1969) who emigrated to Australia and was involved in the Gallipoli landings of 1916: he died in Harrogate; Edith (1891-1981); Arthur (1896-1969) who married Hilda Bailiff on May 3rd 1922: their daughter was Mary; Mary Eleanor born in 1898; Marjorie

James and Sarah Pickles

(1901-1967) who married Percy Hardwick of Garforth in April 1929: their son Gerald was born in 1934 and lives in Harrogate. *Elizabeth Hannah* (1863-1907) who died at Elland. *Henry Greenwood* who was born c1865. *Sarah Jane* born in 1867 and lived at Aiskew. *Arthur Stansfield* (c1870-91) who also lived at Aiskew.

James Henry Pickles died after a stroke on Monday March 26th 1934 and was interred at Whitkirk on Wednesday March 28th. The service was conducted by Rev C Sharpe and in addition to the family members there were a great number of colleagues and friends. These included Walter Roberts, John Roberts, Charles Mart and Albert Davidson representing Roberts Mart & Co. Albert Davidson commenced working for Roberts Mart on May 26th 1913 and died on March 31st 1946. Friends included Philip Marsden of The Grange Whitkirk, Thomas Piercy of Ivy House Whitkirk, Reggie Knight of San Remo and Margaret wife of Vincent D'arcy Massingberd. His wife Sarah Emily Pickles died on Easter Sunday April 9th 1939 aged 80.

Roberts Mart & Co had its origins when William Roberts traded as a rag and paper merchant in Swinegate Leeds in 1852 when he was 28 years old. In the 1860's he moved the business to Alfred Street Boar Lane where James Henry Pickles started his work for the company. He installed a steam powered printing press to overprint the paper bags he manufactured. In 1870 the business was flourishing and the family moved to Allerton House at Moor Allerton. William Roberts employed travelling salemen and one of these was William Mart of Derby. When William died in 1877 William Mart became general manager and when son John Roberts was 21 the firm became Robert Son & Mart. In 1890 Roberts Mart became a limited company and were now paper merchants, lithographers, printers and paper bag manufacturers. In 1898 the remaining portion of Bank Mills was bought and the extension was started to become New Mill. In 1891 the business transferred to part of Bank Mills which was once run by Hives & Atkinson. William Mart died in 1897 and his three sons took part in the business; William Roberts died in 1906 and John Roberts died in 1925 when Walter became chairman: he died in 1947. The firm continued in the Roberts family with father and sons Peter (1914-2000) and John who is the present chairman and managing director. In 1980 a new warehouse was built and in 1983 Romar Packaging Ltd was formed as a subsidiary company. In 1991 a patent was granted covering the manufacture of a roll pack carrier bag. In 2002 Roberts Mart celebrated 150 years of trading in Leeds and in summer 2004 the company moved to newly built premises at Thornes Farm Business Park.

PINFOLD COURT

The cul de sac of Pinfold Court was built from February 1939 by George

Winstanley Airey who also created the new street: there are two blocks of four town houses. There is also a later semi-detached bungalow and a detached house on the street. William Jowitt had placed plans in 1945 for four through houses and two semi-detached houses.
Prospect Gardens was built by Headrow Housing as 16 flats (9 one bed & 7 two bed) for the Retired Person's Scheme on the site of the demolished Chestnut Grove. The housing was opened on May 1st 1978.

PINFOLD LANE

Pinfold Lane was once Pinfold Road and is an ancient street of the village connecting Cross Field Road/Chapel Street (1840) with the turnpike road. Pinfold Lane was once continued on the other side of Selby Road as Baynes Intake Road now represented by a ginnel. An early version of Pinfold was "pynd fald".

In 1783 Ann Wray died holding lands known as Pinfold Garth in Crossfield together with other lands in Stocking Roods, Garthend Field and some land in New Field. A sum of £40 was paid to the Steward of the Manor of Temple Newsam for the extinguishment of manorial incidents in respect of land in Pinfold Lane transferred in 1928 from the Hunslet Rural District Council to the Leeds Corporation.
The Halton Parochial Hall was built in 1908/09 near the site of the original village pinfold where stray animals were collected and on payment of a fee were released to the owners. There was a report of stones from the pinfold being found in the gardens of houses on Pinfold Lane. The 1908 map shows the pinfold walled site and four semi-detached houses which were at first known by individual names. 1 Pinfold Lane was the old post office demolished in 1931 and now part of the green and road junction: the changes were made due to the continual traffic problems on this corner. In 1929 the Council bought the area on the corner for £656. The more modern houses were built in the inter-war years. Prior to the housing the lane ran through open fields and was initially just a track. The field on the west side became the new premises for Templenewsam Halton Primary School in September 1967. This area was sold by auction on June 27th 1878 and included the fields tenanted by butcher William Swift north of the old school and west of the old almshouses. George William Fenwick built some of the semi-detached housing on Pinfold Lane in 1929. The footpath on Pinfold Lane and kerbing was introduced at a cost of £3155 in July 1957. The land on the corner of Pinfold Lane and Selby Road which is now grassed with a public seat was the gift of Hon Edward FL Wood in 1925.
Some of the earlier residents of Pinfold Lane were 3 *Engadine* William Richmond whose daughter Ethel married Leonard Ramsden of London at All Saints Church in 1925. George William & Fanny Jones with daughter

Frances Ann and sons Milton,Edwin and Roy. 5 *Glenburnie* John Walker and later Herbert Powell. John Walter Powell died aged 74 in July 1951; Clara Powell died in September 1971. 7 *Beechurst* James Henry Pickles: he was born in 1861 living first on Graveley Mount with his wife Sarah Emily. Their children were Emily (1877), Mary (1887-1894), James William (1890), Edith (1891), Arthur (1897) and Marjorie born in August 1901. Son Arthur married Hilda Bailiff of Leeds at All Saints Church in 1922. James Henry died aged 73 on March 26th 1934 and Sarah Emily Pickles died on Easter Sunday April 9th 1939. Dentist Reynold LB Forshaw: Kenneth Rowland Cowell who was the son of Alec & Kathleen Cowell married daughter Norma Forshaw who was born in 1928 on July 16th 1948. Norma's younger sister was Pauline Margaret born in 1931: she married Hans Jakob Haffter of Marstetten Switzerland at Whitkirk Church on June 6th 1952. He had been studying textiles at Leeds University and after their marriage they moved to live in Zurich, where she was a governess. Robert & Helen Mattock with their sons Andrew and Ian moved from Gilsyke House where Dr Mattock was in practice with Dr JA Young from 1946 to 1971. 9 *Oakdene* built in the early 1930's: engineer John Berry; Annie, George Vernon Crosthwaite and Kathleen Crosthwaite; 11 Ashbrooke; 15 *Fernville;* 17 *Fairmount* Harold & Olive Bell whose daughters Olga was born in October 1907 and Zara Crosthwaite Bell was born in September 23rd 1910. They were followed by John Stuart White and family. 19 *Brynmor* George & Mary Crosthwaite had plans passed for the houses in 1903 and they were complete by 1908: their daughter Isabel Clara was born at the house in 1914. Wright Popplewell of the Thrift Stores came to live at Avondale in Stanks and then moved to Brynmor by 1920. Joshua and Ethel Popplewell whose son Edward Wright was born here in 1916 with

Margaret born in 1918. Wright's daughter Frances Gertrude was married to Edward Stockwell Lawson on July 17th 1922: he was the son of carpet manufacturer John Lawson. The Naylor family and Emily Crossland followed the Popplewells at Brynmor. In later times the house was home of Lawrence Steel: Walter Henry Steel died in February 1931 aged 78 and Eliza Ann Crawford Steel died in 1945; John Frederick Steel died in June 1945. 23 was built in 1978 as a private house and became the Walsingham Nursing Home from 1987 until closure in May 2001. The house is now a private dwelling again. 25 *Denistoun* built by 1908 with 27; Vera Wilhelmina Austin died at Denistoun aged 4 in March 1908. In 1923 James Wright Popplewell lived at Denistoun: in 1947 James Wright Popplewell was a director of the Thrift Stores and lived at Oak Hill Linton Road Wetherby. Later residents were Edward Stockwell Lawson who married Frances Popplewell and Walter & Elsie Bateson who left Fairfield Primrose Lane in 1935. 27 *Hazlecroft* Thomas & Mary Newns: Thomas Whitmore Newns was a printer in Leeds and was chairman of the Leeds Branch of the South African War Veterans Association. He enlisted in the Argyll & Sutherland Highlanders and became a Leeds special constable for 24 years. He was Master at Headingley Lodge Freemasons and a member of the Temple Newsam Conservative Association; he died aged 74 in August 1952. 41 *Seathwaite*: George Henry & Lizzie Botterill until his death in 1937 and his son Charley (1911-69) and his wife Constance (1911-1983 49 *Craythorne:* Adeline Morritt who was the widow of Thomas Morritt: she was born in 1871 and died in January 1941.

PINFOLD SQUARE

Residents of the two houses on this small cul-de-sac once included George Wraith (1) and Henry Daniel (3): Emily Daniel died in October 1943. James Russell lived at 1 by 1938: he was a prisoner of war in Italy while a member of the Green Howards. The houses were demolished and Pinfolds was built on part of the site which included a brickyard and piggeries. The present garages were completed in 1949 by Kathleen Cowell: the Cowell family owned the two semi-detached cottages on Chapel Street. Joiner Fred Pawson had his workshop in Pinfold Square: he lived at 3 Orchard Terrace. Pinfold Square was once the workshops of Turnbull's Builders and property repairs: the residence was on Windsor Avenue. They had a fireplace showroom at 28 Butts Court Leeds and then by 1961 had moved from Halton to Queens Court Call Lane; by 1964 Turnbulls were based at 131 Albion Street Leeds.

PINFOLDS

Pinfolds is a residential home for children aged 10 to 18 years of age with learning disabilities. The plans for a £280,000 home were placed in

November 1982. It was opened on July 16th 1986 by Leeds City Council Social Services. It was officially opened by the Rt Hon Dennis Healey MP on March 4th 1988 in the presence of the Lord Mayor Coun Doreen Wood, Chairman of the Social Services Committee Coun Bernard Atha and the Director of Social Services for Leeds Derek James.
There was a hostel in Harehills known as Nowell House and there was a need to establish a purpose built home in East Leeds as well as Broom Court in Belle Isle Middleton in South Leeds, where the children from Nowell House were transferred. When the Meanwood Park hostel closed in the late 1980's referrals were to Leeds Social Services and not Meanwood Park. These referrals included children being sent to Pinfolds in Halton.

POLICE

There are mentions in the records of police constables in Halton: PC Henry Yeadon (1861), Sgt Thomas Hirst who served the village from 1862 to 1870, PC James Punton who married Mary Turner in 1875; PC Joshua Pease and PC Mark Noble in 1881, PC Edwin Firth (1882), PC Edwin Birch (1885), Samuel W Bryant (1891) and George Toyne (1901). Police Sergeant Haigh lived at Primrose Road in 1919: his son was Gunner Stanley Haigh. PC Arthur Taylor also served the village and moved to Selby in 1919 to be replaced with PC Robinson of Colton.
Halton had a village police station at 20/22 Primrose Road. Police Sergeant William Holyland of the WR Constabulary based there met his death on December 5th 1925, due to blood poisoning as a result of a compound fracture of the right tibia and fibula accidentally sustained by being knocked down by a car: the verdict was accidental death. His replacement was PC John E Elvidge of the WR Constabulary who became Halton based. He retired on March 1st 1929 after serving Halton for three years. He served at Gildersome, Todmorden, Knaresborough and Harrogate. PC 640 Albert Cannon was appointed to Leeds Police Force in March 1928 from West Riding Constabulary. Sergeant Albert Cannon was married to Rose Elizabeth: their daughter Elsie married Ernest Seagrove in September 1933 and daughter Mona married John Potter on August 12th 1929. 20 Primrose Road was the home of the sergeant and 22 was the home to the constable. When Albert left the Halton police he lived with his wife at 36 Woodland Road, Whitkirk.
The will of Margaret Morkill dated May 1839 included 20/22 Primrose Garth in The Nookin where there was a butcher's shop. She died in October 1841 and on October 24th 1942 the property was transferred to the new tenant John Morkill. On January 31st 1877 Mrs Meynell Ingram sold the property to John Morkill of Killingbeck, the third son of Thomas Morkill of Kippax. In September 1913 John W Morkill of Newfield Hall

Malhamdale sold the property and land to the West Riding County Council for use as a police station. In 1925 the house was let to Leeds Corporation from the West Riding Joint Committee. Arthur Cowper was the son of PC James Cowper who married Esther Ball: daughter of greengrocer Gerald Ball on December 29th 1941.
In November 1952 the start was made on a new police station built by the Irwin Arms public house which opened on December 30th 1953. It was used as a section station until closure by the end of 1965 as it *"had outlived its usefulness and with the early redevelopment of the area the site was passed to the Town Planning and Improvements Committee"* and demolition in 1965.

POST OFFICES

The development of post offices followed the introduction of Sir Rowland Hill's Penny Post on January 9th 1840

From 1822 William Wigglesworth was a village messenger/walking postman serving Halton, Whitkirk and Temple Newsam. There were six foot carriers serving the villages which included Halton. In 1837 William Wigglesworth ran a mail carriage service to Halton and Whitkirk every day but Tuesday. The first mention of a district post office was at Whitkirk in 1851: William Green was the postmaster. Letters came to Whitkirk from Leeds at 7am and at 2pm. In the 1861/71 census Thomas Stockdale was the postmaster/grocer in Halton. In 1883 there was a wall letter box at Whitkirk and in 1897 boxes were also at Austhorpe, Halton Hill, Swillington Common and on Green Lane. The Post Office Controller for the area in 1891 was William Henry Roberts. The first post office for the village was at the corner of Woodman Street run by *William Bell* in 1893, who also sold groceries and beer: this became the property of son Ossie Bell. Ossie's elder brother Alexander was a post office clerk with 14 year old William Daniel and George Longdon as Post Office errand boys in 1891. In 1901 the Post Office was run by 59 year old grocer William Bell whose wife was Ethel and his four children including 18 year old GO Bell. By 1903 the post office had moved to 2 Primrose Road run by *Arthur and Grace Tyzack*: Grace then married George Batty of Barker's Row who was a joiner born in 1857; they ran the post office and confectioners. There was an application to establish a postal telegraph office in 1904 but this was turned down due to the low number of potential customers in Halton: the underground line was later laid on the main road. In 1920 the Batty family were followed by Charles Edward Bolton who moved to an old house at the bottom of Pinfold Lane by March 1925, when a new Post Office sign was erected by Hunslet RDC. In August 1925 plans were presented to acquire this post office for demolition and improve the corner for traffic: problems with this corner were already being voiced in 1911. These plans were passed and the Leeds CC bought the land in early 1927 with agreement to build a house as alternative premises in 1928. This was 21 Chapel Street and the present post office at a new address of 1 Pinfold Lane with the address changing c1955 to 3 Cross Green Lane. The new post office was opened in March 1931. *Charles Bolton* had obtained planning permission on December 9th 1930 for a new shop and house; the plans were passed on January 13th. 1931. The 536 square yards of land was sold by the Council ata rate of five shillings a square yard. On January 30th 1931 a news item was *"The present post office at the junction of Pinfold Lane and High Street will shortly be moved up the street to intended new premises"*. When the new post office was opened George Fenwick was offered £15 by the Council to demolish the old corner building.

The property remained with the Bolton family (Charles died in 1949) until 1966 when it was bought by the Francis family. The sub-postmasters leasing the building were *George Smith* who also ran a drapery business: wife Gertrude died aged 52 on June 23rd 1937 aged 52; *Arthur Field Allott*: his wife ran the Barcley Corsetry Service; *John C Fenton* who retired to Filey in June 1970 after 18 years at Halton and *Bryan & Irene Hall*. *Tony and Jenny Nicholson* started at Halton Post Office on August 31st 1979. In August 1999 they marked 20 years at

Left to Right: Jenny Nicholson, Mike Ingle, Tony Nicholson and customer Jean Pickersgill.

Halton and Tony was presented with a certificate marking his 40 years working for the Post Office by network manager Mike Ingle.
The post office has a blocked side entrance which was once the access for the postmen: where the counter is today was the sorting office. The present garage was once a hen coop and retains the sorting boxes which were only used in periods of heavy use such as at Christmas.
The sorting facilities were transferred to Halton Ring Road in c1946 to the former premises of the Ministry of Agriculture, Fisheries and Foods and moved in 1991 to the Coal Road estate at Seacroft.
The ***Crescent Post Office*** was opened on March 1st 1930 and closed on October 30th 2002. The first postmaster was *Robert William Edmanson* with his wife Doris. Doris died in September 1943 aged 51: she was a respected singer and was in Halton Methodist Church choir. She started worshipping at Quarry Hill Methodist Chapel and moved to Harehills Avenue Chapel. The Edmanson family were followed by Stanley Burley who came in 1947. The next postmaster was *Stanley & Annie Shaw* who advertised the sale of Hornby trains, Meccano and toys. Later sub-postmasters were *Harry & Beryl Clarkson, A Howieson and Joseph & Audrey Smith.* The closed shop at 3/5 Oak Crescent was the subject of planning permission in February 2004 for the alteration to dwellings.
Rookwood Post Office at the bottom of Halton Hill was opened in 1930 with George Campbell. ***Halton Moor Road Post Office*** was built by William Jowitt and opened in 1931 with postmaster Harry Burnett.

POST OFFICE COLLECTING BOXES

There are more than 115,000 postboxes in Britain and were first introduced onto the streets in 1853 as a tall box with large cap:the types we see today were introduced in 1879.

The earliest post box in Halton is not in use: a garden feature of the Old School House on Selby Road is a box from the Victorian age inscribed VR. The box outside the closed Post Office on Oak Crescent is one from the age of King Edward VII, who ruled from 1901 until 1911. There is a King George VI posting box at Whitkirk by the old Co-op building and the others are from the age of our present Queen Elizabeth. There are boxes at Cross Green Lane (Halton PO), Field End Road, Halton Moor Road (PO), New Templegate, Primrose Lane, Selby Avenue, Templegate and Woodland Hill.

PRIMROSE LANE

This is one of the oldest streets of Halton and first known as Back Lane and Occupation Lane (Cross Street to Green Lane until 1901)

There was at one time a row of houses with a corner shop run by Albert Scarfe (1856-1930) & Mary (1864-1940) who later lived at 83 Morritt Drive. The corner shop was later run by Thomas & Alice Bonsall and was demolished to build the Halton Clinic which opened in May 1984. Their daughter Agnes married Ronald Cowell in 1929. The adjacent shop on ***Primrose Terrace*** was that of shoe repairer Arthur Whitaker, later Herbert Greenfield who died in March 1951 and shoe repairer R Middlemass in the 1960's. James Woodhead had a greengrocer's shop here in 1908. In these houses in 1901 were also Sarah Thompson (fried fish shop), Benjamin Smith (lamplighter) and Mary Butler (baker). In later years Janet McDonald ran her hair salon on Primrose Terrace. In 1929 Primrose Terrace was home to the Bonsall family (8), John Maher and Harry Dawson (10), Thomas Hardcastle (12) and bricklayer Walter Eastwood (14). Walter & Mary Eastwood's son Donald was born in June 1914. In 1933 John Longden was at 8 and Harry Pawson at 10: the Bonsalls had moved to the shop on the corner (20 High Street). The end house on this row later became a betting shop run by Edward Hayes: the son of Charles Hayes of Grove Road. 3 Primrose Lane was the business of J Cass Painter & Decorator established in 1899.

The corner of Primrose Lane and the main road was proposed for a £168,000 junction improvement scheme in 1979 which was delayed for a few years until the junction was improved with traffic lights and a widened road. ***Newsam Square*** was the first group of old brick built housing to the left off Primrose Lane.

The land to the rear of the Parade was once a narrow strip of allotments and later was the site on Ingram Avenue for an electricity sub-station in the form of a black and white timber framed house. The inscription over the door was LCED (Leeds City Electricity Department): the site is now the goods entrance for Matalan. It was in February 1931 that a plot of land measuring 630 square yards was sold by JA Bonner to the Electricity Committee of the LCC at a cost of two shillings a square yard.

To the east side of the start of Primrose Lane were four rows of houses: ***Orchard Terrace*** demolished in 1968, ***Britton Terrace, Dial Row*** demolished in 1970 and ***Barker's Terrace*** adjoining 21 Primrose Lane. ***Dial Terrace*** demolished in 1966 was a continuation of Dial Row leading into Graveley Square. In 1872 all the houses in Dial Row belonged to Halton's John Rollinson.

Squire Swift lived on Orchard Terrace: he was a butcher who sold the site for the Halton Co-op shop at the end of the 19th century. Squire was born in 1836 and died at Pear Tree House in February 1931; he lived with his wife Mary who died aged 94 and sons Robert and Raymond. Charles Arthur Smith died in March 1943: he was one of the nine children of Squire and Mary Swift of Orchard House. Thomas Priest was a chemist who lived on Britton Terrace and John Petch was a flour miller on Dial Row (1901). Another well known Halton resident on Dial Row was John Walter Briggs who died aged 76 in 1922: he had been singing bass for St Mary's RC Church in Leeds for 33 years. Dial Row was on the line of the man made embankment between the centre car park and Brooksbank Home: the houses towards Graveley Square had long gardens. Walter Mark Dobson lived on Barker's Terrace: he was born in Colton in 1856 and married at Whitkirk Church in 1878. These properties were cleared for the Halton Centre and Brooksbank Home developments. ***Morritt Grove*** and ***Primrose Garth*** are developments from 1936 and were declared as highways in April 1938. Primrose Garth was surfaced by contractors W Elam in 1936/37. There was public pressure to have a crossing on Primrose Lane at the junction with Morritt Grove: a plan agreed by the LCC in 1936 at a cost of £65. One of the residents of Primrose Garth was Henry Mexted who died on November 24th 1957 aged 89. He was a veteran of the South African War and a private in the 8th/15th Hussars. He had enlisted in February 1899 and discharged in 1902, awarded the Queen's Medal for the South African Campaign and the King's Medal.

The allotments on the west wide were proposed to be the site for a £5.25 million council housing scheme, which was approved in 1976. There were to be 493 houses on land which was to include the sports ground. The scheme was later abandoned.

Primrose Lane Nurseries on the east side by Primrose Road provided the needs of the gardener: they were nurserymen, seedsmen and florists. The business was Elijah Dobson (1860-1924) of 18 Primrose Road who married Hannah Clarkson in August 1887 and later the Nurseries were run by Thomas Barkley of 19 Graveleythorpe Terrace. The nurseries were run by A McGrath & Co with the proprietor being R Hardwick. Alexander and Charlotte McGrath who died February 1925 lived at 2 Graveley Street *Alexander McGrath* was at first a pork butcher in Holbeck and he died aged 77 in October 1952 and was buried in Killingbeck Cemetery. The nursery was run by Joseph & Nancy Timmermans who lived at 61 Primrose Lane: in 1965 he won an award at the Leeds Paxton Society Early Autumn Flowers and Vegetable Show. The Lane becomes an unmade track with Halton Deans on the north side with the sports facilities and Pickering Lodge dating from 1820 on the south side accessed from Primrose Drive and Long Field Drive. There was for many years the Acme Jam Factory, in the fields at the end of Cross Street with foundations barely visible. The factory started c1890 and was sold on June 24th 1902 by Heppers of Leeds: the building was of corrugated iron comprising warehouse, boiling room and two copper pans by Brierley: Leeds Town Water was used at this factory. The purchaser was gardener/traveller Samuel Heathcote who later lived with wife Mary together with Samuel Cyril born 1899 and Cyril Heathcote born March 27th 1898, Millicent May (1902-1990), Millicent born February 1909, Elsie born June 1911 and Constance Mary born in August 1913 at 17 Graveley Street. Samuel Heathcote was born in Derbyshire in 1868 and died in 1937; Maria Heathcote died in late February 1935. The firm invited members of the village to bring clean jam jars in exchange for a penny. Many workers lived in the village including Fred Cavanagh of Field Terrace who worked as a jam boiler and Charles Daniel of Chapel Street with Emily Watson of Newsam Square and 13 year old Mercy Wikely Parkin of Britton Terrace. Samuel and Mary Heathcote's daughter Ivy who worked as a forewoman in the jam factory married Leonard Brownridge on December 28th 1923, whose father Thomas William ran the family firm of furniture removal specialists; son Samuel Cyril born in 1900 married 26 year old Nellie Drury of Oak Road on May 30th 1936. The family later moved from the village to live in York. The building became a car repair shop which moved to Whinmoor.

The junction of Primrose Lane with Cross Street was originally where Back Lane became Garth End Road. The road ran across Garth End Field and was linked by a footpath with Cross Field Road. Prior to being made into a part of Primrose Lane it was Occupation Lane in 1900.

The surfaced road passes 1930's housing on the left with the detached Carlton House on the right built in 1929. This was the home of the Batty family: Charles' son Sydney married Agnes Stott on June 6th 1923. His sister Annie Batty married Joshua Appleyard at Halton Methodist Church: the son of Henry Appleyard of Austhorpe Hall. Charles Batty died aged 76 in April 1938.

Park View Terrace faces onto Primrose Lane and on the south side beyond Park Street are four detached houses standing back from the road. These were built in 1923 in a poppy field and at first had no electricity having to use oil lamps. The first residents at Fairfield 155 Primrose Lane were Walter & Elsie Bateson: he was a teacher at All Saints School and later was headmaster of Manston School. Walter's brother was Frederick Bateson who was a benefactor of Manston Church living in Church Lane. Walter Abbott Bateson moved to Pinfold Lane and died aged 66 on August 24th 1950 having retired after 17 years at the school in 1944. Elsie Bateson died aged 96 on July 21st 1985.

The Mannix family of joiners and builders lived on Primrose Lane. Daniel Mannix died aged 72 in February 1948 and Arthur Daniel Mannix died aged 62 in April 1970. Primrose Avenue, Crescent and

Lane with Valley Drive were developed in the 1930's mainly by JW Shippen and the town houses on the south side of Primrose Lane date from 1970 built on allotments. The road from Park Street to Green Lane was surfaced in 1933. In May 1937 the Council agreed that Primrose Lane was to be sewered, levelled, paved, metalled, flagged and channelled as applied by the Hunslet (Temple Newsam) Town Planning Scheme and the Leeds Corporation Act 1927.The section of Green Lane from Morritt Avenue was constructed in 1931/32 at a cost of £774.

PRIMROSE ROAD/GARTH

One of the original lanes of the village

The stocks for the village were sited on the corner of Primrose Road at one time overlooked by thatched cottages. The stocks were remembered by older villagers in 1929, when they saw young lads putting themselves in the stocks in the later years of the 19th century. There were plans to build a cinema for the village on the corner: they were suppressed by Gertrude Bray who built the row of houses on the corner site which was once the private grounds of nearby Hawthorn House: the house driveway is now the widened Halton Drive. Primrose Road was in a poor state of repair in 1910 when Hunslet RDC declared it to be only a footpath and not a designated highway.

The street runs from Chapel Street to Primrose Lane: on the corner was Alfred Tomlinson's radio & TV dealer, electrical engineers, china and fancy goods shop.

2 was the old Post Office run by Arthur & Grace Tyzack and then George & Grace Batty. George was a joiner and wheelwright born at Wilberfoss near York in 1857; Grace was a baker born at Kendal in 1860 who married Arthur Tyzack; George was her second husband. By 1901 their step-daughter Elizabeth Ann Tyzack born in Ulverston in 1883, Hannah Tyzack born in 1887 and Lucy born in 1889 were living at this house. Elizabeth Ann Speight Tyzack of the Halton Post Office married Edward Parkin on August 26th 1903 and Lucy Tyzack married Alfred Mosby of 5 Dawson Square on November 7th 1915. In 1940 this was shop keeper James Maude and by 1954 this was the home of Walter and Alice Kirk.

4 was Frederick Whiteley's hairdressing salon by 1887: he was also a boot and shoe maker. On August 19th 1891 Frederick's son John William married Mary Frances Smales when he was aged 49. In 1904 the hairdresser was T Fowbert. *Leopold Vincent Button* was born in 1889, son of John Button and he lived at the Primrose Road house/shop with his wife Beatrice. By 1951 Leopold Button had lived in the village for 32 years. 2 Primrose Road was blown apart by a gas explosion in December 1971 and the building was later demolished. The site is now council

housing built by Wimpey from 1974 with 46 houses adjacent to five private dwellings. The Buttons were rehoused by Leeds Corporation at 3 Cricklegate and later at 6 Primrose Road. Beatrice Button died aged 65 on October 29th 1952: she was a founder member of the Women's Section of the Halton & Temple Newsam branch of the British Legion, founded in 1932. Billy Button married for the second time to Lily Edwards SRN (born May 18th 1889) on July 16th 1956; he died in February 1978 in a flat at Craigmona Park Street. There was no funeral service and his body was given to medical science; his widow Lily had died in 1977. Annie Elizabeth Button died aged 45 in February 1953.

Primrose Close dates from the mid 1960's with the odd numbers built first followed by the even numbers. The Ballance family who were long standing village residents lived for a time at 12 Primrose Road. Stephen Ballance was born in 1835 and was a miner; his wife dressmaker Mary Ann Ballance was born in 1841. Their children were Jane born in 1863 who married Frank Dodsworth, son of grocer John on September 8th 1888, Benjamin Fryer who was born in 1868, Alfred born in 1870 and Grace born in 1872. Ben and Alfred were boot and shoe makers and repairers. John Ballance born in 1838 was a grocer who ran a shop on Woodman Row with his wife Elizabeth born in 1844.

Annie Ballance was born in 1894 and was married to Henry Britten on January 12th 1924; brothers Edgar was born in 1895 and Cyril Ballance born in 1897 was a Post Office sorting clerk. Cyril married Priscilla Plant on December 15th 1917 at the Methodist Church. Annie and Cyril's parents were Halton shoemaker Alfred Ballance born in 1870 and Annie Isabel Ballance born in 1871. The family later moved to live at 29 Graveley Street. In the 1950's Cyril & Priscilla Ballance lived with their children William and Micheline at 21 Cross Green Lane. Catherine Ballance died at her home on Birch Avenue in September 1949 and Alfred Ballance died in December 1952.

Nookin Cottage dates back 300 years and was probably a thatched cottage on the Temple Newsam estate built for their employees. The Nookin was by The Orchards where the eight terrace cottages have been demolished and replaced with new housing. The Nookin was once the home of miner John Weatherill and lamplighter Ephraim Weatherill who was at Barker's Row. In the early years of the 20th century the Pique family lived at the cottage: they had alterations and additions to their property in 1935.

20/22 Primrose Road was once the police station for the village and the row of houses opposite date from the mid-18th century. They were built as part of the Temple Newsam estate and were constructed with stone staircases, oak beams and Yorkshire stone floors. There was a communal washhouse with outside dry toilets. To the rear there was a header water tank: it was 8 feet across and 12 feet deep lined with horsehair. The

water came here from the reservoir and was distributed around the local cottages.
The cottages on the west side were built in 1869 and the plots given as birthday presents by Hugo Francis Meynell Ingram in the year that he had inherited the Temple Newsam Estate. Primrose Hill is the large house nearby to The Nookin: meaning a corner. Rose Cottage on Primrose Road was a replacement for the demolished gardener's cottage for the Graveley estate, which had been condemned by the Council in June 1928. The new cottage was built in 1929 for Walter Wood JP who died on July 19th 1931 aged 69. He was the leader of the Socialist & Labour Party in Leeds and from the age of 7 worked in a brickyard and became a pit pony driver when he was 10 years old. He became a miner and a gas stoker at York Road Gas Works; emigrated to Canada, joined the Socialist movement and returned to Halton in 1887. In 1913 he was a member for the Armley & Wortley Ward retiring in 1919. Walter Wood was a magistrate and from 1913 to 1919 was a member of Leeds City Council. He was also the local organiser of the Gasworkers & General Labourers Union and was Leeds President. Walter Wood married Mary Ann in Leeds Parish Church on December 25th 1880 and had seven sons, a daughter and twenty grandchildren: he celebrated his Golden Wedding in 1930. Mary Ann Wood died aged 72 on March 8th 1935. One of their sons was Walter Percy Wood who served with the West Yorkshire Regiment in the Great War and was wounded in action. He was a horseman for the Leeds Sanitary Department and lived at 9 Primrose Road and Field End Road, later working as a meter fixer. Denis Wood lived at 7 Primrose Road and was a sheet metal worker: he ran Marwood Portable Buildings with brother Thomas Wood.
Primrose Hill was the home of Rutherford Miller who was a musical instrument dealer and a Music Hall veteran. He appeared at the Princess Palace in Leeds in King Charles Croft in 1879 and he died aged 62 in 1934. He was a collector of antiques and amongst his treasures was a Stradivarius violin. Charles Edward Sykes lived at Primrose Hill: he died on September 11th 1929 and his funeral was held at St James Church Leeds with interment at Woodhouse Hill Cemetery. He was the Secretary of Halton Institute.

PRIMROSE VALLEY

The valley adjacent to the railway was once known as Prospect Valley and at one time had only one substantial building: Valley House. There were a few miners' cottages for the colliery near the old shafts: demolished in the early years of the 20th century. The first reference to Valley House was in 1851 when Thomas Shaw was a beer retailer in the valley, serving the miners at Garside's Killingbeck Colliery. The ale house opened about that time and was known as The Bird in Hand, probably a reference to the bird cage that miners carried for safety. The colliery developed large tip heaps in the valley and closed by 1893; this was followed later by the withdrawal of beer services at the house and the subsequent enlargement of the smallholding, orchard and greenhouses. This was the home of the Almond family: Harry Almond was a coal miner and his wife often served teas from the house. In 1938 Harry and his wife Mary Jane lived at the house with daughters Violet and Ruby. Harry's father was Frederick Almond who was a horse tram driver. Harry married Mary Jane Jewitt of Crook Co Durham who he had met in Durham while working in the pits. Valley House once featured cellars, bar and a bar mirror; Harry retired in c1965 and moved to Harehills. Claude Almond was aged 23 when he married Louie Burn (born 1924) on August 17th 1946. Wilfred and Shirley Almond lived at Primrose Valley Farm and their daughter Karen Lesley was born in January 1959 and was baptised at Whitkirk Church. The house became a ruin and was eventually demolished c1968: only the site and trees remain. The Almond family were well known both in Leeds and suburbs for their fruit, flowers and green grocery shops: they were in the Leeds market and at 51 Selby Road.

Another family living at Primrose Valley was James and Elizabeth Jackson: he was a gardener and was born in 1851. He married Elizabeth and their children were Harriet born in 1871 and Emily born in 1878. In November 1902 there was an application to Hunslet RDC to open a laundry in the Valley.

There was a planning application in 1977/78 to erect houses on Primrose Valley involving the extraction of coal on the site of the allotments and cricket ground. The scheme involved 493 houses at a cost of £5,219,000: it was abandoned in October 1980.

Primrose Valley was the site of not only the Killingbeck Colliery but also Halton Deans which was the site of Halton Cricket Club's pitch. In 1984 plans were submitted for footpaths, sports fields, tennis courts, picnic site, amphitheatre and landscaping: a sports pavilion was planned in late 1987. Negotiations were completed in December 1988 for a bowling green, football pitches, tennis courts with a car park, paths and tree planting. The site was developed by the Council in the early 1990's from being a landfill site and a children's play area was built together with the bowling green and tennis courts. The valley has many attractive footpaths, marshy pond and shrubs with in summertime a blaze of colourful wild flowers; one of the entrances is from Valley Drive near the railway bridge. In late 2003 the Primrose Action Group received a cash boost from ward-based initiative funds for the restoration of Primrose Valley.

PUBLIC HOUSES

There are references through the early directories to public houses in Halton including the ***Piper Inn***-probably on Primrose Road. The ***Bird in Hand*** was an ale house in Primrose Valley: in 1834 John Rollisson was a ale and porter retailer and was a shoemaker. The ***Old Engine Inn*** was mentioned in 1822 with licensee John Atkinson: Henry Atkinson was at the Piper Inn in 1834. ***The Union Inn*** was run in 1822 by butcher John Laycock.

Irwin Arms is an old established inn built to serve the increasing traffic on the Leeds & Selby turnpike opened in 1740; the three inns on the High Street are shown on a 1765 map. It was on the corner site of Irwin Approach (Halton Moor Road) and was a long low building known as The Cock & Coronet and The Cock and Cushion Inn in the 19th century and was also called The Irvine Arms: referring to the coat of arms of the

Ingram/Irwin family of Temple Newsam. There were two attached cottages called Irwin Cottages (3/5 High Street) with private walled gardens, one being the home of a Halton chimney sweep. The old inn had a bowling green: the site was used to build the present inn which opened in late 1936. The Inn was one of three acquired by John Smith's of Tadcaster: the others inns were Robin Hood, Vicar Lane and Fairway at Gipton.

Licensees have included: John Hardwick (1822), Joseph Ash (1828), Richard Vause (1834), William Pawson (1843), William (1800-61) and Isabella Bardon; their son William married Sophia Chadwick in October 1867, Joseph and Rachel Thompson (1889), Phoebe Jane Clarkson (1912/8), Walter Scott (1928/30), Ernest Drake (1938), Sykes Mallinson (1947) and William Armitage in the 1960's. When Mrs Clarkson left the public house in 1918 there was a presentation from the Halton Harmonic Society, Halton Bowling Club and Halton Allotments Association. The Irwin Arms was sold into private hands in recent years: there are plans to redevelop the site. The public house was closed and boarded up on December 24th 2003.

Leodis was opened on October 25th 1967 on Cross Green Lane on the site of some allotments. Planning permission was finally obtained in October 1962 after initial refusal in 1961. The first signing was of a Roman soldier but this changed to become the coat of arms of the City of Leeds. The inn is owned by the Bank of Scotland and serves John Smith (Scottish & Newcastle) beers.

Travellers was built to serve the turnpike traffic: in 1898 it was sold by Mrs Meynell Ingram to Mary Dawson. The property was bought by Tetley's Brewery at a Leeds auction for £7250 from Harold Dawson on March 16th 1925: it was under lease to the Leeds & Wakefield Brewery who sold it with the bowling green, outbuildings and large garden. The bowling green is now the site of the Halton Centre car park. The inn was popularly known as The Middle House and once featured an old railway carriage at the rear in which pigeons were often places in their baskets. The public house was restored

and refurbished in 2002.
Licensees have included: William Hawkshaw (1830's), Richard Senior (1843), George Bowman (1847), Robert Rhodes (1860's), Alfred Spencer & Caroline Briggs who died aged 39 on November 12th 1878, John William Dixon (1912), George Dean (1917), Arthur Stones (1928/30), Walter Hardy (1938/47), Fred Kenworthy, John Bagnall (1971) and Barry Ellis.
Woodman is a turnpike inn and once had stabling, as did the Brown Cow at Whitkirk. It is often regarded as being the oldest of the High Street inns and is said to be haunted. The licensee from 1930 was Edward Bolus whose son Brian Bolus played cricket for Yorkshire and England. Edward moved to live at 10 Park View Terrace where he died on June 24th 1961; he had been at The Woodman for 20 years. In March 1959 the licensees were Ronald and Doris Roberts, whose son Christopher born in 1950 went to Temple Moor School. Ronnie Roberts started his music career in 1926: conductor of the first Old Time Music Hall at the City Varieties. In the wartime Ronnie was in the fire service and in 1949 became the conductor of the Leeds Empire Theatre orchestra. He conducted the first pantomime Cinderella with Albert Modley and Leeds University Rag Revue in 1948: he left the theatre in 1959 and he died in September 1972.

Licensees have also included: John Atkinson (1830), William Green (1834), Esther Sheppard (1843), John Longley/Samuel Longley and William Smith (1860's), Emma Smith (1871), George Fryer (1870's/80's), James Lowe (1897), Abraham Bennett, (1912), Herbert Thornton (1928), John Edward Griffiths (1929) and William Rourke (1950's).
Wykebeck Arms on Halton Hill was opened on April 21st 1939 on the site of Whitebridge Mill at a cost of £6250. The licence had been transferred from The Greyhound Inn York Road: the licence was approved in March 1938. Lizzie Rider was 28 years at this public house

from the opening. She ran the inn with her husband Edwin who died in 1965 and her parents were at The Greyhound. In January 1966 a new public house was suggested at the junction of Templegate Road, Templegate Avenue and Templegate Way, with shops approved in 1970. A new public house was included on the plans for the new Halton Neighbourhood Centre in 1967.

REX FAMILY

Albert Rex was baptised on January 23rd 1902 at St Mary's Church Garforth: he was the son of builder Albert Rex and his wife Mary Hannah of Victoria Cottages Moor Garforth. Albert was schooled at Garforth and on April 1st 1929 he married Edwina Mary Hodgson of Garforth at St Mary's Church: her father was a local grocer and Edwina was born in 1895. They soon moved to live in Whitkirk at a newly built house Solana 58 Woodland Hill and Albert worked for John Clapham Bartle's Whitkirk Auction Market as an auctioneer. Edwina's mother Lily Hodgson was also living for a period with her daughter and son-in-law. Albert was appointed Secretary of the Leeds & Wakefield Branch of the National Farmers Union from 1936 and also secretary of the Leeds Agricultural Show which was held at Whinmoor, Whitkirk and in Temple Newsam Park. He travelled around many farms offering insurance policies on behalf of the NFU. Albert Rex and farmer William Verity were friends: William was the President of the Leeds Branch of the National Farmer's Union which had local offices on Hollyshaw Lane. The offices were opened in 1950 by NFU Chairman HW Wood and were closed in 1989. The two men would travel to the Smithfield Market in London and were often seen together at Whitkirk Auction Market. In 1938 Albert and Edwina Rex with their only son moved to the detached house Grove Lea 42 Grove Road. Albert Rex was a keen bass singer and sang in St Chad's Far Headingley choir and with amateur productions in Leeds and Garforth.

Michael Albert Edward Rex was baptised at St Mary's Church Garforth

on January 19th 1930. He was educated at Cross Gates Boy's School, Leeds Grammar School from 1940 to when he left school in 1949 and at Gonville & Caius College Cambridge University. He researched the respiratory diseases of poultry at the Department of Animal Pathology at Cambridge University and was appointed the Resident House Surgeon at the University of Cambridge Veterinary Hospital. Michael Rex married Gibby Crampin at St James Church Grimsby on August 4th 1961: they had met while Michael was working at the Blue Cross Hospital Grimsby for 18 months. He sailed to Australia after his father's funeral on Thursday August 10th at Whitkirk Church, to lecture in Veterinary Science at Sydney University. Michael Rex was appointed Senior Lecturer in Veterinary Surgery at Massey University Palmeston North in New Zealand and then was Professor of Veterinary Science at Brisbane Queensland Australia.
Edwina Rex moved to Australia on October 1st 1962 to be with Michael and Gibby following the sudden death of her husband on Sunday August 5th 1961 aged 59. Albert Rex had been taken ill in Grimsby where they had travelled for their son's wedding. Albert was buried at Whitkirk on August 10th 1961. Edwina frequently corresponded with her Halton friends including Vi Gilleghan and she died in Brisbane Australia; Michael Rex died aged 70 in 2000 leaving a widow and three children.

RHODES FAMILY

Joseph Armitage Rhodes was born in 1850 at Hunslet Moor Side and eight years later was orphaned and cared for by his grandfather Joseph Armitage. In 1861 he worked for Henry Inchbold Stationer and Beck & Inchbold 44/46 Basinghall Street Leeds and 56 Albion Street. James Beck lived in Harrogate. In 1864 aged 14 he was apprenticed to J Richardson where he stayed for 27 years. He opened his first business in the Bull & Bell Yard on the west side of Briggate above the Imperial Hotel. He moved to 8 Aire Street where the firm remained in business. He started Rhodes & North in 1890 and this became Rhodes & Sons Ltd: his son Thomas Benson Rhodes remained in the business. In 1894 Joseph Rhodes became the proprietor of the Skyrack Courier (Skyrack Express), started in 1866 by Alfred Hobson as the Roundhay Gazette. In January 1922 he sold out to the West Riding ABC Group of Leeds who sold the paper the year afterwards. Joseph Rhodes was the Secretary for Hunslet Cricket Club and a member of Whitkirk Cricket Club, member of the Friendly Society and a member of the Phoenix Lodge (Leeds Unity) Ancient Order of Oddfellows for 40 years. He was a sidesman at Whitkirk Church, member of the Temple Newsam Ratepayers Association and the Leeds & District Master Printers Association. Joseph Rhodes lived at 52 Hollyshaw Lane Whitkirk and by 1929 was at 7

Mayfield Road Halton. He celebrated his Golden Wedding in 1922 and his memories included the opening of Roundhay Park in 1872 and the building of Cross Gates Railway Station. He was an original trustee for the Micklefield Colliery Explosion Fund: the disaster was on April 30th 1896. The fund was represented at his funeral by Alvara Chadwick following his death aged 82 on June 22nd 1933. The funeral at Whitkirk was attended by many members of his family, friends and colleagues including printer RW Crabtree, Reggie Knight and A Mitchell representing Burley Lawn Methodist Church where he was a Trustee. He left a son: his other son AK Rhodes died in 1930, a daughter, three grandsons and two great grandsons.

SCARFE FAMILY

The corner shop on Primrose Lane and Halton High Street 20 High Street/219 Selby Road was run by Albert & Mary Elizabeth Scarfe as Primrose Cash Store. Albert was born in 1865 in Old Manston (Barwick in Elmet) and was baptised at Bramham Church. Albert was the eldest child of collieryman James Scarfe and his wife Caroline: James was born in 1844 and Caroline in 1839. James and Caroline had five children: Albert born in 1865, Emily born in 1868, Arthur born in 1871, Caroline born in 1876 and Caleb who was born in 1880. Caroline married miner Joseph Parker and they lived with her parents for a short time after their marriage. The family moved to Providence Place Swillington Common on the main Selby Road, where James was a colliery banksman and son Albert became a boot and shoe dealer. Albert married Mary Elizabeth Heaton on June 15th 1895 at King Cross Wesleyan Chapel Halifax. They were both 30 years old on marriage when Albert lived at Swillington Common and Mary lived at Helm Street King Cross, where she was the daughter of watchman John Heaton. There had four girls Emily born in 1897, Maud born in 1898, Lillie born in 1901, Ivy born in 1904 and Olive born in 1906. The family moved to live at Field End by 1901 and moved again to run the High Street corner shop by 1912. They left the shop by 1928 to live at 83 Morritt Drive. The shop was taken by

Christopher and Ella Hayes and then by Alice Maria and Thomas Bonsall in 1930. Albert and Mary then moved to 1 Chapel Yard in 1934 where he was a caretaker at the Halton Methodist Church. Albert Scarfe died aged 73 on December 12th 1938 and Mary Elizabeth died on February 17th 1940 after a move to live on Oak Road.

The eldest daughter Emily was born on May 9th 1896 and she married James Edward Monkman in September 1932 at Halton Congregational Church, where he was a founder member. James Monkman was born on October 18th 1895 at Selby with the family moving to Halton in 1900: Edward served in the Royal Flying Corps. He was a local door to door bread and cake salesman and in 1923 sold from a basket on foot before he started van deliveries. Edward was a talented ventriloquist with his doll Sammy and took part in many concert parties at the Congregational Church. James was the son of Charles Edward Monkman and Rose Annie Cawkwell-Monkman who was born in 1866 and died in 1941: they had children James Edward and William. Charles was born at Hunslet in 1862 and moved to live at Springfield Place Halton: he became a porter at Barkston Ash Laundry. On her husband's death in 1938 Rose Annie lived in the almshouses on School Lane. Edward and Emily lived their married life at 18 High Street and later on Cartmell Drive. James Edward Monkman lived for five years at the Brooksbank Home until his death at St James Hospital on June 21st 1981: he was cremated at Lawnswood on June 29th 1981. Edward's wife Emily died in 1964.

The second daughter Maud Scarfe was born in 1900 and she married David Bell in May 1922. They moved to Arnside where David was the head gardener to the Popplewell family of the Thrift Stores who had retired to live at Arnside. In 1923 James Wright Popplewell lived on Pinfold Lane having joined the grocery business in 1918; his brother Joshua moved to Beechwood Arnside in 1923. Wright was at Morecambe and he died on June 19th 1933. David and Maud Bell's sons were Harold and Maurice: Harold was a pharmacist at Bradford and Bramley after qualification at Leeds University. In later years Harold lodged with his elder sister Emily and her husband: he died in 2002. Maurice was a gardener on the Warter Priory Estate: Warter House was demolished in 1972.

Ivy Scarfe was born in 1904 and she married John William Burdekin in August 1924. John was the son of Thomas Burdekin of Beeston Hill and after their marriage they lived at 9 Cross Street. They moved to live on Ingram Road Holbeck and had three children Kenneth, John and Alan.

The youngest daughter was Olive Scarfe who was born in 1906: she married George Arthur Sedgwick on July 16th 1922. George lived on Morritt Drive near the Scarfe family home and was a sheet metal worker. They moved after their marriage to Redcar where he worked for Redwing Coaches. They came back to Halton and lived on Valley Drive: he worked at Barnbow on the tanks. Olive died in 1992 and George died in 1996: they had two daughters Margaret and Dorothy.

SCHOOLS

Halton has had a variety of private schools over the years and these have included M Blackett's Academy (1822) and a small boarding school in Fryer's Yard on the High Street. The 1822 directory lists Christopher Wainwright and George Wigglesworth as Halton schoolmasters. In 1830/34 the schoolteachers included John Barker, Rebecca Neale and Elizabeth Thornton. In 1847 a boarding school was run by Sarah de Putron with Mary Ann Pollard. In later years there was a preparatory school on Morritt Avenue run by Miss Tindale: one of her pupils was Clifford Giddings born in Halton in 1904 and admitted to Leeds Grammar School in 1914 for 7 years. In January 1923 there was a report of *"a private school in Halton of a great many years closed and five children were transferred to Halton School"*.

Corpus Christi School on Halton Moor Road was built with the church and Bishop Cowgill laid the foundation stone on May 5th 1934. The architect was William Broadbent and builders JH Woods & Co. Corpus Christi School opened in 1935 and a new senior school was opened in September 1968: the architects were Langtry-Langton and the cost was £290,000.

Halton Middle School Plans for the new school were approved in March 1972 using 4 acres on the fringe of Temple Newsam Park. Building was started by contractors Tarmac Construction Ltd in February 1973. The school opened in September 1974 although as the new building was not completed in time the school occupied the old Council School buildings on Selby Road from September 1974. The school had a uniform and school badge which featured a Templar cross and started in their new premises on Templegate Walk after February half term 1975. The school was mainly open plan, although dividing screens were soon erected in this two level school with a large assembly hall, drama room, science, language, music, domestic science and technical facilities. The school soon became well known for school plays, outstanding sports teams and school clubs run by a dedicated staff. The school taught the 9 to 13 age range and closed due to the reorganisation of Leeds schools and the closure of the Middle Schools in 1992.

Headteachers of Halton Middle School

John H Rex was born in 1926 and educated at Sir William Turner's School Redcar and at Leeds Modern School. He worked in the Midland Bank on Park Row Leeds and served for four and a half years in the Royal Signals. He was a student at University College Durham University where he graduated with a BA in Geography and History in 1949. He started his teaching career in 1950 at Burnholme Secndary School in York and four years later was teaching at Joseph Rowntree School at New Earswick. Three years later John Rex taught at Easingwold Grammar Modern School and in 1960 came to live in Leeds where he was appointed Deputy Headmaster at Abbey Grange Church of England School. From 1964 to 1973 John Rex was the Headmaster of Brudenell Council School which closed in July 1973. He was a lecturer at Beckett Park College for a year before taking up his appointment at head of Halton Middle School. John Rex retired at Easter 1987 aged 61. He was the Chairman of the Leeds Headteachers Association and in 1978 was the West Yorkshire representative on the Executive of the National Association of Head Teachers; he was elected President of the NAHT in 1984. John and Bett Rex have three children Anthony, Christopher and Joanne.

Margaret A Webb was born in Birmingham and was appointed as Senior Mistress from her previous post at Swarcliffe Primary School. She was appointed Deputy Headteacher at the school and became Headteacher in 1987; Margaret Webb retired at Christmas 1997.

Temple Moor School opened in September 1956 after the Second World War prevented the plans of 1938 being carried out on Soldier's Field allotments. On April 26th 1935 it was requested that *"a new school was urgently needed"*. In 1938 it was suggested that 16 acres were to be used for a new Halton school; the allotment owners were to receive compensation. The Leeds (Education) Compulsory Purchase Order 1937 for the school site was approved in April 1939. The owners were Rt Hon

Temple Moor School

Edward Frederick Lindley Viscount Halifax and Baron Irwin of Kirby Underdale with the Temple Newsam and District Soldiers and Sailors Garden Holding Assocation and the allotment holders included Dr Patricius Ashmore, hairdresser Leopold Button, Alvara Schofield, William Speight and 15 other occupiers. The purchase price was £6250. A petition was obtained from the area in October 1950 requesting the immediate approval of a new school, as there were already 22,000 folk living in Halton. The plans for *"Halton Grammar School"* were refused for the 1953/54 building programme although working plans were completed in 1954. The contract was awarded to the lowest tender of £168,300 and the architects were FRS Yorke, E Rosenberg and CS Mardall working with city architect RAH Livett. FRS Yorke (1906-62), Eugene Rosenberg (born 1907) who escaped from Czechoslovakia after a short career in Prague, Cyril Mardall was born at Sjostrom in Finland and together was formed the YRM Partnership. The firm specialised in schools, hospitals and industrial buildings: Yorke had designed Barclay Secondary School Stevenage, Rosenberg designed St Thomas Hospital and Hull Royal Infirmary while the YRM Partnership designed Warwick University, Boots Headquarters Building at Nottingham and the Wills Complex in Bristol.

Building of Temple Moor Grammar School started in November 1954 with structural engineers Ove Arup & Partners, Quantity Surveyors Davis, Belfield & Everest and builder William Airey. The school was initially a Grammar Technical School for 540 boys and the official opening was by Lord Boyle in May 1957. When the school was opened the junior boys entered by selection at the 11+ while the senior school was composed of boys who had failed their entrance from many parts of the City, whose parents had opted for education at Temple Moor School. The boy's grammar school became a seven form entry comprehensive school in 1972 and co-educational from September 1992. Extensions to the school started in March 1974 with the building of a new block on the front playground. The top floor science laboratories were completely restored with an interlinking corridor between June and October 1992. The new west wing of the school was officially opened by royal author and past pupil of Temple Moor Andrew Morton on October 1st 1993.

There was an idea to build another secondary school in 1964 and land was purchased from Northern Ideal Homesteads for £16,000 off Templegate.

The first school swimming pool replaced the site of the five courts and was opened on July 6th 1967 by PTA founder member JC Pentith. It was built by Swimming Pools Ltd of Middlesex and Blands of Liversedge: the total cost including heating was £10,500. Severe leakage meant closure and a later reconstruction by September 1975. A new £1 million sports hall was officially opened by Geoff Cope of Yorkshire CCC on Wednesday January 14th 2004. The hall is equipped for cricket, netball, basketball,

TEMPLE MOOR SCHOOL STAFF PHOTOGRAPH 1961 .

Back Row: Mike Cave, David Thompson, John Shelmerdine, Michael Barry, Peter Jackson, Ron Purdy, Graham Brown, David Shepherd and Charlie Wilson.
Centre Row: Alan Smalley, Arthur Blamires, Paul Das, Ben Mawdsley, John Gilleghan, Laurie Newby, David Buxton, Stuart Akroyd, and Vic Crowther.
Front Row: John Burdin, Eric Gent, David Harding, Sam Peters, David Breese, Denny Illingworth, John Haigh, Derek Spiers and Terry Popple.

hockey, five-a-side football, badminton, bowls and has a climbing wall. The sports trophies awarded to the boys and houses in the early years of Temple Moor included the Charles Hayes House Championship Cup in sterling silver. The House Basketball and Swimming Cups were originally won in angling competitions by Charles Hayes.

Headteachers of Temple Moor School

David Ian Breese (1956-77) was educated at Oulton High School Liverpool and obtained a degree in Chemistry at Liverpool University. He was a lecturer at Isleworth College and taught science in grammar schools in Essex and Middlesex. In the war he worked for the Ministry of Supply and afterwards was the head of sciences at Hatfield Technical College. He lived with his first wife Mollie in Bramhope and had two sons and a daughter. When Mollie died he remarried and he and wife Doreen lived at Bicton Heath near Shrewsbury; he died aged 79 in October 1994.
Roger Mainds was educated at Chadderton Grammar School near Oldham from 1945 until 1952 and obtained a Geography degree at Liverpool University in 1955. He obtained a post graduate education degree at the University of London Institute of Education in 1956 and spent his National Service in West Germany. In 1958 Roger Mainds

taught for a year at Tennyson School Battersea and moved to Dunraven School Streatham for three years. In September 1962 he was appointed to the staff of Foxwood School Seacroft. Roger was Head of the Geography Department, Head of Lower School and Deputy Headteacher before his appointment as the second headmaster of Temple Moor School in September 1977. The school became a mixed comprehensive school under Roger Maind's leadership and he retired in December 1994.
Philip Pengelly took over as acting-headmaster of Temple Moor School from January 1995 to December 1995.
Ivor Rees was the third Headteacher of the school from January 1996 to July 2001. He trained at Ysgol Uwchradd Llangyllin Powys and University College of Wales Aberystwyth studying History and International Politics. In 1969 he was appointed to Lincoln School and in 1972 was teaching at Frank F Harrison School Walsall. Two years later Ivor Rees taught at The Riland Bedford School Sutton Coldfield and in 1980 became the Deputy Headteacher at Drayton Manor High School Ealing. In 1983 he was an Inspector and Advisor for Wakefield MDC and in 1989 was appointed Headteacher at Almondbury High School Huddersfield. Ivor Rees is now the Headteacher at Oulder Hill Community School Rochdale Lancashire.
Richard Sheriff was appointed in September 2001 and is the present Headteacher of Temple Moor High School. He was born in Arbroath Angus and educated at Andrew Marvell High School Hull, Sheffield City Polytechnic and Leicester University. Richard Sheriff taught at Lancaster Boy's School Leicester. Alderman Newton's School Leicester, City of Leeds School and Salt Grammar School Shipley.

Deputy Headteachers of Temple Moor School

Samuel Saxton Peters was born in Chesterfield on October 18th 1907 and was educated at Chesterfield Grammar School. He won a County Major Scholarship and was awarded a first class honours degree in Physics at Sheffield University and an Education Diploma. Sam Peters taught at Aylesbury GS and moved to Harrogate GS to become the Head of Physics Department. His war service was in the RAF Education Service instructing aircrew in aerial navigation, meteorology and the operation of aircraft engines. By 1944 Sam Peters was demobbed and taught again at Harrogate GS and in 1946 transferred to teach at Keighley GS before his appointment to Temple Moor School as Deputy Headmaster, Head of Sciences and Head of Physics. He had a distinguished sporting record having played football and cricket for the University and being awarded double colours in cricket and soccer. He played for Derbyshire 2nd XI, Buckinghamshire in the Minor Counties League, Aylesbury and at Harrogate.
Sam Peters was married on October 22nd 1955 to Betty Carlin whom he

met while teaching at Harrogate GS: from June 1956 they lived at 68 Templenewsam Road. Sam and Betty's children were Andrew who was born on February 11th 1956 and was educated at Temple Newsam Halton Primary School and Temple Moor School. Andrew obtained a Zoology degree at Manchester University and then trained at Didsbury College. He entered teaching at Aireborough Grammar School and moved to become Head of Science and Head of Biology at Horsforth School. Mark Peters was born on August 26th 1960 and was educated at the same schools as his elder brother; he obtained a degree in Civil Engineering at Manchester University. Mark emigrated to South Africa and worked for Murray & Roberts in the Orange Free State and Cape Town. He has been responsible for the building of shopping centres and of the Table Bay Hotel Cape Town. Sam Peters retired from teaching in July 1972 after a period of illness in 1971 and he died on March 11th 1982; a farewell retirement dinner was held at the Parcmont Hotel Roundhay Park when many previous members of staff attended to add their good wishes. His wife Betty moved from the family home on Temple Newsam Road in 1998 to live in Otley near her married eldest son.

Geoffrey A Strafford was appointed to oversee the change from the Grammar School status to a comprehensive school. He obtained a science degree at Liverpool University and taught at Oswestry, Southampton, Isle of Man and Greenhead Grammar School Keighley. He was appointed Head of School and Deputy Headteacher in September 1972. He was a Moderator for A Level Biology with the Cambridge LES and had written a plant physiology book for schools. He left Temple Moor School in 1976 to be succeeded by *Geoffrey Ingham* and *Terry Clift*.

Philip Pengelly was educated at Devonport High School Plymouth (1956-62), University of Cambridge (1962-65), University of London (part time) 1969-1973 and full time from 1972 to 1973. Philip Pengelly was Deputy Headteacher Ada Secondary School Ghana (1965-67), Senior Teacher Highgate School London (1967-72) and Head of Science at Foxwood School Seacroft Leeds from 1973 to 1982. He was the Deputy Headteacher at Temple Moor High School from April 1982 until December 1991. Philip Pengelly died in 1992.

Maurice Green was educated at Dumfries Academy, Jordanhill University of Glasgow and he taught at Dumfries Academy and Morley High School Leeds prior to being the Deputy Headteacher at Temple Moor High School from September 1994 until July 2001.

Jill Rowett was born at Ackworth and was educated at Pontefract Girls High School, Chester College of Education and Wolverhampton Polytechnic. She taught at Castleford High School, Cantril High School Knowsley Merseyside, Stocksbridge Village Community School, Knowsley and Hough Side High School Leeds. Jill Rowett was appointed as Deputy

Headteacher at Temple Moor High School in 1991.
Robert Williams was appointed Deputy Headteacher at Temple Moor High School in 2002. He was born at Cardiff and was educated at Leeds Grammar School (1977-85) followed by an honours degree in History at Newcastle-upon-Tyne University in 1988. He obtained the Postgraduate Certificate in Education at Newcastle and received an M Litt in 1998. His previous teaching career was at Durham Johnston School (1990-94) and Fulford School York (1994-2002).
The first caretaker at Temple Moor School was *Harry Richmond* who was born in Leeds and with his wife was the caretaker at the Princess Cinema Pontefract Lane (1923-1965) where they worked for 13 years. He worked in the fire service and from 1948 worked for the Education Committee: he was the caretaker at Beechwood School prior to the opening of Temple Moor School. Illness caused his resignation from the school and he died in July 1957 aged 57. The next caretaker was *Wilfred Banks* who was born in Lower Wortley on November 24th 1905 as the son of Samuel & Clara Ellen (Daniel) Banks: Sam Banks worked at Farnley Forge. He started work as a butcher and was the assistant caretaker at the Blind & Deaf School on Blenheim Walk, where he met his future wife Lily Baines, who was the head cook. They were married in 1940 and in the war Wilfred served in the army landing in Normandy on D Day + 4 and was discharged from Hanover in 1945. He was caretaker at Quarry Mount CP, Halton Moor CP and at West Park Secondary School. Wilfred and Lily Banks lived in the school bungalow before their transfer to 288 Selby Road in 1965. Wilfred Banks retired from the school in 1970 and was followed by caretakers *Ronald Pears and Ronald Curtis.* Wilfred Banks was born on November 24th 1905 and he died in May 1973. Lily Banks moved from Selby Road in 1983 to a flat on Primrose Drive and she died on April 12th 2002 aged 93.
Temple Newsam-Halton Primary School/Halton Council School was erected in 1841 on a site conveyed by Hugo Charles Meynell Ingram and the school was opened on October 10th 1842 being built of Colton sandstone; the money needed for the new school was mainly raised by Rev Arthur Martineau Vicar of Whitkirk. Contributions came from Lady William Gordon of Temple Newsam who also provided the stone from her quarry at Colton, Trinity College Cambridge, The National Society and there were many other contributions to the building fund. The school was enlarged in 1851; in 1862 the Whitkirk Boys School was dismantled to enlarge the churchyard and the stone was used for the Infant's School opened in May 1863. There were several treats for the children and in 1866 Mrs Meynell Ingram held a school feast in the Great Court at Temple Newsam House. In 1875 a half acre of land was bought for a playground and the house for the headteacher. On January 13th 1878 the central schoolroom and two classrooms were destroyed by fire

and a week later the children attended classes in the Halton Methodist Church Sunday School. By 1885 gas lights were fitted throughout the school on Selby Road and in 1893-94 extensions were added for increased space for teaching. In 1920 an old army hut 60 feet by 20 feet was erected on the school playground for the use of the Mixed Department followed by another hut in 1951: they were demolished in March 1983. In 1924 a well 50 feet deep and four feet across was revealed by an LICS coal cart backing on to the footpath by the almshouses. The same year in July saw the donation of 3000 four ounce chocolate bars by Miss Rollinson at The Café on the High Street near Gilsyke House. Halton schools were given permission to use the York Road baths in 1923 at a charge of 1½ pence.

In 1929 three acres bounded by The Croft and Chapel Street together with one acre at the lower end of the site were bought from Lord Halifax at a cost of £450 as a playing field for the increasing number of children. In 1951 a new Infants Department was completed and the new Primary School building was opened on Pinfold Lane in September 1967. On April 1st 1928 the school passed to the Leeds Education Committee from the West Riding Education Committee on the absorbtion of Halton and Temple Newsam into Leeds. On the changeover the headteacher Richard Thomas wrote to the WREC thanking them for their support over the years and hoped that this continued under Leeds Education Committee.

The teachers at Halton School in 1904 were Joseph Owrid, Richard Thomas, Lucy Goodall, Florence West, Lily Sunter who died of heart failure on November 10th 1907 and Alice Cowell. By 1908 Charles Backhouse and Lillie Tinker were teaching at the school. In 1923 the teachers were Mary Phillips, Mrs LMA Bell, Claire Harrison who died on July 6th 1926, Mabel Bland, Arthur Chilton and Richard Thomas: they were teaching 323 children on roll.

<u>Headteachers of Halton Council School/Temple Newsam Primary School</u>

William Miller was the first recorded headmaster and he was followed by *George Hallums*. *William Millington* was the successor and he was married to Emma: their twins were Herbert & Ernest born in April 1866. By 1876 *John Lewis Lodge* was appointed at Halton School: his son Arthur was born in December 1878.

Joseph Owrid was appointed as the next schoolmaster on July 1st 1883 having transferred from Colton School where he was the headteacher from 1876 to 1883. He was born on February 5th 1857 at Bowling Bradford and started his teaching career in April 1869 at St James School York Street. At Christmas 1869 he passed the Queen's Scholarship Examination and entered Chester Training College where he obtained a first class Trained Certificate for Teaching in 1872 after a two year course. He taught at Neston National School for over two years and then joined Coppuell NC at Chorley before being appointed to Colton when it opened as a new school in September 1876. The closure of the local West Yorkshire Pit caused a reduction in numbers at Colton and the vacant situation at Halton meant that he started at the school in July 1883. Joseph Owrid retired on February 4th 1916 when there was a leaving party with speeches by County Councillor Dewhirst: the Owrid family lived at Whitkirk. He died aged 71 on January 25th 1922 and was buried on January 27th at Whitkirk; his wife Elizabeth died aged 92 in January 1944 having moved to Hollyshaw Terrace. His children were Oswald born 1875; Eleanor born 1876 who married John William Strickland on August 23rd 1898; Caroline Beatrice who was born in December 1879 and married 28 year old cashier William Siddall Baron on August 29th 1904.

Thomas family at School House

Richard Richard Thomas was the headteacher of Halton

School from 1919 to Christmas 1932. He had been appointed to the school as an untrained teacher on November 18th 1903 from Primrose Hill Council School. When Joseph Owrid retired after 32 years in 1916 Richard Thomas took charge of the mixed department from February 7th 1916. He retired at Christmas 1932 taking over from T Fletcher at Green Lane Council School. Richard Richard Thomas died in April 1959 aged 82.

Ian Brown was the Halton headteacher from January 1933 to 1939. *Leo W Critchley* was the headteacher from September 1940 to 1943: he lived at 88 Cross Gates Lane. *FW Pepper* was the headteacher from 1943 to 1945 followed by *Alfred Granville Prior* from 1946 to 1951: he lived on Stratford Street Dewsbury Road. *Bernard Lester* was at Halton from 1951 to 1954. *Eric Angood* was the Halton headteacher from September 1956 to July 1978. Eric was born on July 19th 1918 and died on March 5th 1992; his wife Jenny died aged 82 on November 6th 2002. Eric & Jenny spent most of their married life in the house at 10 Harehills Park View on the edge of Harehills Park, where they had three children: Sheena,Peter and Derek who himself trained in York and started teaching in 1975 becoming the head teacher at Appleton Roebuck Primary School.

Eric Angood was born in Harehills and attended Brownhill School and Roundhay School. He trained at City of Leeds Training College and taught first at Middleton School in 1938 when the school was evacuated to Rossington near Doncaster. He moved to Middleton Secondary School and then joined the Pioneer Corps serving in Mauritius, Egypt and Italy: he was promoted to be acting major. In 1946 he joined the staff at Coldcotes School and in 1948 at the age of 29 was made headteacher at Grafton School Lovell Road. Eric became the manager of the Leeds City swimming team: he was an instructor, examiner and treasurer of the Leeds & District Royal Life Saving Society. Eric later was made the president and a life member.

The deputy headteacher of Halton School with Eric Angood was *Charles Dodgson* who started his teaching career at a special school and came to Halton in September 1960. Charlie and Ethel lived at the School House before moving to the flats down Halton Hill: he died in 1997.

Jill Robb-Webb was the headteacher at Halton from 1978 to 1985. *Kay Crellin* was appointed in 1985: she previously taught at Garforth Green Lane Primary School.

Whitkirk Primary School was opened in September 1992 in the same building as the closed Halton Middle School.

Temple Newsam Tiny Tots is a pre-school, meeting since 1970 at Whitkirk Primary School. There is also a Tuesday afternoon for older children starting school in September. The Tiny Tots was awarded a gold in the Leeds Quality Assurance Scheme.

Headteachers of Whitkirk Primary School

Margaret A Webb was appointed the first Headteacher in September 1992 following her position of Headteacher at the former Halton Middle School. Margaret Webb took retirement from teaching at Christmas 1997.
Acting Headteacher *Peter Boyle* took over from Margaret Webb until the appointment of *Peter Coverdale* in January 1998.

SCHOOL LANE/ROW

A short cul de sac between the old school house, the 1930's housing of Selby Road and the property belonging to Pinfold Grove. The original name prior to the school was New Houses Lane referring to the earlier almhouses and was also known as The Croft in the 1920's. The field on the corner of Pinfold Lane and Selby Road had a channel about 25 feet wide which disappeared near the almshouses: many folk thought that this was a Roman road. When the schoolhouse garden was being landscaped two Roman coins were discovered which remained in the Thomas family. The almshouses were owned by Lord Halifax and had a rent of 6 pence weekly at one period. The lane had four almshouses which faced south: the site is now gated and part of the school complex. The 1901 census describes it as School Row with the occupants being Jane Goldthorpe (57), Emma Birkin (67), Matthew Britton (79) and Emma Pawson (62). In 1928 the residents of School Lane were Jennie Hardwick (1) who died in February 1931, Elizabeth Hanley (2), Sarah Hemsworth (3) who died in February 1931 and Robert Cullen (4). 1 School Lane was once the home of the maternity nurse Harriet Kitson who reached the age of 70 in 1931: she had come to the village in 1901. In 1938 the residents were Lillie Verity, Susannah Pickersgill, William Butler and Rose Monkman. In 1965 the last residents of the almshouses were Jane and Elsie Bulmer, Venus Hammond and Elizabeth Wraith. The almshouses were demolished in 1967 in the year that the new school buildings were opened. The School House was built on the Temple Newsam Inclosure Award land. When the headteacher Richard Thomas retired in 1933 he moved a few

years later to a house on Selby Road Whitkirk. Following was William Edmund & Annie Elizabeth Morcombe who had moved from Woodland Road.

SCOUTS AND GUIDES

Halton Templars (18th NE Leeds & 13th NE Leeds) was founded in 1921 by Jack Stuart White who was the scoutmaster and his son Jack R Stuart White and L Alcock as the ASM's, later Ralph Padgett was ASM. The Guides and Brownies were formed in 1930. The first meeting place was in a former stable at Holme Lea which had been converted to a garage. The group then moved to a schoolroom and then an old army hut near the Congregational Church provided by JR Miller. The 1st Halton Templars Guides had Mary Sandy as their Captain and chemist's daughter Dorothy Rennard as the Lieutenant; the Brownies were started by Miss C Dixon and had Miss M Fox as Brown Owl and D Sowden at Tawny Owl. The Rangers were formed in 1932 by Miss GH Piercy. Jack Stuart White became the Commissioner for North East Leeds. In 1933 there was a hope that a new steel hut would be built on Pinfold Lane: planning permission was refused.

In April 1934 a Grand Bazaar was opened by Viscountess Irwin and Col Glazebrook. In January 1934 Jack Stuart White applied to purchase land at the corner of Temple Newsam Road and Halton Hill for scout use but the application was refused. The group paid £100 in 1933 for an old mistal at Laurel Farm. The generosity and support of Lord Halifax resulted in the opening of Baden Powell Hall on April 24th 1937. The £450 was raised for the restoration of the building by Dunhill Bros: it was

officially opened by Lord Halifax.
One of the popular features of the Templars was the band: they started with bugles but later had drums, euphonium, horns and trombones with band members wearing special caps and uniforms. The band first played on Christmas Day 1924. In later years the band started by Jack White with conductor FW Hayes suffered dwindling numbers and they ceased playing.
The cubmasters in the 1930's were Denis and George Bellwood and the scoutmaster was Ralph Padgett. The Templars Scout Group included the Sea Scouts run by Reg Walker, Senior Scouts run by Bill Staveley, Rangers run by Mrs Temple and the Cub pack run by the husband of Coun Doreen Wood, Denis Wood and Harry Whyler. David Staveley was the scoutmaster who left in 1974: the Halton Templars Scouts closed in c1979.
Halton Methodist Church started their own scout troop at the church in April 1937 with scoutmaster AS Batty. Christ Church Halton now has Rainbows for girls from 5 to 6 years and the uniformed Brownies for girls between 7 and 10 years old. Boys and girls are catered for with the Junior Church, Junior Youth Club and Senior Youth Club together with the Youth Fellowship.
Temple Moor School (3rd South East Leeds) held the first troop meeting on April 25th 1958 based at Halton Parochial Hall: the scoutmaster was Eric Gent. There were also the Senior Scout Group (Derek Spiers) and Rover Crew (Graham Brown) for older pupils at Temple Moor. There was an active programme of camps and adventures at home and abroad with two representatives attending the 11th World Scout Jamboree in Greece. The first summer camp was held in July 1958 at Middleham Wensleydale. The last camp was held in July 1969 at the Gower Peninsula. The scout troop was closed as both Eric Gent and Derek Spiers moved to other schools.

St. Wilfrid's Church was the 4th South East Leeds and is now the 3rd East Leeds and has the 2nd Halton Guides, Cub Scouts, Brownies and Rainbows. There was a Scout Troop which originated from Halton Templars c1940. A new scout headquarters was opened on Sunday December 8th 1985 called The Fred Turner Memorial Hall. The opening was by Maud Turner and it was dedicated by the vicar Rev Robin Greenwood.

Frank Thorn was a District Commissioner for East Leeds for 25 years: he retired in 1976.

Robert Stephenson Smyth Baden Powell was born at Stanhope Street Paddington on February 22nd 1857 as the son of the Rev Baden Powell who was an Oxford University professor. He attended Rose Hill School Tunbridge Wells and Charterhouse School. Soon after he was commissioned to the 13th Hussars and became their Honorary Colonel for 30 years. He was the Commander of the 5th Dragoon Guards in 1897 when he trained the troops to be scouts. BP fought at the 271 day siege of Mafeking and it was during this campaign that his book Scouting for Boys was published. In 1907 he had an experimental camp on Brownsea Island with 22 boys from varied backgrounds; he retired in 1910 and in 1912 he married Olave Soames. The 1st International Jubilee was held in 1920 in London and in that year BP was made Chief Scout of the World; he was created Lord Baden Powell of Gilwell in 1929. He returned to Africa in 1938 and died aged 83 on January 8th 1941: he is buried in a simple grave at Nyeri Kenya which bears the badge of the Scouts.

The Girl Guides was formed by BP and his sister Agnes (1854-1945) in 1910 and the Girl Guides Association was formed in the UK. In 1917 Olave Baden Powell organised the Guides in Sussex having been appointed UK Chief Commissioner in 1916. In 1918 her title became Chief Guide which she held to her death in 1977. The Wolf Cubs/Cub Scouts were formed in England in 1914. Today the World Association of Girl Guides and Girl Scouts has nearly 10 million members.

SEWAGE SERVICES

Sewage was taken to the Halton Sewage Works on Halton Hill until 1928: there were also sewage works at Killingbeck and on Green Lane Halton. The sewage pipes from the area lead to the Knostrop sewage works. There were extensions at the Works in September 1904 costing £2500. In 1909 the Halton Sewage Works were valued at £145 with both rhubarb and grass being sold by the authorities. A new rhubarb forcing shed was erected in 1901. In 1928 plans were submitted for a sewer serving Halton through the lands of Temple Newsam estate. In July 1928 plans were agreed to construct a sewer from Barwick Road to Selby Road and from

Halton Sewage Works to the new Wykebeck Valley Sewer. This enabled the closure of Stanks and Halton Sewage Works which closed in October. The same year saw the connection of the Peggy Lane Sewage Works to the main outfall sewer. The site of the Halton Sewage Works was declared an official open space in 1928. The sewer from the Wykebeck Valley sewer to Knostrop was completed in May 1975. In 1976 the sewer from William Rise Halton Hill to Austhorpe was laid at a cost of £2 million: by November this had reached Green Lane and later was at Barwick Road. The excavations for this 50 feet deep sewer revealed fragments of fossilised trees.

The 26 acres of land at Knostrop were acquired on July 6th 1848 and in 1870 the Council bought a further 26 acres from Mrs Meynell Ingram to extend the low level works. Following Mrs Meynell Ingram's death in 1904 the Council bought 600 acres and included eight miles of new city sewers. A new pumping station opened in October 1923 and the whole Knostrop project was completed in March 1936. There have been further modernisation works and the Knostrop works now cover 500 acres.

The manager of the Halton Sewage Works was Robert Adamson whose job was taken by H Lacey in 1927: Adamson was appointed to Hemsworth RDC and he died two years later.

SKYRACK WAPENTAKE

The name Skyrack was the name of the wapentake in which Halton was included: this old administrative division of Yorkshire was created by the Danish-Norse kings and centred at the Old Oak at Headingley. The word is derived from "bright oak" with meetings being by the tree: the original fell down in May 1941. A new oak sapling was planted in 1985 on the site by the Original Oak Inn. The Skyrack wapentake stretched from the A1 to Otley, Ilkley and Addingham, north to Collingham, Harewood and Arthington and south to the River Aire.

SLEIGHT FAMILY

William and Mary Sleight lived at Firdale 33 Grove Road: William was born in 1900 and was Chief Assistant Planning Officer for the Leeds City Engineers Department. He died suddenly in 1979; Mary was born in 1900 and died in 1982. The family lived at Endor Crescent Burley in Wharfedale and moved to Firdale where they lived from 1945 until 1968 when they built a house at Boston Spa. Mary moved to Wendover in 1979 to be near her two sons Peter and Malcolm.

Peter Sleight was born on June 27th 1929 and was educated at Leeds Grammar School being admitted to the school on September 15th 1938 and leaving in 1947. He won a scholarship to Cambridge University where he graduated BA in 1950 and in 1953 gained MB BChir at Gonville & Caius College. Peter was awarded a Brockenbury Scholarship to St Bartholomew's Hospital Medical College London where he was awarded the Burrows Prize in Pathology, Walsham Prize in Surgical Pathology, Kirke Scholarship and the Gold Medal in Clinical Medicine. He was awarded MD at Cambridge in 1964 and DM at Oxford in 1965. He became the Senior Registrar at St George's Hospital (1959-64) and Consultant Physician at the United Oxford Hospitals (1966-73). From 1972 to 1994 Peter Sleight was the Field Marshall Alexander Professor of Cardiovascular Medicine at Oxford University. He is now the Emeritus Professor of Cardiovascular Medicine University of Oxford and Emeritus Fellow of Exeter College. He is Hon Consultant Physician Oxford Radcliffe NHS Trust. Peter Sleight is a consultant on hypertension having published books and films on this subject.

Peter Sleight married Dr Gillian France in 1953 and they have two sons: Christopher is an electronic engineer living at Chipping Norton: he is married to Elizabeth and has three children Jonathan, Richard and Harriet.

James Sleight is a barrister at the Sydney Bar in 2002.

Malcolm Westmoreland Sleight was born on July 7th 1932 and attended Ilkley Grammar School and Leeds Grammar School from September 1942 to July 1950. While at the school he was awarded his 1st XV colours, secretary of the school science society and awarded the Sharpe Science Prize (Biology). In 1953 he was awarded the Natural Science Tripos (Clinical Studies) at Gonville & Caius College Cambridge. He was awarded the FRCS OBE and was Professor of Surgery in the Royal Air Force. He married Ann and they had four children; Malcolm Sleight died in 1981.

Peter & Malcolm Sleight's sister is Eileen Hastings and lives in Pittsburgh USA: she married the Professor of Mathematics in the University of Pittsburg.

SMOKE CONTROL ORDERS

The smoke control orders were imposed on the area during the 1970's with grants being available for the conversion of the fireplaces. City of Leeds No 90 (Halton-Selby Road) Smoke Control Order 1970 included land from the railway to Knightsway, Selby Road and Irwin Approach. This order took effect on November 1st 1971.

SCO No 104 (Halton-Temple Newsam) included part of Halton with Colton, Temple Newsam and Newsam Green. The order took effect on April 1st 1973 and extended to include Knowsthorpe, Pontefract Lane and Halton Moor Road in July 1973.

SCO No 105 (Halton-Austhorpe) included Selby Road, Halton Ring Road, Station Road and Cross Gates Road. The order came into effect in 1977.

SOME SPECIAL EVENTS

Albert Edward Prince of Wales visited East Leeds on Monday and Tuesday May 18th/19th 1868. He stayed at Temple Newsam with the Meynell-Ingrams and on Tuesday morning was taken by horse and carriage to Leeds via Whitkirk and Halton to open the National Art Exhibition at the new Leeds General Infirmary which was opened a year afterwards. He was taken back to the mansion where there was a ball in his honour in the evening: Halton and Whitkirk were decorated for this royal occasion including a Gothic arch across Selby Road at Whitkirk and a triple archway across the road at Halton. During the royal visit the Halton School was closed and used as a temporary police station. *The Prince of Wales was born in 1841 at Buckingham Palace as the eldest son of Queen Victoria and Prince Albert. When his father died in 1861 Edward undertook many public duties and he succeeded to the throne in 1901 as King Edward VII. He married Princess Alexandra of Denmark in 1863 and they had six children.*

The High Street was decked out with bunting on Saturday September 29th 1906 for the visit of HRH Princess Louise accompanied by the Duke of Argyll. They arrived by train from Liverpool alighting at Garforth station where they were welcomed by their host Hon Edward Wood and his father Viscount Halifax. The party were driven to Temple Newsam House by carriages where they stayed the night. The next day the party was driven by open topped car via Whitkirk, Halton, Harehills Lane, Roundhay Road, North Street, Briggate, Guildford Street and Park Lane to Leeds Town Hall where they arrived at 1pm. The Leeds Rifles formed a Guard of Honour and they were greeted on behalf of the City by Lord

Mayor Edwin Woodhouse. Among those who were presented to the royal couple were Hon Frederick Meynell, Francis Meynell and Sir Nathan Bodington who was the Vice Chancellor of Leeds University. At 3pm the party left for the short drive to Leeds Girls High School where the new building designed by Chorley & Connon of Leeds was declared open. After the ceremony the couple returned privately to Temple Newsam via Chapeltown. They attended morning service on Sunday at St Mary's Church Whitkirk where the sermon was preached by Rev Gerald Sharp (Vicar 1898-1910). The royal party left Temple Newsam in the morning of Monday October 1st 1906 for Studley Royal where they were entertained by the Marquess of Ripon returning to Temple Newsam in the evening; they left for home on Tuesday October 2nd. There was considerable debate about the means of transport on the official day and the royal preference of carriages was overruled by the City Council. The villagers of Halton built a large archway complete with photographs across Chapel Street near the end of Pinfold Lane.

Princess Louise was the fourth daughter and 6th child of Queen Victoria and Prince Albert. She was born at Buckingham Palace on March 18th 1848 and married John Douglas Campbell Marquis of Lorne in 1871. She became the Duchess of Argyll in 1900 when her husband inherited the title of Duke of Argyll. Her husband died in 1914 and she died at Kensington Palace on December 3rd 1939 at the age of 91.

On *September 21st 1909* the marriage took place of the Hon Edward Frederick Lindley Wood, son of Viscount Halifax of Hickleton Hall to Lady Dorothy Evelyn Augusta Onslow of West Clandon Surrey seat of the Earls of Onslow. She was the daughter of the 4th Earl William Hillier who had married Hon Florence Gardner in 1875. The marriage was held at the Church of St Peter & St Paul at West Clandon with one of the bridesmaids being Marcia Lane Fox (niece) and the officiating priest Rev John Wylde of Leeds. The reception was held at Clandon Park and the couple then left for York and onwards to Garrowby Hall. The carriage preceded by the Pocklington Band was pulled by 100 men from the hall gates to the mansion: all estate workers were given 5 shillings each and a day holiday; married workers were given 10 shillings. On the Thursday the couple arrived at Hickleton Hall. The Hon Edward FL Wood became the 3rd Viscount Halifax on the death of his father Charles 2nd Viscount Halifax on January 19th 1934; Charles married Lady Agnes Elizabeth Courtenay in 1869 who died in 1919. The Hon Edward Wood was born in 1881 and was the Viceroy of India from 1926 to 1931, foreign secretary 1938-40 and ambassador to the USA 1941-46. He died on December 23rd 1959 and their children were Charles Ingram Courtenay (1912), Peter Courtenay (1916) and Richard Frederick Wood Baron Holderness (1920). Hon Edward Wood's brothers were Charles (1870-99), Francis (1873-89) and Henry (1879-86).

At 11pm on *September 25th 1916* the Zeppelin came over Leeds; it was invented by Ferdinand Count von Zeppelin (1838-1917).
On *August 18th 1931* the Graf Airship flew over Halton with 24 passengers: the following day the airship was flown over Leeds and City Square prior to a visit to Hull.
The coronations of King George V in 1911, George VI and Queen Elizabeth II were marked by special events in the village. There were special teas and celebrations in the churches and in the village hall: in *May 1937* coronation beakers were given to the village children and the houses of the village were decorated. The same happened in *June 1953* with tins of sweets and mugs and street parties were held for the Queen's Silver Jubilee in 1977. On Friday October 22nd 1965 many Halton folk walked to Cross Gates station to get a glimpse of HM The Queen when she arrived by train to open the new £1.5 million Seacroft Centre. Despite poor visibility the royal party arrived and at a later ceremony 11 year old Patricia Jean Hemingway of Pinfold Road Halton and Parklands High School presented a bouquet to HM The Queen.

SPEIGHT FAMILY

The Speight family were involved in many village businesses including farming, haulage and contracting, shop keeping and an owner of a rag merchant's trade. The family lived at a few Halton locations including a shop on Chapel Street, Gilsyke Farm and Poplar House on Woodman Street.
6 Chapel Street was the home of David Speight born in August 1897 who married Alice. He was a motor driver and Alice ran a draper's business from c1917 and was trading in the 1940's. David was the son of David and Mary Speight of Poplar House. David Speight Snr died aged 74 on December 29th 1932 and his wife Mary died aged 51 on January 12th 1910.
Gilsyke Farm on the High Street was a Speight farming concern for a few years. David Speight was born in Leeds in 1842 and was a paving contractor and farmer; his wife Hannah was born in 1844. Their children were Annie who was born in Leeds in 1865, James born in 1867 who helped at the family business, Sarah born in 1872, John William born in 1874, Emily born in 1876, Amelia born in 1877, David born in 1883 when the family had moved to Halton and Clara who was born at Halton in 1887. By 1905 brothers David and John Speight were farming from Gilsyke. John William Speight was born in 1874 and he married Hettie Rollinson of Holly House on January 30th 1902; their daughter Dulcie was born in September 1910. The farm was once run by the Heworth family and following the Speights became a Verity family concern.
Poplar House on Woodman Street was a Speight residence, with rag merchant David Speight and wife Mary by 1900: Mary died aged 51 in

January 1910. David Speight's parents were grocer and provision dealer William of York Street Leeds who died aged 75 on February 56th 1908 and Elizabeth who died at Poplar House aged 75 in November 1907. The family lived at Holbeck where David and five of his children were born and they moved to Halton in 1889. David and Mary left Poplar House to become the licensees of the Black Horse Inn at Askwith near Otley.
The children of David and Mary Speight were William born in 1879 who served in the Great War in the Vetinerary Corps and came back to Halton to work as a haulage carrier. William lived on Wilfred Avenue and married twice: Mary who died aged 40 in 1921 and Elsie Dobson who died aged 87 in 1988. William and Elsie's children were David born in 1934 and Christine who was born in 1939. David married Dorothy Vickers in 1958 and Christine married Jack Blakey in 1960 and they have two married children.
The other children of David and Mary Speight are Harriet born in 1883, Florence born in 1885, Joseph born in 1886, Emily born in 1888, Walter born in 1890, Arthur born at Halton in 1895 and David born at Halton in 1899. Private Walter Speight of the 12th Battalion Yorkshire & Lancashire Regiment was killed in action aged 27 on May 4th 1917: he was married to Lily and lived at 10 Raincliffe Road East End Park and is remembered at the Arras Memorial Pas de Calais. Walter Speight died from injuries received in action on returning from France in the Great War. Private Arthur Speight served with the 2nd/4th Battalion Royal North Lancashire Regiment. He died aged 21 on October 26th 1917 and is remembered at Tyne Cot Cemetery Flanders. Private David Speight of 2nd Battalion Duke of Wellington's (West Riding) Regiment died on August 8th 1918 and is remembered on the Loos Memorial Pas de Calais, France.
James Edward Speight & Maude Ethel Speight had planning permission for a builder's yard (Speight's Yard) in 1946 off Chapel Street. James Edward Speight was involved in laying the tramlines for the Halton service in 1914/15 and in surfacing many roads in the area. James Edward had his business on Beeston Hill by 1886 and was a pavior and contractor specialising in road making and sewering: he later moved to Manor Street Sheepscar.
Other branches of the family were also involved in contracting including Joseph Speight of Barrack Street and later Chapeltown Road, David Speight of Canal Wharf Water Lane whose residence was Moor Farm Chapel Allerton and William L & Frank Speight of 35 Park Lane.

SPORTS

There were proposals for a Halton Sports Centre in the 1970's and again in 1984: Halton Moor Sports Centre was opened on April 1st 1985.
Athletics Initially there were plans for a new sports arena with seating

for 150,000, parking for 1000 cars and a three track tram siding. The Temple Newsam Athletics Stadium built on an old opencast site was opened in May 1954 by Dr Frank Aaron. The waste from the track construction was used for levelling and filling Lawn Pond.

Bowling In 1907/08 there were 123 bowling greens in Leeds. Chapel Street Bowling Club is based at the council maintained site in Primrose Valley reclaimed from a landfill site in 1992 and is well maintained and has a clubhouse. The club is sponsored by the Chapel Street Social Club who have supplied their shirts. They moved from their original green at Sutton Park and this private ground was converted into a children's play area. The team plays in many leagues including Barkston Ash and the Yorkshire Cup.

In 1935 a bowling green was opened on the Sutton Estate (Sutton Park) owned by the Sutton Housing Trust. Halton Sutton Bowling Club was established and this had great success. The green was floodlit on October 13th 1968. In 1989 Sutton Trust informed the club that it could no longer finance the running of the bowling green and offered the club the site which they could not afford and turned down the offer. The Leeds City Council were building a park in Primrose Valley at Halton Dene which would include a bowling green and on Spring Bank Holiday 1989 Halton Sutton Club moved to the new green and changed their name to Halton Dene Bowling Club. In 2001 the club became the bowling section of the Chapel Street Social Club.

In 1920 two bowling clubs at Halton were *Halton Bowling Club* who competed in the Movley Trophy and the Marsden Charity Trophy together with The *Halton Travellers Bowling Club*. The Halton team who played in the Leeds Amateur Association Preston Shield were G Botterill, A Caine, B Dickinson, W Ginns, W Green, C Lambert, JF Loveday, W Macdonald, W Richmond, H Sykes, F Vince and JW Walker.

The other bowling green in Halton is on Grove Road near the site of the old claypits and brickworks. The Grove Road bowling green was opened in 1961 by Leeds City Council with a club established. The Halton Dene and Grove Road greens are owned and maintained by Leeds Leisure Services. There were also bowling greens at the old Irwin Arms Inn: the site of the second public house and at the Travellers Inn on the High Street: this bowling green site is now part of the centre car park.

Cricket There were two cricket teams in Halton with one known as the Temps (Temperance) and was the Halton Wesleyan CC attached to the Methodist Chapel playing on their ground on the field on Engine Lane (Temple Newsam Road). Arrangements to rent the field on Engine Lane had been made in Summer 1874 and this was to be for a sixth month period from April 1875 from the Stevenson family of Park View Farm. Halton CC were in Division 4 of the Barkston Ash League in 1895 together with Garforth, Manston, Seacroft, Swillington United and

Whitkirk. Their pavilion was in Moor Road and in June 1922 the secretary William Dunhill was having his bungalow built on Grove Road. The team selected to play for Halton Wesleyan in 1920 included G Batty, G Bowers, H Butcher, A Killerby, AW Killerby, W Hall, A Hudson, W Palmer and W Todd. In 1922 the Wesleyan CC was playing in the Barkston Ash Cricket League Senior and included C Batty, S Battye, A Buswell, C Kilburn, A Killerby, G Killerby, JA Popplewell, JW Popplewell, J Sallabank, Reg Thomas and H Wilson.

The other team was Halton CC and was also in the Barkston Ash League which was founded in 1894. In 1892 the Halton CC won the Challenge Cup presented by Coun JM Sagar Musgrave, which was competed for among the clubs in the Barkston Ash Electoral Division. The presentation was followed by a dinner at George Fryer's Woodman Inn. The Halton Cricket Club played on their ground at Primrose Valley, now a part of the landscaped leisure site. The beck in the valley was described as polluted in February 1905 and a report to Hunslet RDC stated that the cricket field had recently been taken by the Parish Council.

The League was divided into four divisions of five teams based on geography: Halton were with Whitkirk, Manston, Seacroft and Swillington. The local derby was between the Temps and Halton CC which always attracted a large attendance. The records of Whitkirk CC show that Halton CC played them on July 1st 1920 with the home team scoring just 26 runs in the Barkston Ash Cricket League. There was a pitch on Temple Newsam Road (Engine Lane) and one of the highlights of the year was the needle cricket match between the two Halton teams. One of the teams selected for Halton Cricket Club in 1920 was N Ball, W Benson, H Bowes, H Collinson, E Daniel, H Dobson, A Dodsworth, H Haigh, E Johnson, A Powell, A Shepherd and C Sunter.

In December 1924 Halton United Cricket Club was formed from the merger of the Halton and the Halton Wesleyan teams.

The year of the merger saw the last teams playing for Halton CC and Halton Wesleyans. The team for Halton CC was G Bowers, H Bowers, C Harrison, C Catlow, T Shaw, R Sharp, W Benson, H Haigh and W Brazil. Halton Wesleyan team was G Killerby, W Killerby, AP Buswell, W Dunhill, W Foster, W Taylor, H Kirkby, B Pratt, F Popplewell, A Killerby and JW Sallabank.

The annual meeting of the Halton CC in 1927 elected the following members: President Harold Bell, First Team Captain JA Burton, Second Team Captain RO Thomas, Secretary V Button and League Representative H Cowell.

In 1929 the Halton Cricket Club team included all rounder Noah Ball and other members were Harry Cowell, G Killerby, H Simpson, J King, H Arnold, L Richards, H Cook, A Buswell, T Shaw, C Arnold, R Panther and T Wood.

After the War in 1948 Halton again played in the Barkston Ash League following being dormant from 1941. The ground was made playable again by the Leeds Corporation and seed was sown in March 1948. There was a temporary pavilion of air raid shelters and huts: the Cricket Club was offered a 7 year lease on their ground in 1947.
The Halton team played in the Senior League (Barkston Ash League) and in May 1949 played Barwick in Elmet (Halton scored 63 and Barwick reached 34 all out). The team for this match was FBooth, T Booth, Cawood, Dart, Marshall, Mounsdon, Nicholson, Parkin, Postle, Stead and Thorley. In 1950 there was a needle match between Halton and Aberford in the League with Aberford scoring 101 and winning by one run. The Halton Junior team was 8th in the Division and the Senior Halton team was 2nd in the Division by June 17th 1950. In July 1950 was played the Halton Cricket Club Knockout Cup Final featuring Bailey & Lockharts versus The Nondescripts. In 1951 the Halton Cricket team was Bevins, Easton, Foster, Haigh, Kennedy, Lawn, Malkin, Marshall, Parkin, Peel and Ware. In 1953 Halton played Bolton Percy in the Barkston Ash League as one of a programme of fixtures.
Football There are two council owned pitches in Primrose Valley; the Halton Institute A Soccer Team played in the Leeds Sunday League. In the 1920's the headquarters of the Halton Football Club was at The Woodman Inn. The team played in the Lane Fox Shield and in the 1919/20 season were in Division 1 placed 4th. In 1921 there was a presentation at the Woodman Inn of the Temple Newsam Charity Cup medals by the Chairman of the Barkston Ash Football Executive. Halton District Football Club played the Leeds Police Cadets in January 1966.
Golf The Lord Irwin golf course at Temple Newsam was opened by Lord Mayor Ald Frank Fountain on July 20th 1923. The course had been designed by Dr Mackenzie and cost £3000 taking four months to complete. Work on the Lady Dorothy course was started in February 1923 and this was officially opened on May 8th 1924 by Ald Sir Charles Wilson. The new golf house replaced a temporary wooden building and was opened on the same day by Charles Gibson.
Land east of the golf course was opencast in 1941 and in 1943 the site of the Lady Dorothy course was severely affected by opencasting; as a result one course was made from the two original courses known as the Composite Course. When opencasting in the area ceased in 1948 the Lady Dorothy course was relaid, landscaped and replanted. The two courses run parallel with the 14th/15th fairways of Lady Dorothy passing Jacob's Well which once provided water through taps on the course. The first professional at Temple Newsam was Sid Wingate who lived at 64 Selby Road and later at Troon House Colton, with his daughter Poppy as the first lady professional. Poppy Wingate married Dr Herbert Eadie and her sister Lily who was born in 1918 married 41 year old Stanley

Heckingbottom on September 8th 1947. Following the completion of the present shop premises, the first professional to use this facility was Percy Alliss father of Peter Alliss. On August 22nd 1979 Lord Mayor and President Christine Thomas opened the new club premises based in the original building.

Howard Keith Clark was born at 1 Milestone Yard Halton on Thursday August 26th 1954. His father James Keith Clark lived on Selby Road in one of the six cottages adjacent to Gilsyke Farm at Field End. On their marriage Keith and Doris Clark moved in 1953 to 1 Milestone Yard which they proceeded to restore but moved after the birth of son Howard to Cross Gates and then moved again to Garforth. Howard Clark attended Royds School Rothwell until the age of 15. His father was a Yorkshire County Amateur Champion in 1955-57 and played at Garforth. Howard took temporary jobs at Leeds Wholesale Market and was for two years a local government officer in Leeds. He played at Cobble Hall course at Roundhay which he once reached on his bicycle. Howard Clark turned professional in 1973 and he married Castleford born Christine Arnold: their daughter Angela was born in 1975 and the family lived in Alwoodley. He was married for the second time to Beverley in 1983 and lived at Moor Allerton; Howard Clark was a tournament professional at Moor Allerton Golf Club. His golfing career started as Intermediate Boys Champion in 1969-71, Junior British Boys Champion in 1971 and Youth Champion 1971-1973. He was the Amateur Champion in 1973 and Yorkshire Amateur Champion in the same year when he also took the Walker Cup. On turning professional Howard Clark won a number of events including the Portuguese Open, Madrid Open, Whyte & Mackay PGA Cup, Jersey Open, Glasgow Open, Cepsa Madrid Open, Peugeot Spanish Open,

Morooco Open, and English Open all between 1978 and 1988. He played six times in the Ryder Cup team in 1977, 1981, 1985-89 and in 1995.

Rugby The Halton Old Boys Rugby Football Club came from Halton Council School and played their matches home on the Rec and away. The boys were Leeds champions in 1914-15 being awarded the shield. A photograph from 1920 shows the Halton Old Boys team photographed by the posts on the Rec. One of the boys who played for the team was Fred Hayes: in October 1914 the Halton team beat Holbeck trades School by 24 tries and 23 goals (118-0) and Fred scored 12 tries and 23 goals. The brothers Dick and Reg Thomas played for the team and Reg played professionally for Hunslet RFC. Dick was selected to play for the City of Leeds RFC who once played a match against Hull on the Headingley ground. Halton played in the Northern RFU Leeds & District Intermediate League and the school joined the Leeds Schools RL Junior

League.

Tennis There were three courts in Halton in the early days: one behind the Congregational Church site, in the garden of Miss Rollinson on High Street and a third by Engine Lane. There were also private tennis courts in the grounds of the Popplewell family on Pinfold Lane and at Clifton House home of the Pindar family. There are three tennis courts laid out in Primrose Valley: council owned but now becoming disused. One of the tennis clubs in Halton during the 1930's was the Welfare Tennis Club whose secretary was JW Crosthwaite. The three tennis courts on Grove Road were unplayable by 1979 and restoration was approved in 1981. This was completed by Leeds Leisure Services in April 1982. The Halton Tennis Club was a result of these newly surfaced courts.

SWIFT FAMILY

The Swift family came from Carlton near Rothwell where they were butchers, farmers and flour dealers working both in Carlton and at Royds Green. The church records show that members of the Carlton butcher family in the 18th century were Thomas Swift (1742-1814), Robert (1745-1833), Thomas (1766-1819), Isaac (1778-1850), Thomas (1783-1839), Hannah (1779-1817), Ann (1785-1851), Jane (1792-1880), Thomas (1809-1889) who married Jane in 1831 and Robert (1831-1867).

Four members of this family were John, Roger, Joseph and William. *John Swift* was born in 1781 and was a cattle dealer & skinner in Carlton and lived there with wife Ann born in 1786 and their children Mark William (1812), Mary Ann (1813), William & Sarah (1816), Ellen (1821) and Elizabeth (1824). *Roger Swift* was a Carlton butcher who was born in 1815 as the son of Roger Swift (1772-1852) and married Sarah Megson on January 19th 1835: their children were Squire (1835), Richard (1838), George & Joseph (1840), Mary (1841), John (1844) and John Megson born in 1846. *Joseph Swift* was a Carlton butcher born in 1777 and was married to Phoebe: their children were Jane (1816), Elizabeth (1817), Richard, Thomas and Elizabeth (1821), Rebecca (1825) and John born in 1827. John married Ann and their son William born in 1855 lived at Halton. *William Swift* was a butcher at Royd's Green and Halton married to Mary Parker on November 18th 1825. Their children were Hannah (1825), Sarah (1828), Elizabeth (1833), Roger (1835-1852), Mark William (1837-1839), Mary Anne (1839 died at 8 months) and William born in 1841. William who died in March 1852 aged 78 was buried at Whitkirk and it is also the burial place for his nephew Mark William (1812-1891) and his wife Jane who died in 1892 aged 92.

William was the first of the family to be in Halton as both farmer and butcher: he was in the village by 1820. A map of Halton in 1821 showed William Swift having his fields west of Engine Lane, land north of the present golf course, two fields from Primrose Lane to the Valley, Laurel Farm Chapel Street, the field on which the Congregational Church was built, land on Green Lane by the Bye Law Men's Field, land by The Mount on Garth End Field which was also in the hands of John Swift and the fields on either side of Selby Road from Pinfold Lane to Wilfred Avenue.

Squire was born in 1836 and married Mary born in 1838. Mark William came to Halton and married Jane running the family butcher's business on the High Street, in a shop where the Co-operative Store was built by the end of the 19th century. His plans for a wooden butcher's shop were passed in September 1899. He was the auditor for the Township of Halton in 1867, farm bailiff from 1864 to 1884, Whitkirk churchwarden from 1853, cattle dealer and one of the village butchers. Mark William

and Jane lived with their uncle William as father had died when Mark was only 10 years old. While in Halton they ran an 80 acre farm and in the 1881 census were employing two farmhands. Mark William Swift was interred at Whitkirk on September 26th 1891 aged 79; Jane died aged 92 and was interred at Whitkirk on April 13th 1892.
Squire Swift's marriage to Mary produced 12 children of whom some died in infancy. Robert Owen (1858-1926), Mark William (1861) and his twin brother Roger (1861-1920) who became a schoolteacher after being a pupil teacher at Halton School. His wife Emma Charlotte King who he married in July 1891 died aged 34 in May 1894. Other children were Martha (1863), Squire Eben (1867), Sarah Megson (1865) who became an assistant mistress at Halton School and married George Coleman in April 1899,Roger (1865) who was a pupil teacher at Halton School in 1880,Eva (1869-79), Charles Arthur (1871), Lucy Jane (1875-76), Frank (1877) and butcher Raymond (1880). Squire Swift lived on Orchard Terrace and then ran the 120 acre Laurel Farm on Chapel Street by 1908 and in his later days lived on Britton Terrace.
In 1884 Mark William Swift married Maria Augusta born in 1861 and they had three daughters: Constance (1885) became a schoolmistress, Gertrude Eveline was born on February 17th 1886 and became a Halton milliner and Gladys May born in 1889. The family lived on High Street, Laurel Farm and later on Graveley Street. Mark William became involved in many aspects of village life, ran a busy butcher's shop and also opened a wholesale meat outlet in Leeds called the Swift Beef Company at 15 Dead Meat Market New York Street.
Squire Eben Swift was born on June 23rd 1867 and he married Susannah Ragg and they had four sons and two daughters, one of whom was the Matron of Bridlington Hospital. Squire and Mary lived all their married lives in Selby; he was a plumber and contractor being involved closely with the life of Selby Methodist Church. Squire Swift died in Selby on Sunday February 15th 1931 at the age of 64: there was a service at Selby Methodist Church and the interment of the ashes was at Whitkirk Church. At the time of his death his mother Mary was still living in Halton and she was then the oldest native Halton resident living at Pear Tree House. Mary died in 1932 aged 94 and her will left £1059; Squire's widow Susannah died on January 11th 1954 at the age of 82. She was buried with her husband in the western section of Whitkirk Cemetery.

SYCAMORE AVENUE

The street was Graveley Street prior to 1928 when Hunslet RDC agreed to the name change and ordered new name plates. It was a part of John Graveley's plan for Graveleythorpe: the street was renumbered together with Chapel Street, Primrose Road, Primrose Lane, Field End Road,

Grove Road and Cross Green Lane in 1935. The east housing (odd numbers) dates from 1878 and together with the housing on Cross Green Lane, Birch Avenue (Graveley Road), Whitkirk View and Wilfred Avenue were all a part of this "village within a village". The other name of Noakes Terrace remembers Dr Samuel Joseph Noake of Gilsyke House who bought the site from John Graveley. The west side of Sycamore Avenue was built in three stages: the four centre houses were built first by John Graveley in c1898 with the five houses down to Cross Green Lane dating from 1934 built by George W Fenwick, for which planning permission was granted in August 1934. Reg Knight offered to sell to the LCC 1424 square yards of land on Cross Green Lane for "the erection of public buildings". The street together with many other Halton streets was passed to the Hunslet RDC in 1904 as agreed under the Order for Private Street Works Act 1892. The surfacing of the road was carried out in 1927 and Hunslet RDC agreed to plant 80 Sycamore and Birch trees on both adjacent roads and on The Crescent.
Residents of Sycamore Avenue have included builder George William Fenwick in the house he built (2); market gardener Alex McGrath (2 & 15) who died aged 77 on September 24th 1952: he was a former pork butcher in Holbeck and was buried at Killingbeck Cemetery. The owner of the Acme Jam Factory on Primrose Lane, Samuel Heathcote (17) who later moved to 21. Harry & Doris Cowell lived at 10: the brother of grocer Alec Cowell who lived for a few years at 19 Sycamore Avenue. 11 Graveley Street was the home of Mrs Gideon Lumb who died aged 81 in January 1918 and was one of the village's oldest residents.

TAYLOR FAMILY

Gabriel Taylor was born in 1700 and lived at Stourton: he married Ann Bell of Barwick-in-Elmet in 1728 who died childless. Gabriel married Mary and there were four children including Jonathan Taylor (1745-1823) born at Garforth. Jonathan married Ellen Jeffries (1754-1835) in 1780 at York. Their only son was William Taylor who was born in 1785 and in 1808 he married Sarah Plows of Seacroft whose parents were publicans.
There were eight children including five boys and the eldest son John was born in 1809. John Taylor was a miner living at Barwick-in-Elmet and he married Sarah Turner at St Mary's Whitkirk on December 13th 1833. There were six children and the second son was Jonathan Taylor who followed his father down the pits. Jonathan Taylor was married to Eliza King and first lived at West Field Cottage Osmondthorpe and later moved to the cottage built to the side of the old Irwin Arms public house with an address of 8 Engine Lane (Irwin Approach).
Jonathan and Eliza Taylor's children were: Elizabeth born at Barwick-in-

Elmet in 1869 and married Harry Nichols. Their children were Evelyn, Freda, Maurice and Dennis who was blind; Ada who died as a child; Annie born in 1875 married Sam Hewitt in 1898; Edith was born in 1876 and married Alfred Burnett in 1901 at Whitkirk Church: they had a son Alfred who died young; Carrie (1878-1970) married Robert Shaw (1878-1963) in 1904 at Whitkirk Church. Robert was a tailor in Woodhouse and in 1926 Carrie Shaw bought Pickering Lodge on Primrose Lane and later lived at South View Cottage at Bardsey and died at their house at Aldborough. Their children were Alex born in 1905 and Carrie born in 1910. Carrie married Claude Pybus at Whitkirk Church in 1930: they had two sons Bryan born in 1931 who married Jean Eva Culley in 1956 and Gerald born in 1932 who married Jean Sowray of West Tanfield. The family lived at Boroughbridge where they had a newspaper and book shop as well as Carrie's beauty parlour: they later moved to Aldborough.
Beatrice (Beattie) married George Osmond Bell of Halton whose father ran the post office on the corner of Chapel Street and Woodman Street. Ossie Bell's sister was Mary Emma Bell who died unmarried at Hopewell House.
Alice married David Speight of Halton and they died childless: Alice died in 1957.
Lawrence Harry Taylor was the youngest son serving in the Great War in

The Taylor family
Jonathan and Eliza King Taylor with
(from left) Alice, Edith, Elizabeth, Harry, Annie, Carrie, Beatrice.

the Battle of the Somme and in Flanders Fields. Harry married Minnie Johnson at Whitkirk Church on December 11th 1915: Minnie's father worked at Powolny's restaurant in Leeds. Harry Taylor was a painter and decorator when he was married and in later years became the village milkman, delivering milk by an open cart pulled by a horse around Halton village. Harry and Minnie also ran the grocery and off licence at 1 Cross Street from 1935 having moved from their previous shop on Cross Green Lane, which was to become Marion Squires confectioner and Gallon's shop. Minnie was the daughter of Tom & Polly Johnson and was born on April 10th 1892 at East End Park and she died on September 1st 1954: she was buried at Lawnswood. Lawrence Harry Taylor was born on October 25th 1888 and attended Halton Council School; he died on November 2nd 1989 aged 101 and was buried at Lawnswood. Harry and Minnie Taylor had three children: *Donald Harry Taylor* born 1922, *Beatrice Alice Taylor* born 1923 who married John William Dixon and they have four children and *Kathleen Mary Taylor* who was born in 1926. Their parents are buried at Whitkirk Church cemetery beside Eliza's parents John and Mary Ward King.

TELEPHONE COMMUNICATIONS

The first Leeds Telephone Exchange was opened in summer 1880 at the Royal Exchange Building on City Square/Boar Lane. The first Leeds telephone directory was issued as one page of 147 subscribers in 1881. The Leeds system was at first run by Blakey & Emmett and this was taken over by the National Telephone Company and the Post Office was the system in 1912. A new Exchange was opened in Basinghall Street in 1913 which could deal with 100,000 lines. There were 98 Exchanges opened in the UK in 1912 and in 1913 220 Exchanges were opened with several running automatically. The Leeds Exchange moved to Burley Street in 1965 and to Butts Court in 1993. The Cross Gates telephone exchange was opened by 1917: the number of Dr Haygarth was Cross Gates 3X. Telephone cables supplied Halton and Whitkirk by 1925 with early numbers being directed through the Telephone Exchange at Cross Gates. Households were connected with overhead wires and there were numerous call boxes found through the village. In 1929 the telephone number of the Halton Pharmacy was Cross Gates 165 and in 1936 this was Cross Gates 85265 which became Leeds 85265 in 1941 and in 1953 645265. In 1995 the STD code for Leeds was changed from 1532 to 0113 with 2 added to the number. Today the technical revolution has seen the mobile phone, opening out of the telecommunications industry, e mails through a computer, texting and videophones. Cable telephones are now used through Halton following the cabling of both Halton and Whitkirk in the 1980's.

The mobile or cell phone was invented by Martin Cooper while he was a project manager with Motorola in 1973. The mobile phone was introduced into Britain in 1985 and works on the division of the country into cells. When a call is made to a cell phone a computer first locates the apparatus by paging it over all transmitters. A frequency is selected for the call which is routed through the nearest transmitter.receiver station. The network was first established in the UK by BT and Securicor (Cellnet). WAP's are second generation mobile phones based on digital technology with 1½ million texts per month being transmitted in the UK: WAP means Wireless Application Protocol.

TEMPLENEWSAM ESTATE OWNERS
1066 to 1922

The story of Halton is closely bound up with the owners of Temple Newsam estate over the centuries. The village was part of this great estate.

1066 William the Conqueror appoints Ilbert de Lacy as the overall Lord of the Honour of Pontefract based at Pontefract Castle. He took over the lands farmed by Dunstan and Glunier.

1086 The Domesday Book records the Manor of Newhusum or Newsam meaning the new houses. The Manor was in the hands of the Viliers family.

1155 William de Viliers gave the Newsam lands to the Knights Templars. Temple Newsam became the site of a preceptory near the River Aire.

1310 The end of the Knights Templars with Temple Newsam being obtained by Sir Robert Holland.

1322 Estate confiscated by the King and Holland was beheaded.

1324 Temple Newsam was with the Knights Hospitallers

1327 Mary Countess of Pembroke

1340 John Darcy founder of the Temple Newsam Darcy line: Temple Newsam emparked in 1344.

1347 Son John Darcy inherited the Temple Newsam estate.

1500 Thomas Lord Darcy and built the first Temple Newsam House: he was beheaded in 1537. He had some children whose descendants became the Dukes of Leeds.

1537 Estate confiscated by the Crown until given to the Earl of Lennox.

1544 Matthew Stuart Earl of Lennox: he married Margaret Douglas and in 1545 their son Henry Stuart Lord Darnley was born who married Mary Queen of Scots in 1565.

1565 Estate becomes Crown property.

1603 Lodowick Duke of Lennox

1622 Bought by Sir Arthur Ingram for £12,000: he was the Comptroller of the Port of London and became the Secretary to the Council of the North at York where he built a house. Sir Arthur first married Susan Brown and then Alice Ferrers whose son married the daughter of Viscount Fauconberg of Newburgh Priory. Sir Arthur Ingram's third wife was Mary Greville.

1642 Sir Arthur Ingram the Younger: he married Eleanor daughter of Sir Henry Slingsby.

1655 Their second son Henry Ingram who became the 1st Viscount Irwin: he married Lady Essex Montagu daughter of the Earl of Manchester.

1666 Eldest son Edward 2nd Viscount Irwin who married Elizabeth Sherard of London.

1688 Youngest son Arthur 3rd Viscount Irwin: he married Isabella Machell. They had nine sons of whom five held the title of Viscount Irwin.

1702 Eldest son Edward 4th Viscount who was born in 1686.

1714 Rich 5th Viscount Irwin who married Lady Anne Howard of Castle Howard.

1721 Arthur 6th Viscount Irwin who was MP for Horsham.

1736 Henry 7th Viscount Irwin who married Ann Scarburgh.

1761 George 8th Viscount Irwin who became a Canon of Windsor.

1763 Charles 9th Viscount Irwin was the son of the 7th son Charles Ingram who married Elizabeth Scarburgh. Charles Viscount Irwin married Frances Gibson Shepheard. He died in 1778 and his wife lived at Temple Newsam until her death.

1807 Their eldest daughter was Isabella who married Francis Marquis of Hertford.

1834 Isabella's sister Frances Ingram Shepheard who married Lord William Gordon.

1841 Hugo Charles Meynell Ingram: son of third sister Elizabeth Ingram Shepheard and her husband Hugo Meynell of Hoar Cross. Hugo Charles Meynell added the Ingram name: he married Georgiana Pigou.

1869 Son Hugo Francis Meynell Ingram who married Emily Charlotte Wood daughter of the 1st Viscount Halifax.

1871 Hugo Francis died and buried at Hoar Cross. Temple Newsam with Emily Meynell Ingram.

1904 Edward Frederick Lindley Wood 3rd Viscount Halifax. He was the son of Emily's elder brother Charles Wood.

1922 Lord Halifax sells Temple Newsam to the City of Leeds. It was opened to the public in 1923.

TEMPLENEWSAM ROAD

This road was once Engine Lane and Halton Moor Road which partly became Templenewsam View. The road once joined with High Street (Selby Road)-now Irwin Approach. Mrs Meynell Ingram gave Engine Lane to the public in 1897: the road from Halton to Hunslet.

Halton Hill was altered in 1923 to create the present Temple Newsam Road link thus making access to the newly opened public park easier for cars and trams. The new road from Halton Moor Road (Templenewsam View) to Lawn Pond cost £16,340 in 1923 and included 18 acres bought from Edward Wood for £1650 to construct this road. In 1922/23 the new tramway known as the Templenewsam Light Railway was approved from Wyke Bridge to the junction of Elm Walk and Sycamore Walk. The naming of Templenewsam Road was passed on May 28th 1925. The road up Halton Hill was made into a dual carriageway in 1936-38 and continued as the Halton By-Pass Road. In May 1937 the Council agreed to maintain the triangular piece of land between Templenewsam Road and Halton Hill at the rate of £30 a year. The Council were initially responsible for turfing and tree planting. It was in the same year that Bray & Park conveyed some land to the Council for the Halton By-Pass Road to *"erect houses and make a footpath on Halton Hill"*. The Halton By-Pass Road was to run round the south side of the village to Whitkirk.
Engine Lane/Halton Moor Road at one period crossed open fields and there are stretches of old stone walls between Plantation Avenue and North Plantation which was a part of the farmland boundary. The area to Grove Road/Peggy Lane which is now a green area was at one time the site of Halton Colliery workings, Halton Clay Pits, Brickworks, refuse tip and a small sewage works. There was a fence and hedge which once surrounded this area which once had a cricket pitch and today there are three tennis courts and a bowling green.
By 1928 there were six semi-detached houses on Temple Newsam Road: in 1933 there were 2 shops and 10 houses numbered unevenly from 1. Two years later 2 to 90 Temple Newsam Road were completed with a subsequent change of numbering.
The shops on this short parade from Oak Crescent have included: 56/58 Harold & Gladys Dunhill had a shop here and the butcher until 1972 was Sydney & Constance Mary Lees: their son Samuel was living there in 1970. This is now Moreno's Moroccan Restaurant.
60/62 Harry Bradley & Alfred Cartmell; confectioner James Dean; Halton Pet & Pigeon Supplies.
66 Temple Newsam Road was *Moor Lynne* built by Dunhills, which became the new home of Herbert & Louisa Rennard when they sold The Halton Pharmacy in 1927. Moor Lynne was 7 but was renumbered in 1935. This was the home of Dr and Mrs William Ronald Jackson whose

surgery was at Dunhill Rise.
68 *Glendaragh* Sam and Betty Peters with sons Andrew and Mark; Sam Peters was the first Deputy Headmaster of Temple Moor Grammar School for Boys.
The road has numerous side streets including Oak Crescent, Sherbrooke Avenue, Broadway and Temple Newsam View to the west and Plantation Avenue and New Templegate to the east. Plantation Avenue was Park Avenue when new housing by Percy Sedgwick was being completed in 1932 and the name was changed in that year. There was an application to change the street name back again but the Council refused this idea.
The housing mainly dates from the inter-war years and New Templegate is from the 1960's: the name was proposed in June 1963 and adopted on October 1st 1964. Halton Moor Road once continued to Hunslet and is now partly represented by Templenewsam View. The Council renamed a section of the road and for example 20 Halton Moor Road became 20 Templenewsam View by 1956. In the late 1950's Temple Newsam Road was widened from Halton Moor Road to take increased traffic following the closure of the tramline in November 1959.

THOMAS FAMILY

Richard Richard Thomas was born on April 18th 1877 at 3 Duffryn Terrace Groeslon near Caernarvon, where his father was a worker in the local slate quarry. He came to Leeds in 1898 to marry Fanny Oliver who was born in 1880. In 1900 he joined the staff of Primrose Hill School Whitehall Street; he lived at Nunthorpe Road Rodley and then taught at Halton Council School from November 18th 1903. They moved to Bellbrooke Grove Harehills in 1907. In his first few years of teaching at Halton he had several periods off work with illness and took leave to attend the funeral of his mother in Wales on February 7th 1908. Richard Thomas was placed in charge of the Mixed Department and acting headteacher in February 1916 having obtained his teachers certificate. The family moved to live at the School House on Selby Road which had been built in 1875. He was appointed headmaster on August 28th 1919 in time for the start of term on September 1st. He left Halton School in December 1932 following his appointment as headteacher of Green Lane Council School Wortley until his retirement. He went back to Halton School in January 1933 to be presented with two lounge chairs by the staff and parents. When he retired in 1937 he arranged with Arthur Wilson to build him a house 475 Selby Road. Richard Thomas died on April 26th 1959. The funeral service was held at Halton Congregational Church on Wednesday April 29th where there was a collection to be placed towards a complementary memorial already in the Church to his wife. Richard's wife Fanny had died of cancer at the School House on

May 30th 1938 at the age of 58 and was buried at Whitkirk Cemetery on June 2nd 1938. Richard Thomas lived at the new house until his death being looked after by his housekeeper Mrs Wilks of 246 Selby Road.
The prayers were led at Richard Thomas's funeral service by AW Roberts from Halton Methodist Church, the lesson was read by Rev Ernest Southcott of St Wilfrid's Church and a tribute was read by Rev R Parmley of Halton Congregational Church. On Sunday March 5th 1961 a memorial to Richard R Thomas was dedicated at the Congregational Church by the minister: a music stand made by William Pease and a pair of silver communion servers.
Richard R Thomas was the leader of the Wesleyan PSA (Pleasant Sunday Afternoons) which he started in 1925, a founder member of the Halton Congregational Church and a senior deacon, a Leeds Councillor from 1945 to 1947, President of Leeds NUT, President of the Leeds Congregational Council and Yorkshire Lay Preachers Association. In 1925 he was elected President of the West Riding Brotherhood & Sisterhood Federation. The family were Richard Oliver, Reginald and Eva Ellen Thomas.
Richard Oliver Thomas was born on March 15th 1902 at 126 Beckett Street opposite the workhouse (St James Hospital). The Thomas family lived there with Fanny's father Robert Oliver and his wife Eva (Charlesworth); Robert & Eva were married at Lady Lane Chapel in Leeds. The Oliver family came from Hurworth-on-Tees near Darlington, where Robert was a farrier. Dick Thomas was educated at Brownhill School and Cockburn High School which he reached on his bicycle via Engine Lane and the Red Road. On April 18th 1927 he married Edna Payne at Whitkirk Church: she was the daughter of Walter & Eleanor Payne of William Avenue. Edna was born in 1904 and the married couple lived at 6 The Crescent Whitkirk. In the year of his marriage Dick Thomas was captain of the Halton Temps 2nd XI Cricket Team and the leader of the Halton Concert Party which gave over 500 performances in Leeds. Dick left Cockburn School to obtain a job at Barnbow in 1916 in the office as a clerk and left in December 1916 as there was a vacancy for a junior clerk in the City Treasurer's Office Leeds: this was the start of his municipal career. He retired in 1963 after 46 years service and 29 years in the City Treasurer's Department. Richard was later appointed the Deputy Director of the City Buildings Department at Leeds Town Hall. Richard and Edna celebrated their Silver Wedding in April 1952. He was a dedicated worker for the Halton Congregational Church being bazaar secretary and treasurer, Sunday School superintendent, organist, choirmaster, PSA secretary and he formed a Youth Club and a Musical Society. Dick Thomas was a talented artist selling many of his paintings for church funds. One of his signed paintings is at Halton Post Office on the wall behind the counter. Edna Thomas died aged 61 on April 1st 1965

in the LGI and was cremated at Lawnswood. Richard Oliver Thomas died on May 14th 1989 and was cremated at Lawnswood with his ashes scattered on May 19th. His last address was Fairview Brooklands Avenue Seacroft which was the home of his friend Alice Wardman. They had no children but adopted a seven year old orphan boy Clifford Alderson who served in the Navy on the aircraft carrier Illustrious and on other ships. On one occasion Clifford was floating in the Indian Ocean for nearly two days before being picked up. He married Mona Jesson of 205 Selby Road: they had a son Alan who became a member of Halton Congregational Church in July 1938 and daughter Lynn who became a schoolteacher. Roland Jesson lived at The Crescent: he died in October 1976 having served Halton Congregational Church for 40 years.
Reginald Thomas was born on August 25th 1903 and on September 3rd 1930 married Edna May Todd, daughter of Louis Edwin (1897-1952) and Emily Todd (1879-1975) of Halton. Edna was born in March 1903 and attended Halton School from 1908 until 1916. Reginald and Edna lived first at 208 Selby Road before redevelopment forced removal to their new home 296 Selby Road. Reg Thomas worked in the City Transport Department and was a local government officer. Their son *Gordon Thomas* was born on January 19th 1935: the child died of meningitis in June 1937 and was buried at Whitkirk Cemetery on June 30th. Their daughter *Patricia Anne Thomas* was born on July 13th 1938 and was baptised at Halton Congregational Church on September 4th. Pat was educated at Halton School and Roundhay School where she met her future husband David Buckroyd of Harehills: they were married on December 16th 1961 at St Wilfrid's Church Harehills. David obtained a degree from Oxford University and started his teaching career at Merchant Taylor's School Crosby. He taught at King's School Pontefract, King Edward VII School Lytham where he was deputy headmaster and was appointed the Headmaster of Ermysted's Grammar School at Skipton in 1982 and retired in 1998. David & Pat's married children are Russell Stuart and Alison Jane.

Reginald and Edna Thomas

Edwin and Emily Todd moved to a semi-bungalow Ashleigh 315 Selby Road after Edwin's retirement; after his death in 1952 Edna Todd lived both at the bungalow and with Reginald and Edna at the house near the bungalow. Reginald Thomas died on May 13th 1987 at a nursing home in Roundhay and was cremated at Lawnswood. He was a member of Whitkirk Bowling Club winning the Championship in 1973; he also played for Hunslet Rugby. Reg and Edna celebrated their Golden Wedding in September 1980.

Edna May Thomas returned to Halton School on Friday July 10th 1992 for the 150th anniversary celebrations which were opened by Leeds Director of Education Stuart Johnson: she died at Skipton on January 30th 2000.

Eva Ellen Thomas (Nellie) was born in 1908 and in 1933 married Edwin Jones second son of Milton & Frances Anne Jones of Cross Gates and Halton Garages. The married couple lived at 14 Templegate Whitkirk. Edwin was born in 1907 and died at Perth Scotland in 1988; Eva died at Ilkley in 1996.

Their children were Anthony Edwin Jones born 1936, Sylvia Thomas Jones born August 25th 1938 and Richard Milton Jones born 1946. Anthony married Patricia Dyson in 1961 and they have three married children Bridget, Rachel and Colette. Sylvia Jones married Malcolm Ryan in 1959 and they have two married children Andrew Mark and Suzanne. Richard Jones married Lynne Holliday in 1968 and they have two children Neil and Claire.

THRIFT STORES

It was *Wright Popplewell* who founded the Thrift Stores and originally traded as Popplewell & Co Ltd. He was born in 1858 and his first shop was at 30 Bath Road Holbeck in 1881 and in 1888 at Wortley Lane New Wortley as provision merchants. He soon opened in Cross Gates, Garforth, 366 Kirkstall Road and at 332 Burley Road. In 1900 the first shop in Halton was opened on Cross Green Lane with a new front added in 1938. The Thrift butcher's shop on Wilfred Avenue was converted from a private house: planning permission was given in October 1934.

Wright Popplewell lived at 8 Stanmore Road Burley and came to live at Avondale in Stanks, retired from Thrift Stores in 1914 and then moved to Brynmor Pinfold Lane Halton by 1920. His son *Joshua Appleyard Popplewell* became the Managing Director of Thrift Stores; he was living at Fernbank 2 Graveleythorpe Halton, afterwards at Denistoun Pinfold Lane and by 1919 moving to Chestnut Grove. He married Ethel Ineson in 1906 first living at Burley. He was a director of the Leeds Co-operative Society retiring in 1901; moved to Kirkstall and in March 1933 returned to Halton to open the Methodist Church Spring Fayre. The chairman of the Fayre was Richard Haste Carr of Craigmona. Joshua & Ethel's children were Ethel Gertrude born in October 1908 who married accountant Louis William Euler, they lived at Ancaster Road; Frederick Harold (1912-14) who died of meningitis, John Alfred (1910-36) who died

of TB, Edward James Wright (1906-96) and Margaret Gwendolen (1918-20). Wright's daughter Frances married Edward Stockwell Lawson a carpet manufacturer of Burley on July 19th 1922. Wright lived in later years at Mayfield Drive Morecambe and he died on June 19th 1933.
In 1923 son *James Wright Popplewell* lived at Denistoun Pinfold Lane having joined the business in 1918 and brother Joshua moved to Beechwood Arnside in 1923. In 1947 James Wright Popplewell was a director of the Thrift & Provident Stores and lived at Oak Hill Linton Road Wetherby. His wife Mabel Popplewell died at Wetherby in January 1928. In 1956 there were 200 Thrift stores in Yorkshire with their headquarters at Bridge Road Kirkstall opened in 1928. The director was EJ Popplewell and the firm had 1083 employees.
In 1926 Thrift joined with Ideal Stores of Wellington Street (1872) and they later acquired RC Hopkinson, Woodcocks, Abbey Stores and Walter Barkers.
The Thrift Store on High Street adjacent to the Irwin Arms public house was opened by shopper Florence Wainwright of Mayfield Road on Thursday July 23rd 1964 who had been shopping at the Thrift from 1918 at their first shop on Cross Green Lane which had opened in 1900. When the new store opened a polythene bucket was given free to any customer who spent more than 15 shillings. The new Halton store had 2000 square feet of floor space with 52 feet of display cabinets together with a large storage area on the upper floor. In 1964 there were 160 branches with 1000 staff of which 25 were working at Halton. In that year the Chairman of Thrift Stores was Oxford graduate Christine Shaddick.
The shop closed when the new store was opened: the Halton Store became House of Holland on closure.
Thrift Stores were mainly closed by 1972 with the headquarters at Kirkstall becoming Clover in 1973. *Together with Gallons Stores the firm was taken over by Allied Suppliers who were an amalgamation of smaller stores. In June 1982 Argyll Group bought Allied Suppliers from James Goldsmith for £101 million. Argyll was started by James Gulliver and by 1987 the group became the 4th largest grocer in Britain.*

TOC H

The Halton & Cross Gates branch of TOC H opened in September 1946. In 1934 TOC H had 3000 members in Yorkshire in 83 units. The TOC H Hostel at Brotherton House North Grange Road Headingley was opened on March 19th 1932 and was closed in 1970. The Yorkshire area office at 65 Oxford Row Leeds closed c1968. The Leeds branch was founded in December 1923 and closed in September 1982: the Halton & Cross Gates Branch of TOC H closed in 1962.
TOC H was founded to the memory of those who gave their lives in war

and peace in the service of their fellow men; providing accommodation for needy people, a legal scheme for the poor, hospital visiting, Christmas parcels and coach trips for the retired. The founder was Tubby Clayton (Philip Thomas Byard Clayton) born in Queensland on December 12th 1885. He was educated at St Paul's School and Exeter College Oxford where he took a degree in Theology. In 1915 he went to France as an army chaplain and in December 1915 he opened Talbot House in Poperinge which was known as Every Man's Club. The club was just behind the lines in Flanders and became known to thousands of soldiers who found a touch of home and respite from war. The house took the name from Lt Gilbert Talbot, brother of Tubby's senior chaplain who was killed in action at Hooge. The nickname TOC H for Talbot House was derived from TH in army signallers code. Tubby Clayton was the Vicar of All Hallows London from 1922 to 1962 and he died on his 87th birthday in December 1972. The earliest statement of the aims of TOC H was to provide members with opportunities to develop a spirit of understanding and reconciliation; to enable members with their varying gifts to serve their fellows; to bring to members the knowledge and experience of others; to work for a better world through the example of friendship, service and fairmindedness. The symbol of TOC H is the lamp.

There were many activities organised by Halton TOC H including week camps for Halton boys at Spennithorne in Wensleydale. Boys from Halton were invited to Spennithorne as guests of the Knights of the Round Table which had been formed by the Rector of Spennithorne in 1950. They also held whist drives and dances at St Wilfrid's Church Hall.

TRANSPORT

Halton is three miles from Leeds and was a distance covered on foot, horseback, coach services and later by trams and buses

In 1845 Halton was served by horse drawn "buses" from the Horse & Jockey on Commercial Street and from the Free Market Hotel Kirkgate. In 1847 there were three services daily terminating at Garforth. The route past the Brown Cow Inn at Whitkirk ran on market days as well as the normal services; the carrier was John Coates. In 1860 John Coates ran his service to Halton from the Horse & Jockey, Ship Inn and Bradford Hotel three times daily and on Sundays. In the 1860's the bus to Kippax was run by Reuben Clough: the Perseverance ran until 1868. This was taken over by Kippax farmer James Binns who ran twice a week: in 1892 the carrier was Thomas Watkinson. In 1920 A Goodhind was advertising two fine charabancs for hire with the slogan *"book now for Pontefract Races"*.

Bus services One of the first services was The Breadwinner which had solid tyres. Bus routes to Halton started in June 1925 by Hartley Bros & Rhodes with the terminus at Colton. There was then a service from Vicar Lane to Garforth, Kippax and Ledston Luck with another to Garforth, Sherburn-in-Elmet, South Milford and Selby. Hartley Bros & Rhodes were bought in 1933 by the West Riding Automobile Co. In 1931 the West Riding service started from New York Road and served the 12 mile route to Castleford via Halton, Garforth, Kippax and Great Preston in 55 minutes.

The Kippax & District service started in 1928 running from New York Road and served Halton, Swillington Common, Garforth, Kippax and Ledston Luck. In 1936 the Kippax & District service ran from Vicar Lane to Selby Road and along Chapel Street and Green Lane to the Ring Road. The last "yellow bus" ran on Saturday March 30th 1968: it had been Watson's Kippax & District Motor Co and was taken over by the LCC and by Wallace Arnold.

Bus routes were numbered in July 1937 starting at 31. The main bus services through Halton were 39 Vicar Lane to Halton Ring Road; 40 Vicar Lane to Stanks and 41 Vicar Lane to Colton via Hollyshaw Lane which had started in 1932. These services moved to the new Central Bus Station which opened on September 1st 1938. In 1924 there were only eight buses running in Leeds while by 1937 there were 210 and in 1953 Leeds was running 416 buses. During the war period services were reduced with route 40 being cancelled until September 1946. In 1950 Limited Stop services were introduced on all three Halton routes.

In 2004 the Halton services through the village are 40 Seacroft and the 18 along Selby Road and 18a through the Templegate estate. Services 163, 164, 165, X4 to Castleford, 140 and X66 to Micklefield, 402 to Selby and 921N to Swillington are operated by Arriva and the 88 route by Black Prince from Bradford to Colton. *Arriva* was formed by Tom Cowie's Sunderland Group who bought British Bus: the holding company was the Yorkshire Bus Group. On privatisation Caldaire Holdings included West Riding Automobile Company, Yorkshire Woollen and Selby & District who held their own operators licences. Arriva took the West Riding Automobile Co to become Arriva Yorkshire with the Yorkshire Woollen as Arriva Yorkshire West. Arriva Yorkshire is based at Belle Isle Wakefield (West Riding HQ). *Black Prince* is based in Fountain Street Morley. In 1968 Brian Crowther started his commercial services with one coach: in 1969 he formed a partnership with Bert Colley and a new name for their firm came from the Black Prince statue in City Square. There was an increase in private hire, school journeys and contracts; Brian became the sole proprietor when Bert Colley died in 1976. In 1975 the firm operated the Blackpool Express under contract to National and after partial regulation in 1981 Black Prince operated this as a commercial enterprise. *First Leeds* is a subsidiary of First Group plc which in 1996 took over

Yorkshire Rider. First Group was based at Bristol and was Trevor Smallwood's Badgerline. Leeds City Transport was taken over by a worker's cooperative in 1986 who were taken by Yorkshire Rider.

In early November 2001 the £16 million Elite Quality Bus Initiative was opened: work had started in January 2000. The route included newly laid reserved guided track for buses on a part of Halton Hill and York Road. The work on Halton Hill revealed the old tram lines last used in November 1959. It was the West Yorkshire Passenger Transport Authority under Coun Mick Lyons who obtained the money for this system. *Mick Lyons was born in 1933 and has been a member of Leeds City Council from 1980 and became chairman of the WYPTA in 1989: he worked in the rail industry from 1946 until retirement in 1996. He was awarded the OBE in HM The Queen's Birthday Honours List of 2003.*

Train services commenced on September 22nd 1834 with the Marsh Lane to Selby line, initially having no stop at Cross Gates. Work started on the new line in 1830; the contractors from Osmondthorpe to Selby were Hamer & Pratt of Goole and during the line building in 1833 the 54 feet high Halton Embankment was the scene of earth slips. Thousands of stone sleeper blocks were hewn from Halton Quarry on Halton Hill and used for the line which required 140,000 blocks. Cross Gates Station was opened in c1850 and it was rebuilt in 1902, when the main line was doubled. The line to Wetherby was opened in 1876 and closed to passengers on September 9th 1963: the line closed in 1964. There was a temporary Saturday stop at Halton Dial for a few years until 1864 and in July 1929 a planning application was placed to build the Osmondthorpe Halt. The station opened in October 1930 and was closed in May 1978.

Tram services Horse trams ran on lines which were constructed along York Road in 1874 originally terminating at The Woodpecker Inn and then to The Greyhound Inn in 1894 and two years later to Victoria Avenue. In December 1912 a newspaper commented that "*The little village of Halton views the intended tram links as the first step to incorporation. Many Halton residents work in Leeds and now walk to Halton Dial or Cross Gates rail station. The trams will bring prosperity to the village but many shopkeepers feel that they will lose business as they will use the tram to go to the shops in Leeds*". Lines were laid to Halton Dial and up Halton Hill (1 in 15.7) as a single track with passing places to Chapel Street terminus by the Institute with construction starting in October 1914. In July 1914 a council statement was that "*The tram extension is from York Road to the boundary of the City at White Bridge and thence to Chapel Lane in the village of Halton with another extension to Manston Hospitals*". The first tram to Halton was on April 30th 1915. This was tramway route 6 to Chapel Street but was route 23 and from October 1929 was route 17. The tram lines had cost £11,689 with the contractor being David Speight of Halton. The original plan was

to continue the line along Chapel Street, Cross Green Lane and Green Lane to Cross Gates. This plan proved impossible due to the severe restriction at the railway bridge, although overhead lines were placed in Station Road from the Cross Gates terminus.

In 1931 route 17 left the Corn Exchange every 20 minutes with 139 daily journeys and 141 on Saturdays and 108 on Sundays. The first tram to Halton left at 4.55am and the last left the village terminus at 11.45pm.

The approval of the Temple Newsam tram service was given in March 1923. The Temple Newsam service was opened with the 10am tram from Corn Exchange to the Golf House on April 18th 1924 and a few days later was extended to the terminus at the mansion. Service 22 left for Temple Newsam in 1931 during the summertime with 13 journeys taking 26 minutes from Leeds to cover the 4 mile route. The service to Temple Newsam was increased for the thousands who visited the Great Yorkshire Show on July 12th-14th 1932; the Halton Dial sub-station opened in May 1932 feeding Gipton, Cross Gates, Halton and Temple Newsam.

The double track up a section of Halton Hill came in 1923 with the whole route from Halton Dial to Temple Newsam made double track from 1936. It was in January 1935 that £32,500 was made available to build the reserved track up Halton Hill with the widening of the bridge over Wyke Beck. The cliff was removed from Elam's farm to Portage Avenue involving 22,825 cubic yards and this was completed by June 1936. The high wall was built to stabilise the ground complete with a set of steps from the pavement to the street above. Work started on the whole project in March 1935: a few months later Councillor Frederick Leach became the new chairman of the Transport Committee. Fred Leach lived on Morritt Avenue and his position lasted until November 1938; he took

over from Coun Donald Cowling and when Cowling joined the RAF in August 1940 Leach took over the chairmanship again until 1945 when Coun John Rafferty was elected to the position.
The end of the tram terminus at Chapel Street was advertised in May 1936 and the last tram used this terminus on November 7th. The reserved track and junction for the Temple Newsam line opened on November 8th 1938. The new tram route number became 20 instead of 17 while the route to Temple Newsam had opened as route 24 in April 1924 and became 22 in 1929. The routes remained 20 and 22 until closure in 1959. The same year that the route to the park was opened so also was the route to the new tram terminus at Cross Gates on a reserved track to a point at the end of Austhorpe Road; this was shortened in September 1938 and further altered in December 1940 to be near The Regal Cinema. Cross Gates Road was widened with a dual carriage way and central tram reservation by June 1937. Safety reasons during the war saw many trams dispersed to the Temple Newsam terminus at a newly laid track parallel to the service lines. This lasted until January 1944 and a long wooden shelter existed at Temple Newsam from 1932 when it was introduced for the Great Yorkshire Show. Most of the shelter was removed in September 1940 in two parts to City Square for sheltering during wartime. Route 15/18 linked Whingate with Cross Gates while route 16/20 linked New Inn with Halton; 20 was the route from Kirkgate to Halton and route 22 was from Kirkgate to Temple Newsam.

The Last Trams in Leeds

The routes from Cross Gates and Temple Newsam/Halton were formally closed on Saturday November 7th 1959. The last service tram left Leeds Corn Exchange for Cross Gates at 4.39pm and was due back in the city at 5.35pm. The last service tram to Temple Newsam was 177 and it was on these trams which ran on the last day in service that passengers obtained a souvenir ticket. The city bus services took over from the trams at that point to serve Halton and Cross Gates. There was a ballot for places on the last trams which were to leave Swinegate Depot at 6pm-6.15pm and were due back at the Depot by 7.30pm: over 1000 applications were received of which half were successful. The first two of the ten Horsfield trams were reserved for invited guests of the City Council and they included the Lord Mayor Gertrude Annie Stevenson and members of the Tramways Committee and City Council who were on the first tram in the procession. The Council issued card invitations and advised that due to available space no spouses could be accommodated. Other guests included the Mayors of Morley and Pudsey, Major FS Eastwood (Regional Traffic Commissioner), AB Findlay (General Manager LCT 1949-60), JG Taylor (Divisional Road Engineer) and representatives from Bradford, Doncaster, Hull and Sheffield. The procession started at

Swinegate where there were TV cameras and flash cameras recording the scene and slowly wended its way up York Road followed by a procession of cars, scooters and bicycles. Many thousands on the road sides watched five trams bound for the Cross Gates terminus at Cross Gates Road by The Regal Cinema and five trams numbered in sequence were 173,176,189,175,160 for the Halton terminus by the Irwin Arms public house and then to Temple Newsam terminus. The Horsfield (RL Horsfield General Manager 1929-31) trams had been the backbone of the Leeds fleet and the driver of the first official tram was Arthur Aisthorpe who had worked for 39 years as a tram driver and on board was the longest serving tram conductress Elizabeth Hoyle who had served for 19 years. The Halton tram procession went before the Cross Gates trams from Halton Dial. The Lord Mayor took her turn at the controls of the last tram 178 and Ald John Rafferty also drove this tram into the depot for the last time. The first and last trams numbers 178 and 160 were decorated in coloured lights and it was a memorable sight in the November murk: like an *"illuminated gondola"*. When the trams had run for the last time the official Council representatives were invited for a special dinner. On the top table at this Civic banquet was a silver plate fruit bowl which had been made from the driver's foot pedal of a Leeds tram and presented to the Lord Mayor. The courses at the dinner carried names which represented this special event in the life of the Leeds transport system. The menu was: Melon Swinegate, Minestrone Kirkgate, Filet of Sole Fares Please, Grilled Chicken Woodpecker, Peas a la Torre, Celery a la Gipton, Potatoes Halton, Pineapple on the Line, Cheese and Biscuits by request and Coffee terminus. On Monday November 9th a Tramway Exhibition with working models was opened at the Leeds City Art Gallery by Ald John Rafferty who was elected Lord Mayor for 1968.

I have a blue ticket from this occasion numbered 14028 and printed "Cross Gates, Halton & Temple Newsam Tram Services. This ticket was issued on the last day of operations Saturday November 7th 1959 to mark the closing down of the tramway system in Leeds. Fare 5d." The reverse of the ticket is printed with: "Tramcar operations in the City of Leeds commenced in 1871. The first line was opened for traffic with horse trams between Boar Lane and the Oak Inn Headingley on 16th September. Steam trams were introduced on the Wortley route on 17th June 1880 and electric trams on the Roundhay route on 11th November 1891. For 10 years three different forms of traction were in operation but the last horse trams ran on 13th October 1901 and the last steam trams on 1st April 1903. From the beginning of the century the electric tramway system grew rapidly as various extensions were made. The era of the electric tram reached its peak in 1933 when the fleet totalled 476 trams running over 324 miles of track".

TURNPIKES AND TOLLS

The ***Leeds & Selby Turnpike Trust*** was started in 1741 with the act passing through parliament on April 30th 1751 running from Leeds along the York Road from Halton Dial. There was a tollbar where the toll gates were approved in March 1751 for Halton Dial and house. The road climbed Halton Hill which was always an obstacle even following turnpiking and through to Peckfield Bar at the crossing of the Ridge Road. The route passed through Monk Fryston after the crossing of the Great North Road passed another turnpike bar at Hambleton before arriving at the final toll bar at Gowthorpe on the outskirts of Selby. Initially the Gascoigne coal pits at Garforth did not pay a toll although in 1950 this was revoked.

Paterson's Roads by Edward Mogg (1822) gives the route via Black Bank from Leeds to Selby and then Halton, Whitchurch, Garforth,Peckfield Common, Boot & Shoe, Monk Fryston, Hambleton, Thorp Willoughby and Selby. In 1842 the rent for the Selby & Leeds Turnpike Trust was £1274 a year; the business was sold by auction on a few occasions. The tolls on the turnpike roads were completely abolished on December 31st 1870 and toll bars were banned from 1873. The old Leeds/Selby toll bar at Halton Dial was converted into Waites's shop, vacated on July 12th 1929 and subsequently demolished.

VERITY FAMILY

The Verity families were farming parts of Upper Nidderdale in the 19th century. In the 1840's Bouthwaite Farm was with Thomas and Elizabeth Verity with their four children; West House Farm with William and Ann Verity with their three children; Southfield was with William and Jane Verity with their two children; Riggs Farm with Thomas and Jane Verity with their three children; Heathen Carr was with John and Hannah Verity; Stonebeck Up was run by Thomas and Mary Verity with their seven children; Miles Verity with his wife Elizabeth was farming from Middlesmoor: their children were William, Catherine, Thomas, Isabella and Margaret.

Thomas and brother Peter Verity were farmers at High Riggs Farm Stonebeck in the 1870's and at nearby Low Riggs Farm were John and Mary Verity. Heathen Carr was a 350 acre farm run by John and Mary Verity with their children Matthew, William and Jane. William and Ann Verity were at Stonebeck Up and at Stonebeck Down was John and Elizabeth Verity with Thomas, James and Hannah. At Stean Farm were Matthew and Ann Verity with their children William, John, Jane and Mary Ann. The families were tenant farmers on the Yorke estate, which was sold in 1924.

It was Miles Verity who decided to leave his Nidderdale roots following the decision to construct Gouthwaite reservoir. Miles was born in Upper Nidderdale in 1825 and he farmed at Gouthwaite Hall from c1877, following the Weatherhead family. A few years later he and his wife Hannah with sons William born in 1866 and Robert born in 1873 brought all their stock to Halton Hill by track and road including the cows and hens. The search for a new farm living was brought about by the construction of Gouthwaite Reservoir. The first sod for the new reservoir was cut by the Mayoress of Bradford on September 13th 1893 with opening in 1901.

Gouthwaite Hall was built in the early 17th century and was a seat of the Yorke family of Bewerley Hall. In the late 19th century the old Hall was divided into three houses for the tenants. The Hall was demolished and some of the stone were re-used to build the present Gouthwaite Hall, which was above the level of the reservoir. The Hall site was submerged in 1900, although the empty Hall had been flooded in October 1899.

William was a teenager when he came to Halton and a few years later was courting Annie, daughter of Thomas and Mary Freer. Annie was the youngest of three children: her sister was Fanny and brother Richard. The Freer family were Halton hay and straw dealers of Town Street (High Street); Thomas was born in Tadcaster in 1839 and Mary was born in Thorner in 1844. They married in 1893 when William was 27 and his wife was 23 years old, running Whitebeck Farm after his father Miles died on June 11th 1893 aged 68 and his mother Hannah died on September 12th 1898 aged 53.

William and Annie Verity

William Verity died aged 63 on August 6th 1929 and his wife Annie died aged 87 on August 30th 1957, while living with Miles and Mary at 364 Selby Road.

The children of William and Annie Verity were Miles who was born in 1894, William born in 1896, Annie born in 1898, Mary Hannah born in 1900 and youngest child Thomas Richard born on November 15th 1913.

Miles was educated at Ampleforth

College and ran Gilsyke Farm: he remained a bachelor. William Verity married George Whitfield's daughter Mary of Grange Farm Colton in 1928. Their children were William Edward who was born in 1925 and Christine Mary born in 1929 and died in 2001. Edward married Audrey Margaret Proctor at St Mary's Church Old Sharelston in 1954 and their children are Jennifer Mary who is a dentist with John William and Gillian Frances who now run Hollinthorpe Farm. Audrey lived at the Green Tree Inn Hatfield Woodhouse and moved for a short period to live at Colton Mill before moving to Sharleston Farm and then to Swillington.

Miles Verity came from Whitebeck Farm to Gilsyke Farm until ill health forced his retirement in 1948 on the recommendation of Dr Jack Young of Gilsyke House. Miles moved to 364 Selby Road where he died on April 10th 1956 aged 62;l he was cremated at Lawnswood on April 12th and the ashes were interred at Whitkirk.

William Verity moved from Whitebeck Farm to Laurel House Farm on Chapel Street. His wife Mary died aged 35 on April 18th 1933 and William moved to live at Hollinthorpe Farm Swillington Lane in 1935. The Lowther's Swillington estate was sold by Bartle & Co on December 11th 1935 at the Swillington Welfare Institute and included 12 farms with Hollinthorpe and Leventhorpe, Little Preston Hall and 119 cottages. William Verity died on Wednesday June 8th 1960 in the Brotherton Wing at the LGI and there was a service held at Halton Methodist Church on June 13th.

Annie Verity married Lorenzo Schofield who was a Latin master at Cheltenham Grammar School. Annie Verity died on January 21st 1958 and her husband in 1962; their children are June, Jonathan and artist Simon.

Hannah Mary Verity remained single living with the Halton family and for a period moving to live in London. Mary died on January 10th 1980 aged 79 in The Retreat York.

Thomas Richard Verity married Alice Rhoda Hanson at Halton Methodist Church on January 6th 1940; their son is Malcolm. Thomas was a farm labourer at Gilsyke Farm for a period before moving to Dewsbury to run a newsagents shop.

VICTORIA CROSS HOLDER

Sergeant Albert Mountain of the 15/17th West Yorks Regiment (Prince of Wales Own) won the Victoria Cross in 1918. Albert Mountain was born in Halton on April 19th 1895 with his home at Field Terrace and 140 Selby Road. Early in the War he joined the Leeds Bantams and later transferred to the Leeds Pals. On March 26th 1918 at Hamelincourt France when the situation was critical Albert Mountain with a party of ten attacked an advance patrol of about 200 men with a Lewis gun killing half of them. He then rallied his men in the face of overwhelming

numbers of the main body of the enemy to cover the retirement of the rest of the company. This party of one NCO and four men held at bay 600 of the enemy for half an hour. Sergeant Mountain later took command of the flank post of the battalion holding on for 27 hours until finally surrounded. His son was Brian Mountain who lived at the Selby Road house. In the Second World War he volunteered for Home Guard duty and was a special constable. After the War he was the chauffeur to the Lord Mayor of Leeds and later was the licensee of The Miner's Arms at Garforth living on Aberford Road Garforth. In 1956 Albert was one of 400 surviving holders of the VC and he went to London for the VC Centenary Parade which was reviewed by HM The Queen and Prince Philip. He died on January 7th 1967 and was cremated at Lawnswood.

A replica of Albert Mountain's VC is displayed in the Regimental Museum of the Prince of Wales Own Regiment of Yorkshire Tower Street at York. There is a copy of the citation with a photograph showing Albert wearing the VC and the Leeds Pals 17th West Riding Regiment Prince of Wales Own cap badge. Albert Mountain was also awarded the French Croix de Guerre and the Medaille Militaire. The original VC awarded to Albert Mountain is held in a York bank for safe keeping.

The Victoria Cross was instituted in 1856 and there have so far been 1354 awarded: the first was on June 26th 1857 when Queen Victoria decorated 62 officers and men who had fought in the Crimean War against Russia. Since 1945 the VC has been awarded 11 times: two in the Falklands War of 1982. The medal is inscribed "For Valour". The VC has been given to 116 Yorkshiremen or servicemen with Yorkshire regiments since 1857: one of the first was Bombardier Thomas Wilkinson of York. He received the VC for his outstanding bravery at the Battle of Sebastopol and he died in York aged 55 and was buried with full military honours.

The other holders of the Victoria Cross are also remembered by a bronze plaque in the Garden of Remembrance on The Headrow, which was unveiled in November 1992. Louis Aaron, Alfred Atkinson, William Boynton, William Butler, Laurence Calvert, David Hirsch, Edward McKenna, John Pearson, Charles Ward, George Sanders, Frederick McNess, Charles Ward and Jacob Weiss (Jack White). Holders of the VC who were not born in Leeds but are buried in the City are Harry Daniels,

Wilfred Edwards, Charles Hull, Arthur Poulter, John Raynes and Kirby Ridgeway.

WARTIME IN HALTON

The Boer War would have been felt in the village with a few being taken for army service and the Great War certainly influenced the population with so many being remembered on the various war memorials in the village. Great Britain declared war on Germany on August 4th 1914 for violating the Treaty of London. The Parochial Hall became a temporary VAD (Voluntary Aided Detachment) hospital with iron bedsteads and a team of voluntary nurses. The south wing of Temple Newsam House became a VAD hospital with Lady Dorothy Wood as the Commandant. There were many Belgian refugees who were accommodated in the stable block, which later became the refreshment rooms. Many young men from Halton were part of the armed forces especially the West Yorkshire Regiment Prince of Wales Own. So many never returned and were buried in France and Belgium or are remembered in memorials such as those at Tyne Cot Cemetery and on the Menin Gate. On June 18th 1919 the Germans signed a peace treaty in the Hall of Mirrors in the Palace of Versailles a few miles from Paris. In Halton there was a Peace Festival held at the Halton Recreation Ground in July 1919 when the Halton Philharmonic Society (leader John Briggs) performed to great acclaim. Over 400 gathered on the field and there were school races with a tea served later at the school. Over 10,000 men from the Leeds area were killed in this War and so many Halton families lost a generation.

There were both searchlights and anti-aircraft guns in Halton: the two searchlights were down Colton Road in a field near North Lodges and the guns were a fixed site near Queensway and on The Smilings: junction of Woodland Road and Temple Walk. The guns were commanded by actor Henry Ainley who often called in at the schoolhouse on Selby Road to talk with Richard Thomas. Dick Thomas remembered when the gun was fired on three occasions: one was when a Zeppelin came from Garforth on the way to the Munitions Factory at Barnbow. The anti-aircraft gun started firing and the shells burst in the front of the airship which changed course.

In the 1920's Richard R Thomas of Halton School organised the Boots for Bairns and in 1924 33 pairs of boots were presented to needy children.

The Second World War affected village life with the military service taking away the men to serve our country. Blackout of windows was ensured by teams of ARP wardens, rationing of clothing and foods, limitation to the goods offered for sale and the occasional black market selling. Permits were issued for the supply of milk at 2d a pint. Identity cards were issued on September 29th 1939 and rationing started with

bacon, ham, sugar and butter on January 8th 1940 followed by meat on March 11th 1940, tea, margarine, cooking fats, cheese on July 1940, jam, marmalade, treacle in March 1941, concentrated milk in November 1941, dried milk in December 1941 and a points scheme for sweets from July 27th 1942 and bread was rationed in July 1946. Soldiers were billetted in Halton and used the Parochial Hall and Mission Room for meetings which was also used by the Home Guard.
War broke out at 11am on Sunday September 3rd 1939 and locally there were thousands of sand bags issued and when the War started the blackout meant that no lights were to be shown after 7.30pm. The cinemas and theatres were closed and were suggested as air raid shelters. On Friday September 15th the cinemas were re-opened and in Leeds the Paramount (Odeon) was showing Beau Geste and the Leeds Grand Theatre was to re-open on Monday September 18th with two performances of They Walk Alone. The Empire Theatre Leeds opened again with Big Bill Campbell and The Ovaltineys appeared at the City Varieties. The Theatre Royal had performances by the Arthur Brough Players. The News Theatre at City Square was advertised as *"Leeds Safest Cinema"*.
Locally the Ritz Cinema Cross Gates re-opened after a few days with Wings of the Navy and The Regal Cross Gates re-opened on September 16th with Will Hay in Oh Mr Porter and the following week was showing Little Tough Guys in Society.
The local school was closed for three months and re-opened when the air raid shelters were placed; the school hosted lectures for Air Raid Wardens.
Anderson Shelters were designed for garden use in corrugated iron with prefabricated components often semi-sunk into a metre deep pit covered with soil and a steel door. The sheds with their 14 corrugated iron sheets were distributed free of charge to those families who were earning less than £250 a year otherwise there was a charge of £7. There were eventually over 2.3 million shelters erected to those homes with garden areas: they were 6 feet high, 4½ feet wide and 6½ feet wide long buried to a depth of 4 feet and covered with 15 inches of soil. By the mid-war years there were over half a million in the country. *The name remembers their inventor Dr David A Anderson and not as is often supposed Sir John Anderson (1908-65). The idea was presented to engineer William Paterson with Oscar Carl Kerrison in November 1938 and in February 1939 the first shelters were delivered to householders in Islington North London. Morrison shelters were built with 219 parts for 16 people. Sir John Anderson Morrison was born in 1882 becoming Home Secretary from 1939.*
Halton was in Sector 103/107 Civil Defence. There were two large concrete blocks opposite Dial House on Chapel Street and another two

blocks on Selby Road were intended to deter possible enemy tanks. There were several air raid shelters in the village including the Halton Congregational Church Sunday School, a brick shelter in the road on Wilfred Avenue was built in August 1940 and at Halton Methodist Church. At the Methodist Church there were two air raid shelters with one under the stage in the hall: an air raid siren was placed on the roof. The church was also the First Aid Post for the village: notices were issued and the local chemist displayed the Air Raid Precautions card which stated that the ARP Warden's Post was at the Parochial Hall and the nearest First Aid Post was at the Methodist Chapel. The two posts were always manned during air raids. There were also ARP posts at the old Mission Hall and at Hawthorn House.

Gas masks were distributed in the village from October 1938: they were being manufactured from 1935. Baby gas masks were issued in October 1939: over 1½ million were ready to be used by January 1940. The Halton Knitting Circle started in early 1940 and raised money for wool to be used by a band of knitters for men on active service: the meetings were held at Clifton House and Mrs Blaydon Jones held whist drives in support at Hawthorn House. In a few months of work 73 scarves, 104 pairs of socks and 85 pairs of mittens were finished and distributed. The Circle ended in July 1941 when there was a lack of wool and their proceeds were sent to the Red Cross Fund. War Charities were also supported by whist drives held at Milton Jones's house on Pinfold Lane. A Rest Centre was established at the Congregational Church to receive the homeless after an air raid.

Leeds was bombed nine times with only five of the raids producing fatalities. The first raid was on Sunday August 25th 1940 when four bombs fell on Whitehall Road. On Saturday August 31st York Road was hit with much damage around Quarry Hill Flats including The Woodpecker public house, when a bomb landed on the pavement outside the doors and St Patrick's Church. The worst raid was on Monday March 14th and Tuesday March 15th 1941 when 40 enemy planes dropped incendiary bombs and high explosive bombs on the city. The raid started at 9pm and 116 fires burned around Leeds: the all clear was sounded at 3.12am. There was a noise of anti-aircraft guns from their emplacements at Boggart Hill and Wellington Hill. In this raid there was severe damage caused to the City Museum, Town Hall, Schofield's Arcade, Mill Hill Chapel, Kirkgate Market, Royal Exchange, Wellington Road Goods Yard and Leeds General Infirmary. The war in Leeds had 77 fatalities.

Nearly 30,000 children, teachers and mothers from Leeds were evacuated in trains and buses to the Yorkshire countryside including Pateley Bridge, Wakefield and Lincolnshire. *I took an evacuation card home from Cross Gates Boy's School.* The first children to be evacuated from the city were taken to their schools on Friday September 1st 1939

with their cases and gas masks. By the following day 28,902 people had been evacuated and in November 1944 a train from Lincoln brought home the last of the evacuees from Lincoln.
In August 1944 there were 75 evacuees at the Congregational Food & Rest Centre and they were later billetted in Halton. There were also centres at Temple Newsam Café and St Wilfrid's Church. Parties of Fire Fighters were organised and Halton Templars Scouts were trained to erect indoor shelters provided by the Ministry of Home Security: they were erected in a half hour by teams of boys. In charge of training the scouts was JR Stuart White. In November 1941 the first meeting took place of the Halton, Cross Gates & District Unit of the Womens Home Defence and volunteers were sought to be medical orderlies, switchboard operators and clerical staff. Trenches were dug for protection: in 1938 these appeared on Mayfield Road which were railed off later. The underground air raid shelter on Mayfield Road still exists.
Teams of men with cutting equipment started the task of removing iron railings in 1941 and by 1944 there was over a million tons collected: most removed at a rate of 10,000 tons a week remained unused. The blackout ended on September 17th 1944 after VE Day on Tuesday May 8th 1945: the surrender took place on May 7th.
There were village celebrations when the War ended on VE Day and on VJ Day August 15th 1945 there was a party for 100 children for the residents of Wheaton Avenue, Charlotte Grove and Wilfred Avenue. The Day brought a bonfire and fireworks and a Victory Garden Fete at the Congregational Church by the Youth Fellowship.
Rationing ended with bread taken off in July 1948 and this was followed by the de-rationing of jam in December 1948, tea in October 1952, sweets on February 5th 1953, eggs in March 1943, cream in April 1953, sugar in September 1953, butter, cheese and margarine all in May 1954 and meat was the last item to be taken off the ration on July 3rd 1954. Clothes were rationed on June 1st 1941: Utility CC41 was issued at 66 coupons a year and a civilian man's overcoat was 16 coupons. Coal had been restricted from 1939 and this was lifted in July 1957.
There were a few Halton men who did their National Service: conscription extended to peacetime with the 1948 National Service Act. National Service was 18 months with four years in reserves. In 1950 the Korean War led to a 2 year National Service. Call up ended on December 31st 1960 with the last serviceman leaving in May 1963. The last serviceman to be demobbed was Geoffrey Williams of Oulton Leeds who joined in November 1960 and left on May 12th 1963 at the age of 24 years.

Personal Memories of wartime and afterwards in Halton

I was only three years old when war broke out with memories rather dim. I remember being told of the air raids on York Road in August 1940 when

I had just turned four years old and on the city in March 1941 as my brother and I were taken to the relative safety of the cellar under our shop. The cellar was down a flight of stone steps and my parents had altered a third of the area to be equipped with bunks next to the coal store. I remember the air raid sirens sounding in Halton and a man tapping on the shop window asking us to make the blackout of the windows more secure. I started at Cross Gates Boys School when I was five years old in September 1941 and walked from the shop down Park Street and Valley Drive across the valley bridge to the back gate for the school. I wore grey shorts, grey shirt, long socks which often drooped around my feet and topped by the red school cap with a blue gates on the front above the peak. I remember how kind Miss Norah Lancaster and headmaster James Harrison were to the children and how I was sometimes a little late having to find a way underneath the iron bars of the fencing around the school precinct on Bridlepath. My school report for Christmas 1944 in Class Standard 2a shows me at position 5 out of 45 in the class with a score of 151 out of a total possible of 170.
When I was 9 years old I obtained entry to the Junior School of Leeds Grammar School where I started at Sheafield in Clarendon Road at Easter 1945: I left Cross Gates on March 28th . I went either by tram from the Irwin Arms or bus from near the shop and then either a tram or bus up Woodhouse Lane and a walk along Reservoir Street past the main school buildings; sometimes Dad gave me a lift in the car. I was in J3 with Miss Hilda Jones (LGS 1918-55) who always had a small Missionary Box on the teacher's desk and then J4 with Miss Hilda Christie: I always remember having my side hair pulled by "Ma Chris" when I was speaking out of turn or not saluting in the street. Miss Christie had taught at the school from 1915 and retired in 1952: she wrote a book about her LGS experiences called "Please". We walked up to the main school for lunch in a crocodile and back again for more playtime. School ended at 4pm and if Dad did not meet me in the car I either walked down Woodhouse Lane and called in to see my grandfather at 159 Woodhouse Lane or I walked down Mount Preston to the tram in City Square: number 20 for Halton. I remember deciding to go home by West Riding bus one afternoon and ended up lost in Castleford. I was brought home by kind Ivy who was the conductress on the Yellow Bus to the relief of Mum and Dad.
I went to the main school in Form Middle 2 with my form master Wilf Batty (LGS 1944-75) and after three Sixth form years left for Bede College Durham University in July 1955 at the age of 19.
My parents kept a newspaper cuttings book and I still treasure those two volumes of wartime Britain. There were few emergencies when I was at school both at Cross Gates and at Leeds Grammar School as the raids took place at night. I had my own ration books and still have my gas

mask and these precious books with the coupons removed week by week. The earliest Child's Ration Book RB2 I possess is dated October 23rd 1939 and is for meat with S Lees Templenewsam Road Halton and for Bacon, Butter, Margarine and sugar where the retailer was J & F Rhodes of 61 Boar Lane Leeds (the July 1940 book shows that the branch registered was at 45 Otley Road Headingley). There is no retailer mentioned for cooking fats and all those coupons remain intact. I have a Ration Book Supplement issued in July 1941 with retailers names of A Cowell 15 Cross Green Lane and fruit from S Rowley at 1 Oak Crescent. I have a red Clothing Book dated 1947-48 with no magenta coupons remaining and one supplementary orange coupon. My last Ration Book is from 1953-54 and most of these coupons are still intact.

I used to help Harry Taylor distribute the milk from a large milk churn on his horse drawn cart which was pulled around Halton delivering to houses: I would wait for the jar to be presented at the cart and measure carefully from a can which was hooked over the lid. I remember helping the village lamplighter to put on the gas at the lamp posts with his long pole. We had a stirrup pump and using the water filled bucket I managed to water the plants in our small garden at the rear of the shop which also had a shed for my tricycle and later bicycle. The garden had four small flower plots on a concrete surround and a high privet hedge on the Park Street side. The rear of the premises was an unmade back street where I used to play with the other children and it was also the parking place for Dad's car, until we bought the garage and land on Wilfred Avenue with Alec Cowell.

During the wartime and afterwards the good folk of Halton were so friendly. Everybody seemed to know everybody else and helped each other through the dark years of war. I was in Whitkirk Church choir when I was at Cross Gates Boy's School and then I transferred to the school chapel choir, where I remained until I left Leeds Grammar School in July 1955. I also attended Sunday School which was held in the Cross Gates Bowling Club hut on Station Road, presenting my attendance book for the picture sticker.

I went to Cross Gates Library which I joined soon after it opened in December 1939. The Junior Library was wonderful and I loved Enid Blyton's Adventure series and Captain WE Johns' Biggles books. I always remember the kindness in later years of librarians Mrs Levitt and Mrs Monica Hemming who allowed me to stamp the outgoing books after we had listened mesmerized to her stories told to a large group of children.

The radio was an important part of life at home and on VE Day Tuesday May 8th 1945 (the surrender was signed at 2.41am on May 7th) Winston Churchill broadcast from 10 Downing Street at 3pm: hostilities ended at 12.01am. The Home Service on May 8th included broadcasts by Joe Loss and the Lew Stone Bands, a concert by the BBC Symphony Orchestra together with an address by HM The King and the Archbishop of Canterbury. The General Forces Network broadcast the Oscar Rabin Band, Itma with Tommy Handley, Jack Train and Dorothy Summers with Sandy Macpherson on the organ.

The end of the war in Leeds was marked by the play Pink String & Sealing Wax at the Grand Theatre; Francis Laidler's Humpty Dumpty at the Theatre Royal starring Norman Evans, Betty Jumel and Kirby's Flying Ballet; the Empire Theatre presented Old Mother Riley with Arthur Lucan and Kitty McShane. There were films being shown at the Assembly Rooms, Scala, Majestic, Tatler, Odeon and Gaumont. The Ritz Cinema in Cross Gates was showing Rita Hayworth in Cover Girl and The Regal Cinema showed Eleanor Powell in Sensations of 1945.

My 9th birthday on July 28th 1945 was marked by the General Forces Network broadcasting from 5pm with the Jack Payne Band, Jack Benny comedy and the Promenade Concert. The Home Service featured the Harry Davidson Orchestra and Those Were the Days. Two days before this day Labour had won a landslide victory at the general election and Clement Attlee (1883-1967) became Prime Minister. Five years later in 1950 I was listening avidly to Dick Barton Special Agent at 6.45pm on The Light programme. There was one TV station broadcasting from 5pm to 6pm for the children and from 8.30pm to 10.30pm with mainly news programmes: we got our first TV set for the Coronation in June 1953.

We used the large cellar not only for coal and a temporary air raid shelter but also for the storage of winchesters of medicines and shelves of bottles with a small fridge to store the penicillin on a shelf at the bottom of the cellar stairs. There was a stone table in the middle of the cellar on which was a mesh cupboard for items of food and it was on this table that I was allowed to churn the milk for the butter. There was a large copper pan which Mum used to make the jam: I enjoyed scraping the butter bowl and jam maker when it was nearly finished. Of course I also enjoyed scraping the cake mixture bowl in the kitchen and kneading the dough for the bread.

There were happier memories when the war was over with VJ Day in 1945 and I was taken to St Anne's on Sea and Scarborough staying at boarding houses. We visited my aunts in Barnsley, especially Ethel Gilleghan who had married my grandfather's brother Arthur and Herbert's sister Emma Winter who always provided some appetising teas. It was in 1950 that I went abroad for the first time with my school visiting Switzerland and staying at the Hotel Felsenheim at Sachseln with instructions to bring back some tins of Libby's fruit and chocolate.

I was in the Kangaroo Patrol in the School Scout troop and went to my first camps near Scarborough and in Chatsworth Park at Baslow. Later years saw me become a Lance Corporal in the school Combined Cadet

Force. I put blanco on my gaiters and belt, brasses were polished and the boots were like a mirror: every Friday evening prior to parade on Saturday mornings at school. In 1952 my school was in the Yorkshire-Lille Exchange and I had three weeks at my friend's schoolhouse at Templemars near Lille. Claude Leboef came over to Halton for three weeks and we went exploring our area on bicycles and trams. This was also the year of the death of the King on February 5th and I was taken to London for the declaration at Temple Bar: I appeared briefly in the cinema film A Queen is Crowned. I was taken to London to see Oklahoma at the Theatre Royal Drury Lane in 1947 and to see the Crazy Gang at the Victoria Palace. These were the first of many future visits to the London theatres and I still go down annually to enjoy the shows.

WAR MEMORIALS

An inaugural meeting for the erection of a war memorial took place at the Halton Council School on November 15th 1918. The original idea by Hunslet Rural District Council was to include all the names of local men who had fought in the war but this proved to be too many for the intended bronze plaque. A committee was formed headed by the chairman Hon Edward Wood of Temple Newsam and Philip Saltmarshe Marsden of The Grange as treasurer: a few meetings took place at The Grange over the next few months. Members of the committee included Reginald Knight of San Remo Halton.

Hon Edward Wood promised the gift of any land site on Selby Road and the first to be considered was south of the main road between *"the cemetery and watertower"*. This was followed by a proposal for The Crescent site (waterworks reservoir) but the final site was to be in the *"east corner of Gun Field":* on the soon to be created Queensway.

There were seven varying designs submitted with one featuring sculptured men of the armed forces. The architects engaged were Kirke & Tomlinson of Albion Street with builders Thompson & Sons. They charged £488 with the architect's fee being £25: the total cost was £603. The subsequent need for more funds resulted in a general appeal to the local community which was to wipe off the deficit.

The work started in March 1920 and the bronze plaque on the 15 feet high Portland Stone cross was unveiled by Lady Dorothy Wood on the opening evening July 3rd 1920 at 6.30pm when two hymns were sung and prayers said by the Vicar of Whitkirk. It was a cold evening when the chairman Edward Wood gave his address prior to the memorial being unveiled by his wife. There were over 2000 at the ceremony which a newspaper report of the time said was *"by an old water tower now being removed"*. Those present included the vicar Rev Ernest William Wilson (1915-23), Rev J Miller Hamilton Pastor of the Whitkirk Baptist Church whose son was killed in the Great War, Rev W Phillipson of Cross Gates Wesleyan Church, Philip Marsden chairman of the Executive Committee, Walter B Pindar who was Clerk to the Hunslet RDC together with children from both Halton and Colton schools. A report later said that *"the isolation of the war memorial adds to the impressiveness with no view blocking"*. Hunslet RDC took over the maintenance of this war memorial in November 1920.

The site was planted with shrubs and was originally nearer the road. The gates were given by Nurse Elsie Dacre on her retirement as District Nurse: they were unveiled in July 1959 and council approval had been obtained in August 1958.

The site became the property of Leeds City Council on April 1st 1928 who continue to maintain the property. The holly wreath has been purchased with funds from the Halton Branch of the Royal British Legion but this was disbanded in 2001. The wreath for 2002 was provided with residual funds and the help of the Leeds 15 Community Association. The wreaths in 2003 were provided by the East Leeds Historical & Archaeological Society and the Leeds 15 Community Association with the Cross Gates Branch of the Royal British Legion. There is a short service at the War Memorial on Remembrance Sunday led by the clergy, choir, members of Whitkirk Church and uniformed organisations.

The Great War Memorials

The "Temple Newsam" War Memorial , Queensway, Whitkirk

Charles Ascott, Anthony Austin, Edgar Balance, Enoch Ball, Arthur Barraclough, Fred Bateman, Arthur Bennett, Herbert Berry, William Bevins, Thomas Booth, Jack Bowers, Fred Boyington, Horace

Brockhouse, Clifford Brooke, Victor Butler, Fred Childerson, Fred Clayton, Ernest Coleman, John Coleridge, George Collis, Percy Coultas, Sam Cousin, Edgar Dale, Herbert Dale, Arthur Dobson, George Dobson, Thomas Dodsworth, Rowland Ellis, George Farndale, Fenny Fountain, Charles Goodall, Walter Goodall, Harry Guest, Stanley Haigh, Bernard Hamilton, Eldred Hardwick, William Hargreaves, Alan Heywood, James Hunt, Ernest Ingle, Arthur Kaye, William Laycock, Clarence Leer, Ralph Lucas, Eric Mackay, Edgar Nichols, Fred Nicholson, Harry Pullan, Herbert Rollinson, Fletcher Russell, John Shaw, Frank Simpson, William Smales, David Speight, Walter Speight, Reginald Spencer, Kenneth Stott, Harold Sunter, Rowland Sunter, Thomas Tate, George Taylor, Henry Temple, Rupert Tinker, Louis Todd, Norman Turner, Sam Whitfield, Sam Woodhead, Percy Woodward and Roy Worsnop

Ethel Jackson and Maria Rowley died at the Barnbow Munitions Factory in 1916. Albert Kettlewell of New Row Colton was killed at an accident at work. He was a boilerman at the Clarence Iron & Steel Works run by Messrs Taylor Bros when a beam fell on him and died in October 1916 at the age of 23.

St Mary's Church Whitkirk Porch Memorial

The following names are in addition to those on the Queensway Memorial:

Charles Cawood, Fred Hardcastle, John Kettlewell, Alfred Knoakes, Reginald Marsden, Harry Myers, Matthew Roberts, Henry Temple, Herbert Turner. Other names have been changed: Goodall to Goodhall and Victor to Albert Butler.

Whitkirk Church War Memorial was unveiled on the wall of the north aisle on June 19th 1931 remembering 79 men of the parish who had lost their lives in the Great War. Amongst those present at the unveiling was the mother of Ethel Jackson: her daughter was killed in the Barnbow Explosion of 1916. The Halton Templar scouts and guides together with the Silver Band were present at the service. This painted tryptych memorial is now on the south aisle wall.

Halton Methodist Church War Memorial Plaque (not now on display)

War Memorial at Halton Methodist Church includes the names Herbert Berry, William Bevins, Tom Booth, Jack Bowers, Frederick Boyington, Victor Butler, Frederick Childerson, Stanley Haigh, Eldred Hardwick, Ernest Ingle, Arthur Kaye, Herbert Rollinson, Frank Simpson, Harold Sunter, Roland Sunter, Louis Todd, Roy Worsnop.

The memorial was unveiled on September 5th 1920 by Rev W Eastwood of Collingham. The brass tablet was designed by James Thompson of Dodsworth Court Briggate Leeds.

St Wilfrid's Church War Memorial Plaque (in the north transept)

Herbert Berry, William David Bevins, Thomas Booth, Jack Bowers, Fred Boyington, Victor Butler, Fred Childerson, Stanley Haigh, Eldred

Hardwick, Ernest Ingle, Arthur Kaye, Frank Simpson, Herbert Rollinson, Harold Sunter, Roland Sunter, Louis Edwin Todd and Roy Worsnop.
There are 1.7 million entries over the two world wars found in the records of the Commonwealth War Graves Commission and mention of 23,000 cemeteries and memorials.

Details of some of the above men are to be found in the records of the Commonwealth War Graves Commission:

First World War

Private Anthony Austin of the West Yorkshire Regiment Prince of Wales Own died on November 10th 1917.

The regiment originated in 1685 as the 14th/15th Foot. They served in Canada 1745-59 including the storming of the cliffs at Quebec on September 13th 1758 with General Wolfe. The 4800 British troops defeated the 7500 French on the Heights of Abraham on which Wolfe was buried. The regiment fought in the American War of Independence 1775-83, West Indies 1785-1810, Waterloo June 18th 1815, Crimea 1855, Maori Campaign New Zealand 1860-66, Boer War 1899-1902 and the Great War when 20,000 men died in the 52 battalions that were raised and Second World War. In 1908 the TA was formed and on show in the regimental Museum at York is a drum major's mace from the 3rd Voluntary Prince of Wales Own Leeds Rifles together with a black officers tunic and hat.

From 1876 to 1881 the 14th (Buckinghamshire or Prince of Wales Own) Regiment of Foot and from 1881 the regiment became the Prince of Wales Own West Yorkshire Regiment. The name from 1920 to 1958 became The West Yorkshire Regiment The Prince of Wales Own. Soldiers from the PWO have served in Northern Ireland, Cyprus and the first Gulf War and formed part of the international force in Bosnia. The regiments have been honoured with six VCs and the French Croix de Guerre. The present Colonel-in-Chief is HRH Duchess of Kent. The freedom of the City of Leeds was also conferred upon the West Riding Regiment Prince of Wales Own on July 1st 1945.

From 1782 to 1881 the 15th (York East Riding) Regiment of Foot; 1881-1935 The East Yorkshire Regiment (The Duke of York's Own). The Prince of Wales Own Regiment of Yorkshire formed in 1958 from The West Yorkshire Regiment The Prince of Wales Own 14th of Foot and The East Yorkshire Regiment (The Duke of York's Own) the 15th of Foot. They marched through Leeds in May 1988 with the salute taken by Lord Mayor Doreen Wood. The Regiment is to be disbanded in plans announced in November 2003.
Private Arthur Barraclough of the 10th Battalion West Yorkshire

Regiment Prince of Wales Own was the son of James & Kate Barraclough. He died on April 23rd 1917 aged 25 and was buried at Arras. He worked at Joseph Town & Sons Albion Street Leeds and lived at Colton Mill.
L/Corp Arthur Bennett of the 1st/7th Battalion West Yorkshire Regiment Prince of Wales Own died on October 9th 1917.
Sergeant William D Bevins was in the 6th Battalion King's Own Yorkshire Light Infantry and died aged 22 on May 30th 1916 and was buried at Agny near Arras. He lived with his parents John & Sarah Bevins in Colton Road Whitkirk.
The King's Own Yorkshire Light Infantry was raised on January 7th 1756 as the 53rd Regiment of Foot. They were at first stationed in Exeter and moved to Leeds where recruiting took place on March 16th 1756. Their base was at Pontefract Barracks and a regimental depot at Strensall. The regimental name KOYLI came in 1881 and in 1968 they were amalgamated with the Somerset & Cornwall Light Infantry, King's Shropshire LI and the Durham LI to form the Light Infantry Regiment. The KOYLI were given the Freedom of Leeds on June 7th 1945. In 1979 the KOYLI freedom was transferred to the Light Infantry; 49th (Yorkshire) Signals Regiment Royal Signals (TA) who were formed in 1861 as 2nd West Riding Royal Engineers Volunteers on April 1st 1967; RAF Church Fenton was granted the Freedom of Leeds on April 29th 1971.
Rifleman Thomas Booth of 1/7th Battalion West Yorkshire Regiment Prince of Wales Own (Leeds Rifles). He died on October 9th 1917 and was buried at Passchendaele New British Cemetery Flanders.
Jack Bowers of the 10th Battalion West Yorkshire Regiment Prince of Wales Own died on July 1st 1916 and was remembered at Thiepval Cemetery Somme.
Thiepval is the largest memorial to the missing from any war in which British soldiers died: 72,000 British soldiers from the Battle of the Somme with no known grave. The cemetery was designed by Sir Edwin Lutyens and was unveiled by the Prince of Wales and the President of France on July 31st 1932.
Private Fred Boyington was in the 1st Battalion West Yorkshire Regiment Prince of Wales Own and died on September 20th 1914. He was buried at La Ferte-sous-Jouarre Seine et Marne.
Horace Brockhouse of the 9th Battalion Lancashire Fusiliers died aged 32 on August 16th 1917. He came from Bramley and lived with his wife Ethel.
Sergeant Clifford Brooke was in the 13th Battalion East Yorkshire Regiment. He died on March 31st 1918 and is remembered on the Arras Memorial. He was the son of Frederick and Ada Brooke and the husband of Annie Brooke.
Lance Corporal C Cawood of the 8th Battalion West Yorkshire Regiment Prince of Wales Own died on July 20th 1918 and was buried at Marfaux

British Cemetery Marne.

Private Frederick Childerson of the 283rd Mechanical Transport Company VII Corps Heavy Artillery of the Army Service Corps. He died aged 40 on Sunday April 14th 1918. He was the son of Harry & Charlotte and husband of Edith and was buried at Namps-au-Val British Cemetery Somme.

Private Fred Clayton of the 2nd Battalion West Yorkshire Regiment Prince of Wales Own died aged 19 on August 25th 1916 and was buried at Fauborg d'Amiens Cemetery Arras. He was the son of E Clayton of 5 Stanley Terrace Halton; his brother Victor Clayton of the 5th West Yorkshire Regiment Prince of Wales Own was reported missing but returned home from the War in December 1918 having been a POW from April 1918.

Sergeant John William Coleridge was in the 2nd Battalion King's Own Yorkshire Light Infantry. He died on February 6th 1918 and was buried at New Irish Farm Cemetery Ypres in Flanders.

Private George William Collis of the 10th Battalion West Yorkshire Regiment Prince of Wales Own died on February 15th 1916 and is remembered on the Menin Gate Ypres.

Private Percy Coultas of the 15th Battalion West Yorkshire Regiment Prince of Wales Own died aged 24 on January 31st 1919. He was the son of James & Maria Coultas of Belmont The Avenue (Morritt Avenue) Halton. He was buried at Longuenesse St Omer Souvenir Cemetery Pas de Calais.

The 15th Battalion (1st Leeds) Prince of Wales Own West Yorkshire Regiment were known as The Leeds Pals. The idea was that the men would serve with friends, relatives and workmates. By September 1914 the Battalion had enlisted 1275 men many of whom were sportsmen. Training was held at Colsterdale in the Dales and in 1915 some of the pals set sail for Suez. In March 1916 the Pals sailed for Marseilles and were to be involved in the Battle of the Somme. On July 1st 1916 24 officers with their Pals went over the top: 750 out of 900 were killed. A memorial cairn was erected at the site of the first camp in Colsterdale and was unveiled on September 28th 1935.

Sergeant Sam Cousin of the 8th Battalion West Yorkshire Regiment was killed aged 45 on March 16th 1915 and buried at Lawnswood (grave W438). Sam is also remembered on the Lawnswood Cemetary War Memorial. He was born at Pool Wharfedale in 1869 and lived with his wife Edith born in 1873 at 5 Cross Street Halton. Sam was a tailor machine cutter.

Private Herbert Dale of 8th Battalion West Yorkshire Regiment Prince of Wales Own died on September 27th 1918 aged 20. He was the son of William & Jane Dale of 14 Temple Walk Halton and a native of Colton. He was buried at Lowrie Cemetery Havrincourt Pas-de-Calais.

Rifleman AS Dobson of 1st/7th West Yorkshire Regiment Prince of Wales Own. He lived on Meynell Road Colton and died on December 26th 1918 and was buried at Leeds General Cemetery. He is remembered on the screen memorial for the Great War at Lawnswood Cemetery.
During the First World War major hospitals in Leeds were 2nd Northern General (1800 beds) and East Leeds War Hospital (1900 beds). Rifleman Dobson is one of those remembered on the memorial devoted to those who were originally buried at Leeds General Cemetery (opened in 1835). Lawnswood Cemetery was opened as Headingley Cemetery on December 20th 1875 by the Bishop of Ripon.
Private George Dobson of 8th Battalion Duke of Wellington Regiment (West Riding Regiment) died on September 14th 1916 and is remembered at the Thiepval Memorial Somme France. He lived at 14 High Street Halton and was a hay and straw dealer who later lived at 3 Dawson Square.
Private Thomas Dodsworth of the 2nd/4th Battalion King's Own Yorkshire Light Infantry died aged 21 on August 28th 1918. He was buried at Ligny-sur-Canche British Cemetery Pas-de-Calais. The cemetery was started in August 1918 by the 3rd Canadian & 19th/43rd Casualty Clearing Station: there are 80 Great War burials. The cemetery was designed by WH Cowlishaw. Tom Dodsworth lived with his parents at Field End.
Lance Corporal George Farndale died on May 3rd 1917 and is remembered at Arras Memorial. He was in the 15th Battalion West Riding Regiment Prince of Wales Own.
Fenny Fountain emigrated to Canada while still young and was one of the first to volunteer to serve with the Canadian Grenadier Guards: he died in 1916.
Private Charles Augustus Goodall of A Company 8th Battalion King's Own Yorkshire Light Infantry died aged 26 on July 9th 1916. He lived at 15 Graveley Street: the son of Charles Edward & Sarah Ruth Goodall. He was buried at Etaples Military Cemetery Pas de Calais where there are 10, 769 burials.
Private Walter Hubert Goodall of the 2nd/7th Battalion West Yorkshire Regiment Prince of Wales Own died on February 26th 1917 aged 28. He was the son of Charles Edward and Sarah of Halton and husband of Jenny of Beeston Hill; he worked as a tram conductor and lived on Upper Accommodation Road. He was buried at Wimereux Communal Cemetery Pas-de-Calais where there are 2845 burials from the Great War.
Gunner Harry Guest of B Battery 83rd Brigade Royal Field Artillery died on August 22nd 1917 aged 19. He was the son of John & Mary Hannah of 20 Overdale Terrace Halton and is remembered at Tyne Cot Cemetery.
Private Stanley Haigh of 1st/7th Battalion Duke of Wellington Regiment. He died on November 17th 1916 and was buried at Foncquevillers Military Cemetery Pas-de-Calais.

Lieutenant Bernard St George Hamilton of the 15th Company Machine Gun Corps died on June 28th 1917 aged 25 and was buried at Arras. He lived at 3 Carter Terrace Whitkirk with his parents Rev & Mrs John Miller Hamilton. His father was the Cross Gates Baptist Church minister from 1912: his wife Ellen died aged 91 in April 1937. Their son is remembered on the family grave in Whitkirk Cemetery.

Private Eldred Hardwick of the 16th Battalion West Yorkshire Regiment Prince of Wales Own died on May 3rd 1917 aged 21. He was the son of Walter Hardwick of Field End Road Halton and worked at Garforth Colliery. He is remembered at the Arras Memorial Pas-de-Calais.

Lance Corporal William Hargreaves of the 11th Battalion Northumberland Fusiliers died on June 19th 1917 aged 39 in hospital in France and was buried at Mont Huon Military Cemetery Le Treport Seine Maritime. He was the husband of Louisa of 4 Sunny Hill Halton. He once worked for the London & Leeds Fire Insurance Co in Leeds.

Lieutenant Alan CA Heywood lived at Glendorgal Halton and was in the Royal Air Force. He died aged 23 on June 20th 1918 and was buried in Cairo Egypt. He had been educated at Drax Grammar School.

Private Arthur Kaye of D Company 25th Battalion Royal Fusiliers died aged 38 on August 3rd 1917. He was the son of Joseph & Mary Ann of Huddersfield and husband of Florence Kaye of Dial House Chapel Street Halton. He was killed at Dar-es- Salaam when a member of the Legion of Frontiersmen and is buried at the British & Indian Cemetery in Tanzania. When he was working Arthur was at Blackburn's Aeroplane Factory on Roundhay Road.

Lance Corporal William Laycock was in the 2nd Battalion Scots Guards. He died aged 21 on November 24th 1918 and was buried at Le Cateau Cemetery. He was the son of David & Ellen Laycock of 6 Wilfred Avenue Halton.

Ralph Lucas of the 9th Battalion West Yorkshire Regiment Prince of Wales Own died aged 31 on September 25th 1917. He was the son of Sam & Charlotte Lucas and husband of Annie of 5 Barkers Terrace Halton and is remembered at Tyne Cot Cemetery.

Rifleman Eric Sutherland Mackay of the 8th Battalion West Yorkshire Regiment Prince of Wales Own died on July 31st 1918 aged 18. He was the son of Robert & Eleanor Mackay of 26 Hollyshaw Lane Whitkirk and was buried at St Sever Cemetery Extension at Rouen where there are 8363 burials.

Private Harry Myers of 10th Battalion West Yorkshire Regiment Prince of Wales Own. He was the son of Martha Rawdon Myers of Prospect Street and died on July 1st 1916 aged 21.

Private Edgar Nicholls lived with his family on Temple View and was employed at Leeds Corporation Meter Department Whitehall Road. In 1914 he joined the East Yorkshire Cyclists Battalion and later was transferred to the West Yorkshire Regiment Prince of Wales Own: he died aged 21. His brother was TP Nicholls the well known and talented cyclist.

Sergeant Frederick Nicholson was in A Battery 94th Brigade,Royal Field Artillery. He lived on Overdale Terrace and once was a miner at Micklefield Colliery; he died on October 6th 1916 and was buried at Bulls Road Cemetery Flers Somme.

The Battle of the Somme was a fierce encounter which saw the loss of 57,000 British troops during the first day of hostilities and went on to claim more than 415,000 lives.

Private Harry Pullan of 1st Battalion East Lancashire Regiment died on May 13th 1915 aged 21. He was the son of John & Mary Pullan of Parlington Kennels Aberford. He is remembered on the Menin gate at Ypres.

Private Herbert Rollinson of 9th Battalion King's Own Yorkshire Light Infantry died on October 14th 1917 and is remembered at Tyne Cot Cemetery.

Private John Edward Shaw of the 2nd Battalion West Yorkshire Regiment Prince of Wales Own died on April 5th 1918 aged 20. He was the son of Thomas Riddin and Polly Shaw of 7 Newsam Square Halton and was buried at Hangard Communal Cemetery Extension Somme.

Private William Smales of the 10th Battalion Lancashire Fusiliers died on September 2nd 1918 aged 29. He was the son of Charles & Ada Smales of 4 Britton Terrace Halton and the husband of Agnes of 4 Rose Cottages Romanby Northallerton. He was buried at Vis-en-Artois Cemetery Pas-de-Calais.

Private David Speight of 2nd Battalion Duke of Wellington Regiment died on August 8th 1918 and is remembered on the Loos Memorial Pas de Calais.

Private Walter Speight of the 12th Battalion Yorkshire & Lancashire Regiment died aged 27 on May 4th 1917. He was the son of David Speight of The Poplars and was the husband of Lily of Raincliffe Road East End Park and was buried at Arras.

Private Reginald Spencer of 1st Battalion King's Own Yorkshire Light Infantry died on October 6th 1918 and is buried at Etaples Military Cemetery Pas-de-Calais.

Private Kenneth Stott of N Company (Ripon) Royal Army Medical Corps died on December 25th 1916 aged 24. He was the son of Walter & Lucie Alberta Stott of Halton and the husband of EF Pearson (Stott) of Ben Rhydding. He was buried in Ripon Cemetery.

Private R Sunter of 9th Battalion Duke of Wellington Regiment died on September 18th 1918 and was buried at Villers Hill British Cemetery Guislain Nord France.

Thomas Tate was Driver 209149 of 139th T Company Royal Engineers who died on February 17th 1919 aged 30. He was the husband of Clara Tate of 3 Fryer's Yard Halton and was buried in Whitkirk Cemetery.

Corporal George Henry Taylor was in the 2nd/7th Battalion West Yorkshire Regiment. He died on February 16th 1917 aged 21. He lived at 33 The Drive Halton and worked for his father James Taylor in his perambulator and mail cart factory Hunslet. He is remembered at the Thiepval Memorial Somme.

Lance Corporal Henry Henderson Temple was in C Company 9th Battalion West Yorkshire Regiment. He died on October 9th 1917 aged 33 and is remembered at Tyne Cot. He was the son of Adam & Maria Temple and the husband of Lily Temple and he lived on Shakespeare Street.

Lance Corporal Rupert Henry Tinker of the 10th Battalion West Yorkshire Regiment Prince of Wales Own died on September 18th 1918 aged 21. He lived with his parents Henry and Sarah Tinker on Meynell Road Colton and later of School Lane.

Rifleman Louis Edwin Todd of the 1st/8th Battalion West Yorkshire Regiment died on August 13th 1916 aged 19 and is remembered at Thiepval Memorial Somme. He was the son of the FT Todd of Primrose Road and enlisted at a recruiting rally at Roundhay Park in August 1915: he was a member of Whitkirk Church choir until he was 17 and also a keen member of Halton Cricket Club.

Lieutenant Herbert Norman Turner was in the West Riding Regiment and died aged 22 on July 14th 1916. He was buried at Flatiron Copse at Mametz Somme and lived in Wortley. He was the son of Arthur & Clara Turner of Balks House Wortley and was educated at Leeds Grammar School where he was a member of the OTC. He was an accountant articled to HW Blackburn of East Parade.

Sergeant Sam Whitfield was in the 16th Battalion Cheshire Regiment and died on October 22nd 1917 aged 37. He was the son of Thomas & Charlotte Whitfield and is remembered at Tyne Cot and lived in Halton.

Private Samuel Woodhead of the 1st Battalion East Yorkshire Regiment died aged 20 on April 25th 1918. He was the son of Edwin & Jane Woodhead of High Street Halton and is remembered at Tyne Cot.

Rifleman Percy Woodward of the 2nd/8th Battalion West Yorkshire Regiment Prince of Wales Own died on September 29th 1917. He is buried at Favreuil British Cemetery Pas-de-Calais.

Rifleman Roy Worsnop of B Company 1st/7th Battalion (Leeds Rifles) West Yorkshire Regiment Prince of Wales Own was the son of Abraham Naylor and Margaret Worsnop of Glageon 38 Oak Road Halton. Roy was a POW in June 1918 and he lived at Thelma Royd Halton Hill. He was buried at the Glageon Communal Cemetery Extension Nord 40 miles east of Cambrai.

The Leeds Rifles were raised on Saturday November 5th 1859 when the

Volunteer Force was formed to meet an invasion from France: the volunteers joined at Leeds Town Hall for the oaths of allegiance. The Corps was the 7th Yorkshire, West Riding (Leeds) Rifle Volunteer Corps. In 1887 they became a Volunteer Battalion of The Prince of Wales Own West Yorkshire Regiment. The home of The Leeds Rifles was Carlton Barracks and in 1908 they became two Battalions 7th/8th Leeds Rifles POWO WYR.. The first line battalions (1/7th) served in Flanders from April 1915 to the end of the War mainly serving to hold the Ypres Salient as well as on the Somme, Passchendaele and the final advance to victory. Some 2050 members of The Leeds Rifles died on active service in France and Flanders. The Commanding Officer of 8th Battalion West Yorkshire Regiment Prince of Wales Own from 1921 to 1925 was Lt Col Hugh D Bousfield CMG DSO TD. Col AR Glazebrook served with the 7th Battalion at Carlton Barracks.

The War Memorial at Leeds Parish Church was designed in Portland stone by Sir Edwin Lutyens as a memorial to the men of the 7th and 8th battalions of the West Yorkshire Regiment (Leeds Rifles). The dedication was held on November 13th 1921 and it was unveiled by Captain G Sanders VC MC.

Graves from the Great War in St Mary's Whitkirk Cemetery Selby Road:

Private AH Dodsworth West Yorkshire Regiment Prince of Wales Own died on June 16th 1920.

Lance Corporal William Laycock of the Scots Guards died in France on Sunday November 24th 1918 aged 21. He was the son of David & Ellen Laycock and is buried at Le Cateau Communal Cemetery east of Cambrai.

Sgt Thomas Hindson Mellish of the Royal Scots was killed in action at Ypres on October 22nd 1917 aged 23 and is remembered at Tyne Cot. His father William died on December 15th 1942 and his wife Sarah died on July 23rd 1929 are buried in Whitkirk Cemetery. The family lived at Fairview Carter Terrace Whitkirk.

Men who died in the Great War and not mentioned on the memorials

Private William Chadwick of the West Yorkshire Regiment Prince of Wales Own died on March 9th 1916 and buried at Chatko Military Cemetery in Alexandria Egypt. The cemetery has 2259 First World War burials with 503 from the Second World War.

Private Clarence Lea of 10th Battalion West Yorkshire Regiment Prince of Wales Own died aged 19 on July 3rd 1916. He was the son of Samuel and Elizabeth Ann Lea of 7 Hermon Terrace Halton. He was buried at Daours Communal Cemetery Extension on the River Somme 6 miles east of Amiens. The cemetery was designed by Sir Edwin Lutyens and has 1225 burials.

Lance Corporal Arthur William Platt 6th Battalion Dorsetshire Regiment who was born on November 8th 1871 and died at Arras on September 5th

1917. He is buried at Sunken Road Cemetery Fampoux Pas-de-Calais on the north bank of the River Scarpe 7 miles east of Arras. Fampoux was taken by the British on April 9th 1917, lost in March 1918 and retaken in August 1918; the small cemetery has 196 burials. He was the second son of the Whitkirk vicar Rev George Moreton Platt who died of pneumonia at the vicarage on May 13th 1898: his wife Emma had died on February 13th 1896. He was the vicar of Whitkirk from 1863 until his death.

Lt. Frederick Williams of the Royal Air Force died in 1918 having been a talented athlete. He was the son of Frederick of Bannycroft Morritt Avenue Halton. He had joined the Royal Engineers in 1914 and obtained a commission in the RAF: his father was the manager of Gallagher Tobacco Merchants Leeds.

Lance Corporal Walter Wood 6th Battalion King's Own Yorkshire Light Infantry died on September 16th 1916 and is remembered at the Thiepval memorial.

Percy and Thomas Woodruff: their brother George of the Kings Own Yorkshire Light Infantry was wounded aged 22 and awarded the Croix de Guerre.

The Second World War Memorials

St Mary's Church Whitkirk

The lychgate memorial designed by Charlton & Crowther was dedicated by the Bishop of Ripon on June 26th 1949 in the presence of the vicar Rev WJ Crick. The structure includes stones from famous buildings damaged during the Second World War including Coventry Cathedral, Houses of Parliament, St Paul's Cathedral, Leeds Town Hall and Leeds City Museum; the timber came from war ships. Following vandalism the memorial had iron locked gates fitted and the name plaques were re-inscribed. The restored lychgate was dedicated on April 3rd 1988.

Kenneth Adams, Arthur Anderson, S Armitage, John Ashmore, HI Austin, Maurice Ball, Roger Batley, I Beeger, HSF Bishell, William Bowes, DA Canham, Peter Cariss, GM Carnall, Colin Comins, George Cooper, E Cotterill, JH Dacre, S Eccles, GM Fairbanks, PH Fairbanks, FV Gott, W Hall, J Hardcastle, Frederick Hyde, Frank Noel Jenkin, Dennis Jones, N Kenny, R Linley, John Nelson Movley, CW Myers, Robert Noble, Dennis Pease, LD Peel, W Prince, SM Ramsden, WS Robson, WH Rollinson, Rodney Rushton, Leslie Saycell, Harry Thorley, Charles Edwin Trott, Dennis Turrell, JJ Wadkin, L White, DJ Wilson, Donald Windle and J Yeoman.

St Wilfrid's Church Halton on the south nave wall:

Arthur Anderson, William Bowes, Alice Briggs, Donald Cowell, Arnold Dobson, Eric Fletcher, Harry Haley, Keith Hepburn, George Heseltine, Owen Jones, Cyril Murray Gordon Parker, Harry Petty, William Prince,

Albert Pyrah, Walter Scarfe, Ronald Smith Sydney Spence, Harry Stead, Allen Sykes, Ernest Tate, Dennis Tordoff, George Trowles, Harry Varley and "to those who died in Seacroft Military Hospital".

The War Memorial Queensway has an additional inscribed marble plaque remembering the men lost in the Second World War.

Graves from the Second World War in St Mary's Church Cemetery

Sub-Lieutenant Peter Cariss RNVR died May 24th 1943 aged 20

Sergeant James Clifford USAAF who was killed on air operations over Germany on June 30th 1948 aged 25

Lance Corporal Reginald Kay 2nd Derbyshire Yeomanry Royal Armoured Corps March 3rd 1942 aged 26

Lance Corporal John Nelson Movley of the Coldstream Guards who was killed in action in Italy on February 19th 1944 aged 24. His father Mawson Movley was the licensee of the Brown Cow public house who died aged 71 in 1958

Sgt/Bdr Ronald Smith RAFVR died December 1st 1943 aged 20

Aircraftsman 2nd Class J Tasker RAF died on March 5th 1945 aged 32

Private Ernest Tate RAMC died aged 19 on October 5th 1943: he was the son of George Tate who died aged 73 in 1967

Leading Aircraftsman Harry Thorley RAF Auxiliary of Woodland Road died on August 14th 1940 aged 37 in the Battle of Britain: he was cremated at Lawnswood on August 20th.

Aircraftsman 1st Class J Yeoman RAF May 11th 1944 aged 21: he was the son of Arthur & Doris Yeoman

Details of some of the above men are found in the records of the Commonwealth War Commission:

Second World War

Private Ken Adams of the 1st Battalion East Lancashire Regiment died on August 12th 1944 aged 19. He took part in the D Day Landings in Normandy on June 6th 1944. He was the son of William and Charlotte Adams of Woodland Road. He was buried at Banneville-la-Campagner War Cemetery Calvados where 2170 Commonwealth men are buried.

Gunner Arthur Anderson of Royal Artillery died aged 22; he was a baker working in Horsforth.

Captain John Barrett Ashmore of the Royal Army Medical Corps. He died on February 7th 1944 and was buried at Taukyan War Cemetery Myanmar.

Flight Sergeant Herbert Ingle Austin of W Op/Air Gunner 429 (RCAF) Squadron died aged 39 on April 23rd 1944. He was the son of Herbert & Emily Ingle Austin and husband of Olive of Halton. He was buried at Herkingen General Cemetery Zuid Holland.

Sergeant Observer H Stuart Bishell died aged 22: he lived on Selby Road

and was an accountant in Leeds. He is buried in Dusseldorf Cemetery.
Guardsman William Bowes of the 1st Battalion Grenadier Guards died on August 3rd 1944 aged 21. He was the son of Gleniss and Dorothy Bowes of Halton and was buried at Tilly-sur-Seuilles War Cemetery Calvados near Bayeux where there are 990 Commonwealth burials.
Radio Officer Donald Arthur Canham of SS Wayfarer (Liverpool) Merchant Navy. He died on August 19th 1944 aged 22 and is remembered at the Tower Hill Memorial London.
Sub-Lieutenant Peter Cariss served on HMS Runcher and died on May 24th 1945 aged 20: his ashes were interred at Whitkirk Cemetery on May 30th. He was the son of James and Elsie Cariss of Sherbrooke Avenue Halton: James died in October 1967 and Elsie died in March 1983.
Sergeant George Mitchell Carnall of 254 Squadron RAF Volunteer Reserve. He died on July 9th 1941 aged 20. He was the son of George Charles and Mary McIntosh Carnall of Austhorpe and Far Headingley. He is remembered at the Runnymede War Memorial.
The Air Forces Memorial at Runnymede Sussex commemorates 20,352 fliers from Britain and the Commonwealth who have no known grave. HM The Queen opened the memorial on October 17th 1953 in front of 24,000 people. The airmen served in bomber, fighter, coastal, transport and flying training squadrons and flew from bases in Britain and north and western Europe. The memorial is maintained by the Commonwealth War Graves Commission. HM The Queen laid a wreath at the Stone of Remembrance on October 17th 2003.
Captain Colin Frederick Innes Comins was a Quartermaster with the 122nd Field Regiment Royal Artillery. He died aged 38 on April 14th 1942; he was the son of Frederick Innes & Nora Jane Comins and was buried at Kranji War Cemetery Singapore.
Stoker 1st Class Edward Cotterill of HMS Wakeful RN. He died on May 29th 1940 and is remembered at the Chatham Naval Memorial.
Leading Aircraftsman Donald Cowell of 511 Squadron RAF Volunteer Reserve died on October 6th 1946 aged 23. He was the son of John William & Nellie Cowell of Halton and is remembered at the Runnymede Memorial.
Sergeant James Harold Dacre of the RAF Volunteer Reserve died on April 4th 1944 aged 19. He was the son of Albert & Elsie Dacre of Bramley and was buried at Harehills Cemetery.
Private Arnold Dobson of the 1st Battalion West Yorkshire Regiment Prince of Wales Own died on March 7th 1942 aged 23. He was the son of John & Ada Dobson of Willow Well Road Halton and was employed at Gallon's Store. He is remembered at the Rangoon Memorial Myanmar.
Corporal Stanley Eccles of 2nd/4th Battalion King's Own Yorkshire Light Infantry died aged 30 on February 2nd 1945. He was the son of Horace &

Lily Eccles and husband of Dora and was buried at the Padua War Cemetery in Italy.

3rd Officer Gordon Maguire Fairbanks of SS Refast (London) Merchant Navy died on June 6th 1942 aged 28. He was the son of Richard William and Norah Christine Fairbanks of 613 Selby Road Austhorpe and the husband of Lilian. He is remembered at the Tower Hill Memorial London.

Sergeant Philip Haig Fairbanks was a W Op/Air Gunner with the Royal Air Force Volunteer Reserve and he died on September 10th 1942 aged 20. He was the son of Richard William & Norah Christine Fairbanks of Whitkirk and was buried in the Reichswald Forest War Cemetery Kleve at Nordhein Westfalen Germany.

Sergeant Henry Stuart Fell was a naval bomber of 106 Squadron RAF Volunteer Reserve and he died on March 12th 1943 aged 22. He was the son of Rev Charles & Beatrice Fell of Scarborough and was buried at Reichswald Forest War Cemetery Kleve Nordrhein Westfalen. This is the largest Commonwealth War Cemetery in Germany where there are 7579 burials.

Sergeant Frank Vennard Gott of the 460 Squadron Royal Air Force Volunteer Reserve died on May 28th 1944. He is remembered on the Runnymede Memorial.

Lance Corporal Harry Haley of 7 Armoured Division Provost Company Corps of Military Police died on March 30th 1943 aged 31. He was the son of Mary & Mary Haley and the husband of May and was buried at Sfax War Cemetery Tunisia.

Private Wilfred Hall of 2nd Battalion East Yorkshire Regiment died aged 20 on July 18th 1944. He was the son of John and Hilda May Hall of Whitkirk and was buried at Ranville War Cemetery Calvados.

Sergeant Jack Hardcastle of 105 Squadron Royal Air Force died on October 28th 1940 and was buried at Whitkirk Cemetery.

Sergeant George Heseltine of the RAF Volunteer Reserve died on December 31st 1943 aged 19. He was the son of Arthur and Dora Victoria of Haltonand is remembered at the Runnymede Memorial.

Flight Lieutenant Noel Jenkin of 59 Squadron Royal Air Force Volunteer Reserve died aged 27 on February 24th 1944. He was the son of Thomas and Agnes Emily of Halton and husband of Margaret Inez of Austhorpe. He is remembered on the Runnymede Memorial.

Lance Corporal John Nelson Movley 2660110 of the 2nd Battalion Coldstream Guards died aged 24 on Saturday February 19th 1944. He was the son of Edgar Mawson and Isabel Movley of Whitkirk and was buried at Minturno War Cemetery in Italy. This cemetery is 50 miles north of Naples and has 2049 Commonwealth burials who lost their lives during the battles across the Garigliano river. He is also remembered on his parent's grave at Whitkirk.

Lance Bombadier Charles William Myers of 73 Anti-Tank Regiment (RA) died on July 27th 1942 aged 28. He was the son of George & Annie Myers of Whitkirk and the husband of Alice and is remembered at the Alamein Memorial Egypt.

Gunner Robert Noble of 72 Field Regiment (RA) died on June 4th 1942 aged 36. He was the son of William & Sarah Noble and the husband of Edna May of Halton. He is remembered at the Knightsbridge War Cemetery Acromal Libya.

Steward Gordon Parker of HMS Hood died on May 24th 1941 aged 22. He was the son of William Ernest and Mary Parker of Kyffin Avenue Halton. He is remembered at the Portsmouth Naval Memorial.

Gunner Dennis Pease of the 41st Battalion/15th Lt AA Regiment RA died aged 22 on January 19th 1943. He was the son of Walter and Alice Mary Pease of Colton and Halton and is remembered at the Alamein Memorial Egypt.

Gunner Leslie Douglas Pewel of 134 Light Anti-Aircraft Regiment (RA) died on March 13th 1943 aged 20. He was the son of Frank Leslie and Annie Smith Peel of Temple Walk and was buried in Sheffield General Cemetery.

Lance Corporal Albert Edward Pyrah of the 4th Battalion Royal Welsh Fusiliers died on December 7th 1944 aged 25 and was the son of Timothy & Jessie Pyrah of Halton Moor. He is buried at Leopoldsburg War Cemetery Limburg Belgium.

Walter Scobie Robson was a W/D Pilot in 37 Squadron Royal Air Force Volunteer Reserve and he died aged 27 on October 20th 1944. He was the son of George Scobie and Frances Ann Robson and husband of Anne of Halton. He was buried at the Budapest War Cemetery in Hungary.

Gunner William Henry Rollinson of 203 Battalion/68 Lt AA Regiment RA died aged 35 on August 7th 1944. He was the son of Herbert & Emily (nee Frame) of Halton and husband of Beatrice of Leeds. He was buried at Bayeux War Cemetery Calvados.

Sergeant Rodney Rushton of 77 Squadron Royal Air Force Volunteer Reserve died aged 19 on August 11th 1943. He was the son of Henry and Lauretta Rushton of Halton and was buried at Chievres Communal Cemetery near Mons Holland. This cemetery has 50 graves of those killed in the attacks on the nearby Luftwaffe airfield.

Sergeant Leslie Saycell of the REME died aged 25 on January 31st 1943 and was the son of Thomas and Mary Saycell and husband of Dorothy of Upton Pontefract. He was buried at Tobruk War Cemetery Libya.

Corporal Walter Scarfe of the 1st Battalion Yorkshire & Lancashire Regiment died on January 21st 1944 aged 24. He was the son of Arthur and Eliza Scarfe and the husband of Dorothy Ayrton. He is buried at the Minturno War Cemetery Italy.

Squadron Leader Ronald Smith of the RAFVR was the son of Basil & Sarah Ann Smith of William View Halton. He died aged 20 on December 1st 1943. His father died aged 84 in 1980 and mother died aged 81 in 1976.

Sergeant Sidney John Spence of the Royal Artillery Service Corps died on October 13th 1945 aged 33. He was the son of Joseph & Minnie Spence of Halton and was buried at Harehills Cemetery.

Private Harry Stead of the 2nd Battalion East Yorkshire Regiment died aged 21 at the Normandy Landings on June 6th 1944. He was the son of Nellie Stead and stepson of George Dyer; he was the husband of Dorothy and lived in Halton. He is buried at Ranville War Cemetery Calvados.

Leading Aircraftsman Harry Thorley of 609 Squadron RAF (Auxiliary Air Force) died on August 14th 1940 aged 37. He was the son of Bentley and Mary Thorley of Woodland Road and was the husband of Edith of Halton. His ashes are interred at Whitkirk Cemetery.

The 609 (West Riding) Auxiliary Air Force Squadron was based in Leeds and was one of the most successful fighter units: it was the first Spitfire unit to shoot down 100 enemy planes. The Squadron was based at RAF Yeadon from 1936 with 55 Belgian pilots serving with the unit. They served in the Battle of Britain fought over southern England between July 10th and October 31st 1940 between RAF Fighter Command and the German Luftwaffe. On September 15th the RAF inflicted losses that convinced the Luftwaffe the battle could not be won: the day is now Battle of Britain Day. In the battle 2353 British men and 574 from overseas took part and an estimated 544 were killed including Harry Thorley. A memorial in honour of the 609 Squadron was unveiled in the Belgian town of Waremme on September 8th 2003 in the presence of Squadron Leader Brian Waite, officer commanding the present day 609 Squadron and nine other reservists; they provide ground support for the RAF. A memorial was also unveiled on March 29th 1968 at Leeds-Bradford International Airport (Yeadon Airport).

Carpenter's Mate Dennis Albert Tordoff of HMS Dasher Naval Auxiliary Personnel Merchant Navy died on March 27th 1943 aged 21. He was the son of Benjamin and Alice Maud Tordoff of Halton: Ben was a police sergeant and the family lived on Morritt Drive. Dennis is remembered at the Liverpool Naval Memorial.

Sapper Denis Turrell of 553 Field Company Royal Engineers died aged 25 on July 1st 1944. He was the son of Frederick and Alice Turrell and the husband of Joan of Halton. He was buried at St Manvieu War Cemetery Cheux Calvados.

Private Harry Varley of the 2nd Battalion Yorkshire & Lancashire Regiment died on August 25th 1944 aged 21. He was the son of Harry and Margaret Varley of Halton Moor. He is buried at Digboi War Cemetery in India where there are 200 Commonwealth burials.

Private Leslie White of 8th Battalion Argyll & Sutherland Highlanders died on November 4th 1943 aged 30. He was the son of Walter and Edith White and the husband of Irene. He is buried at Sangro River War Cemetery Italy where 2617 Commonwealth servicemen are buried.
Aircraftsman 1st Class Jack Yeoman of the Royal Air Force Volunteer Reserve died aged 21 on Sunday May 11th 1941. He was the son of Arthur & Doris Yeoman of Whitkirk.
There were a number of civilians who died in Leeds due to enemy action and they included Fireman Frederick Smith of Primrose Lane Halton who died on February 8th 1945: his wife was Sarah Jane Smith.

WATER SERVICES

The first supply came from the many wells in Halton: there were at least 12 wells between Pinfold Lane and along Chapel Street to the High Street. There were also wells in the squares and yards and the kitchen of Gilsyke House had a 30 feet deep well. In April 1875 George Westerman of Halton sought permission to sink a new well for drinking water. In 1893 Hermon Terrace and Mount were supplied by a 21 feet deep pump well near the main street. The main supply for the village later came from the reservoir at the bottom of Halton Hill which was supplied from Wyke Beck. A water wheel was built at Whitebridge Mill in 1859 for the pumping of the water up Halton Hill to a holding reservoir on Selby Road: the site of the large green at The Crescent. The water was pumped to a tower which had been built on Selby Road opposite the end of Wilfred Avenue and distributed to Temple Newsam and later Halton and Whitkirk. The Halton mains supply from Leeds was turned on in 1893 and the village residents were asked to contribute costs for this water if they wished to be connected. The Graveley family at Hawthorn House decided not to take the Leeds water as their well supply was sufficient. The whole of the Halton Waterworks could have been leased from the estate in 1889 including water tower, pumping station, reservoirs and pipes. The costs involved would have been £3500 for the tower and reservoirs, £2000 for the pumping station and water wheel and the pipes cost more than £3000. In 1891 there was concern over the pollution of Wyke Beck especially in the section from Great Heads Beck. In 1892 the creation of a new water company was suggested as well as a possible water supply from the disused coal pits at Killingbeck, Prince Arthur on Hollyshaw Lane, West Yorkshire at Austhorpe and the workings in Primrose Valley. The agent for Mrs Meynell Ingram informed the Hunslet RDC in late 1892 that unless agreement could be reached, she would cut off the supply of water to Halton in March 1893. There was much legal concern over the use of the waterworks and a court case resulted in a compromise with both parties paying costs. The Council made their decision to accept water from the Leeds high level supply and in May 1893 tenders were accepted to construct a new Halton water supply with pipes across Wyke Beck. The contract for manufacture was with Clay Cross Co and Glenfield Co with a clerk of works appointed at a wage of two guineas a week. There were 52 applications for this post and it was Thomas Nunneley who was successful. The work was finished quickly and the clerk was laid off in November 1893 when the water was turned on. There were many complaints over the cost of the new Leeds water with many insisting that their wells were to be their source. In 1901 the reservoir was suggested to be on a lease to Hunslet RDC at £30 a year to the Temple Newsam Estate. The water tower was taken down in 1920 as the area was supplied by the mains system: the houses near the site are named Tower Cottages where the waterworks managers lived. The site of the tower was used for the present bungalow built in 1925 by the Townend family. The reservoir was filled in and 22 houses were built around the site: in 1915 a refuse tip was suggested for the old reservoir site with soil a foot deep and in 1919 the concrete which lined the reservoir was sold.

WHEATON AVENUE

Wheaton Avenue is the back cul-de-sac to the odd numbers of Wilfred Avenue while Wilfred Street is the back cul-de-sac of the even numbers. Wheaton Avenue, Charlotte Grove and parts of Wilfred Avenue were surfaced in 1912. The old cotton mill became the premises of tailor Ken Thompson: demolished in June 2003 to prepare the site for a development of housing. Wheaton Court is part of the Headrow Housing flats built on the site of San Remo.

WHITE FAMILY

John Stuart White was born in Dunedin New Zealand in 1877 as the eldest of seven children: his father was a Dunedin lawyer. He came to England by boat in 1907 around Cape Horn with his wife Frances Turner and their son Jack in order to learn the motor trade. He worked at the Rover Car Factory and then teamed up with R Purdy as agents for selling explosives to Yorkshire colliers and quarries. He joined up in the Great War and was sent out to the Workshop branch of the ASC (RASC) in France where he became a staff sergeant. After the war Purdy and Jack White carried on their business but sold out to ICI in 1934: John became the ICI sales manager in Yorkshire until 1940. In 1922 Jack White was in Halton forming the Halton Scouts (18th SEL) and became the District Commissioner. In 1941 he was awarded the Medal of Merit when scoutmaster of the Halton Templars. In the Second World War Jack

White joined the Home Guard and was appointed the ammunition officer for the area, visiting and checking ammunition dumps and stores. He was a keen gardener and grew his own vegetables until he was over 80 years old. He always had a great love for motor bikes and sidecars: prior to the Great War he toured Europe on his machine and later took part in trials including the Scott Trial from London to Edinburgh. At the age of 78 John Stuart White entered the Veterans Event at the Ilkley Motor Club in August 1955. The previous month he had taken his son and grandson David educated at Sedburgh School on a ride through France and Switzerland: they rode separate machines travelling 100 miles a day. John Stuart White died in December 1969 at the age of 92: a memorial service was held at Halton Congregational Church on January 3rd 1970. Frances Lorraine White wife of John White died aged 85 on November 11th 1962.

Their children were Jack Stuart White and George White who also lived for a few years at the family home Brynmor 17 Pinfold Lane Halton.

John Rowarth Stuart White was born in New Zealand on January 1st 1905 and moved to Chestnut Avenue Cross Gates when his parents emigrated in 1907. He was educated at Leeds Central High School and the Leeds University Dental School where he graduated as a Bachelor of Dental Surgery in 1928. Jack opened his Halton surgery at 17 Chapel Street in 1929 and lived at Holme Lea with his parents until his marriage to Mary Barrand Sandy on May 11th 1935. They met through a shared interest in Scouts and Guides: he was the son of the South-East Leeds Scout Commissioner and ran the Halton Templars Silver Band, while Mary was the Captain of the 1st Halton Templars Guides and Rangers. Mary

Sandy was the daughter of Henry and Elizabeth Sandy of The Grove Halton where a reception was held after the wedding at St Mary's Church Garforth. One of the bridesmaids was Mary's sister Pat Sandy who was born in 1920, while the best man was his brother George Stuart White (1911-1985). The Halton, Colton and Garforth Guides formed a Guard of Honour and the Scouts arched their troop colours at the church gate.
He acquired his first motor bike in 1920 and became an active member of the Vintage Motor Cycle Club, the Vintage Sports Car Club and the Veteran Car Club. It was not unusual for him to be seen arriving at work disguised in leathers on his 1926 Scott motor bike and his 1929 Brooklands Riley Lulu. The married couple lived on Wayside Avenue Scarcroft where their son David was born in 1936: he also qualified as a dental officer and served for 30 years in the Royal Navy; their daughters were Elizabeth born in 1942 and Penelope in 1945. In 1939 Jack White joined the Royal Naval Volunteer Reserve and was called up in 1940. He became a naval dental officer at HMS Ceres Wetherby, Hayling Island and Royal Marines Lympstone. The highlight of his war service was on the cruiser HMS Norfolk mostly on Russian Convoy escort duties. He was appointed in 1945 to HMS Aorangi to provide denture work for the fleet. He sailed for the Far East until the Japanese surrender ended the War enabling him to tour New Zealand visiting relatives. He returned to his Halton practice after the War and the family moved to Thorner in 1946 where they had five addresses including Woodthorpe, Hillcrest and Sandhills House. Mary died at the last Thorner address Redroofs at the age of 69 in 1979. Soon after Jack moved with Pat Sandy to live at Leeds Road Barwick-in-Elmet and in 1989 moved to Richmondfield Drive. Jack White died in Seacroft Hospital on Friday October 13th 2000. In 1954 he was a founder member of Cross Gates Rotary Club and was President in 1961. In 1968 he was elected the chairman of the Leeds District Branch of the British Dental Association and was a member of the Leeds Local Dental Council. He retired from dentistry in 1976 and sold the practice to Peter Rider who moved from Dial House to a newly built surgery on Selby Road in 1992. Jack White enjoyed travelling, photography and gardening; he was a member of the Vintage Motor Cycle Club, Vintage Sports Car Club and the chairman of the North East Veteran Car Club. In 1961 he won his class in the Leeds Veteran & Vintage Car & Motor Cycle Rally from Roundhay Park to Temple Newsam Park.

WHITKIRK VIEW

This is a row of eight terrace houses from Park Street built in 1878 by John Graveley. 1 to 8 Whitkirk View was renumbered in 1935 to 38 to 52 Cross Green Lane.
In 1881 the recorded residents were Thomas & Martha Hill, George and

Eliza Peters and William & Elizabeth Riley. In 1891 there were William James Cout, Leonard and Eleanor Curzon, Thomas and Elizabeth Johnson, James and Martha Warren, James and Margaret Yates. One of the early residents was William Morritt who married Mary Jane and their daughter was Audrey Mary Morritt born on June 29th 1916.

1 was bought by Herbert Rennard in 1907 and the house was converted into the Halton Pharmacy. In 1927 the shop and house were bought by Herbert Gilleghan for his son John and wife Violet who he married in 1928. Jack Gilleghan died at the age of 53 in 1958 and the family sold the business to Ronald Blass who sold to Edward Broadley. The property was sold in 1987 to Robert Sidebottom of Garforth who opened Past n Present in the premises.

7 was sold on March 25th 1879 by John Graveley to Thomas Hill as part of the original Martinmas Lands on the Cross Field. In 1891 Thomas Hill sold it to William & Ann Watson who sold it to Mary Elizabeth Ward in 1928. In 1937 this house together with 5 Whitkirk View were sold to Alec Cowell who had the corner shop on Cross Green Lane/Wilfred Avenue. The residents for many years of this house were the Green family and Joyce Green maintains their link with the house.

The last of the houses on Whitkirk View was Gerald Ball's greengrocer's shop from 1928. Gerald Ball, Dorothy and Harold lived at the house/shop which was converted again to a private house in 1978 retaining the shop window. In the 1950's Charles Winston and Marjorie Murgatroyd lived here. In November 1977 plans were presented to convert this off-licence and grocery into a fish & chip shop and in April 1978 these were changed to convert the shop back into a house.

The cul-de-sac of Back Whitkirk View was connected at the end by a footpath to Primrose Lane. In 1927 the Hunslet RDC ordered that this path was to be cleared and kept open: the path today is blocked off with no access.

WILFRED AVENUE

A new street was proposed by RS Wigin in January 1892 to be completed "near the waterworks". The two rows of ten terrace houses were built in 1902 by Wheatley and Easton of Cross Gates. The land had been bought by Leeds solicitor RS Wigin of 83 Albion Street from the Temple Newsam estate. The Thrift butchers had one corner shop and on the east side was Alec and Kathleen Cowell's confectionery and grocery shop. This was the home of Emily Bean when it was first built and she lived there until 1923, when the house was converted to a shop and run by John & Lilian Weatherill. When the Thrift store was opened by the Irwin Arms in 1964 the Wilfred Avenue butcher's shop and the grocery on Cross Green Lane were closed. One of the residents of the street was Herbert Emery (12)

who died on January 13th 1968: he was born at Swillington Common and worked as a boilerman at Barkston Ash Laundry. Annie Emery worked at the Premier Fruit Stores on Chapel Street. Noah and Florrie Ball lived first at 4 Hermon Street prior to moving to 10 Wilfred Avenue: Noah died in 1961 and Florrie moved to a flat at Seacroft having worked for many years for the Gilleghan family at the shop.
Houses were built in 1936 on Wilfred Avenue and W Elam was contracted for the new street works. There was a large open field and garage on the right: the land was once the orchard of Orchard Villa and later tennis courts, used by Halton Congregational Chapel and a bowling green used by owner Joseph Thomas. These were to be used as allotments with the garage and greenhouse bought by Jack Gilleghan and Alec Cowell in 1949. Signalman Thomas Kay who lived at 32 Wilfred Avenue was a gardener employed by the new owners. The land was sold to Clarkson Ltd in January 1961 who developed the site with new housing. Thomas Kay's son Reginald was killed in the Second World War: he was in the 2nd Derbyshire Yeomanry (Royal Armoured Corps). He was only 26 when he lost his life on March 3rd 1942 and he was buried with full military honours in Whitkirk Cemetery. There was a long procession headed by a band from their home in Wilfred Avenue along Selby Road to the cemetery on March 7th 1942. His father Thomas Moss Kay died aged 76 in February 1959.
Orchard Villa was built in 1913 for the owner of the Barkston Ash Laundry and became the home of the Pease family in 1934. The present owner is Margaret Pease who was educated at West Leeds School and took part in the 1922 Children's Day at Roundhay Park. She trained for teaching at Leeds Training College and taught at Middleton Secondary Modern School in 1930, Osmondthorpe Junior Girls School and Cross Gates Primary School from 1935. Margaret was one of the first to be

trained at Leeds Town Hall in 1939 as an ARP warden. She was responsible for planting forget-me-nots at the War Memorial, played hockey for the Halton team and was a member of the WRVS.
Further towards the main road on the right side was the Barkston Ash Laundry. The houses opposite were built in c1963: there is an electricity sub-station adjacent.

WOODLANDS AND GRAVELEYTHORPES

Woodland Road dates from the 1934 with a few builders including Eastwoods, Lawsons and Richard Cooper (1939). Woodland Hill was built from 1936 by Robert and Edward Lawson of Dewsbury Road, Fairweather & Longbottom (1938) and Frank Horsman: Graveleythorpe Road also dates from this period. Near the bottom of Woodland Hill once flowed a muddy stream which flowed across the road in 1949 but was then restricted to a pipe under the road: the site is seen by a slight dip in the road today.
The corner shops/houses which front both Woodland Hill and Cross Green Lane were built on the Temple Newsam estate. The land was conveyed from Charles Lord Halifax who died in 1934 to his son Edward Lindley Wood in 1926. In March 1950 Lord Halifax conveyed the land to a Trust headed by Sir Arthur Horace Penn of Saxmundham, London chartered accountant Stanley Spofforth and Col Hugh Delabere Bousfield. *Col Bousfield lived at Weetwood Court: he was a member of the Leeds Rifles from which he retired in 1925 after 29 years service. He fought in the Boer War and was wounded in the Great War at Passchaendale, where he became a POW. When the Colonel died on July 5th 1951 aged 69 his place on the Trust was taken by Arthur Rimington Glazebrook a solicitor of Butts Court Leeds and who lived at Colton Lodge Meynell Road Colton and at Grove Cottage Woodlesford. The son of Sir Richard Glazebrook,Col AR Glazebrook married Joan Anne Marsden of The Grange Whitkirk on November 12th 1929.*
In December 1952 the land was sold to Mark Haley Builders. Mark William Haley of 65 Ivy Street also built 22 semi-detached houses on Woodland Hill, Cross Green Lane and a newly created street Templestowe Gardens in the same period. The other director of the building firm was George William Haley with his base at Bennett Road in Headingley.
The first occupants of the 7 shops included grocers Malcolm and Joan Bell in 1956: they sold in 1961 to the Bennett family of Harrogate and David Orange started his TV business in 1987 in the corner shop at 67 Cross Green Lane.
Woodland Hill:
2 Haley's Butchers ran the shop in the 1960's, selling meats, pork pies

and bacon. The business closed by 1979 when there were plans for conversion and there was planning permission to open a fish & chip shop. It is now Regal Chinese Takeaway.

4 Goldfinch Wines were a business in the 1960's. Woodland Wine Store took over the shop together with 6 Woodland Hill.

6 Patricia's shop sold knitting wools and ladies childrens and gents wear in the 1960's, followed by Jeanne's wool shop. June Stockwell had a cake business from 1997: she taught at Temple Newsam-Halton Primary School. The plans for the enlarged house and shop from two original shops were passed in June 1998.

8 Hardware shop was run by Alex Smith in the 1960's and sold paints, electrical goods, stationery and greetings cards. A launderette followed and this was converted into a shop again in late 1987. A kitchen tile shop followed and in 1990 became offices. It became Juste Nous Catering with Clare Guymer in 1997: an outside catering business. Plans were passed for the conversion in January 1997.

10 George Harrison ran a chemist's shop for a few years and later this was K&J Harrison off-licence and confectioners. This became Elizabeth's Salon in early 1960 and is now Julie's Hair Studio.

Templestowe Crescent is on Woodland Road near Green Lane and built by Fairweather & Longbottom and George W Fenwick in the late 1930's. Graveleythorpe Road was developed by Dunhill's Builders from 1946 who also built houses on Knightsway and Woodland Road. Templestowe Hill was built by Mark Haley and in 1956 the builders made up the road prior to passing it over to the City Council.

WOODMAN STREET

The old established street started as Woodman Road became Woodman Lane and in 1933 was Woodman Street.

Vine House dates from the mid-17th century and was the chandler's house where tallow candles were made. The house had been built by the Temple Newsam estate to serve the house. The present kitchen and car port was the original croft. Vine House was home to plumber John Fox (1871), Dr Frederick William Pogson (1899), teacher Jane Mattinson (1901) who lived with her sisters Elizabeth & Minnie; Clarence & Lucy Bell. William Bell of Vine House died aged 67 in 1908: his wife Ellen died aged 81 in 1925 while their daughter Camilla was born in 1887 and died in 1899. William Bell applied to Hunslet RDC in 1905 to make extensions to Vine House to be used as offices. The plans in 1905 to widen Woodman Street were abandoned by the Council. In 1934 this was the home of Thomas Percy and Maud Nicholls with Arthur Pickersgill. In 1939 the householders were Eric & Maude Jennings who had a confectioner's shop on Chapel Street: Eric Jennings died aged 41 on June

18th 1948 and was buried at Harehills Cemetery.

The Poplars/Poplar House is a 17th century house with stables and was altered in the 18th century. It was the home of coal miner Samuel Ambler who was born in 1836 with wife Ann: their children were Emily, Ann, Kate, Celia and William. In 1885 it was leased from the Temple Newsam Estate to John Gordon and William Frankland Dean and in 1922 was sold by Lord Halifax to builder George Edward Smith, who leased the property from 1920 following John Henry East. George Smith died aged 73 on August 6th 1941 and was buried at Harehills Cemetery. It became the home of rag merchant David Speight and his wife Mary. In 1920 Poplar House was home to motor dealer Arthur Goodhind who lived here from 1942 to 1950 and Leeds master baker Horace Lindill came in 1954 followed by coal merchant Jack Wigglesworth. It is now known as Woodside House and the present owner bought the property in 1971.

Hopewell House was built by the Bell family in 1913/14 being the home of Mary Emma Bell, who died in April 1940 aged 65. The family ran the first Halton Post Office, bakery and grocery shop. In later years it became the dwelling for the caretaker at Halton Methodist Church:it was sold in March 1971 to the Church, who sold it in April 1986: it has had several changes of hands in recent years.

WORLD WIDE WEB

There are many web sites which can be accessed with relevant available information concerning the area of Halton. ***leodis.net*** is the Leodis database website of the Leeds City Council and provides a wealth of photographs of Halton from Wyke Bridge to Cross Gates. This is a digital photographic archive managed by Leeds Library. The database has a collection of photographs taken between 1890 and 1960: the site is continually being upgraded and has additions and amendments from those who access the site. There were 289 entries on this website on 29 pages in 2004.
Other sites including references to Halton are by logging on to the *Google* search engine and typing *Halton Leeds* which brings nearly 10,000 references. Other useful sites include the web page for Whitkirk at ***btinternet.com/whitkirk*** and ***friends reunited.co.uk*** for local schools; ***ukvillages.co.uk/uk villages.nsf*** is of some interest and many of the organisations in Halton have their own websites.
Family historians may find the following web sites helpful:
yorkshirebmd.org.uk has a database covering the Yorkshire births, marriages and deaths from 1837 to 1950. freebmd.rootsweb.com

provides free Internet access to the Civil Registration Index for England and Wales and will cover 1837 to 1983. cwgc.org is the site of the Commonwealth War Graves Commission. familysearch.org is the site of the Mormon Church resources with records extracted from church records. archives.wyjs.org.uk is the site for the West Yorkshire Archive Service.

Births, Marriages and Deaths

The dates given for births may either be the actual date of birth or the date of baptism according to church records.
The dates given for deaths may either be the actual date of death or that of burial according to church records.
The dates given for marriages are taken from church records.

Acknowledgements:

John Gilleghan would like to thank the following for their kind help in writing this story of Halton

Barnsley Local Studies Library
Halton, Cross Gates and Morley Branch Libraries
Leeds Co-operative Society Ltd
Leeds Grammar School
East Leeds Historical & Archaeological Society
Leeds City Council Development Department
Leeds Local Studies Library
Leeds Skyrack Express
Regimental Museum York
Bradford, Harrogate, Skipton and York Reference Libraries
Halton & District Local History Society
Temple Moor High School
Tony Stevens
Temple Newsam Halton Primary School
Thoresby Society Leeds
Wakefield Local Studies Library
West Yorkshire Archive Service Leeds
West Yorkshire Federation of Women's Institutes
Yorkshire Post Newspapers

Many members of the Halton community, past residents and those interested in local history who have so willingly given their time and memories in the preparation of this book

Books written by John Gilleghan MBE

Scenes from East Leeds
Highways and Byways from Leeds
Worship North and East of Leeds
Leeds-An A to Z of Local History
Introducing the Yorkshire Dales
Time Traveller in the Dales
The Magic of the Yorkshire Dales

ISBN 141202945-7

9 781412 029452